A New Woman of Japan

Transitions: Asia and Asian America

Series Editor, *Mark Selden*

A New Woman of Japan: A Political Biography of Katô Shidzue
Helen M. Hopper

Japanese Colonialism in Taiwan: Land Tenure, Development, and Dependency, 1895–1945,
Chih-ming Ka

Vietnam's Rural Transformation, edited by
Benedict J. Tria Kerkvliet and Doug J. Porter

Privatizing Malaysia: Rents, Rhetoric, Realities,
edited by Jomo K. S.

The Origins of the Great Leap Forward: The Case of One Chinese Province,
Jean-Luc Domenach

The Politics of Democratization: Generalizing East Asian Experiences,
edited by Edward Friedman

Our Land Was a Forest: An Ainu Memoir,
Kayano Shigeru

The Political Economy of China's Financial Reforms: Finance in Late Development,
Paul Bowles and Gordon White

Reinventing Vietnamese Socialism: Doi Moi *in Comparative Perspective,*
edited by William S. Turley and Mark Selden

A New Woman of Japan

A Political Biography of Katô Shidzue

Helen M. Hopper

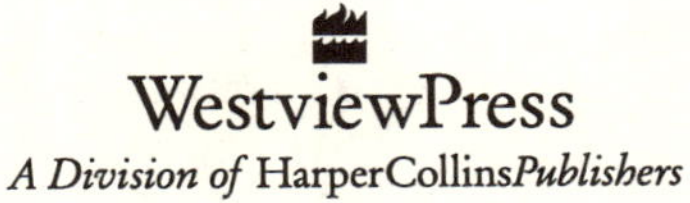

For Paul

Transitions: Asia and Asian America

Published in 1996 in the United States of America by Westview Press, Inc., 5500 Central Avenue, Boulder, Colorado 80301-2877, and in the United Kingdom by Westview Press, 12 Hid's Copse Road, Cumnor Hill, Oxford OX2 9JJ

Library of Congress Cataloging-in-Publication Data
Hopper, Helen M.
A new woman of Japan : a political biography of Katô Shidzue / Helen M. Hopper
p. cm.
Includes bibliographical references and index.
ISBN 0-8133-8971-2 0-8133-3422-5 (pbk)
1. Kato Shidzue, 1897– . 2. Statesmen—Japan—Biography. 3. Women in politics—Japan—Biography. 4. Feminists—Japan—Biography. 5. Women's rights—Japan. I. Title.
DS885.5.K33H66 1996
952.04'092—dc20
[B] 95-25165
CIP

The paper used in this publication meets the requirements of the American National Standard for Permanence of Paper for Printed Library Materials Z39.48-1984.

10 9 8 7 6 5 4 3 2 1

Contents

Photographs

Preface

Katô Shidzue, born into an upper class family at the turn of the century, was educated to become a traditional "good wife and wise mother." While her father brought home Western trinkets from his professional visits to Europe, her mother made sure that Shidzue's decorum remained proper for an aristocratic Japanese woman. When, at seventeen, she married the Baron Ishimoto Keikichi, she seemed well on her way to fulfilling the subservient feminine role required of her. Her husband, however, insisted that Shidzue become a "new woman" of Japan; that she school herself for independence and militancy in a world he hoped would come to reflect his ideals of socialism and Christian humanism. Trying to be the woman Keikichi demanded, in 1919 she left their two infant sons in the care of her mother and followed her husband to New York City to study the liberated ways of Western women. There she met the socialist radical Agnes Smedley and the crusader for birth control Margaret Sanger, and determined that she, like these Americans, would become an advocate for a new society. She would press for the liberation of Japanese women from oppressive feudal family law by joining the "new women" of Japan who were struggling for their human rights. Over the next few years Shidzue began her life's work for political and social equality and family planning education. Her campaigns would intensify during the early thirties, become muted during the late thirties, necessarily fade during the forties, and rise to new heights at the war's end. Now at ninety-eight, she can reflect on a lifetime of activism in which struggles against government opposition and social inequality have brought some substantive improvement to the lives of Japanese women.

While Shidzue became most famous for her family planning activities, her political contributions went far beyond that single issue. As a "new woman" of the twenties Shidzue saw her sisters oppressed by a family system which subordinated their roles to that of "good wife and wise mother," a government which barred them from political activities, and a social milieu which jeered at, while at the same time exploiting, their desire to work outside the home. All of this made little practical sense in the environment of a rapidly industrializing and urbanizing nation. The conflict and confusion over the social changes which had accompanied the end of World War I in Europe and America had not bypassed Japan. The industrial era demanded a socially modern Japan which employed men and women fairly and distributed rights and power more evenly. Like their sisters abroad, Shidzue and her circle decried their lack of political rights, their economic inferiority, and their sexual exploitation. In the home, Japan's "new women" saw traditional marriage as a convenience for linking families and producing a male heir. They denounced it as a desecration of the romantic love and sexual freedom which they had read about in Western books by Margaret Sanger and Havelock Ellis, as well as in modern Japanese novels. Less outspoken women remained reticent on the subject of free love but vicariously enjoyed the public debates by the "new women" and the fiction published by women writers which was often frankly confessional and sometimes even salacious. The "new women" with whom Shidzue associated discussed all of these topics in study groups, prepared pamphlets, wrote articles and crusaded for change. While not uniform in their vision of Japan's new society, they knew that change was needed.

By the mid-twenties, while Shidzue's thinking emphasized yet greater personal and public freedom, her husband, Keikichi, made an about face, and he demanded that she give up her liberated ways and become a traditional wife. Keikichi then joined imperialist adventurers seeking fortunes in China and the colonies, and by 1932 he had pledged his allegiance to the militarist goals of Imperial Japan. Abandoned, Shidzue was left to raise and provide for her two teenage sons alone. She refused to surrender her vision of a democratic society even though in the thirties it became increasingly difficult for anyone to question Japan's official policies. More and more frequently liberal and socialist organizations were hounded by the increasingly powerful "thought" police. As the decade progressed "dangerous thoughts" became the frightening key words, and proclamation of liberal ideas perilous. Shidzue continued to study, write, and preach emancipation for women, thereby placing herself in jeopardy. The thirties became an exhilarating, if sometimes frightening, experience which included two lecture tours to America, founding a birth control organization, and advocating women's rights from left-wing political platforms. This pioneering work was aided and inspired by a growing friendship with Margaret Sanger and others in the American birth control movement. Her intellectual life was encouraged by her American mentor, Mary Beard, who motivated her to write her own story in English and to research the lives of women from Japan's past. Throughout the thirties

Shidzue's thinking matured through her reading of Japanese and Western literature and philosophy. In short, she tried to contend against the prevalent atmosphere which continuously narrowed the opening available to democratic thought and feminist aspirations. Privately this was a period of personal fulfillment through an intimate liaison with the proletarian party leader, Katô Kanjû. Although both were married to others, their unity of political purpose and mutual determination to thwart Japan's insistent move to the right gave them the courage to quietly challenge social mores. Their association put Shidzue in danger when at the end of 1937 the Japanese "thought police" rounded up and imprisoned the leadership of the left.

The late thirties was a period of conformity for most Japanese as the militarists won the political day and forced society into their imperialist mode. Most political leaders, writers, and activist women, if not in fact fascist, had by this time outwardly accepted the policies of the authoritarian state. Shidzue, however, continued some family planning activities, displaying an extraordinary window of liberal thought and action until the war with America began. Afterwards she quietly sustained an inner spirit of democracy and bided her time.

Shidzue's story is also that of a mother of two sons, weathering economically trying as well as politically oppressive times. She had been raised to enjoy wealth, but learned to use her talents outside the home to provide support for herself and her children. During the war, however, none of her cleverness could provide what did not exist, nor overcome the illness and want caused by the dedication of the nation's resources to total war. She watched helplessly as one son slowly wasted away and the other was soldiered off to war. Toward the end of the war, completely alone, she sought a new life through marriage to her beloved Kanjû. Their personal joy was increased by the birth of their daughter amidst the 1945 fire bombing of Tokyo.

In the impoverished but stimulating immediate postwar period both Katôs, determined to help usher in a democratic revolution, sought political office. Shidzue became the first woman to announce her candidacy for the House of Representatives in November, 1945. Elected in the first balloting, reelected the following year, and elected in 1950 to the first of four six-year terms as a Senator in the House of Councillors she set about to see her pre-war dreams of equality and freedom for women become law. As a Diet member she worked for birth control legislation, abolition of the feudal family code of 1898, establishment of a separate women's bureau, environmental protection, and, in foreign affairs, strong ties with the United States and improved relations with previously colonized peoples, particularly the Koreans. She believed that women would make a difference in the new democracy and that the social and political movements begun by women in the twenties would come to fruition. Though she watched her larger vision of a democratic revolution fade, she persevered in each of her causes, using her national prominence to gain public attention for each issue.

Probably Shidzue's most significant, though least acknowledged, progressive agency occurred during the years of American Occupation, 1945-1952. At this time, she was poised to play an influential role on both the American and the Japanese sides. On the one hand she was familiar with American culture, knew English well, and had friendships among the American officials; on the other, she was an elected member of the Diet with an influential role in the revived women's movement. She combined these attributes to have a voice, and exert leverage in both camps. In the liberating light of the new constitution, the promise for Japanese feminism seemed bright. Shidzue could not have predicted in 1946 that the cold war atmosphere would cause abrupt changes in American goals for Japan, or that conservative male leadership would quickly regain political control, making it impossible for women to attain the leadership they seemed destined for. During those early Occupation years women were on the march and first and foremost among these was Katô Shidzue.

After the war she was restored to her American friends, and Margaret Sanger, once again, became important to Katô's revived birth control activities. Conversely, in the later part of Sanger's life, she found an adoration and respect in Japan that she had never experienced at home. This relationship, detailed in numerous letters, reveals a side of Sanger not apparent from her American experiences. A second friendship begun in the twenties and rejuvenated after the war was that with the historian, Mary Ritter Beard. In late 1945 Katô found a third admirer in Lt. Ethel Weed, Chief of Women's Affairs with the Allied Occupation. These two worked together to bring about opportunities for women. American connections proved vital to Shidzue's political practice and ideological foundations.

Throughout her lifetime Katô Shidzue formed associations with prominent Japanese who influenced her thought and social activism. She read the socialist writings of Yamakawa Kikue during the twenties and remained an admirer of her after the war. Her paths crossed occasionally with Ichikawa Fusae, noted for her leadership in Japan's suffrage movement, though after the war a competitive relationship developed between them that limited cooperative activities. During the twenties and thirties Katô esteemed the writer Miyamoto Yuriko, but they clashed ideologically soon after the war and parted ways. Shidzue interacted with many other women, less known outside Japan, in her struggles to advance the cause of women's liberation; however, there was never a unified Japanese women's movement nor was there easy agreement between Japanese feminists either in the twenties or after the war. Thinking and action ran the gamut, while organizations often focused on single issues. The period of greatest unity was immediately after the war when it appeared that women would be consulted and would gain a share of the political power. Unfortunately the limits to Japanese feminist power were evident all too soon after the heady ascension of the first class of women to elected office. Katô Shidzue shared in the early show of strength, and then moved on, necessarily, to a more independent road.

The particular issue that Katô Shidzue came to focus on was family planning. This choice was a natural outgrowth of her relationship with Margaret Sanger and of her own accomplishments in the birth control movement of the thirties. Katô's belief that women could not be economically or politically free unless they had control over decisions about procreation formed the basis of her political agenda. A woman's choice about when and how many children to have was related to the entire question of family authority. This, then, determined the subordination of wives and the imprisonment of mothers to the financial needs and daily care of husbands and children. In 1945 Shidzue saw the issue of family planning as essential to the liberation of women. That her attempts to change existing Eugenics Laws were not fully successful was a grave disappointment to her. It reflected the successful wresting of power over this issue by conservative male legislators and greedy physicians who were more interested in maintaining female subservience and making a financial profit than in considering the needs of women. Again the campaign for real gender equality in Japan came up against the entrenched power of conservative men, who fought hard against relinquishing their control over the shape of postwar Japan. Still, determination and persistence on Shidzue's part signaled that she would not be silenced.

In the fifties Katô Shidzue entered the arena of international politics as well. Here was where she felt her greatest contribution would be. She ignored the preachings of the Socialist Party and independently sought closer ties with previously colonized peoples, particularly the Koreans. Through her independent actions and her insistent support of the United States she incurred considerable criticism from her party and from the Japanese left wing in general. Such criticism moved her yet further along her private road and made her appear to be a political maverick. She never regretted her actions, and always claimed that she worked for a wider cause in the international arena. Here, as in the thirties, she proved to be heavily influenced by her several years in the West. Thus, at a time of upheaval in Japanese relations with America in the early sixties, it is not surprising that she would be right in the thick of the debate, nor that her husband's leadership role in the Socialist Party, and her own membership in it, would have little influence over the pro-American position she would publicly pronounce.

The years from 1960 have been quieter ones for Katô. She has continued to work diligently as president of the Family Planning Federation of Japan and has, also, contributed to the heightened discussions over conservation and environmental protection. In this she has not been so different from others in the women's movement who have found their voice in broader issues, not exclusively women's problems, and have organized around the practical militancy of consumer movements and citizen protests. Unfortunately, the power of women as a group has thereby been diffused. Katô Shidzue does not personally find this a disadvantage, since she no longer describes herself as a "feminist", and, in fact, like so many other Japanese women, carefully avoids that term. She sees herself rather as a citizen of the world, interested in leaving her part of that vast environment a better place.

Strangely, there has yet to be a biography of Katô in Japanese. There are few references to her in standard Japanese histories or women's histories. For example, none of the three Japanese women named above (Yamakawa, Miyamoto, and Ichikawa) make more than passing reference to her in their copious writings. This apparent lack of interest in one so obviously influential over such a long period of time is curious at least, and makes researching Katô Shidzue's contributions difficult. Many of the relevant documents are ephemeral, often stored in out-of-the-way places and printed on by now excruciatingly fragile paper. Fortunately the many letters exchanged between Shidzue and her American friends spanning the years from 1920 through the sixties are accessible in the Sophia Smith Collection and the Library of Congress. Moreover, numerous references to Shidzue's influence and accomplishments during the Occupation era can be retrieved through careful perusal of the myriad of papers collected during the U.S. Occupation, and housed in the National Archives. Shidzue herself has written several autobiographies, and in the early days published her arguments in newspapers and magazines. The present biography examines the several sources available in an attempt to fill a significant void in Japanese women's history.

Two women in Japan have helped me in this venture. One, Ashino Yuriko, is the Deputy Executive Director of the Family Planning Federation of Japan, and has enjoyed a twenty-year association with

Katô Shidzue. The second, Funabashi Kuniko, translated Katô's 1935 autobiography into Japanese, has published a Japanese translation of some of the correspondence between Sanger and Katô, and has transcribed and edited Katô [Ishimoto] Shidzue's diary of 1937-1938. These two women and I are in agreement that Katô Shidzue has made a significant lifetime contribution to her society, which should be recognized through public discussion. We are equally astonished that this discussion has not yet taken place. Indeed Katô Shidzue is frequently interviewed, and continues to appear on television (the latest examples were an October, 1994 commentary in the *Asahi Newspaper* and a fall television appearance for "Old People's Day," and television appearances and speeches in 1995). Yet she has never been seriously reviewed. Sitting around a table in Ashino's apartment in October, 1992, we speculated on the reasons for this. One suggestion was that the Japanese are uncomfortable writing a biography of someone who is still alive. Another was that birth control as a cause or a subject has never really interested the Japanese public, and it is therefore deemed sufficient to say, simply, that she was an important birth control advocate. Furthermore, unlike some contemporaries such as Yamakawa, Ichikawa, and Miyamoto, Shidzue has not published a body of work defining a theoretical position or discussing her political perspectives. We all further noted that she has been a political maverick in a country whose political parties, until the most recent years, have not been tolerant of rebels. During her years in the Diet she was a member of the Japan Socialist Party, but often she annoyed party officials by publicly ignoring or opposing party policies. There are many Socialists who would privately criticize her and do publicly ignore her. To these speculations I would add that many of Katô's most important contributions are recorded exclusively in the archives of the American Occupation. Supporting this conclusion is my colleague, Koseki Shôichi, a noted constitutional scholar, who, like me, believes that Katô's performance on the Constitution Committee and her other activities during the early period of the Occupation were particularly notable. I would add that I have found very few Japanese scholars of the Occupation (almost all seem to be male) who have shown any interest in women's contributions during this period, necessarily a handicap if Katô's performance is to be fairly reviewed.

In my longtime study of Katô I have many people to thank for support and help in addition to those mentioned above. First of all, of course, I would express my deep appreciation to Katô Shidzue, herself, who generously answered questions during a week of personal interviews and phone conversations in 1978. At Mrs. Katô's invitation, the interviews were conducted in her daughter's condominium and covered many hours of reminiscing. At that time she was eighty-one.

In addition I want to thank Mrs. Katô for selecting photographs in the summer of 1995, and to Ashino Yuriko and Katoh Taki for forwarding them to me.

Several colleagues and friends have offered commentary on different sections of the biography or have given me other sorts of advice and assistance and I would like to thank them for their support: Dick Mitchell, Brett de Bary, Victor Koschman, Tom Grunfeld, Miles Fletcher, Sally Hastings, Scottie Faerber, Frank and Nobuko Itoh, Patricia Steinhoff, Alice Cook, Thomas Burkman, Barbara Ramusack, Delmer Brown, the staff at the Sophia Smith Collection, and members of the Midwest Japan Seminar, who have provided an environment of intellectual excitement.

One colleague in particular has read and reread the entire manuscript offering thoughtful suggestions and providing new ways of conceiving different aspects of Katô Shidzue's life. For this generous help I particularly thank Mark Selden. I would also like to express my appreciation for financial support from the Empire State College Foundation of Empire State College, State University of New York, and from two travel grants provided by the Northeast Asia Council of the Association for Asian Studies.

My most heartfelt gratitude is reserved for my husband, Paul, who has provided continuing encouragement for this project for far too many years. His intellectual, emotional, and technical support for my research and writing of this biography has been irreplaceable. I dedicate the book to him with abiding love and heartfelt thanks.

Helen M. Hopper

1

Good Wife, Wise Mother (1897–1920)

In January, 1920 the Baroness Ishimoto Shidzue, daughter of a wealthy Japanese engineer and wife of a Japanese Baron, found herself abandoned in New York City. She had a single room in the home of a middle class American couple at 157th and Broadway while she studied across town at a secretarial school. Before leaving her alone in this strange environment, her husband, Baron Ishimoto Keikichi, had chided his wife to meet only with Americans and admonished her to study hard, learn English, and become a Western-style, independent woman. Shidzue was lonely and cold, and missed her family in Japan and the ease of her aristocratic life in Tokyo. Most of all she longed to hold her two baby sons, whom she had entrusted to the care of her mother. During that especially miserable winter in New York City she had much time to lament her decision to leave her babies behind and follow her radical husband abroad on his revolutionary quest.

During the brief month which Shidzue and Keikichi had lived together after her arrival in America the previous September, her husband had made little effort to help her adjust to New York or find new companions. He did introduce her in passing to a few of his radical friends, one of whom, Agnes Smedley, briefly rescued Shidzue from her isolated life that day in January. Since Shidzue's husband clearly had approved of an association with someone of Smedley's political persuasion, Shidzue felt bold enough to approach her. The Japanese woman wanted to know if Smedley had heard of a remarkable person called Margaret Sanger, of whom Shidzue had been told unbelievable tales. Yes, Smedley said, she was well acquainted with her. Later, Smedley repeated the exchange to Sanger, describing Ishimoto as an exotic, independent young Japanese woman who was married to a radical Japanese aristocrat, well-known in socialist circles. Sanger was intrigued. She immediately invited the Baroness to be her guest of honor at a tea.

On January 17th, Smedley accompanied Shidzue to Sanger's apartment, where the young Japanese first met the woman who was to become her mentor and lifelong friend. The meeting was one filled with immediate mutual admiration and respect. As Shidzue wrote in her 1935 autobiography, "Quite contrary to my imagination, when she received me at the door of her studio, I saw a delicate little figure with charm of a thoroughly feminine type. Still her strong will power was evident in her bright shining eyes. And her thick shining hair gave a touch of eternal youth to her appearance. I felt instantly her magnetism and my respect for her deepened as she talked about her difficulties." It was at this moment, Shidzue claimed, that she inwardly declared, "I will carry the banner for Birth Control in Japan!"[1] Even though she felt inferior in character and courage to the older woman, Shidzue believed, in retrospect, that her own strength lay in a "knowledge and conviction" that would assure her success in such a formidable undertaking. She believed, in fact, that she had found the cause that would motivate her toward the lifetime of social activism that her husband had decreed for her.

Family and Education

Hirota Shidzue[2] had married Ishimoto Keikichi on December 23, 1914, when she was seventeen years old. It was a magnificent wedding appropriate to the joining of two wealthy, aristocratic families. The Baron Ishimoto's father, Lieutenant General Ishimoto Shinroku, had served the Meiji Emperor with distinction in the Russo-Japanese War of 1904-05. The Emperor had rewarded his loyal subject by conferring upon him the noble title of Baron and, further, in 1911 had welcomed him as Minister of War in Prime Minister [Prince] Saionji Kimmochi's cabinet. Unfortunately the new War Minister died in 1912 after serving only briefly in the government. He left a wife, six sons and one daughter, of whom Keikichi was the eldest.

Shidzue was also from a distinguished, if untitled, family. Her father, Hirota Ritaro, was born in 1866 into a samurai family which served the Abe Clan in Western Japan. After a childhood of private tutoring in classical Chinese and Japanese studies he entered the highly selective Imperial University in Tokyo to study science and mechanical engineering, thus accumulating the knowledge which would permit him to play a part in Meiji Japan's remarkable industrialization. Shidzue described her father as "wearing a Western suit and hat, understanding English well, designing factories in modern style, but in his private life thoroughly imbued with the feudalistic ideology. He was during my childhood, and he still [1935] is, a samurai, not with sword girded at his side, but with the engineer's ruler in his pocket."[3] Hirota Ritaro was also honored by the government after the Russo-Japanese War. He was decorated by the emperor in recognition of his procurement of munitions for the military through his trading company in London. He was further celebrated by the Imperial University which granted him an honorary Doctorate of Engineering and a university chair. It was he who sought out the Baron Ishimoto to be his daughter's husband, and it was he who convinced her of the appropriateness of the match.

Shidzue's mother, Tsurumi Toshiko, the eldest of ten children, came from a notable and highly educated family. She had attended a Canadian mission academy in her youth where she had studied English and other Western topics. In spite of this background, she exhibited no Western veneer whatsoever. In 1935 Shidzue described her as the quintessential traditional Japanese mother and wife. "My mother uses polite words only, never liking to pick up the vulgar words spoken in the street. She never betrays unpleasant feelings. 'Endurance' and 'repression' are her greatest ideals. She says to me, 'Endurance a woman should cultivate more than anything else. If you endure well in any circumstances, you will achieve happiness.' She never loses her temper with the servants, but is always dignified and gentle, however, stupid or slow they may be.... She has managed the household admirably, and has brought up her six children well."[4]

Growing up in comfort and style in Tokyo at the turn of the century Shidzue was surrounded by quiet luxury, exposed to culture and learning, and provided with every convenience and opportunity appropriate to an educated girl in an upper class environment. She was born on March 2, 1897, and named by her father for the Noh drama *Shidzuka* he had been attending at the moment of her birth. Her father wrote the name in the Japanese *katakana* syllabary rather than choosing Chinese characters, *kanji*, to represent the sounds. At the time of Shidzue's birth the family still lived just outside the Imperial palace on the grounds assigned to the Abe family for whom they had been retainers during the feudal era. Soon after, however, they moved to Kojimachi, an exclusive area in Tokyo, close by the Imperial Palace, the government buildings and the present-day Meiji Shrine. "In the neighborhood of my father's home, all the residences occupy large tracts of land; from the gate to the house door there is usually a long avenue, and at the back of the house a spacious garden. Each house is surrounded by a six-foot wall of plaster or wood and only the top of the house can be seen from the street."[5] In 1912 her father tore down his Japanese house and built a Western style house designed by a German architect. Even before this modern change, when the family lived in purely Japanese style, and the children were raised by their mother's traditional hand, their father filled the house with Western furniture and inventions. He brought home a piano, desks, a sewing machine, and other useful and aesthetic items from his business trips to Europe. Consequently, Shidzue enjoyed both Japanese and Western influences in her early education and material surroundings.

Shidzue's household included her parents, an elder brother, Kôichi, a younger brother, Yôji, twin younger sisters, Kiyo and Kayo, and the youngest brother, Hirô. In addition, her mother's younger brother Tsurumi Yûsuke lived with the family for much of Shidzue's childhood. The large estate also accommodated a number of servants. During the summer all of the children and some servants went to Kamakura, a full day's journey from their Tokyo house, to stay with their grandfather for three months. Shidzue described the trek. "A train of several rikishas would carry mother, elder brother, myself, younger brothers and sisters and maids - two youngsters would ride in a rikisha together, and one or two rikishas carrying big trunks of bedding, spare kimonos and accessories, books and toys all wrapped up in the big square green furoshiki (cloth for wrapping) would follow in the rear of the procession. The rikisha men ran with speed on the flat roads along the moat under the hanging branches of willows or down hilly roads between the brick government buildings to Hibiya Park, but they were slow when they climbed hills, making zigzag curves while the persons who were riding would bend their bodies forward trying to cause these men less strain."[6] The rikisha ride to the train station at Shimbashi would take forty minutes, and then the train ride to Kamakura with its eleven stops en route another three hours. Her grandfather's house was built on a cliff and from it one could see the entire town and the seashore. She remembered her summers as filled with swimming, nature walks, reading and listening to her grandfather tell samurai stories of fighting for his lord just before the overthrow of the feudal Tokugawa shogun in the 1860s.

In 1902, at the age of five, Shidzue was enrolled in the Peeresses' School which had been founded by the Empress just ten years after her husband, the Emperor Meiji, had established the Peers' School for boys in 1877. The Peeresses' School was an institution for children of the nobility and such others from upper class families who were deemed suitable to associate with royalty. Until she was twelve Shidzue studied, and played with the young girls of the school, learning the appropriate manners and etiquette for members of the overthrown feudal aristocracy whose style of life endured within their own closed circle. In 1909 she graduated to the higher school, where for the next five years, until her marriage in 1914, she studied arithmetic, algebra, geometry, physics, chemistry, Japanese and foreign geography, and history, and all forms of Japanese reading and writing as well as some Chinese. Most of her time, however, was spent on the arts appropriate for a proper wife; calligraphy, painting, drawing, music, sewing, embroidery, and cooking. In the few moments left she received training in ethics, with emphasis on loyalty and filial piety, and participated in exercises and athletics.

In spite of the time consuming nature of Shidzue's formal education and the broad coverage which it appeared to embrace, she has credited her social training and "mental awakening" to two other sources. It was her mother whom she considered the greatest influence on her aspiration to become "a good wife and wise mother" in accordance with the ideal of the seventeenth century neo-Confucian moralist, Kaibara Ekken. On the other hand, she emphasized, "My young uncle, Tsurumi Yûsuke, was the one who first developed the intellectual side of my life."[7] Tsurumi came to live in his older sister's home in 1908 when he was twenty-three and studying at the Imperial University. Uncle Yûsuke became Shidzue's great favorite and she never tired of hearing his stories which ranged from tales of ancient Japan, to the heroics of Joan of Arc, the novel, *Uncle Tom's Cabin,* and the political oratory of William Jennings Bryan. Tsurumi Yûsuke was a follower Dr. Nitobe Inazô, the Christian humanist and interpreter of Japanese *bushidô*, or the way and spirit of the warrior. Uncle Yûsuke joined with a group of other students including Ishimoto Keikichi to form a study society which met in Nitobe's home and pursued their mentor's teachings of Eastern moral philosophy and Western learning, reading such authors as Goethe, Wordsworth, Tennyson, Carlyle, Dante, Milton, Kant, Longfellow and Victor Hugo. Once the group met at the Hirota house and Shidzue was permitted to sit silently in the back of the room and listen. She was tremendously moved by, though did not fully understand, the recital of the thinking of great European and American minds. Dr. Nitobe, married to an American from Philadelphia, was at ease in both Japanese and Western customs and thought. He gave Shidzue a number of books and she became "baptized by the spirit of humanism." She believed that while Uncle Yûsuke was her mentor, Dr. Nitobe was her "reverend minister."[8]

Early Married Life

When Shidzue's father brought her the good news that the Baron Ishimoto Keikichi's family sought her as his bride, she was far from delighted. Her fears, however, were somewhat allayed by her Uncle Yûsuke's opinion of this man. "What a lucky child you are!" he told her. "You would be the most fortunate woman in Japan if you were to marry the young baron!.... Baron Ishimoto is one of the brightest disciples of Dr. Nitobe and I have known him for quite a while."[9] He then went on to explain that Ishimoto was a student of Christian humanism, a gifted honor student at the Imperial University, who aspired to become a social reformer to help Japan's ill-treated laborers. To this end he was completing an engineering course and would use his education and talent for social causes. Shidzue and Keikichi, ten years her senior, met, and consented to the match.

The formal Shintô wedding, which followed an equally ritualistic betrothal ceremony, included the preparation of an extensive and expensive trousseau, "befitting the baron's rank." This was comprised in part of bedding, cushions, clothing for all seasons and occasions, furniture, hair ornaments, and jewelry,[10] and required "four two-ton motor trucks" to transfer the entire collection of goods to the Baron's mansion five days before the wedding. At the conclusion of the ceremony on December 23, 1914, Shidzue would leave her family and join her husband to live in her mother-in-law's home and learn her ways. Her trousseau must provide all of her personal needs for much of her life to come. The wedding itself took place in the grand reception room of the Ishimoto mansion and was solemnized by the "three-three-and-nine times exchanging sake cup ceremony"[11] which united the Baron and Baroness in marriage. For each event over the course of the day Shidzue wore appropriate ceremonial wedding kimono and hair style with all of the expensive accompanying ornaments. It was a grand and traditional affair out of the previous era. In deference to the modern period the Baron wore white tie, tails and a top hat.

After graduation from the Imperial University and his marriage to Shidzue, the Baron joined the Mitsui Mining Company as an engineer and was sent in January, 1915, to the island of Kyûshû to supervise workers in the Miike Coal Mines. Bride and groom, married not yet a month, traveled by train along the coast parallel to the Inland Sea from Tokyo to the southern tip of the island of Honshû, then crossed the Straits of Shimonoseki by boat, and connected with a train destined for an interior section of northern Kyûshû where the mines were located. Here they began their life among chimney's puffing black smoke, the dust and dirt of the company town, and the black underground coal mines. It was a startling change from their accustomed rich cultural life amidst the best homes and gardens in Tokyo. Much to Shidzue's surprise her executive husband did not move into a gentleman's office but conducted his work from the pit surrounded by common laborers and was, in fact, required to do physical labor and not merely shuffle papers.

A further shock to her were the quarters which would be their first home. She described the place, a company owned residence, as a "hut" with small four mat rooms and a narrow ladder to a tiny attic. The hut, which was thatched with straw, had a minimal amount of electricity in the evening, but no private bath. The Baroness had to use the public bath like everyone else. One maid had accompanied them to Kyûshû, and she proved invaluable, working hard at scrubbing down the filthy hut and, in general, helping Shidzue to survive her wretched environment, which she described in 1935. "Rats ran about freely regardless of the social rank of the new occupants. When it rained, buckets, washtubs and bath towels of every kind were quickly assembled to catch the water which dropped wherever it pleased through the leaky roof, upon our heads, into my closets where I kept the bed quilts and even on my beautifully polished chest of drawers brought from Tokyo. Luckily I had packed only the worst possible kimonos chosen from my gay trousseau."[12]

Life in this mining area was miserable for the miners and their families and only somewhat better for Shidzue. Her husband began his breakfast of steamed rice, *misô* soup and boiled eggs at five each morning. The hour was early but his meal more nourishing than those of his workers. While he ate Shidzue would read the Bible to him. He then walked to the mines and headed down to the pits to supervise his workers. Like them he had an hour for lunch at noon and then would return home at the end of the day so late that he only saw daylight when he worked the night shift. His salary was low and it was difficult to stretch it through the month, even though rent was free. Their lives improved somewhat when they moved to a larger, better house. Early in 1918, after just two years in the field, Keikichi was ordered back to Tokyo because his health had deteriorated under the grueling conditions of the coal mines. Just six months earlier, in June, 1917, Shidzue had given birth to their first son, Arata.

The two years at the Miike Coal Mines were both miserable and enlightening for the privileged Shidzue. She was shocked by the tragic existence of the fifty thousand miners and their families and emotionally moved by those who managed to persevere amidst continuous hardship. She had visited the cramped, stuffy, dusty, narrow pits and knew something about the adverse conditions her neighbors endured. She observed the women, burdened with many children but without the means to care for them. She saw the squalor in which they were forced to live and die. She heard even more from her husband about both the realities of the miners' dismal lives and the theories of why this was so, for his socialist ideals led him to fixed conclusions about the evils of capitalist management and its oppression of the people. Shidzue claimed that at the time of her first visit with Margaret Sanger her determination to take up the cause of birth control education was based, in part, on the tragic impressions the wretched women in the company villages of the Miike Coal Mines had made upon her. It was then, in 1920, she associated her experiences during the first years of her married life with the humanistic teachings of her husband and Dr. Nitobe, and concluded that her contribution to the alleviation of human suffering would be through propagating Sanger's message for the liberation for women through birth control education.

When the Baron, Baroness, and infant son returned to Tokyo they moved to Kamakura to be close to Keikichi's new job with a chemical laboratory, a subsidiary of the Mitsui Company. Their return coincided with the excitement caused by major international events. Among these, the most inspiring for Keikichi and other intellectuals and activists in Tokyo was the Russian Revolution. This cataclysmic foreign news was followed in the summer of 1918 by rice riots at home which rocked Japan and frightened the conservative government. Fast moving events were causing liberals and radicals, especially student, labor, and intellectual leaders, to think forward to sweeping political and social changes within Japan. Keikichi went obediently to his laboratory each day, but in his free time he studied labor problems and the relationship between the contribution of workers to the wealth created for owners like Mitsui in the new capitalist industries. He read excitedly the works of Marx, other communist and socialist thinkers, and Russian literature. His reading and his study of events unfolding in Japan and throughout the world brought him to the conclusion that good intentions of even the best individual were not adequate to rescue the poor for whom the world refused to show mercy.

Reeducation in the West

Keikichi lectured his wife, "To find solutions to Japan's labor problems one must personally study the thought and action of revolutionary leaders." As his thinking led him to more and more radical beliefs his dissatisfaction with the dull routine of his work increased. In an effort to understand the emotional and intellectual stress her husband was experiencing, Shidzue began to read some of the literature he suggested to her, and she, too, began to sympathize with his particular brand of humanism, stimulated by the successful Russian Revolution. She, too, felt the exciting influence of revolutionary thought.[13] She could understand why he wanted desperately to do something more rewarding, more exciting, more pertinent to the changes he saw occurring in the world. She was not surprised when he finally acted. Determined to somehow play a role in the earth shaking events, Keikichi decided to travel abroad and study first hand the revolutionary socialist activities which were firing up the intellectuals he read and the workers they wrote for. Mundane family and company responsibilities paled in comparison with the possibility of joining the revolution. On February 13, 1919, Keikichi sailed for America, the first stop in his pursuit of radical transformation. The preceding October a second son, Tamio, had been born, and so he left behind a wife and two infants.

The excitement of the new environment completely enveloped Keikichi as he traveled about America. He sent home postcards and letters which described something of what he was experiencing, and he invited his wife to join him in his revolutionary quest. He warned her, however, "Don't come abroad if you seek pleasure and new fashions in clothes or are planning to spend your time only at the theaters or motoring like other 'bourgeoises mesdames'. Come to me if you will educate yourself, to feed yourself with knowledge of the world, to prepare yourself to swim abreast the world's new tide."[14] Shidzue, abandoned and lonely, made up her mind to leave her two babies and follow her husband to America. She sent the boys, Arata, then just past two, and Tamio, just one year old, with their maids to her family home in Kamakura, where they would be cared for by her mother and other family members and retainers, while she sailed on August 15, 1919, for America. A month before she left she wrote in her diary of the pain of leaving her babies behind. She ended the entry, "I much prefer to stay with my darlings but I believe firmly that it is my duty to endure this trial of separation in order to study more while I am young so that some day in the future I can carry out a mother's duties to them in manifold measure." She had begun to reinterpret her role as traditional "good wife and wise mother" in the light of her husband's radical requirements for her life.

The trip started in joy and comfort, for Shidzue's father accompanied her to her destination. The arrival in San Francisco made an exquisite impression upon her, and she believed that a dream had come true. Her husband met the ship and the three of them took a room at a hotel in Berkeley. Keikichi then told her father, while Shidzue listened, of the things he had seen and the dreams he had dreamed for changing the lot of the laborer. She observed that while both men had been educated at the same university and in the same field, one had "strictly limited his interest to the sphere of mechanical power, and the other proposed to utilize its productive power in the interest of general human happiness. I recognized," she continued, "a thousand mile gap between the father and the son-in-law, and I thought that in that distance lay the progress of the younger generation."[15]

The three then proceeded by train to New York City. Once there her father checked into a hotel in Washington Square and Keikichi took his wife to his cheap, dirty room where she encountered bed bugs, shabby furniture, and substandard facilities. The day after their arrival he showed her how, for a pittance, she could get a cup of coffee and a muffin at a Sixth Avenue cafe. She was scandalized. Why must she live in such an impoverished manner, she thought, given her station in life and her money in the bank? She was downcast and miserable. Her Uncle Yûsuke, also in New York, exclaimed that Keikichi had finally truly become a Bolshevik and, strangely, this comment made in jest, explained everything to Shidzue. One week later Keikichi took his wife to the Y.W.C.A. to consult with an advisor at their Training School explaining to those in charge and to Shidzue that he wanted her to gain professional skills, learn English quickly, and thereby become an independent, self-supporting modern woman.

Beginning the first of October she entered the Ballard School in the Y.W.C.A. building and registered for a secretarial course. She worked so hard for the next few weeks on her stenography, bookkeeping, secretarial duties, and typewriting that she was able to ignore the squalor of her living environment. She enjoyed the atmosphere of freedom and candor at the Ballard School, especially the fact that her teachers were all women and made her feel comfortable asking any question, no matter how elementary. She felt at ease speaking aloud in class, even though she had to use English.[16]

Just one month later Keikichi went off to Washington D.C. to the first meeting of the International Labor Organization. Before he left he encouraged his wife to find herself new quarters, thereby taking her first steps toward the independent life he envisioned for her. She advertised in the newspaper and the next day a southern American woman and her husband offered her a room in a more suitable middle class area of New York. Thus, the quality of her material life improved substantially, while her loneliness increased several fold, after her husband left. He returned briefly to spend Christmas vacation with her, but essentially they were separated from October until Shidzue joined him in Europe early in the summer of 1920. By that time she had received a certificate of graduation from the Ballard School accompanied by a report card grading her A in each of the four secretarial subjects.

The year in America was a mixed one. Shidzue studied hard and learned both English and a marketable skill, but she was intensely lonely for her family and for the friendship of other Japanese, and exhausted by the continuous need to speak in English. At one point in 1919, in direct defiance of her husband's command that she meet only with Americans, Shidzue had tea with the Japanese chief of the New York City branch of the Yokohama Specie Bank, (present-day Bank of Tokyo). Their conversation, far from stiff and formal, turned quickly to the subject of love and, more specifically the contrasting attitudes Japanese and American women held on this intimate topic. The banker told Shidzue that American women, unlike their Japanese counterparts, were interested in experiencing the freedom to enjoy all aspects of love. At that point he brought up Margaret Sanger whom he described as a beautiful person, who crusaded for birth control. Shidzue was completely in the dark. She had not heard of Margaret Sanger, nor did she know what "birth control" meant. Her companion went on to explain Sanger's crusade for planned children, as well as her attitudes toward free love. He also eagerly related stories about Sanger's battles with the authorities as she carried out her mission.[17]

Shidzue had been quite taken with her frank discussion with the banker and decided to ask her acquaintance, Agnes Smedley, for further information about the curious and remarkable woman, Margaret Sanger. Smedley, who had been held in prison for possible seditious acts until the end of World War I, was one of Shidzue's few acquaintances in New York City sanctioned by her absent husband. Happily for Shidzue, in January, 1920, Smedley was in charge of Sanger's new journal, *Birth Control Review,* and the two American activists were close friends. This, then, was the chain of events which led to Sanger's tea, held on an icy January day in New York City to honor the Baroness Ishimoto.[18]

When Sanger greeted the Baroness at the door to her apartment on January, 17th, she shattered the mental image which Shidzue had formed during the earlier conversation with her banker friend. Sanger was not strong minded, big boned, man-like, with short hair and a large voice, as she had imagined. After all, wouldn't these be the mental and physical characteristics of someone who fought the authorities, the Japanese woman had thought. Instead Margaret Sanger was beautiful, had thick, abundant hair, big blue eyes, a lovely voice and a warm manner. She seemed to glow with kindness, and Shidzue's strongest impression was that here was a woman filled to the brim with a mother's love.[19] A mutual admiration and empathy was kindled by this meeting. The women had more in common than they realized, for at that moment both were suffering from illness, loneliness, and personal despair and both would leave New York at the beginning of the summer for Europe in search of emotional and intellectual restoration.[20]

Shidzue does not mention whether she and Sanger met again during that winter, but the inspiration emanating from this one meeting was dramatic. Sanger's personal demeanor, her birth control message to mothers, and her loudly proclaimed attitudes about the fulfillment of women's emotional and sexual desires all made an impact on the dejected young Japanese woman's heart. Whether Shidzue did, in fact, determine at that moment that birth control education would become her particular social cause, she certainly became enticed by the desire to somehow free women from male oppression and to improve the quality of married women's lives.

The new information conveyed by Sanger and her friends meshed readily with Shidzue's husband's humanistic teachings and his insistence upon her own acquisition of independence and self-sufficiency. She saw a connection between male sexual domination and female social and economic dependence. Here was the place for her to start. A woman would never be free, she reasoned, as long as she did not achieve personal independence. She described her new goals in a school letter-writing exercise. The training at Ballard would enable her to take up a position in the business world. This would free her economically. More importantly, however, her American education had given her a broader purpose in life. She would "work for the independence of all Japanese women." She continued, "I believe that every woman whether she belongs to the upper class or to the lower class, married or single, should not be dependent upon the man, economically or intellectually."[21] During the next two years she would logically tie the achievement of female independence to a woman's need to control the size of her family. In her husband's absence Shidzue had learned the lessons he had forced upon her very well .

By contrast, the Baron's frenzied travels to America, from there to Mexico, back to America, off to Stockholm, from there to Germany and England and other points in Europe, all in search of an understanding and application of Christian humanism proved disillusioning. His ultimate goal had been to travel to the new Soviet Union, to observe the manifestation of his revolutionary beliefs in all their glory. He had begun his quest with great excitement and idealism. Before Shidzue had joined him in America, Keikichi had sailed to Mexico in his continuing search for revolutionary enlightenment. Curiously, this trip is recorded in the military intelligence files of the U.S. government. It seems he was not considered simply an idealistic romantic but a possible trouble maker, and so he was tracked. The brief note sent to the office of the Secretary of State said, "Kerkicki Ihimoto

[sic], a Japanese said to be figuring on a contract with Carranza to supply ammunition, speaks English fluently; now enroute to Havana on *Morro Castle*. Uses typewriter incessantly."[22] There is no evidence that Ishimoto was on such a sensitive and explosive mission. He did tell Shidzue that soon after his arrival in the U.S. he left for Mexico under the auspices of his employer, the Mitsui Company, to inspect the mines in that country. It is doubtful that this was cover for something more sinister. Other, more suspect, aspects of his American stay, including a meeting with the labor leader, Bill Haywood, of the International Workers of the World (IWW), who had recently been released from prison, and with the Japanese socialist, Katayama Sen, curiously, were not cause for security sensitive comment.

These radical contacts contrasted strongly with Keikichi's more conservative participation in the International Labor Organization's [ILO] first meeting in Washington in October, 1919. He went on his own to the meeting but once there he assisted, so he claimed, the official Japanese delegate, Masumoto Uhei. The choice of Matsumoto as the Japanese delegate had created considerable conflict in Japan. In accordance with their signing of the Versailles Peace Treaty the previous June, the Japanese government had agreed to permit the establishment of labor unions. Pointing to this pledge several labor union leaders insisted that a delegate chosen from the workers should be elected to fill Japan's allotted ILO Conference slot.[23] In fact the government manipulated the election and secured the selection of a member of management, an engineer. Thus, upon the occasion of the Washington ILO Conference, the socialist-humanist, Baron Ishimoto, resurrected his Mitsui engineering and management affiliation and his noble title to join his privileged compatriots.

The Baron returned from Washington for a brief Christmas stay with Shidzue, but his restlessness would not let him be tied down. He had tired of his American travels and associations. On January 3, 1920, he sailed for Europe. Once there, his primary goal was to enter the USSR and meet with Lenin and Trotsky, who were "carrying out the socialism which has shaken the world since Karl Marx advanced the new idea."[24] His dream, however, became a nightmare. In spite of introductions from Katayama and other socialists, Soviet officials refused to issue him a visa. The primary obstacle was his title; a revolutionary could hardly be addressed as Baron.

By the time Shidzue joined her husband in England early that summer, he was sullen and irretrievably distraught. He gave no sign of passion or even interest in their reunion. There was no doubt that his disappointment over his exclusion from the USSR had changed him. His disillusionment was plain, and this had changed his character irrevocably. Shidzue was determined to enjoy her new experience despite her husband's dark manner, and, in truth, became enchanted with her tour of Europe. She was delighted with the exoticism and beauty of London, Paris and Rome, interested in conversations with the new women voters in England, fascinated by social discussions in Germany, and shocked and amazed by the disruption workers caused the general public as they participated in strikes in Italy. There were moments of returned joy to their marriage as they both enjoyed the natural beauty of the countryside and the historical and cultural treasures of the cities. But there was no doubt that Keikichi had begun to lose his romantic idealism just at the time that Shidzue had discovered the personal ideal of free love and the public social cause of women's liberation.

At the end of the summer husband and wife returned home[25] where their sons were being cared for by Shidzue's mother. The two boys did not remember their mother, for in her absence their grandmother had become their caretaker and refuge. Arata was now just past three and Tamio would be two in one month. It would take time to renew their confidence and trust. Meanwhile the Ishimotos circle of friends were interested to learn about the couple's exotic travels. Shidzue and Keikichi became newsworthy and were introduced about as representatives of the "new man and woman" of Japan.[26] Keikichi wrote articles for the newspaper about his exotic experiences and for a brief moment forgot his disappointments.

Shidzue had not forgotten her promises to herself to seek economic independence and to propagate birth control education, but she had to find some way to accomplish this within the constraints of social class and family responsibilities. Reality and her dreams did not mesh easily. She sought out employment and found an appropriate part time job which would allow her to care for her sons, earn a small income, and use her new professional skills, but would not cause too much opposition at home. She became private secretary to the Y.W.C.A. entertainment hostess, Miss Anna Birdsall. The salary was fifty yen a month and the hours flexible, allowing her to fulfill her proper role as mother and wife. She enjoyed her job, which primarily consisted of introducing Western visitors to Japan's culture and people, but before a year had passed Miss Birdsall returned to America and Shidzue returned full time to her traditional role as "good wife, and wise mother." She appeared to have taken a step backwards.

Keikichi, meanwhile, found his dreams stifled by his work environment. He had managed, to some extent, to pretend that his travels were the fulfillment of a professional assignment as a representative of the Mitsui Company, and in that spirit, he reported on his "findings" to his superiors, then once again, he took up his tiresome duties. In apparent conflict of interest, but in accordance with his sympathies for the worker, he joined the mining division of the new labor union, Sôdômei,[27] where he established a subgroup to study labor questions. Soon, however, he recognized that his labor interests and his role as a Mitsui engineer/manager were antithetical to his own beliefs about the disaccord which existed between the interests of the mine owners and laborers. Mitsui's management, as well, found Keikichi's two roles at odds. He was informed that his union work was inappropriate and reproved by his superiors.[28] He resigned his job. Although, for the moment, he had adequate wealth to keep the family economically secure regardless of whether he worked or not, he needed a focus and wanted additional income, albeit not employment which conflicted with his ideology. He found his answer in the establishment of a book store which stocked imported foreign books. Whereas Shidzue seemed invigorated with her fledgling ventures into the public world, Keikichi, still discontented, was establishing a pattern of both financial failure and instability in his professional life. This was just one of the first signs of an inconstancy which would push him from project to project, casting him as a wanderer with uncertain focus.

In one of his many restless moments Keikichi decided that he and Shidzue would take a trip to Korea and China and so for two months in the fall of 1921, just one year after their return from the West, they set sail once again.[29] Shidzue was obviously conflicted over what she saw on this Asian trip. She moved back and forth between interpretations of the Koreans and Chinese which were less than complimentary and those which were sympathetic and showed great concern for the oppressed and impoverished workers and mothers. Her evaluation revealed a naiveté and confusion which reflected a conflict between her upper class interests and an egalitarianism produced by her recent socialist education; between her pride in country formed by her family's accomplishments and her nation's advancement, and her newly embraced internationalism; and between her repugnance for the dirt and squalor, so distant from her own way of life, and the empathy which her newly embraced humanism engendered.

Thus, in little more than one year this young Japanese woman, trained in the traditional ways of a lost era, had become radically reeducated toward thoughts of liberation for herself and for her female compatriots. Shidzue had begun to weave an activist future from the intellectual and emotional threads she had taken up in 1920 and 1921. The fabric would take the entire decade to weave, and its design and character would change in accordance with personal associations and national policies, but the pattern was clear. On the personal level, economic independence would become both a cause and a necessity; intimate relations with a man would have to include mutual respect, romance and love; and child raising, though it would continue be an important focus, would not be all consuming. The outmoded ideal of "good wife and wise mother" was not adequate to sustain this new woman. On the public level, social action for birth control would be intertwined with a determination to free women from oppression; international cooperation would take precedence over national self-interest; and political and social action would be demanded to achieve the first two goals. Within these contexts Shidzue would find that she would build on her association with Margaret Sanger and with other Americans, and she would make strategic use of her growing knowledge of Western culture and the English language. Facing both East and West she would be challenged by personal and public excitement as well as turmoil and confusion in the decades to come. Her way would not be smooth nor without personal tragedy, but her influence and contribution both nationally and internationally would be substantial.

Notes

1. Ishimoto/Katô, 1935, p. 183. (Katô Shidzue's own writings will be referenced by publication date only.)

2. From 1897 Shidzue was known by her father's name, Hirota. After her first marriage she became Baroness Ishimoto Shidzue. When she married Katô Kanjû she took his family name, Katô. She prefers to romanize her given name with a "d," Shidzue, though others have written it Shizue. Her father wrote the name with *katakana* letters rather than *kanji*, or Chinese characters, but sometimes she is referred to by two *kanji*. I refer to her as Shidzue when using her family name might cause confusion.

3. 1935, p. 6.

4. 1935, p. 11.

5. 1935, p, 19.

6. 1935, p. 32-33.

7. 1935, p. 87.

8. 1935, p. 97.

9. 1935, p. 105.

10. 1935 provides ten pages listing the trousseau.

11. *sansan kudo*. The bride and groom each sip three times from three different cups, or nine sips. This signifies the marriage ceremony. The marriage is legalized when the bride's name is stricken from her father's register, and written in the groom's family register.

12. 1935, p. 149.

13. 1981, p. 41.

14. 1935, pp. 171-176. In the 1981, pp. 41-44, version of this decision Shidzue sounds less hesitant, more determined to go to America specifically to learn, armed with a personal plan, not merely following her husband's wishes. The earlier version would appear to be closer to what actually happened.

15. 1935, p. 176.

16. 1981, p. 44. Since her teachers had always been women, probably the emphasis should be on freedom to speak out.

17. 1981, pp. 45-46.

18. In 1948, p. 55, Shidzue identifies Smedley as famous for her writings about the Communist Chinese Eighth Route Army. See the 1981, p. 46 version of the meeting which elaborates somewhat on the 1935 description.

19. In 1948, p. 56, Sanger is described as *onna-rashii,* suggesting the ideal of Japanese womanhood. See also 1981, p. 47. The picture of Sanger filled with mother's love would hardly fit that suggested by Ellen Chesler, Sanger's latest biographer, *Woman of Valor,* Simon & Schuster, 1992.

20. See 1935, 1948, & 1981 for a picture of Shidzue, and Ellen Chesler, *Woman of Valor,* Chapter 8, for a picture of Sanger during this period.

21. From the Ballard School files as reproduced in "The Baroness Learns Shorthand," by Louis A. Leslie in *The Gregg Writer,* February, 1933, 25:6, p. 272. Box 235J, Sanger Archives, Library of Congress. [Referenced, Sanger, LofC.]

22. The message is signed Foster and copies were sent to the General Staff War College and to Operations. MID-1766-1044, May 11, 1919, Ishimoto Keikichi file, Office of Strategic Services (OSS), National Archives.

23. See Sheldon Garon, *The State and Labor in Modern Japan,* University of California Press, 1987 pp. 43-44. Interestingly in Shidzue's 1935 comment, p. 189, Masumoto and his two advisors, Ooshima and Dômae, are "industrial laborers." She implies that Keikichi was welcomed because he knew English. In fact, they were management, and he was welcomed as a Mitsui manager.

24. 1935, p. 191.

25. 1948, pp. 61-64 and 1935, pp. 205-207.

26. 1948, p. 61.

27. General Federation of Labor in Japan [Nihon Rôdô Sôdômei].

28. 1948, p. 62.

29. See 1935, pp. 213-219.

2

A "New Woman" of Japan (1921–1928)

When Shidzue returned to Tokyo from her travels in China and Korea, she thought once again about her determination to achieve economic independence. Fortuitously, a friend who imported yarn from America, convinced her that she could profitably run a retail yarn shop. Seizing this opportunity Shidzue, found suitable space in the building which housed her husband's book store, and opened the Minerva Yarn Store, named after the imported wool product. With great vision she added a section which sold finished products knitted on a piece-work basis by women working in their homes, and provided space for a knitting school in an adjacent room.

An aristocrat playing the role of a merchant was news and the *Sunday Mainichi Newspaper* and the *Weekly Asahi Newspaper* ran feature stories about the wife of the Baron Ishimoto and her new store. This free advertising proved invaluable for soon the Minerva Yarn Shop was frequented by "elite" customers, including a famous, trend setting Kabuki actor. On the other hand the Baron's brothers criticized Shidzue and made disagreeable remarks that such independent behavior was inappropriate for an upper class woman. Such cryptic remarks as, "Ishimoto has changed in an odd way;" or "She's a little bit strange, isn't she?" implied that one of her social status should be at home performing the role of "good wife and wise mother", rather than imitating the lowly merchant class and winding up the common subject of newspaper articles.[1]

Shidzue became labeled in the press and by her compatriots as a "new woman".[2] This term grew out of the "bluestocking" movement of intellectual women which had taken shape at the end of Meiji Period [1868-1912] and during the early years of Taishô [1912-1925], around 1911-1916. The Bluestocking Society [Seitôsha], and its magazine, the *Bluestockings,* were founded by Hiratsuka Raichô and invigorated by other intellectual women and a few supportive men.[3] Many women, often wives of well known literary men, contributed articles to the magazine and participated in the intellectual and social discussions of the day, including the issue of just what constituted a "new woman". While Shidzue was never associated with this society, which had disbanded before she returned from America in 1921, she was interested in the arguments which the group had generated on such subjects as marriage, love, the state's responsibility toward women and children, and, of course, birth control. She was also acquainted with several of the women who had participated actively in the society's discussions, most notably Hiratsuka Raichô, Yosano Akiko, and Yamakawa Kikue. These women, predominately, though not exclusively, upper class, were well educated and enjoyed debating the political and social issues of the day. They were acclaimed or branded, depending on one's point of view, as "new women". For Shidzue's in-laws and most members of her social class the title suggested impropriety, especially in attitudes toward love, marriage, and the family. For her associates, who were representatives of this group, it was a title of honor.

Meanwhile, Shidzue's venture into the business world, another arena in which she represented the avant guard, was succeeding in all of its three phases; retailing yarn and finished knitted products, and teaching knitting. She was able to turn a profit for herself, employ a few of her upper class friends who wanted part time work in a respectable business, and pay wages for piece work to less affluent women who could not leave their homes. At the same time Shidzue authored and sold a practical book of knitting instruction and traveled throughout the country giving knitting lessons. Describing this business venture in 1948, Shidzue commented that it gave her and a few other women the opportunity to be at least partially reliant upon their own strength and resources, and that it enlightened a few members of her social class, who by tradition would automatically disparage merchandising. She also noted sadly that her successful enterprise began to serve as a wedge between her and her husband, driving them further apart as he became more and more unsympathetic to her strivings for economic and social independence. The freedom and enterprise which he had insisted that she embrace had proved too successful along side his own failed projects. It seemed that the more her business prospered, the shakier her marriage became and this caused her great pain and anguish.[4] Two catastrophes beyond her control temporarily solved her problem. The September 1, 1923, earthquake which destroyed so much of Tokyo gave her an acceptable excuse to close down her two year old business, while competition from cheap American finished wool products provided significant economic motivation to do so.

Pioneering for Birth Control

Shidzue had not forgotten the primary cause, women's emancipation, for which she had promised to work upon her return from America. She was not seeking just personal economic independence but wanted to help free women in general from their feudal family chains. Furthermore, she believed that promotion of Sanger-style birth control was necessary to the achievement of this goal. Circumstances propelled her project forward. First, she saw it as an opportunity for her and Keikichi to work together on a project. Secondly, she found the public already interested in the subject and eager to learn more about it.

Keikichi, always looking for something to fasten his footloose existence to, seized upon his wife's project and began to study the issue of birth control. In addition, he continued his interest in labor issues, and frequently entertained labor activists at home, while Shidzue, playing the proper wife and hostess, interjected her presence into the group. Among Keikichi's visitors were Sôdômei labor union leaders Suzuki Bunji and Katô Kanjû, and the Christian-Socialist, Professor Abe Isô. Keikichi and these labor organizers discussed the connection between the impoverished living conditions of workers, their fight for just wages and benefits, and their inability to control the size of their families. Birth control education based on a "scientific" study of family limitation, and its relationship to more prosperous and healthy workers, seemed necessary to any discussion of labor reform.

Meanwhile, Shidzue acted independently, as well, to stir up public interest. She had already gained some fame through an *Asahi Newspaper* article of September, 1920, which linked her with Margaret Sanger. It seems that during her stay in New York she had told an *Asahi* reporter about her meeting with Sanger, and believing this newsworthy, he had sent off a report which was published just before Shidzue returned from Europe.[5] In the spring of 1921 Shidzue, published her own two-part article on the importance of birth control education in a Tokyo newspaper. Birth control was a hot issue.

On May 10th, just nine months after Shidzue had returned from her year abroad, she and her husband gathered together a group of interested people for a mid-day discussion about propagation of birth control ideas in Japan. The missionary, Elizabeth Coleman, was included in the group to provide first-hand information from America. Excited by this event Coleman immediately wrote her friend Margaret Sanger, sure that she would be "interested in our very first birth control conference here in Japan." She exclaimed about the charming Baroness Ishimoto who, because of her newspaper articles, was being called "control" by students at the university, and further commented "that one feels very glad to have a leader like her?" She went on to inform Sanger that those gathered had appointed a few of their numbers to "draw up a statement that could easily be circulated, and each of us were to enlist the cooperation of people who would be willing really to come in caring honestly for the movement, and when we have 50 such people, we are going to have a meeting and put out some sort of formal propaganda. It is all very interesting, and one felt quite like a pioneer. The Ishimotos are so unusually radical and progressive for Japan."[6] Both the luncheon and Shidzue and Keikichi proved a great success.

The Ishimotos were not the first to discuss birth control in Japan nor were Shidzue's articles the first to attract the public's attention. In fact interest in this subject had boomed after the end of World War I, generated by the same economic problems which brought about the 1918 rice riots, and by the realization that Japan's population was increasing well beyond the capacity of its natural resources. Women's magazines, newspapers, and other publications featured numerous articles on birth control beginning as early as 1918. Articles in the well circulated *Housewife's Friend, [Shufu no tomo]* ran the gamut from advice about and ads for contraceptives, to discussions of ways to prevent venereal disease.[7] Many articles in various magazines appeared about the work of Marie Stopes in England, well known due to her residence in Japan early in the century. Once in a while the lesser known American, Margaret Sanger, was also mentioned. By the time Shidzue's articles appeared, birth control was a subject which had generated great interest, if little understanding, among the literate and intellectual classes. Consequently, the guests at the Ishimoto house in May were not being introduced to the topic of birth control for the first time.[8] Rather they had gathered to found a working organization which would systematically promote birth control education. The practical outcome of this meeting was establishment of The Birth Control League of Japan, which was patterned after the plans for the soon to be established American Birth Control League. The parallel structure was provided by Elizabeth Coleman's hand written notes in English about the probable configuration of the new American organization. Although the fledgling Birth Control League of Japan predated the official inauguration of its American foremother, it did not last very long. Just the same its fleeting existence was sufficient to highlight Shidzue's name in both Japan and America.

During the summer of 1921, Shidzue sent an essay to Margaret Sanger which set forward in English the case for birth control propagation in Japan. Impressed by this foreign tract, and undoubtedly pleased by its similarity with her own stand, Sanger ran the commentary in the

September issue of *The Birth Control Review*. The article was filled with information about the importance of bringing population growth into sinc with the limited resources available in Japan, limiting births with the eugenic goal of improving the quality of the population, and using birth control measures to improve living standards for individual families and for the country as a whole. Ishimoto's most poignant plea, however, appeared to be how important birth control would be for "the emancipation of women.... The Japanese woman must be liberated to develop freely.... Japanese women must have time and money to seek self-development," she proclaimed. Proving her case, she stated that women, both married and single, spent an inordinate amount of time devoted to child rearing, and, additionally, serving their husbands and in-laws. In addition women had to sacrifice all discretionary money to the needs of their children, leaving nothing for their own cultural and educational advancement. Birth control, then, was essential to the physical and spiritual freedom and independence of women and to the "perfection of man" as well. "By Birth Control, men and women awaken spiritually to their independence." Furthermore, she insisted, "To improve spirit and body is to improve mankind." To those who would call the use of contraceptives immoral she countered, "At the present time, it does more harm to society to have too many underdeveloped children and too few well developed. Morality demands that we act with less harm to the next generation."[9]

Establishment of the fleeting Birth Control League of Japan and Shidzue's publication in *The Birth Control Review*, inaugurated what was to become a long association between Shidzue, the American Birth Control League, and the League's primary spokeswoman, Margaret Sanger. In the fall of 1921, Shidzue was invited to join the League's National Advisory Council, an honor she gratefully accepted, while vowing to work harder for her own fragile organization.[10] The twenty-four year old Ishimoto Shidzue had taken to heart a cause which she would actively propagate for seven more decades.

Sanger Aids the Cause

Shidzue, meanwhile, was busy preparing for a visit from her mentor, Margaret Sanger, who had accepted an invitation from Kaizô publications to visit Japan and lecture on birth control.[11] In 1920 Kaizô had established a five year program to bring an outstanding world figure once each year to lecture to the Japanese public. They had already presented Albert Einstein and Bertrand Russell. Looking toward 1922, Margaret Sanger's name was forwarded to Kaizô by a famous artist, the sculptor, Ishigaki Eitaro.[12] Ishigaki had met both Sanger and Agnes Smedley during a stay in New York City, and had been impressed by Sanger's advocacy of birth control. Already planning a tour of China and India, Sanger accepted immediately. Shidzue was overjoyed; it was a dream come true. The word went out in headlines everywhere, "Margaret Sanger, Birth Control Pioneer, Is Coming."

Sanger prepared carefully for the trip by reading whatever was available about Japan's demographics, history, economics, and territorial expansion. She added to this knowledge on the journey by interacting with her ship companions, the Japanese military and foreign office officials returning from their tough and disappointing bargaining over naval reductions at the nine power international treaty conference in Washington D.C. Not only did Sanger rub elbows with such important luminaries as Foreign Minister Shidehara Kijûro and Admiral Katô Tomosaburô, Naval Chief of Staff, but she gained the respect and interest of the Vice Minister in the Foreign Office, Hanihara Masanao, who was able to help her when she landed at Yokohama. In fact many of the Japanese as well as other passengers asked questions of her and on February 23rd, she gave an invited two hour lecture to the first class passengers, and later other lectures to those in second and third class.

When the ship docked on March 10th, her reception was less hospitable. Authorities, urged on by a large block of conservatives in the House of Peers, the upper house of the Japanese Diet, refused to permit Sanger a visa to land. Many in the civilian government as well as military leaders saw Sanger's visit, which directly followed the forced treaty reduction of the Japanese naval fleet at the Washington Conference, as yet another attempt by the West to limit Japan's power and prestige. The only difference was that this time it would be through population control. Consequently, the military sympathizers among those in power opposed lectures on techniques which could be used to limit births. Such information might subvert Japan's national policy to strengthen its industrial and military might.

Sanger was met, as well, by friends. "Baron Ishimoto fortunately was there early to advise me and also came Mr. Yamamoto and his group from Kaizo....", she wrote in her Diary. "Baroness Ishimoto came in her native costume. Very tall and lovely to look at. Speaking clear and fine English." Also present was "a delegation of six women representing the Women's Movement in Japan. These adorably perfect doll women came in costume, bowing so stately and courteously from the waist to the floor almost, took ones thoughts away from the difficulties of officials & the trials of the day and brought first the perfumes of a fairy land with gnomes & delightful wise old ladies to the realization that these little new women in Japan are the instruments to carry out the real dreams of an emancipated womanhood in Japan."[13] And thus Sanger began her affectionate, if sometimes condescending, relationship with a Japanese people, both real and mythical, who accorded her more adoration and respect than she ever received at home. The meeting also represented the reconfirmation of her association with the "Margaret Sanger of Japan", as the Baroness Ishimoto had been christened in the press.

Only after Sanger had signed an agreement not to speak publicly about birth control was she finally permitted to leave the ship. According to this document she could not explain practical methods of contraception, suggest how to obtain birth control literature, or introduce birth control as a method of limiting population in any public forum. The authorities privately admitted that there was not much they could do about prohibiting these banned topics in small gatherings at private homes. In fact, until Sanger became seriously ill on the 21st, she participated in a whirlwind of social events at which she privately discussed prohibited topics while publicly lecturing on acceptable topics. Because of the fiasco over her disembarkment, and the government prohibitions, the press was even more interested in her, and reporters followed her everywhere quoting her daily in their newspapers. During most of her activities the Baroness Ishimoto, at whose home Sanger stayed while in Tokyo, was at her side, sometimes as translator, but primarily as hostess and friend. At all public events, which included dinner parties, teas, and receptions, a large contingent of police, present to monitor her words, also, joined the elite company of guests who gathered to listen to this now infamous celebrity.

During her ten active days in Japan, Sanger participated vigorously in several events each day. In all of these she appeared to be more impressed by the titled male elite interested in her cause. She seemed less certain of the accomplishments and future potential of Japan's "new women", and was highly stereotypical in her descriptions of even the women with professional qualifications. The only woman who received higher accolades than the adoring men was the Baroness Ishimoto. In this instance, a "new woman", eclipsed her titled husband. Sanger commented, "I would not consider him as quick, nor alert as Baroness. She seems to me more intelligent. He's not so experienced. She will come to London Conference in July."[14] Stereotypes established during this visit set a pattern which Sanger altered only slightly during two more pre-war and several post-war tours of Japan. Despite visible evidence to the contrary, Ishimoto Shidzue was the only Japanese woman whom Sanger credited with characteristics and accomplishments which met her own peculiar Western measure.

Sanger's first dinner party was held in Yokohama "with eight Japanese gentlemen. The Baroness went home to care for children.... Then home to Baron's house where fires in fireplaces cheered us after a long fatiguing day." She was pleased to find that Mrs. Coleman, a friend of the American birth control movement, was a neighbor of the Ishimotos and would be hosting "a Birth Control dinner" in the next few days. Sanger took in a lecture in English by the "well known Japanese", Tsurumi Yûsuke (Shidzue's favorite uncle), which was a "very instructive balanced address on New Japan." The Ishimotos held a special dinner party on the 15th which included Suzuki Bunji, Abe Isô, and Kaji Tokijirô, a gynecologist. "These three men agree on principles and have formed nucleus of a good substantial Birth Control League here." Even Shidzue, the inspiration behind this group, missed out on this accolade. On the 16th the Baroness held a reception with "about one hundred & twenty present. Prominent Japanese women doctors. I spoke for half an hour on B.C. Baroness Ishimoto was Chairman. Imperial Theater later until 9 pm." She then commented that it would be difficult to describe the "effect the theatre had on me. Weird music, orchestra, Weird dances, and Weird plays. Gloomy, simple, primitive & realistic.... The dresses of Baroness Ishimoto are elegant, her taste is so simple but the combinations are lovely."

The next day she had a private discussion with Dr. Kaji, one of those practical talks without police listening in. "Dr. Kaji told of the methods of B.C. he found successful - plain soft Japanese paper folded & inserted against cervix - then as this absorbs the sperm it is removed & a clean piece wet in antiseptic solution & wiped the vagina dry & clean. 1000 cases no failures."[15] Kaji had recently been to the U.S. and had met with physicians who advocated birth control. He was himself a strong supporter of birth control education, and he opened a birth control clinic shortly after Sanger's visit.[16]

Later that day Sanger met at the Peers Club with "a select group. We spoke very frankly - talked of methods & the art of love — It was very inspiring to hear their questions & to hear their perfect English. Baroness Ishimoto sat throughout the discussion very bravely." She enjoyed a dinner with twenty-five of the men, "no wives". This stimulating, frank camaraderie with upper class men whom she saw as her intellectual equals could be contrasted with her "luncheon with Mrs. Ishimoto['s] mother & sister. Both ladies understand English very well, speak a little. Such lovely demeanor between mother & daughter we Western nations could well copy." It was the "doll" like demeanor of these attractively attired "tiny" women which attracted her. And again, her meeting that afternoon at a hospital where she lectured to fifty nurses and doctors, including the woman doctor, Yoshioka Yayoi, proved less than overwhelming. "They [the female nurses and doctors] are a very insignificant looking group of nurses and only the lead physician Dr. Yoshioka Yayoi looked really intelligent — this doctor thought that using the pessary caused irritation - very reactionary, behind some of the men physicians".

Just before she left Japan Sanger concluded, "The women here are too low voiced to ever do anything. They are trying too hard 'to be or not to be' proper. One hears much of the 'New Woman' but one seldom sees her. It seems only those women who have turned Christian are able to think independently or to do anything with their lives. It also seems that to be a Christian means to be a rebel or a radical of some kind. One tells it with great secret pride."[17] This evaluation of Japanese women, like those Sanger would make in the thirties, show that she was not as observant of the people Shidzue had gathered to talk with her or knowledgeable of the variety of "new women" actively discussing women's roles in the "new Japan", as she believed. The commentary on Christians is particularly amusing since the woman she admired, Shidzue, had abandoned her interest in Christianity by this point, and the one who was afraid to frankly translate Sanger, Gauntlett Tsuneko, suffered this affliction on behalf of her Christian puritanism. Of course, Sanger was dependent on this translator, whose accuracy she could not verify, and on other English speaking women who had attended schools run by Christian missionaries. This undoubtedly prejudiced her thinking. Although Sanger used the title "new woman" in her diary, she seems to have missed the discussion which framed this term.

Sanger's visit was a triumph. She was constant copy for reporters, revered by all who hosted her, and even received adulation from some officials who prevented her from speaking publicly about birth control. For the Baroness the American was a godsend, a morale builder, an inspiration with practical advice and materials for advancing her chosen cause. Ishimoto Shidzue, "Madame Control", was now given a new title by the newspapers which was echoed loudly by the members of the public; she was called the "Margaret Sanger of Japan." She did not wait long to capitalize on her enhanced recognition. In May a group met at her house to form a Birth Control Study Society which included her original associates in the Birth Control League with a few prominent additions, the marxist woman activist, Yamakawa Kikue and her husband, Hitoshi, and Drs. Majima Kan and Kaji Tokijirô.[18] The group declared as their primary goals further personal study, and production of practical literature for birth control education. They began by translating several of Sanger's pamphlets for distribution, then published a periodical called *Small Family*, which lasted only one issue, and, more successfully, wrote their own pamphlets. Shidzue's contribution was a tract called "Observing the Birth Control Question from Different Angles", while Keikichi contributed, "The Problem of Japanese Population and Birth Control" both of which were later published in Sanger's *Birth Control Review.*

Shidzue had been particularly concerned during Sanger's lectures by the conservative caste given the translation of her more frank comments about women's sexuality, sexual love, and methods of birth control. The official translator, Gauntlett Tsuneko, a Japanese married to an Englishman, had, from Shidzue's perspective, interjected a puritanical Christian conscience into her translating chores. A few times Shidzue had interceded and retranslated a statement, but this was not enough to recast the misrepresentation. After Sanger left Shidzue determined that education was necessary on all fronts and began by giving Gauntlett some of Sanger's writings on both freedom to love and birth control. According to Shidzue, these caused her friend to change her views and join the Study Group.[19]

Another Mentor from America

Tokyo of 1922 was an exciting and exhilarating place, and it had a forward looking mayor who wanted to make it livable and modern as well. The mayor, Viscount Gotô Shimpei, was one of Japan's most revered Meiji/Taishô statesmen. He had completed his medical studies at the University of Fukushima, north of Tokyo, and had gone from there to the University of Berlin where he studied and observed Germany's public health system. He returned to Tokyo in 1892 a firm believer in Bismarck's "state socialism". From this point on he continuously held important bureaucratic positions, at both the local and national level, from which he constantly looked for ways to improve living conditions for the people. A contemporary scholar has called Gotô "one of the most visionary and politically ambitious higher civil servants in prewar Japan."[20]

In 1910 Count Gotô's daughter, Yoshi, married the new Imperial University graduate, Tsurumi Yûsuke, who was to gain national recognition as a bureaucrat, politician, intellectual, writer, novelist, lecturer, and unofficial ambassador to the U.S. This, of course, was Uncle Yûsuke who had so significantly influenced Shidzue. In 1918, when Gotô was in America consulting at the New York Bureau of Municipal Research, he became acquainted with the famous historian Charles A. Beard, one of the bureau's researchers, and with his wife, Mary Beard. The following year when Tsurumi was in New York, he also met the Beards, who were always interested in interacting with foreign guests. Thus, when the city of Tokyo unexpectedly came into a large sum of money to establish a Bureau of Municipal Research both Gotô, and his son-in-law, Tsurumi, thought of Charles Beard. In February, 1922, Mayor Gotô officially invited Beard to come to Japan to offer advice on modernization of the city's government and services.[21] Tsurumi, who was once again in New York, acted as go-between. Convincing Beard to come was not difficult, for both he and his wife were eager to visit the Far East. More importantly, Charles was excited and challenged by the mammoth project which urban planning for a modern Tokyo would present.

Charles, Mary and their two children arrived in Tokyo on September 14th. Charles, who had come to learn and consult, insisted that he pay all their expenses. During the six month stay, he generously lectured throughout the country, consulted with Gotô and other Tokyo officials, discussed municipal planning with several mayors, and, in spare moments, enjoyed thoroughly the entertainment and cultural displays provided him and his family by the grateful elite of Japan's officialdom. When he lectured and observed outside Tokyo, he was accompanied by Tsurumi as his translator and confidant.[22] Meanwhile, Mary Beard gave at least one lecture, and was entertained by Ishimoto Shidzue, acting at her uncle's behest. Shidzue's knowledge of English and her familiarity with the West made her a perfect host. As a bonus, Shidzue was a representative Japanese "new woman" and was, therefore, of intellectual interest to Mary Beard, an observer and writer about women's lives.

As Mary erroneously remembers it, on one occasion Shidzue took her, to Tokyo's licensed prostitute quarters. They were accompanied, on this trip, by the "feminist editor", Hatano Akiko.[23] The women were escorted by "an elegant gentleman" dressed in traditional kimono, who had made arrangements with a particular establishment to receive the foreign guest. Calling the place, "one of the most exclusive houses", Beard described the scene in a 1947 letter. "Well at this house the whole hierarchy was exhibited to us, informally. As we sat on the floor served foods by young geisha, the Madame sat in a corner as 'hostess.' The tiny girls were brought in—truly sold and bought little slaves. They did little things to demonstrate their training. All the grades and ranks of the system were there for us to see. Two or three geisha sat with us talking. The oldest of the group spoke very frankly and said that it would be better for the entertainers to be paid by the public for public dancing, etc., than by private patrons. She was known as 'an intellectual' to patrons of this house." As can be surmised Beard had actually been taken to a geisha establishment, with the intent of showing off a group of Japanese women with particular artistic accomplishments. This was not a trip to observe government licensed prostitutes, as Beard thought, and as Shidzue had, in fact, done a few months earlier for Sanger. From Beard's perspective, however, there was no difference. "While Japanese men almost universally denied to me, when the matter came up, that the geisha is a prostitute; that the system signified sex slavery; these men were patrons of the houses and thus justifying themselves. How else could the women be maintained in such segregated quarters? The papers were beginning to discuss the sex slavery aspect before we left Japan and the vice of getting municipal revenue from the segregated districts. Wives were rarely, if ever, so naive as to think there was no concubinage in the geisha relations of their husbands."[24] For Beard, and, in fact, for Shidzue and her "new women" associates, there was no real difference between the services provided by the geisha and those of the licensed prostitute.

The meeting between Mary Beard and Shidzue had been fortuitous. In the future there would be yet another contact in America and a new mentor from whom to learn Western ways. In the thirties Mary would be an important conduit for writing projects which would help to keep Shidzue intellectually stimulated and economically solvent during the traumatic years of militaristic repression.

A New Political Freedom for Women

Shidzue and other activist "new women" were exhilarated in 1922 to finally be able to organize politically without fear of government interference or possible arrest. They spent the next few years organizing and joining groups as they tested the political freedoms which the parliament had finally voted them. Before this time the 1890 revision of Article Five of the Police Security Regulations, and its amendment of 1900 had prohibited women from joining political parties, organizing or participating in political groups, assembling or joining meetings which discussed political topics, or acting in any manner which might be considered political.[25] In fact women had been illegal political participants for years, especially since World War I when the numbers of activist women's groups had increased dramatically. But these groups had existed at the behest of the authorities. The Home Ministry, which controlled the police, and other bureaucratic government divisions, had the power to interpret and execute the many public peace and police laws and ordinances, to the detriment of individual women and groups which the authorities deemed political. In February, 1922, the Diet amended the Public Peace Police Law to permit women to attend and organize political meetings and discussions. This milestone recognized the contribution of women activists and inspired them to take additional steps toward the social and political reform necessary to secure full civil rights.[26]

Although she had many public and private projects in hand during 1922, Shidzue did not permit herself to overlook the benevolent responsibilities of a proper upper class woman. She had gone into the yarn business, in part, to earn funds for a leper hospital, and this was not her only philanthropic involvement. In 1921 the Soviet Union had suffered a terrible famine with starvation so sweeping that the Soviet government encouraged the world renowned writer, Maxim Gorky, to publicly plead for foreign aid. Inspired by the leadership of the U.S., which set up a famine relief organization headed by Herbert Hoover, several nations, including Japan, responded sympathetically with generous donations of food and money. At this time Shidzue belonged to the Wednesday Club, several members of which formed the core of the Women's Volunteer Organization for Russian Famine Relief during the summer of 1922. The group gathered at Shidzue's shop where they discussed their strategy and launched their appeal. A few of the women who participated were the socialist leader of the banned Red Wave Society [Sekirankai], Yamakawa Kikue; poet, feminist, and political activist, Yosano Akiko; the young, celebrated novelist, Chûjô Yuriko (later Miyamoto Yuriko) who had recently returned from New York City; Kawasaki Natsu, Shidzue's friend and associate in birth control activities, and Shidzue; all "new women".

Working energetically the group managed to raise a few thousand dollars which was forwarded through the Japanese foreign office to the Soviet Union.[27] This money, a minuscule amount compared with the government's total donation, represented a great sum to the few women involved. More significantly the fund raising meetings brought activist women of different political perspectives together for discussion while they selflessly served a non-controversial human cause. The range of political thought within this group was broad, encompassing both Yamakawa's outspoken marxism and Shidzue's quiet liberal humanism. The group's ability to work together is especially noteworthy since several of the women had vehemently disagreed in public debate over controversial social topics and feminist issues in the late teens and early twenties.[28]

In addition to the political and philanthropic organizations which Shidzue spearheaded, in May, 1922, she and a few close friends formed a private society to discuss social, political and literary questions of the day. This group, called the Coming Light Society [Raishôkai],[29] was made up of both men and women, many of whom were artists. It included, among other writers, the popular and successful novelist and social critic, Arishima Takeo. His novels, *A Certain Woman* [Aru onna] and *Grab Love with Abandon* [Ai wa shiminaku ubau], had established him as an intellectual concerned about the "new woman's" social and sexual life. He was particularly lauded for his ability to delineate the conflicts and confusions which the "new woman" experienced as she sought sexual and personal freedom. In his writings he philosophized about the contradiction which necessarily arose between morality and instinctive living and both revered and criticized what he termed, in English, the "impulsive life."[30] A second important member of Raishôkai was Shidzue's dear friend, Hatano Akiko, an editor at the popular women's magazine, *Women's Review* [Fujin kôron]. Hatano and Arishima caused a scandal in March, 1923 which implicated Shidzue and scarred her birth control movement.

Arishima, a widower, and Hatano, married to a prominent businessman, had, for some time, been involved in a secret love affair. Shidzue, as Hatano's confidant, had discussed the illicit liaison in the context of Japan's male biased adultery laws, which automatically punished the woman, and the code of Japan's "new woman", which celebrated sexual and emotional freedom. Both Hatano and Shidzue had been heavily influenced by Arishima's writings about love, and by the more sexually explicit foreign writings of Margaret Sanger, Marie Stopes, and Havelock Ellis. Shidzue said later that she had advised her friend to end the affair. Neither Hatano nor Arishima, however, had the power to break off their relationship and their sad solution was double "love" suicide. Hatano left a note for Shidzue, who was then implicated and met public disapproval for not having restrained her friend. In the end Shidzue suffered ostracism by many within her social status, and notoriety in the newspapers. Furthermore, her advocacy of birth control was criticized by those who associated the practice of birth control with "comfortable sex" declaring that bourgeois women prevented conception so that they could "play." The entire affair was a sobering one for Shidzue, who not only lost a dear friend, but found herself the focus of unwanted celebrity and her cause in disrepute. She was angry that society permitted illicit sexual alliances on the part of men but held adultery by women to be a heinous moral transgression as well as a legally prosecutable crime.[31] She would have cause to ponder this more personally in the future.

Another member of Shidzue's Coming Light Society was Katô Kanjû, labor leader, who lectured the group on "The History of the Japanese Labor Movement" and "Problems of Women Factory Workers." A labor leader with the union, Sôdômei, he had been a regular visitor to the Ishimoto household during Keikichi's attempts at labor organizing.

Kanjû, also a member of the Birth Control Study Group, was respected and his company enjoyed by both Ishimotos. After one of the Coming Light Society discussions in 1923, Kanjû invited Shidzue to join his labor organizers and speak to the miners and their wives about birth control at the Ashiô Copper Mines, located to the north, near Nikko, about eight hours by train from Tokyo.[32] Shidzue agreed, though she had never lectured to a group of workers before and was apprehensive. Happily her friend and neighbor, and associate in the birth control movement, Elizabeth Coleman, volunteered to accompany her. This quieted Shidzue's fears.

The two meetings held at the mines on March 31, and April 1, 1923, drew large crowds, for the miners were curious as to whether "the Baron's wife could understand the pain of such lowly people". Drawing from her experiences in the Miike Coal Mining area in Kyûshû seven years earlier, and her observations, then, of the pain and suffering of those women, she spoke about unplanned children and the associated impoverishment of families. Four days later she wrote to Sanger to tell her about the event. "Two large meetings...at the theatre of Ashio town...were attended by 1200 to 1300 miners and their wives. I gave the address on the subject of Birth Control, and even though I was interrupted several times by the authority of the policemen, I succeeded in delivering the thought which I wanted to propagate.... I was called the 'Japanese Sanger.'" She then included a photo from the newspaper which pictured her lecturing to the miners with Mrs. Coleman standing nearby as her "chaperone".[33] Shidzue later called this event a turning point in her life which she would never forget.

Upheaval by Nature and Man

On September 1, 1923, Tokyo suffered a cataclysmic earthquake, one of the most devastating natural disasters in history. It was followed by hundreds of aftershocks, and wildfires, which rampaged out of control consuming all wooden structures in the way. Fortunately, Shidzue was at her shop when the tremors hit. The newer concrete buildings did not sustain major structural damage, and she and her frightened workers came through safely. After dismissing her employees, she and Keikichi, whose book store was in the same building, managed to drive their car through the city to her father's house. There she found her family only slightly injured and the house reasonably in tact, though soon to be threatened by fire. She and Keikichi were living in Kamakura, however, and her great worry was her children, who were at home. In a heroic effort to locate his sons, her husband drove and then walked for hours arriving finally at a city almost totally destroyed by earthquake, fire and tidal waves. At his own home, however, he found Arata and Tamio safe, in a house which, though damaged, was still standing. Unfortunately there was no way to get this good news to his wife. It was another week before the frantic Shidzue was able to get to Kamakura traveling partly on land and partly by sea, to discover that her sons were fine, if somewhat tired of their continuous diet of macaroni. The entire Hirota-Tsurumi-Ishimoto clans escaped any serious injury or loss in this disaster which killed over one hundred thousand people and destroyed much of Tokyo.[34]

After the September 1, 1923, earthquake Viscount Gotô resigned as mayor of Tokyo to accept the more prestigious position in the national cabinet of Home Minister with its new responsibility of rebuilding the destroyed capital. His first action was to cable Charles Beard, "Earthquake fire destroyed greater part Tokyo. Thoroughgoing reconstruction needed. Please come immediately if possible, even for short stay." Beard cabled back, "Lay out new streets, forbid building without streetlines, unify railway stations."[35] He also agreed to come. He and Mary packed a tent along with their clothing and were back in Japan one month after the earthquake.[36] They stayed two months. As before, Charles claimed that he was there primarily as a sounding board, and that Japanese planners, engineers, and scientists would have to make the decisions and plan the new city. He insisted that they were far more capable culturally and intellectually to accomplish this job than any outsider.

For Mary Beard this second visit within one year was an opportunity to continue her study of Japanese women and their efforts, which she felt were substantial, toward breaking the feudal chains which bound them. She traveled throughout devastated Tokyo, and out into the countryside. The resilience and the power shown by the women impressed her. She stated in 1947, that it was based on these visits and her observation and companionship with Ishimoto Shidzue, that she began to realize the inadequacy of feminist theories of the twenties which spoke about oppressed women as if they had contributed nothing to feudal and early modern society. She was particularly struck by what she considered the erroneous thinking of the "feminist" and marxist/socialist, Yamakawa Kikue, and a specific 1922 tract in which she had, Beard felt, denied any contributions of women to the long history of Japan. She felt that her own observations of the "living demonstration of woman's share in primitive culture" as exhibited in rural Japan of 1922-23, decried suggestions that women had yet to achieve any semblance of power, or that equality was a necessary prerequisite to historical contributions by women. It was this interpretation, enhanced by her 1922 and 1923 Japan experiences, which would lead her in the thirties to urge Shidzue to write her own story and the story of other Japanese women to show the impact that women had on both modern Japan and Japan through the historical ages.[37]

After the earthquake, Shidzue determined at first to reopen her store which had not suffered damage. Signs of unanticipated discontent appeared in Keikichi, however, and she decided to close the Minerva Yarn Shop and return full-time to her family. This appeared to be what her husband demanded of her. She did not, however, abandon her determination to study and to work for social causes. She continued to participate in the birth control discussion group contributing information from the *Birth Control Review*, which she received regularly from Sanger, and she aided the practical work of the birth control movement by obtaining contraceptives from the American Birth Control League. The years 1922 and 1923 had been significant in her life. On the positive side, she had been successful in her first business venture, had greatly expanded her social and intellectual interactions, was moving forward in her efforts to propagate birth control education, and had enjoyed inspiration from two American mentors, Margaret Sanger and Mary Beard. On the other hand, she had begun to realize that her marriage less and less resembled the romantic ideal of the "new woman." Not able to achieve his own political goals Keikichi was growing more and more restless. His socialist quest no longer interested him, his career efforts had all failed, and he seemed unable to find a new goal. His answer, as always, was to travel, in effect, to run away. Once again leaving their sons, Arata almost seven and Tamio, five and a half, they sailed for America in April, 1924.

Once in America they were entertained by old and new friends including Margaret Sanger, Mary and Charles Beard, and the feminist, Carrie Chapman Catt, who inscribed a gift copy of her book, *Woman Suffrage and Politics*, "To Baroness Ishimoto who, I predict, will lead the women of Japan to their emancipation from outworn traditions." After about two months they sailed off to England, where they enjoyed a social whirl which included a lunch with Professor John Maynard Keynes, and meetings with the British Malthusian League, and on to the Continent, where highlights included meeting Agnes Smedley in Berlin and in Geneva, their old friend and mentor, Dr. Nitobe Inazô, now an administrator with the League of Nations. In August it was back once again to New York to more gatherings, highlighted for Shidzue by her further opportunities to be with Margaret Sanger.[38] Finally in the late fall of 1924, after nine months away from home, Shidzue and Keikichi returned to Tokyo to face a life without the glamour and constant stimulation of travel.

After her return Shidzue focused on her family responsibilities in accord with Keikichi's wishes. She did, however, continue some involvement with groups seeking new avenues for women. It was just at this time that several women's groups joined together to form the Women's Suffrage League.[39] The most prominent leaders of this federation were Kubushiro Ochimi and Ichikawa Fusae, who had just returned from studying in America. In December, 1924, Shidzue joined the League's central committee as finance chairman. The organization which she brought to the alliance was the Bright Sunshine Society [Reijitsukai], a study group interested in discussion of cultural, social, and political issues. After December the society's primary objective became providing moral support and raising money for the League as it sought enfranchisement for women. According to Shidzue's report of February, 1925, her associates pledged themselves to practical money raising activities to aid a unified effort to fight for women's suffrage. The Bright Sunshine Society as organized by Shidzue consisted of nineteen women including the writers, Yosano Akiko, Chûjô (later Miyamoto) Yuriko, Okamoto Kanoko, Fukao Sumako, Hiratsuka Raichô. Their first charitable event brought together famous men, artists and writers, who raised a substantial sum of money for the Women's Suffrage League. For this effort the Bright Sunshine Society was publicly thanked by an appreciative core of the League, most prominently Ichikawa, Yamakawa Kikue, and Gauntlett Tsuneko.[40]

The year 1925 was an exciting one filled with economic promise and romantic titillation for women who dreamed of personal independence and sexual freedom. Many middle class women were seeking and obtaining jobs, sometimes to provide needed income for a family but sometimes simply to give themselves a sense of independence and freedom.[41] Both women and men were reading literature and articles which praised the new liberties urban women were experiencing and even conservative women, who remained in traditional roles, enjoyed vicariously the autobiographical and fictional experiences which the new writers portrayed. The first chapter of *Nobuko*, Chûjô (Miyamoto) Yuriko's novel about her unfulfilling marriage and her search for personal independence and freedom from family duty and responsibility, was published in a popular magazine in 1924. That same year Tanizaki Junichirô's novel *A Fool's Love [Chijin no ai]* was serialized in the *Osaka Asahi Newspaper* with the final installments coming out in 1925 in the popular women's magazine, *Josei*. Here was a female character, Naomi, who seduced readers with her sexual freedom and total lack of personal and familial responsibility. These works and many others became popular as both women and men of this period were intrigued by the sexual attributes of the variously described "new woman" and "modern girl."[42]

Politically women were encouraged by the passage of the universal manhood suffrage law in March, 1925. This gave them hope for their own cause as they optimistically saw women's enfranchisement as the obvious next step in Japan's democratic development. The countervailing law, also passed in March, did not seem to garner much interest among the women, but would loom large in Ishimoto Shidzue's life a few years into the future. This was the Peace Preservation Law which added further weight to previous rescripts, regulations, and laws designed to permit the state to control the social activities of its citizens and, thus, protect the nation from the negative consequences which might be brought about through "dangerous thoughts."

For Ishimoto Shidzue, personal circumstances made it difficult for her to share in the general excitement of the mid-twenties. She limited her political activities and retreated further into her home. In the beginning her withdrawal was balanced by her desire to press her depressed husband into an active political life. She had suggested and Keikichi had agreed that he seek a Diet seat in the House of Peers. His success in this endeavor was so important to Shidzue that she took the advice of those who told her to refrain from all political activities, especially advocacy of birth control, if she expected her husband to have any hope of election to that conservative body. She must, they told her, appear to be a proper wife.

According to the 1889 Meiji Constitution, the House of Peers was an hereditary body, and, thus, the members did not seek popular election like their counterparts in the House of Representatives. Rather, the upper house consisted of a set number of members who represented the five ranks of nobility and were elected by their peers within each rank. Baron Ishimoto, who was of the lowest rank, could seek one of the sixty or so seats allotted to barons. He put himself forward as a candidate, but he did not win a majority of the approximately four hundred other barons eligible to vote. The loss was devastating.

From this time onward the distressed Keikichi in effect abandoned his family responsibilities and sought solace in adventure and, on occasion, employment in distant parts of the Japanese Empire, first Korea, later Northern China and Manchuria. Shidzue remained at home with her growing sons, every so often joined by Keikichi, who would return briefly in a whirl of apparent glory. For Shidzue, the late twenties was a period of decreasing wealth, and increasing depression. Although she did on occasion join with her friends for discussions, and at even rarer moments add her physical presence to the continued fight for women's suffrage, more and more she became a political and social recluse. In her autobiographies, which each end with a chronology of significant events, these years are simply omitted.

Notes

1. 1988, pp. 70-71.
2. The term "new women" undoubtedly came from similar discussions in the West both at turn of the century and during twenties.
3. See Miyamoto Ken, "Itô Noe and the Bluestockings," in *The Japan Interpreter*, 10:2, 1975; Laurel Rasplica Rodd, "Yosano Akiko and the Taishô Debate over the 'New Woman'," in Gail Bernstein Ed., *Recreating Japanese Women, 1600-1945*, University of California Press, 1991. See contrast between the "new woman" and the "modern girl" in Barbara Hamill Sato, "The *Moga* Sensation: Perceptions of the *Modan Gaaru* in Japanese Intellectual Circles during the 1920s," in *Gender and History*, 5:3, 1993.
4. 1935, pp. 208-211 for a straight forward description, and 1948, pp. 65-69, for a more reflective one. More information on new middle class working women contrasted with upper class adventurers or, "professional women," in Barbara Hamill Sato, "Cultivating a Different Modern: Women and Shûyô [cultivated professionals] in the 1920s," Paper, Association for Asian Studies, 1994.
5. Interview, 1978.
6. Coleman to Sanger, 5/16/21, Reel 18, Sanger, LofC. Elizabeth was the wife of the missionary Horace Coleman.
7. Margaret P. Haas, "The First Birth Control Movement in Japan, 1902-1937," undated, unpub. ms., pp. 5-7.
8. Professor Abe Isô had lectured on "Neo-Malthusianism" in the Hawaiian Islands. See letter from an editor of Japanese newspaper, *The Daily Nippu Jiji* to Anne Kennedy, Executive Secretary, of the *Birth Control Review*, 11/17/21, Reel 18, Sanger, LofC. See writings of Abe Isô, Ooto Tenrei, and Majima Kan, all important figures in the birth control movement.
9. Baroness S. K. [sic] Ishimoto, "A Japanese View of Birth Control," in *The Birth Control Review*, 9/21, pp. 6 and 17.
10. For the American Birth Control League's establishment in 1921 and Sanger's leadership which emerged shortly thereafter see Ellen Chesler, *Woman of Valor*, Simon & Schuster, 1992, pp. 199-209. Ishimoto to Kennedy 1/10/22, Reel 18, Sanger, LofC.
11. The Kaizô organization published the liberal magazines, Kaizô [Reconstruction] and Kaihô [Liberation]. Information about 1922 Japan trip comes from Sanger folders at Sophia Smith Collection, Smith College, Northampton, Massachusetts, [Smith]; the "World Trip Journal," Reel 18, Sanger, LofC; the reports of Sanger's trip in *The Birth Control Review*, May and June, 1922; Katô/Ishimoto, 1935, pp. 224-231; 1981, pp, 51-57; 1988a, pp, 72-87; and 1978 interview.

12. 1988a, p. 72. Chesler, p. 245 credits Agnes Smedley with generating the invitation. In fact the prominent Japanese secured the invitation.

13. Diary, "Trip to Japan," 1922, Box 29, Folder 218, p. 9&10, Smith.

14. Diary, March 25, 1922, Box 29, Folder 218, p. 55, Smith. The last comment contrasts with Sanger's report in *Birth Control Review*, where she credits only men with leadership in Birth Control League of Japan, even though it was Shidzue who was instrumental in forming League.

15. Quotes from 1922 Japan Trip Diary, Smith.

16. 1988a, p. 80.

17. 1922 "Japan Trip," pp. 32, & 49, & p. 57, Smith. Yoshioka Yayoi became a famous and successful. In the early post-war era she was acclaimed one of the three richest women in Japan. She gave most of her fortune to charity and founded hospital for women's diseases and women's medical college.

18. 1988a, p. 79; 1935, p. 230, and *Nihon fujin mondai shiryô shûsei*, Vol. 10, entry for May, Taishô 11 [1922]. Each source adds an additional participant.

19. 1988a, p. 77-78; 1981 p. 56. In 1981 version Gauntlett is not named, but described as a Christian imbued with puritan ethics.

20. Sheldon Garon, *The State and Labor in Modern Japan*, University of California Press, 1987, p. 27.

21. Ellen Nore, *Charles A. Beard: An Intellectual Biography*, Southern Illinois University Press, 1983, pp. 102-107.

22. See Charles Beard's introduction to his book, *The Administration and Politics of Tokyo*, The Macmillan Company, 1923. He reported on this research and reproduced his heavy lecture schedule there.

23. Descriptions of visit are from a letter of 7/30/47, Mary Beard to Dorothy Brush, Beard Files, Smith.

24. See Sheldon Garon, "The World's Oldest Debate? Prostitution and the State in Imperial Japan, 1900-1945," in *American Historical Review*, 98:3, pp. 710-732.

25. Sharon L. Sievers, *Flowers in Salt*, Stanford University Press, 1983, pp. 52-53 & 99-101.

26. For laws, which affected men's as well as women's activities, see Richard Mitchell, *Censorship in Imperial Japan*, Princeton University Press, 1983. Yamakawa Kikue's Red Wave Society, which experienced escalating pressure from police after the socialist May Day activities, 5/1/21, is important example of forced dissolution. For discussion of amended law, Sheldon Garon, "Women's Groups and the Japanese State: Contending Approaches to Political Integration, 1980-1945," in *Journal of Japanese Studies*, 19:1, 1993, pp. 17-19; and Dorothy Robins-Mowry, *The Hidden Sun*, Westview Press, 1983, pp. 65-69. One organization most active in efforts to revise Article Five was the political rights group, New Women's Association [Shin fujin kyôkai], founded in 1919 by Hiratsuka Raichô, who was soon joined by Ichikawa Fusae and Oku Mumeo. The New Women's Association, much weakened by internal dissension and disagreement, Ichikawa Fusae's 1921 departure for America, and outside criticism, particularly from Yamakawa Kikue, was dissolved in 1922. Shidzue was never an official member of this group.

27. 1935, pp 211-212 mentions event and lists three women but gets the dates wrong; a better source is *Nihon fûjin mondai shiryô shûsei* , Vol. 10, p. 100, references 516 and 601. This entry comments on event and lists all group members. I suggest a range for donations because Ishimoto claims almost 8,000 yen, while *Nihon fûjin....* states just under 4,000, (four or two thousand dollars).

28. A primary argument existed at this time between Yosano Akiko, Yamakawa Kikue and Hiratsuka Raichô, all of whom figured in other twenties women's associations. Ishimoto did not publicly participate in the early twenties debates on feminism, which centered at this time on the role of the state in protecting mothers. See Jennifer Shapcott, "The Red Chrysanthemum: Yamakawa Kikue and the Socialist women's Movement in Pre-War Japan" in *Papers on Far Eastern History*, 1987; and Laurel Rasplica Rodd, "Yosano Akiko and the Taishô Debate over the 'New Woman'" in Gail Lee Bernstein Ed., *Recreating Japanese Women*, University of California Press, 1991, pp. 174-198. For Miyamoto [Chûjo] Yuriko's participation see Susan Phillips, "Beyond Borders: Class Struggle and Feminist Humanism in Banshû heiya [the Banshû Plain]" in *Bulletin of Concerned Asian Scholars*, 19:1, 1987, p. 57 which specifically mentions Miyamoto's twenties charitable work; Masao Miyoshi, *Off Center*, Harvard University Press, 1991, 197-206; others who have commented on Miyamoto's literary works of the twenties and later are Kyoko Irye Selden, Noriko Mizuta Lippit, Brett de Bary, and Yukiko Tanaka.

29. 1935, p. 233; 1988a pp. 79-86. In 1935 Shidzue refers to the Raishôkai or Coming Light Society, but in 1988a she uses Reijitsukai. Probably Raishôkai was original name for the private social group which met in members' homes for discussion, while Reijitsukai was public group which became women's political as well as social group. The fact that some of membership overlapped, and that Shidzue seems to combine the two, causes the confusion.

30. See Tatsuo Arima, *The Failure of Freedom: A Portrait of Modern Japanese Intellectuals*, Chapter VI, "Arishima Takeo: Bourgeois Criticism," Harvard University Press, 1969.

31. 1988a, p. 86. In fact the adultery laws in the 1898 Civil Code provided punishment for men who carried out sexual liaison with a married woman, which was the case in this instance, as well as for any woman married or not who committed an adulterous act. In this case the press, the public, close friends of the couple blamed Hatano and excused Arishima

32. 1935, pp. 233-236; 1948, pp. 62-64; 1981, pp. 58-60.

33. Ishimoto to Sanger, 4/5/22, Reel 18, Sanger, LofC.

34. See Edward Seidensticker, *Low City, High City*, Alfred A. Knopf, 1983, pp. 3-9 for general description; Shidzue, 1935, pp. 244-254, for her family's story.

35. Mary Ritter Beard, *The Making of Charles A. Beard*, Exposition Press Inc., 1955, pp. 25-26.

36. Ellen Nore, *Charles A. Beard: An Intellectual Biography*, p. 108.

37. Beard to Lt. Weed, 2/25/47, Smith; Mary Beard, "The New Japanese Woman" in *The Woman Citizen*, 1/12/24; Yamakawa tract which engendered specific criticism, 9/22 issue in English of *Shakaishûgi Kenkyû (A Monthly Study on International Socialism and Labor Movement)*, "Woman in Modern Japan VI. The

Woman's Movement" by Yamakawa Kikue. For a similar comment about Beard's ideas on equality, emancipation, and women's contributions to history see Nancy F. Cott, Ed., *A Woman Making History: Mary Ritter Beard Through Her Letters*, Yale University Press, pp. 25-26. Unfortunately Mary Beard destroyed most of her private papers making reconstruction difficult.

38. See 1935, pp. 257-262; and three letters of this period between Sanger and Ishimoto Shidzue, Reel 18, Sanger, LofC.

39. League for Attainment of Women's Political Rights [Fujin sanseiken kakutoku kisei dômeikai] later shortened to Women's Suffrage League.

40. See Ishimoto Shidzue, "Reijitsukai hôken," 2/23/25 in Ichikawa Fusae, ed., *Nihon fujin mondai shiryô shûsei* [*Collection of Documents on Japanese Women's Questions*], Vol. 2, pp. 251-254, and "Fujin mondai kenkyûsho sôritsu shuisho [Prospectus of the Formation of the Group for Study of Women's Problems]," November 19, 1924, pp. 256-258, for oversight group of which Ichikawa and Ishimoto were two of five officers.

41. See Barbara Hamill Sato, "Cultivating a different Modern: Women and *Shûyô* in the 1920s"; and Margit Nagy, "Middle-Class Working Women During the Interwar Years" in Bernstein, ed. *Recreating Japanese Women*, University of California Press, 1991, pp. 199-216.

42. Retitled *Naomi*,, translated by Anthony H. Chambers, Alfred A. Knopf, 1985. See Barbara Hamill Sato "The *Moga* Sensation," and Barbara Hamill Sato, "Modan gaaru no jidaiteki imi [The Modern Girl in a Historical context]," Minami Hiroshi, ed., *Gendai no esupuri - Nihon modanizumu* [Present-Day Spirit - Japan's Modernism], 188, 1983, pp. 84-85; and Miriam Silverberg, "The Modern Girl as Militant" in Bernstein, ed., *Recreating Japanese Women, 1600-1945*, University of California Press, 1991, pp. 239-266.

3

Independence (1929–1935)

Shidzue described her life of the late twenties as one of emotional and economic limbo. She had permitted her husband, Keikichi, to determine the course of their lives since the mid-twenties in the hopes of saving her marriage. Somehow Keikichi, who ten years before had insisted that Shidzue become a free and independent "new woman", had done an about face and reverted to the traditional role of feudal lord whom she could no longer love or respect. As Keikichi roamed abroad, it became more and more evident that he had abandoned Shidzue and his family responsibilities. She decided it was time to determine her own future and return to an active life.

Although Shidzue had declared after her first meeting with Margaret Sanger in 1920 that educating women about birth control would be her lifetime work, her husband's political about-face had compromised this project for several years. Finally, in the fall of 1929, Shidzue could write to Sanger informing her of recent advances by the Japanese birth control movement and of Shidzue's own efforts to bring this about. She explained away her low profile over the past few years saying, "I regret that my poor health keeps me away from social activities for years, but my ardent prayer for the purpose has never changed."[1] Sanger responded sympathetically and offered to publish Shidzue's report on birth control clinics in her *Birth Control Review.*

To Shidzue and other family planning activists, Japan of 1929 appeared to be hospitable to birth control as one approach to solving the recent population upsurge and the poverty which accompanied that increase. Clinics sprang up all over Tokyo in response to a declaration by the assistant mayor that birth control was the best hope for decreasing the high infant mortality and increasing the health prospects for those in the lower classes. As Shidzue reported to Sanger, "The Health Department of the city of Tokyo is considering setting up birth control clinics in the Municipal Health Advice Stations, and eight have already been established in the slum districts in Tokyo."

She continued that there were already thirty-two social workers who were teaching the poor the "evil of prolific births", advising them to use contraception, and sending them to the clinics for appropriate instruction. Shidzue emphasized that B.C. was now a politically acceptable topic for it was the majority party, the conservative Seiyûkai, which proclaimed that birth control was an appropriate means to solve Japan's population problems.[2] The Seiyûkai's decision to advocate birth control, in spite of opposition by the party's leader, Tanaka Giichi, was based on population and food pressures, and on the growing problem of venereal disease in the military. A cabinet report recommended creation of offices which would provide for consultation on marriage, birth, and contraception; regulation of improper advertisement, sale, and distribution of contraceptives; and research into eugenic aspects of contraception.[3]

In her report to Sanger extolling the bright future ahead for the birth control movement in Japan, Shidzue underscored this important official approval. She pointed out that the "strong central power" and better facilities at both the national and local governmental level would mean successes in birth control propagation that were simply not possible within private associations. For example, in Tokyo "clinics [would] be run by competent experts, and safe, correct contraceptive methods [would] be developed in Japan," she said. Another benefit of public regulation would be their power to banish the "social parasites" who were presently "selling poor mothers ineffective [contraceptive] medicines or injurious instruments at exorbitant prices."[4]

The next year was a good one for birth control advocates. It seemed that the B.C. movement would receive both endorsement and substantive help from government bureaus. One of Shidzue's B.C. associates, Dr. Majima Kan, established his own clinic, which provided contraceptives not previously available in Japan. Shidzue contributed new ideas on birth control through her exchange of information with Sanger and B.C. materials brought to Japan by foreigners. The birth control movement in Japan increased its membership and broadened its program. In accordance with advice from New York, Shidzue asked the Women's Suffrage League to endorse birth control advocacy, which they did. She also received support from Hiratsuka Raichô, an influential "new woman", Yamamoto Sugiko, a physician who represented other women medical doctors, and from others associated with the labor movement, the Y.W.C.A., and the Young Women's Buddhist Association. On behalf of the Birth Control League, she arranged a meeting for physicians who expressed a willingness to study contraceptive methods. She also convinced the social division of the Municipal Bureau of Tokyo, the Salvation Army and several hospitals to send representatives as well.[5]

Government enthusiasm for birth control, however, proved fickle. In less than two years, on January 10, 1931, the Home Ministry issued a qualifying directive which stated that intrauterine contraceptives could not be sold, displayed, or stored for sale because they were liable to cause injury. The document further stated that birth control was a private matter and that the government did not intend either to condemn or condone the use of contraceptives. Birth control was not outlawed, contraceptives, such as condoms, could be sold, and intrauterine devices could be provided in clinics; however, the government appeared to be modifying its previous wholehearted support. This public hesitancy motivated Shidzue and her associates to reform and expand their private endeavors in birth control education. Accordingly on January 17, 1931 the Birth Control League of Japan held an organizational meeting attended by about 150 people including leaders of labor and women's movements, social workers, physicians and pharmacists. Shidzue was named president, Dr. Abe Isô, honorary president, and Dr. Majima Kan, chairman. The League's announced purpose was to survey clinical research and make recommendations about appropriate contraceptive methods; to monitor all publicly available contraceptive devices and protest against those which the League considered dangerous and "unscientific," and to join the International Birth Control League.[6]

Shidzue began to redefine her own role in the B.C. movement pledging to seek common cause internationally and to educate women, especially poor women, in safe and effective methods of birth control. She told Sanger, "I wish to be a real friend of the suffering women and their poor children." To achieve this she sought to propagate safe methods of birth control, and tried to prevent charlatans from preying on the needs of poor women. Practically she tried to gain removal of the countless "quack remedies" for abortions which appeared in newspaper and magazine advertisements under the heading of "birth control" and which were posted on billboards along railway lines. One such medicine was labeled "Sanger", a fact which shocked and angered Margaret, who asked Shidzue to prevent the pharmaceutical company from using her name. Since it was at the municipal level of government that laws governing contraceptives, abortion, and birth control clinics were enforced and illegal dealers prosecuted and jailed, Shidzue sought help from the Tokyo and Osaka police.[7]

Since birth control education and clinics were not illegal in Japan, Shidzue and her colleagues felt confident about the future. The Birth Control League was flourishing in 1931, and a number of physicians in major cities felt comfortable opening independent clinics. Some disagreement arose, however, for by 1932 the original organization had been disbanded and a new group piloted exclusively by "influential women" had replaced it. As Shidzue told Sanger, "We excluded men from the committee, but of course have asked a large number of them to act as medical advisors and to give us financial support." In May, 1932 this new group opened a branch in Osaka.[8]

Abandonment and a New Love

Shidzue's public activism, however, continued to be overshadowed by her problems at home. By 1931 she had finally acknowledged that her marriage could not be saved and determined that she must secure a divorce. The decision was not a sudden one. After Keikichi and Shidzue had returned from Europe in 1924 the two had moved apart in both their attitudes toward marriage and their thinking about Japan and the world. Periods of physical separation had lengthened as Keikichi attempted various business schemes in Manchuria and Korea, while Shidzue and their sons remained in Tokyo. Even before the "Manchurian Incident" of September 1931, which sealed Japan's imperialist policy, it was obvious that Ishimoto Keikichi had joined the ranks of those calling for colonial expansion. With the sudden forced inclusion of Manchuria within the Japanese imperial sphere, he became even more eager to be a part of the glorious future he saw for the Japanese Empire. In the fall of 1931 Shidzue was dismayed and depressed by both her nation's act of conquest and her husband's enthusiasm for it.

On September 18, 1931, Japan's Kwantung Army contrived hostilities in Manchuria by blowing up a section of the South Manchurian Railroad. Three days later the Japanese army widened the war by occupying the seat of the provincial government in Kirin and then moving on to Mukden. Taken by surprise, the government in Tokyo blustered about looking for a solution to the Manchurian question that would not cause a war with the USSR or any other Western power. Eventually Tokyo accepted the army's action, and in February 1932 the new state of Manchukuo declared its independence under the protective custody of Japan's Kwantung Army. At home extremists assassinated two leaders, one a former finance minister and one an important industrialist, while ultranationalists praised their country's newest imperialist adventure, and the public, whipped up by newspaper accounts of army victories, praised their gallant troops and called for conservatism at home and aggressive military action abroad. Baron

Ishimoto was firmly in the jingoist camp. As he left his family once again, he explained to his wife the necessity behind Japan's conquest: "America and the Soviet Union are so much larger than my country and they are rich in natural resources. Japan is a narrow land with few material resources. Consequently we can't become a great country within our own boundaries. We must develop Manchuria and Mongolia economically, and so I am going off to construct a Utopia in Manchuria."[9] The Baron told Shidzue that she should feel honored to serve the family in Tokyo while he served the nation abroad.

For the previous six years Shidzue had put aside her own liberated views and tried to be the "good wife and wise mother" which her husband demanded. She could not in good conscience, however, support his move to Manchuria or the political motivation behind that decision. Describing this event in 1948 she said, "His activities had created a great gulf between us.... My husband had made a 180 degree conversion from his position as an intellectual humanist and pacifist and had embraced the theory that it was natural for Japan to undertake imperialist aggression in Manchuria and Mongolia. He felt that his private life should not interfere and confuse this situation. He considered this a way to make a living while aiding Japan's national policy of opening up new lands. He would not look back to his home."[10] In a November, 1931 letter to Margaret Sanger she commented, "The political situation is very serious here in Japan over the Manchurian problem and reactionary movements are getting powerful...."[11] She did not mention her husband's politics.

The years 1930-32 were a time of great economic hardship and emotional pain, and Shidzue was "distressed about her household and husband."[12] Only by borrowing a little money from her father and a bank did she manage to keep her family going. Once her father rescued her from creditors who threatened to carry off the family's art treasures to pay for yet another debt her husband had incurred. Sympathy from her mother was hard to come by. She reminded Shidzue of her role as the wife in a noble family and of the responsibilities she was expected to fulfill. "My mother did not believe in consolation. She just said that women received a cruel stick. Because Mother had not known hardships she absolutely did not understand the lives of women who must confront economic problems and loss of property. She simply wondered why her daughter was grumbling.... There was no one but myself to rely on. I had to manage everything alone. I did not have time to stream with tears. My spirit died."[13]

Shidzue knew the kind of behavior which was expected of an upper class Japanese wife, but she had internalized a different ideal about the relationship between a husband and wife, one greatly influenced by her reading of Margaret Sanger and Havelock Ellis on male/female equality, sexual fulfillment and free love. Therefore, she experienced severe anxiety over the inadequacy of her marriage. She believed that "serious relationships of couples must be absolutely bound by both respect and love. And of these the loss of respect is fatal to the couple's relationship. Consequently, it is not possible at all to save a relationship which has lost both respect and love."[14] Her inevitable conclusion, then, was that her marriage had failed. Keikichi blandly accepted this and gave her permission to seek a divorce. Unfortunately the custom governing those in the upper ranks of society and Japanese family law under the Meiji Civil Code of 1898 made divorce impossible. "I was just the wife and mother and had no rights of my own", she commented in 1978.[15] In fact, had she been able to obtain the divorce, her sons would have remained in her husband's family and she could not have expected much, if any, financial settlement. These facts were of little importance, however, as she was unable to secure the necessary permission from any two required relatives among father, brothers, or brothers-in-law. Also, her husband's family opposed a divorce. "And so", she lamented, "while Ishimoto disappeared abroad, I was reproved at home."[16] Although prevented from legally divorcing her husband of seventeen years Shidzue initiated an exchange of letters with Keikichi which resulted to her satisfaction in an informal agreement of the dissolution of their marriage. From that time on, she considered her marriage to the reactionary, tyrannical Baron ended, and she accepted responsibility for her own support and for that of her sons, Arata, 14, and Tamio, 13.

In this time of personal trial Shidzue's intensified work with the birth control movement and her continued participation in the Women's Suffrage League provided her with some sense of intellectual and social satisfaction. The public activities, however, could not fill the void created by a loveless marriage. The longer she was alone the more acutely she became aware of her loss of male companionship and love, and, though she tried to console herself and fill many lonely evenings reading love poems from the Japanese literary classic, the *Manyoshû*, and romantic stories and novels by contemporary Japanese and Western writers, this proved inadequate. In March, 1931 Shidzue had turned 34.

Fortunately, that fall Shidzue once again experienced love, and thus, was able to create some balance between her private and public lives. Although her new liaison complicated her existence because of the secrecy it demanded, it gave her the emotional fulfillment she needed to survive. After having spent eight increasingly lonely years, from 1923 to 1931, attempting to sublimate her emotional needs in loyal service to an increasingly oppressive husband and then in intellectual endeavors and social activism, she found herself free once again to love and be loved.

The prologue to her diary of 1937-39 includes an entry from May 1, 1932, the day she went to watch the May Day Parade in order to see "him", her beloved Katô Kanjû.[17] In this joyful entry she includes a reference to a date six months before. She writes "October 22, 1931 was a memorable day. It was the day in which I announced my separation from an anguished life and a history of tears. Accordingly I changed from a life of self-sacrificing devotion and began anew to receive passionate love. It was a powerful resurrection. From that time on I grew in pride day by day. Shidzue has become a fortunate woman."[18] This diary entry celebrated the private liaison between Shidzue and Kanjû. On this date Shidzue, still the wife of the absent Baron Ishimoto Keikichi and responsible for their sons, and Katô Kanjû, who lived with his wife Kimi, his son Nobuyuki and daughter Sumiko, determined to ignore adultery laws and family and class sensibilities in favor of personal desire.[19] The May 1st date, a day of solidarity for socialists, also reflected the couple's public left-wing political alliance, a truth which would significantly affect their lives as their country became more and more militarist and reactionary.

Shidzue had known Kanjû since she and her husband had returned in 1920 from their first trip to America. At that time Katô Kanjû often visited the Ishimoto home, for he and Keikichi held similar liberal views. The two men shared an interest in the labor movement and Kanjû lent his name and energy to the birth control movement which both Keikichi and Shidzue espoused. It will be remembered that at Katô's urging Shidzue bravely spoke in 1923 on his labor union's platform at the Ashio Copper Mine in celebration of the successful strike which Katô had engineered. Kanjû had also joined the Ishimotos in several study groups before Keikichi had made his about face and joined the reactionary nationalist cause. Shidzue reminisced many years later that she had felt warmly toward Kanjû finding him "a reliable man" in contrast to her husband. It is not surprising, then, in the lonely and conflicted atmosphere of 1931 Shidzue permitted her association with a man whom she liked and respected to grow intimate.

After Shidzue's abandonment Kanjû became a frequent visitor to Shidzue's house. As she revealed years later, his presence had a calming effect on her "desperate" family. "He brought a warmth to the family just at the point when we were snapping," she said, and then went on to contrast her husband's coldness and uncaring attitude toward her and their sons with the concern which Katô showed all three of them. "I believe that Katô understood the pain and hardship that people suffer." As Katô spent more evenings in the Ishimoto household, her sons came to respect him while their mother's love for him grew. He became a part of the family.[20]

Lecturing in America

Ishimoto Shidzue's successful return to birth control advocacy and her intimate relationship with Katô Kanjû did not solve her practical problems. Theoretically she knew her most pressing need was to become economically independent. Only then would she be truly liberated. "I had to become a working woman", she explained. "Because of my experiences with the painful workings of the family system, the feudalistic discrimination against wives, and with an irresponsible husband, during my younger years, I had taken up an interest in theories about the emancipation of women and about socialism. I can remember being well guided in those days on the issue of liberation for women by Yamakawa Kikue's writings on women's history."[21] She discovered, however, that it was not so easy to convert intellectual theory into cash to pay the bills.

Late in 1931, an avenue for financial independence suddenly appeared in the form of a letter from Uncle Tsurumi Yûsuke, who was once again in New York City. He suggested that Shidzue follow his example and come to the United States to earn money through lecturing. She was both enthusiastic and apprehensive about this proposal, for while her knowledge of English made this a possibility, she was unsure whether it was adequate to the task. Also, although she had been traveling about the country giving birth control lectures, she knew nothing about the expectations of a foreign audience, nor how to go about engaging such a tour.

It was her good fortune that her uncle was able to provide an introduction to Feakins Lecture Bureau in New York City, his tour sponsor. Feakins not only invited Shidzue but wanted her to come immediately. Her reduced economic circumstances helped her to overcome her nervousness. Feakins had offered her prepayment of all travel, daily expenses, and a stipend. They specified that she should tour selected cities throughout the United States and lecture on the activities of women's groups in Japan and on Japanese customs and culture. Hurriedly Shidzue began writing speeches and translating them into English while making arrangements for her departure and for the care of her two sons, now ages fifteen and fourteen.

Shidzue had no difficulty booking passage on a ship bound for California, but getting a passport was a more complicated issue. She explained, "Because I was the wife of a Baron from a noble family, I could not leave my country without my husband's written permission....In those days a wife had absolutely no freedom of travel."[22] Since Baron Ishimoto was in Manchukuo (Manchuria) working for the glory of the fatherland, Shidzue had to write him requesting his written permission by return mail, so that she could obtain the passport necessary to begin her journey. In her letter she explained the circumstances of her trip and the urgency of a speedy reply. She worried she might not receive a reply in time, for there had been times when she had not know where her husband was, and months when he chose to remain completely out of touch. Just the same she made her plans, took care to register her plans in the official family register in accordance with the law, and found an older woman to look after her sons. Her husband's permission arrived just in time for her to make the booked September 28th sailing.

Shidzue arrived in San Francisco on October 14, 1932, and spent almost a full year in America. Her lecture tour took her to cities in California, to New York City, Boston, Dallas, Palm Beach, several cities in between and a few cities in Canada. She spoke at churches and synagogues, small and large lecture halls, and over the radio. It was a grueling trip with many unexpected and even jolting experiences. She had developed lectures on three topics: "The Japanese Aesthetic Sense", "The Birth Control Movement in Japan", and "The Women's Liberation Movement." At the close of each formal lecture her audiences were permitted to ask questions on any topic, and they did so enthusiastically. Often people asked about Japan's conquest of Manchuria, sometimes in a hostile manner. Consequently Shidzue found herself forced to speak on Japan's imperialist actions as frequently as on her prepared subjects. It was a trying experience both because of the anti-Japan and even anti-Japanese attitudes she encountered, and because of the strain of discussing such complex issues in English.

She had been forewarned. In a letter inviting her to make her New York headquarters at her home, Margaret Sanger had said, "[The tour] will be very interesting but I warn you it will be very strenuous. All foreign lecturers are nearly killed by publicity and interviews, etc. Really, [though,] I do not think we are any harder on people than other vitally interested individuals!"[23] The president of Feakins Inc., William B. Feakins, was also aware of the difficulties which his guest speaker would incur. He included a note of concern in a letter to Sanger. "It doesn't seem a very propitious time for a Japanese to be booked in America; but we are keeping in mind to emphasize the fact that the Baroness is not talking politics, but is speaking about the women of Japan, the children and the artistic life. If we can get into peoples' conscientiousness [sic] the fact she has done so much along social lines for her people, a great many organizations will be able, I hope, to forget what is now so well entrenched in their minds."[24] And yet, in the press release of October, 1932, Feakins stated that one of Baroness Ishimoto's lecture topics would be "The Manchurian Question and the Birth Control Movement." The Baroness was described as a woman who "has worked indefatigably for woman suffrage and birth control, and many other movements. She claims that birth control rather then emigration is the key to Japan's destiny."[25] The expectation was created that Shidzue would tie birth control to the "Manchurian Incident" and Japan's foreign policy in general. Feakins solved his "poor timing" by featuring the primary foreign policy disagreement between the U.S. and Japan. It would be up to Shidzue to handle the confrontational questions.

After the war Shidzue wrote that she had been adamantly opposed to Japan's militaristic advances from the early 30s. She had feared what she saw as a growing fascist attitude in Japan. Her activities for social causes, her knowledge of electoral politics through her associations with Katô Kanjû and others in the political left-wing, and her work in the women's suffrage movement had all lead her to embrace a liberal political perspective. The outlawing of the Communist Party in 1928 and the mass arrest of many on the political left, the rise of the ultranationalists 1928-1932 which created a politically difficult atmosphere for anyone who opposed nationalist demands, and the popular acceptance of militarist actions in Manchuria, had made her fearful of the political direction the government was taking. While there is little doubt that her postwar perceptions accurately portrayed her inner feelings at the time of her lecture tour, on the road in America she was somewhat circumspect about her public criticism of government policy. She tried to hedge her position and speak in a manner which would present her primary concern, the need for birth control, address issues about Japanese foreign policy which worried Americans, and yet not entangle herself in a battle with her own government.

In one oft-repeated substantive critique of Japan's Manchurian policy, Shidzue said, "Overcrowding causes imperialism and imperialism causes war. The solution to overcrowding, and therefore to war, is reduction of the birth rate. Even in the case of my own country, I believe birth control is a better answer to the Manchurian problem than either emigration or imperialistic expansion."[26] On the other hand, when asked how she and other Japanese women felt about Japan's withdrawal from the League of Nations over its criticism of Japan's actions in Manchuria, "Baroness Ishimoto remarked that in emergencies like that the women of her country are inclined to blame the delegates from other countries and to imagine that their own men are in the right. 'As long as England has India and the United States has the Philippines and other countries have outside territory, we think Japan has a right to have Manchuria,' the Baroness argued, with as much conviction as if she were not a pacifist at all."[27] Walking the tightrope of international affairs during a period of deteriorating relations between the U.S. and Japan was not easy.

There is little doubt that the Baroness was much more comfortable when speaking about Japan's feudal family system, the progressive activities of Japanese feminists, her own social activism, the birth control movement, and the artistic accomplishments of Japanese women, a topic often demanded by the public. Audiences found her attractive and reporters spoke of her as "gentle, soft-voiced and assured, with the poise of generations of Oriental aristocrats," "the diminutive Baroness," and "a captivating little Japanese aristocrat." When she told her own story, Shidzue gave credit for her education to her husband, a liberal humanist, and spoke of the work which both of them had forged in their attempt to help the poor women of Japan achieve a better life. When she spoke about the oppressed lives of Japanese wives "under Japan's ancient family system," she did not personalize this issue by describing her own oppression nor admit that her husband had deserted both his earlier liberal beliefs and his family to follow the imperialists in Manchuria. This was not a topic for public or private discussion.

In March, *Vogue* printed Ishimoto Shidzue's "Kimono Into Décolleté" in which she described the way that Japanese women moved back and forth between traditional Japanese and modern Western culture. She spoke ideally about the sophistication and artistic accomplishments of the well-mannered and well-dressed upper-class Japanese woman. She painted a canvas of a benevolent Japan, devoid of political conflict, but filled with the charm of the old and the comfort of the Western new. She moved in travelogue fashion from the "kimono as a work of art" to creative and fashionable Western dress, from the "national passion" for flower-arrangement to the leisure activities of tennis and golf, from the celebrated art of Kabuki theater to "the movies which give [a woman] the rest and forgetfulness she craves." Even when she spoke of the "ancient and unalterable tradition of family" she managed a little joke within the context of describing the "utmost deference" which a woman owes her family within which "the man is the undisputed lord." "Very often Americans, struck by the complete absence of the dreaded 'middle-age spread' in Japan, ask why a Japanese lady never gets stout. She will tell you the secret: 'Bow to your husband frequently - you will get real exercise.' Would this be a popular way of reducing in America?"[28] Shidzue played with her role as visiting Japanese aristocrat during her tour of the United States. She moved back and forth between a kind of myth and truth as she tried to fulfill the social, economic, and political goals which she had broadly conceived before she left Tokyo, provide her audiences with the pictures they wanted to see, and not clash needlessly with official Japanese policy.

Shidzue was an invited guest of honor at many social events. Though she preferred Western clothes her audiences and friends loved the traditional Japanese look, and so she always wore a kimono. This traditional attire, which she considered confining and uncomfortable, became her costume for both work and leisure. It seemed contradictory that Western feminists like Margaret Sanger, who lobbied for women's emancipation, praised this native dress. To Shidzue the kimono, though beautiful, represented the traditional subjugation of women in Japanese society. Shidzue, who dressed as her hosts expected, spent her off-duty hours shopping for Western fashions which would form the core of her Tokyo wardrobe for the next several years.

Dinners, cocktail parties, and teas frequently held in her honor were welcomed by Shidzue. She had come from a Japan in the midst of depression and financial stress caused by world and national economic crises and Japan's militarist adventure in Manchuria. Shidzue had grown up in an atmosphere of upper-class wealth and culture, and she had experienced and enjoyed the splendor of lavish entertainment. Her social activism and liberal thinking had not diminished her taste for beautiful surroundings and elegant parties. It was luxurious to be able to forget the borrowing and penny pinching so necessary for everyday life and participate in gala events abroad where she was not forced to make choices based on either personal finances or political appearances. She enjoyed the company of the social elite who preferred an elegant ambiance to an intense intellectual or political exchange.

In between the sometimes rude questioning Shidzue experienced from the podium and the luxurious formal dinners hosted by the wealthy, she enjoyed informal gatherings with birth control advocates. In a letter to "Havelock dearest" Margaret Sanger described a tea she gave for her Japanese friend on November 28, 1932. "Yesterday I had fifty people in to tea for Baroness Ishimoto who is visiting me & studying clinics so as to establish them in Japan....She is lovely & in native costume makes a delightful impression. She lectures in English & gets paid for it too! Even tho its depression."[29] Shidzue enjoyed total relaxation during a day out with Florence Rose, Sanger's secretary. "'Rose' was all devotion. Feeling that I needed diversion, she bore me off to Coney Island later one afternoon and we had a very lively time there, indeed, running to catch boats and trains, riding on merry-go-rounds, shooting the chutes, and seeing the resort as others see it while enjoying ourselves in similar style."[30] As a last refuge she had the warmth and comfort of meetings with Uncle Yûsuke who oversaw her tour with the care of a favorite relative and the knowledge of a successful Feakins lecturer.[31]

The lecture tour filled Shidzue's empty purse, and renewal of American friendships gave her great pleasure. But her happiest moment came at the end of the trip when, her lecturing over, she seized the opportunity to study the organization and operation of the Margaret Sanger Clinic. During this three month period of observation she hoped to learn enough to open her own clinic. She was especially impressed with Sanger's case history method. The system involved writing case history information about clients on cards and then applying this documentation in a systematic way toward birth control advice on an individualized basis, and Shidzue hoped to introduce it in her own clinic. At the end of her intensive study Sanger complimented her on her accomplishments and said that there was nothing further which she could teach her. Shidzue must return to Japan to become Sanger's "beautiful offshoot."[32]

New Projects

During Shidzue's stay in New York, she was invited by Mary Beard, to visit her Manhattan apartment. When it came time for Shidzue to return to her hotel, Beard walked with her. For two hours these two discussed the style of life and status of contemporary Japanese women.[33] Beard had spent much of her life writing and speaking on women's historical roles and devising a world-encompassing theory on that subject. She was interested in just how Japanese women fit into her scheme. Beard commented that her own 1924 article, "The New Japanese Woman"[34] was one of very few English writings on that subject. She believed that a book based on the life of a contemporary Japanese woman would be a good way to interest American readers in this topic. Suddenly she turned to her Japanese guest and exclaimed that she should write that a book.

While Shidzue demurred at the thought of becoming an author, she did begin to describe her concerns about impressions left by other Japanese women who had visited America. She particularly pointed to the image of Japanese women portrayed in the New York City performances of "Madame Butterfly" which starred a famous Japanese soprano in the leading role of Chôchô-san. She thought about the image she had tried to convey during her lecture tour, and about the manner in which she had presented herself. She had tried to show the traditional Japanese woman dressed in kimono and sensitive to the traditional arts, but had spoken frankly about the importance of the modern birth control movement and other subjects which she felt suited a feminist position. She warmed to Beard's idea. She recognized the contribution she could make if she used this as an opportunity to expose the exploitive family system, and the lordly manner of Japanese husbands, and not just describe women's artistic accomplishments, manners and customs. She would do it! Later, Beard introduced her to Reinhart Publishing Co. On the basis of their success with Sanger's book, and Beard's agreement to help edit Shidzue's English, a contract was signed with delivery of the manuscript set for one year latter.

When Ishimoto Shidzue docked at Yokohama in August, 1933, she had been away for almost eleven months. The excitement of the trip, financial success of the lecture tour, intellectual stimulation of her study at Sanger's clinic, and the exhilaration of the book contract enhanced the feelings of freedom and independence she had begun to experience in 1931. Immediately upon her return she physically severed her ties with her past by moving out of the house she has shared with her husband. Ishimoto Keikichi had left again for Manchuria, and it was not known when he would return. She rented a smaller house from a friend and began a new life with her two sons. The defining moment for Shidzue was putting a nameplate on her gate with only her name, "Ishimoto Shidzue," on it. From this point on Shidzue considered the separation from her husband final, and wrote him to that effect. In her mind she was free. Settling into her new home, she decorated her sons' room and her own with inexpensive items she had brought back from America and felt that she could "set off on a working life serene in appearance and heart."[35] In reality she remained the Baroness Ishimoto, for neither her family nor her husband's would agree to a divorce.

Shidzue focused her intellectual and political efforts for the next two years on first, her autobiography, and then a reinvigorated family planning campaign. Immediately upon arriving home she began writing her story, working sixteen hours a day for almost a year. First she completed a Japanese version, then laboriously translated that into English, and, finally, she typed the finished manuscript. Her inspiration for the exhausting work came both from her desire to provide the American public with a frank view of the women in her country, and her urgent need to secure income. When she mailed off the finished manuscript she felt as if had "given birth." In August, 1935

Facing Two Ways: The Story of My Life,[36] was published simultaneously in the US, England and Sweden.[37]

Before publication Beard took the manuscript in hand for careful editing, a fact which Shidzue did not acknowledge until after the war. In 1948 she described Beard's contribution as one of correcting "imperfect expressions in English" and helping her to phrase difficult intellectual ideas. In 1981 she commented that Beard had taken time from her very busy life to read through the completed text "brushing up" the English. She further credited her with seeing the project through from beginning to end and expressed herself "truly thankful" for this and for the American's continuous "warmth and friendship." In 1984 Shidzue fully acknowledged Beard as her "intellectual leader" and "editor."[38]

In September Margaret Sanger sent Shidzue the reviews of the book, which were highly favorable, and wrote her own personal "review." "It is beautifully & charmingly written and I think that you have presented to the American public and even to the English speaking world a vision and a picture of the Japanese woman, especially the cultured woman, in a most illuminating way."[39] These comments seem so bland considering the revelations Shidzue made about her deteriorating relationship with her feudal husband that one wonders whether Sanger had read the book. The description on the book jacket was more enticing. "Even when her husband withdrew all sympathy," it proclaimed, "and when the mad wave of imperialism swept all liberal reforms aside, her convictions did not waver and her labors did not cease."

When the book appeared the *Mainichi Newspaper* commented that "A Japanese woman writer has become a best seller. Regardless of what one thinks of the text, Ishimoto Shidzue's *Facing Two Ways* is having an extremely promising sale." Shidzue was immensely gratified. That moment, however, was also filled with sadness for her much beloved father had died of encephalitis at aged seventy-one just before the publication was released. Shidzue, heavyhearted that he could not share in her accomplishment, placed a book jacket in his casket.[40]

Facing Two Ways was such a commercial success that Farrar and Rinehart followed it in 1936 with an abridged, less expensive version, *East Way, West Way: A Modern Japanese Girlhood*. Shidzue's financial bonanza from these two publications was, however, short lived. Her intention had been to find a secure investment opportunity which would bring her a steady annual income. She automatically turned to her friend and confidant, Katô Kanjû, for investment advice. As she explained in 1947, "He had an unusually bright boy in his factory, one in whom he had a great deal of faith, a boy who wanted, in short, to establish himself in his own enterprise. Since Mr. Katô had

100% confidence in him and I had equal if not greater amount of faith in Mr. Katô, I agreed to invest money in the plan. A small sized factory was built, but though the young man had considerable technical knowledge, he had never had any experience in handling great sums of money. As a result he spent it without knowing what he was doing and I was ruined. It was a terrible time. I ran here and there trying in vain to take care of the problems that arose out of this situation. Finally, I decided to give everything up. The young man ran off to Manchuria and I was left with nothing but trouble. My confidence had been betrayed in every way....However, there was nothing to do but forget it all...Which I tried to do......"[41] Once again Shidzue suffered at the hands of a man who abandoned his financial responsibility to her and ran off to Manchuria.

During this same period, Shidzue reconstituted her birth control organization toward more effective advocacy. In the fall and winter of 1933-34, she helped to form the Women's Birth Control League of Japan. Joining forces with Hiratsuka Raichô, Kawasaki Natsuko, Niizuma Itoko, and Dr. Yamamoto Sugiko, as well as other members of "progressive" women's groups, she embarked upon a movement to enlighten Japanese women about birth control using the educational materials she had brought back with her from the Margaret Sanger Clinic. The women of this new league opened information bureaus in hospitals in four villages in which Shidzue and the others conducted question and answer sessions with women who had just given birth, and provided practical birth control information. Shidzue also wrote articles for women's columns in newspapers trying to generate interest throughout the country in the practice of birth control. She was apparently quite successful, for she received more than a thousand letters within the first six months from women around the country who wanted answers to questions ranging from choice of contraceptives to how to care for their children during illness.

The activities of The Women's Birth Control League found resounding support at the Fifth Annual Women's Congress held in Tokyo on February 18, 1934. Conference delegates, representing many progressive groups throughout Japan, passed a resolution supporting the idea of birth control as a method for helping women eliminate unwanted births and overcome poverty. At the same time they drew a careful line between contraception and unlawful abortion, condemning the latter. The resolution directly contradicted government preaching which admonished against birth control and praised increased births for national strength.

Shidzue recognized the political nature of her clinic work and connected birth control with women's liberation from feudalism. "I was saddened by the tired and unhealthy appearances of the women [in the hospitals]," she wrote in 1948, "and by the fact that they seemed to have so little time off between pregnancies....I believed that the distress of these women could not be solved without social liberation from the feudal yoke and economic pressures they experienced. Although I believed it was important to understand this fundamental truth, I, also, felt that the practical knowledge of birth control would improve the welfare of these women on a daily basis and would save them as individuals. Consequently I introduced the same sort of information bureau in my own Tokyo neighborhood...." This was in fact the clinic opened March 1, 1934 by a few of the members of the Women's Birth Control League of Japan. Shidzue's role in the clinic's work was to lecture to groups of women on birth control methods. She explained her approach, "As an introductory lesson to teach contraceptive methods to sexually ignorant women I used a model of the female reproductive organs which I brought back from America. With this model, which was a dissection of the reproductive organs cut away in such a manner that you could have both an internal and external view, the women were able to understand the process of conception. Thus, I was able to introduce them to birth control methods and I could teach them about the variety of contraceptive methods available." After her lecture Shidzue would send the women to speak individually with a physician who would work out a plan for the birth control method which would most effectively meet the needs of that woman.[42]

In a letter Shidzue told her mentor, Sanger, that the newly established Tokyo birth control clinic had been set up according to the methods applied at the Sanger clinic, which she studied less than a year before in New York City. "Margaret Sanger's spirit is living in this clinic, and Dr. Stone's technique is leading the medical side of the work....The clinic is located in the densely populated quarter in Tokyo, placed in a doctor's office. It is only five weeks old but we have already asked for cooperation with the social center of the City Bureau."[43] She wrote her friend Florence Rose less formally, saying, "I wear my white gown over my American suits, when I instruct mothers [at the clinic]. I sit on the silk Japanese cushion in the green mats-room. There is a low table in the center and an alcove on the north side of the room. Always a beautiful rolled picture is hanging on the wall according to the season...and a few branches of cherry blossoms were arranged [yesterday] in a beautiful vase. We bow politely every time before we begin instruction.... We have no nurse at present to take care of the children so I am busy taking histories of patients, instructing, nursing everything at once."[44] In November of the same year her group moved their clinic to a donated house in Nihonbashi, "the Forty-Second Street and Broadway" of Tokyo, and secured the services of a gynecologist with several years of practice and a medical degree from Tokyo Imperial University to ensure that this clinic would be run on a "scientific basis." By that time the group had also opened a clinic in the rural north of Japan which would serve "peasants' wives...whose living standard is unspeakably poor..." and laborer's wives who in conversations with their neighbors exclaim that "they are regaining peace in their family since they succeeded in removing the constant fear of undesirable babies by having a field clinic in their crowded community to solve their keen problems." Shidzue proudly stated, "Though our footprints are still very faint, I can assure you that we are on the way to progress."[45]

The period between Shidzue's return to Japan in August 1933, and her second lecture tour to America in December 1936, was one of hard work for little remuneration. Even the autobiography, which had originally brought in substantial royalties, had turned into a financial disaster. Just the same she persevered in her several projects even though their liberal political content, placed her in some personal jeopardy under the Peace Preservation Act of 1925. At the same time, privately, she enjoyed an emotionally satisfying personal life highlighted by her clandestine love affair with Katô Kanjû. She carried on her intellectual and political missions either by publicly ignoring the political changes and declaring the legality of her work, or by carefully concealing activities which were more obviously dangerous. Her personal life was necessarily kept very quiet.

She was often tired and complained in letters to her American friends of periods of illness. She also commented briefly on her larger worries brought on by her government's actions at home and abroad. She wrote Sanger, "It has been very hard for me to adjust myself again to this conservative and reactionary country after spending the most delightful months in a democratic country mingling among the most progressive people. I have to encounter many difficult and unpleasant problems in promoting my work here." And writing to a friend in the American Birth Control League she stated, "It is hard at present to promote any progressive movement as we are in what they call an extraordinary moment anticipating serious international problems.... However, birth control is needed with acuteness whether the authorities believe in it or not." To another she said, "The general attitude of the public here toward birth control is hard to be expressed in one word. It has been obvious that Japan is controlled by the military influences, so it is natural to encourage more population as an expression of the nation's strength." Answering a question posed by an American acquaintance, Shidzue explained in January, 1935 that "[clinic] regulation of the Home Department has been revised recently and the doctors [no longer] have the freedom to indicate contraceptive treatments as one of their specialities, so the public has no means of knowing [this is available]."[46] It was wearying to be continuously battling the authorities as she fought for her right to provide public clinic facilities and educational materials on family planning.

Notes

1. Ishimoto to Sanger, 10/12/29, Reel 18, Sanger, LofC.
2. Ishimoto, "B.C. Clinics in Japan," 10/12/29, Reel 18, Sanger, LofC.
3. Margaret P. Haas, "The First Birth Control Movement in Japan, 1902-1937," undated, unpub. ms., p. 34.
4. Ishimoto, "B.C. Clinics in Japan," Reel 18, Sanger, LofC.
5. Ishimoto to Sanger 6/5/31, Reel 18, Sanger, LofC.
6. Constitution of Birth Control League of Japan, 1/28/31, Reel 18, Sanger, LofC.
7. letters between Ishimoto and Sanger, 1930-31, Reel 18, Sanger, LofC; Smith.
8. Ishimoto to Sanger, 6/1/32, Reel 56, Sanger LofC. Might be one cause of rift between Shidzue and Majima Kan which lasted well into the postwar era.
9. 1981, p. 72.
10. 1948, p. 78.
11. Ishimoto to Sanger, 11/20/31, Reel 18, Sanger, LofC.
12. 1981, p. 71.
13. 1984, p. 104.
14. 1948, p. 79.
15. 1978, interview.
16. 1981, p. 72.
17. 1988b., diary, 1937-1939, includes 1932 segment.
18. 1988b, p. 1. From diary entry for 1931.
19. 1988b, p. 364., ed., Funabashi Kuniko comments on family situations.
20. 1984, p. 106.
21. 1948, p. 80.
22. 1981, p. 75, and interview, 1978.
23. Sanger to Ishimoto, 12/18/31, Reel 18, Sanger, LofC.
24. Feakins to Sanger, 5/3/32, Reel 18, Sanger, LofC.
25. Memo for Press Release, 10/19/32, Reel 56, Sanger, LofC., includes handwritten note: "300 copies sent to Press from Coast to Coast."
26. *New York American*, 1/2/33.
27. *New York World Telegram*, 6/23/33.
28. *Vogue*, 3/15/33.
29. Sanger to Ellis, 11/29/32, Smith.
30. 1935, p. 371.
31. Several letters, 1931-32, Reel 56, Sanger, LofC.

32. 1981, p. 63.

33. Discussion between Beard and Shidzue is recreated in 1981, pp. 79-82.

34. Published in *The Woman Citizen*.

35. 1948, pp. 89-90.

36. Baroness Shidzue Ishimoto, *Facing Two Ways*, Farrar & Rinehart, 1935.

37. Fifty years after publication, 1985, a partial translation by Funabashi Kuniko, appeared. Funabashi told this author that she omitted the sections which would be "too familiar" to the Japanese reading public.

38. Beard confided in 1951, "I put her former book [*Facing Two Ways*] through the press and had to put it into English which could 'pass' as well as clarify a lot of parts in it, etc. I was glad I could do all this. I did not 'profit' myself out of that publication although the publisher made me take 1% or so of the royalties, bringing me in toto about $5.00. So I have done my bit for Shidzue's story." Mary Beard to Ethel Weed, 8/22/51, Smith.

39. Sanger to Ishimoto, 9/12/35, Reel 18, Sanger, LofC.

40. 1981, p. 85.

41. Ethel Weed to Dorothy Brush. interview June/July, 1947, Smith.

42. 1948, pp. 90-92.

43. Ishimoto to Sanger, 4/12/34, Reel 18, Sanger, LofC.

44. Ishimoto to Florence Rose, 4/17/34, Smith.

45. Ishimoto to Stella Hanau, Publications Director, American Birth Control League, 11/1/34, Reel 18, Sanger, LofC.

46. Ishimoto to Sanger, 4/12/34; Ishimoto to Mrs. F. Robertson Jones, 4/15/34; Ishimoto to Stella Hanau, 11/1/34; Reel 18, Sanger, LofC; Ishimoto to Miss Kaufman, 1/10/35, Smith.

4

"Dangerous Thoughts" (1935–1936)

In the mid-thirties Japan was a nation in flux. Unlike Europe and America she had experienced a substantial recovery from the world-wide depression. To some extent this resulted from military demands for manufactured goods created by Japan's new imperialist foreign policy. It was also tied to Japan's advantageous position in world trade as she devalued the yen to accommodate a thriving export industry. Economically the nation seemed to be improving rapidly even while many citizens were still suffering from inadequate personal income, low living standards, and lack of public programs and welfare provision. Politically the nation was moving more to the right as the military gained greater formal power within the cabinet, and its actions were applauded by a majority of the public. Assassinations in the early thirties of public officials including the prime minister significantly weakened the strength of party government and, unknown at this time, would end party determined cabinets until after 1945. The 1925 Peace Preservation Law had given the Home Ministry and Justice Ministry and the "special higher police" [Tokkô] the power necessary to wipe out the Communist Party by 1935. The increased numbers of these specialized "thought police" and other investigative units checking on those who did not conform to accepted political conduct meant that non-communists on the left, or others engaged in activities which threatened the policies supported by an increasingly strengthened military power, became suspected of "dangerous thoughts."

At the same time labor continued to organize, though at a slower rate than at the turn of the decade, and there were still strikes for better working conditions, though again at a much reduced level. Women, who had seen their hopes for even local enfranchisement dashed at the beginning of the decade, continued to agitate for women's emancipation, but in a more modulated manner. The birth control movement, with its several branches, marched on, but with a careful eye to laws which drew a fine line between legal birth control and illegal abortion. Most women, in fact, joined national and local organizations which applauded Japan's troops in China and supported the nation's economic policy. The Greater Japan Federated Women's Association [Dai nihon rengô fujinkai] and the Patriotic Women's Association [Aikoku fujinkai] numbered memberships in the several millions and claimed a following down to the smallest villages and hamlets. The government encouraged these women to provide kits to send to soldiers in Manchukuo, to learn savings methods and, in general, to "rationalize their lives" in accordance with national goals. There must be a moral reawakening with women leading the way.

The pressures of the "thought police," the emphasis on "dangerous thoughts," the government's push for total acceptance of a military driven public policy, the suppression of anti-imperialist speeches, the manipulation of nationalized unions and the male-dominated women's groups, all would appear to predict a totalitarian Japan. Strangely, those on the left did not see this as an accomplished fact. They still had hope for democracy. In 1932 several legal left-wing political groups joined in a coalition to form the Social Masses Party [Shakai taishûtô] and pushed forward in their determination to influence the next elections, sure their time would soon come. There were still labor and political leaders who dared to speak out against national policies, and women who continued to work for their equality and independence. It was amidst this atmosphere that Ishimoto Shidzue pushed forward in her determination to educate women in family limitation, and her beloved companion, Katô Kanjû, decided to go to America as a spokesman against Japan's imperialist policy. Both of these activities threatened official policy, but neither was illegal.

Questionable Activities

In the winter of 1935 Katô Kanjû was invited by a committee of the American Federation of Labor to visit the United States on a fact finding and speaking tour. Since his English was minimal, and he had never visited the U.S. before, he relied upon Shidzue for help in improving his English and for first-hand information about lecturing in America. The summer stay in America would prove vital to Katô's leadership role in building a radical socialist movement in Japan. Unfortunately, it would also give the "special higher police" an excuse to tie him to the Communist Party USA two years later.

When Katô set sail May 23, 1935, it was the American authorities he needed to convince of the benign nature of the visit. They were concerned about the prospect of a socialist politician, the Chairman of the National Council of Japanese Labor Unions [Nihon rôdô kumiai hyôgikai known as Zempyô], coming to America to meet with the Unemployment and Insurance Committee of the AFofL's most radical wing. Katô overcame American suspicions by obtaining the sponsorship of the Methodist Federation for Social Service.[1] Unexpectedly, the Japanese Home Ministry and its "special higher police" did not oppose the voyage at all. After his arrival in Seattle on June 4th, Katô traveled across the U.S., accepting engagements as they were offered. These included sessions with the AFofL's radical opposition committee with whom he exchanged views on union tactics, and workers' well-being under capitalism,.[2] He also gave public lectures using a set speech entitled "Capitalism and Labor Classes in Japan."[3]

Although Katô was never a member of the illegal Japan Communist Party, there was no doubt about his radical credentials, nor the anti-government intentions of his American efforts for his primary goal was to speak out publicly against official Japanese foreign policy. His speeches emphasized the importance of international opposition to Japan's imperialist actions in China and urged the building of a united international labor movement directed toward averting a widened war. One representative gathering was that of June 24th in Manhattan sponsored by the Committee to Promote Friendly Relations Between Japan and the American People.[4] On that evening Katô alerted the audience of about five hundred to the growing danger of Japan's China policy. He warned that the hostilities could spread and that eventually America could be brought into a full fledged war. "The war spirit has been inspired by imperialists and is being carefully nourished by them.... The ambition for territorial expansion in Japan belongs to the Japanese capitalists. They are pushing war preparation in spite of all we can do." He insisted, however, that Japanese labor opposed the war. His purpose in coming to the United States was to secure bonds of friendship between American and Japanese workers. Hopefully this would translate into a peace movement to counter militarist and capitalist efforts to convert labor to the policies of the imperialist classes through conjuring up patriotic feelings.[5]

All of Katô's lectures became a part of the public record and they would return to haunt him after his arrest. They would also be a part of the trials visited upon his intimate friend, Ishimoto Shidzue, for the "special higher police" would associate her own travels in the U.S. with Katô's trip based on the couple's intimacy. Suspicion of "dangerous thoughts," let alone a possible tie with the Communist Party USA, would be reason enough in the late thirties for an arrest.

Fortunately for Kanjû, an even more incriminating aspect of this tour was not discovered by the "special higher police" This was an unplanned secret meeting in New York City with one of Japan's most radical leftists. As revealed almost three decades later, Katô conferred in August, 1935 with the twice imprisoned Japanese exile Nosaka Sanzô, who was a leader of the underground Japan Communist Party. The consultation was lengthy and intense. Katô gave Nosaka concrete details of the state of affairs in Japan and Nosaka informed Katô about international developments and pressed for a "popular front movement" in Japan.[6] Nosaka had attended the Seventh Comintern Meeting in Moscow during July and August as a member of the executive committee and so spoke with knowledge, authority, and urgency about the Comintern's deliberations supporting a "popular front movement," which would provide an umbrella for all socialists, including left-wing non-communists like Katô.[7]

Katô returned to Japan from his lecture tour on September 5th, and began working for a "popular front." At first he worked through the union, Zempyô, which he had formed in 1934 and which he chaired. Zempyô, however, focused, quite properly, on economic issues and Katô wanted a political base for "popular front" activities. By this time, he and some of his union colleagues had become dissatisfied with the socialist position espoused by the Social Masses Party, and felt the time was right to establish a more radical socialist party.

In January, 1936 Katô, Suzuki Mosaburô, and a few others gathered together to organize the "anti-fascist" Labor-Agrarian Proletarian Council, known as Rôkyô [Rônô musan kyôgikai] Katô hoped to use this as a base to build a proletarian movement which would either win over the Social Masses Party or replace it as the more powerful party of the left. In the meantime Katô supported the Social Masses Party and congratulated them on winning eighteen Diet seats in the January, 1936 election. He hoped this victory and his own new party would represent the beginning of a "popular front" movement. The hope for a socialist future was immediately blunted, however, when, on February 26th right wing, lower level military officers attempted a coup. The next day martial law was declared. The insurgents capitulated in defeat, but the tense climate created by martial law affected the left as well as the right. For Katô and his colleagues, this event proved to be a preview of more extensive repression to come.

Katô clearly expressed his opposition to Japan's capitalist and militarist policies in his American speeches, his political campaign of February, 1936, and his writings of 1936. As he wrote that September, "To pave the way for a front populaire in Japan, the Labor-Agrarian Proletarian Council (Rôkyô) has been recently organized, in the hope that this new body will prove powerful enough to lead the Social Mass Party to become the central force of the proposed anti-Fascist movement."[8] Katô expected his party to publicly oppose government policies, especially militarism, and to gain strength through cooperation with others who were left of center. Though dangerous, such political activity was not illegal in 1936 as long as it did not include the illegal left, the Communist Party, and did not advocate "altering the *kokutai*" (national polity) or "denying the system of private property," activities specified as illegal in the Peace Preservation Law of 1925.[9] In 1937, after Japan's escalation of hostilities in China, the interpretation of this law would be broadened and such activity would become illegal.

The winter of 1936 was a significant period for Ishimoto Shidzue as well. Margaret Sanger, who was on her way home from India, docked briefly in Tokyo. Shidzue, of course, was there to meet the ship. She was exhilarated by even a brief encounter with her American friend and mentor. Sanger's ship arrived shortly after the insurrection of February 26th, and as Shidzue casually commented in a letter, "Tokyo was then and is still under martial law, and no public meeting was permitted, but she [Sanger] had no trouble landing in Yokohama..." In fact, she was more upset that the institution of martial law prevented a public rally featuring Sanger, than any political ramifications of this action. This time it wasn't Sanger or her birth control message that the government feared, but rather the possibility of public disorder created by any crowded public rally. Shidzue was placated, however, by the extensive news coverage which Sanger received. "A big picture of Mrs. Sanger and me is posted in shop windows for this week's [March 20th] photo news in Tokyo and throughout Japan under the title 'Sangers, American and Japanese'," she wrote. She was pleased that the *Hochi Newspaper* intended to publish a fifteen day series on Sanger's views, theories, fights for recognition of birth control, and the current status of her movement. This would do much to publicize the birth control cause. At a small gathering a reporter interviewed Sanger, and a few birth control sympathizers asked her questions. Shidzue was grateful for this opportunity to catch up on the latest technical developments in contraception noting especially Sanger's description of a new formula for foam powder which was in use in India. There was also word of a new medical magazine to which Shidzue's clinic might want to subscribe.[10] At the end of the meeting Sanger generously contributed the 100 yen which she received from the press to the clinic.[11]

In May and June, 1936, under quieter circumstances, Shidzue received two visits from Edith How-Martyn, an English feminist who ran Sanger's international operation, the Birth Control Information Center, in London. She had stopped by Tokyo to meet with Dr. Majima Kan, Dr. Oota Tenrei, and Ishimoto Shidzue. In her report to Sanger she told of the difficulties which doctors, who wanted to provide legal, practical birth control devices for women, had in gaining recognition for their contraceptives. Laws prohibiting abortion made it difficult for the authorities to distinguish between legal contraception and illegal abortion. Dr. Majima, for example, had been imprisoned two years before under suspicion of performing an abortion, when he claimed to be providing contraceptives. Understandably, he had become extremely cautious. How-Martyn commented, however, that the authorities were not without some justification for she met one doctor, who, did not seem to recognize a difference between these procedures. He claimed that his method of birth control was to "scrape the inside lining of the uterus monthly and added that 1000 women are coming regularly to him!"[12]

A Secret Liaison

The years 1935 and 1936 had been invigorating years for Shidzue and her beloved Kanjû. During that time Kanjû had visited the United States, consulted with the most radical members of Japan's legal and illegal left-wing, chaired a labor union, organized a new left-wing socialist party in Tokyo, and campaigned for an anti-fascist "popular front." All of these activities except the meeting with Nosaka were publicly acknowledged and, though representative of the most radical viewpoints in Japan, were within the bounds of legal, if dangerous, political activity. During this same period Shidzue had published her autobiography, begun another writing project, helped found and work in several birth control clinics, and campaigned actively for birth control and for women's emancipation. These too were legal activities, though birth control was, at best, frowned upon by the government.

Together Shidzue and Kanjû secretly enjoyed an intimate personal relationship, and publicly supported each other's political activities emotionally, intellectually, and practically. Kanjû invited Shidzue to join him in his quest to undo the imperialist actions of the nationalist/militarist government. She accepted. She had opposed the government's foreign policy beginning with the Manchurian Incident, and found government domestic policy anathema because it oppressed women. Sharing Kanjû's platform offered important public exposure for own advocacy of family planning and women's liberation. Of course, she would never be permitted to actually participate in party deliberations. Although changes in Article Five of the Peace Preservation Law promulgated in 1922 had given women the right to gather for political purposes and to join political parties, in the thirties, tradition, custom, and anti-feminist attitudes, which persisted even on the left, would preclude active participation in Katô's political organizations.

Describing her relationship with Kanjû during this period Shidzue explained many years later that while Kanjû struggled for an independent political base, the two of them had had many opportunities for "intimate relations" which included "instruction from him in matters of political combat and questions of social concern." She also commented that both her private and public association with Kanjû and her active participation in causes sanctioned by his political party had received approval from her two sons, high school students at the time, and old enough to understand the political and social implications of her activities. In her remembered past, Arata and Tamio were in ideological agreement with her, and respectful and admiring of Kanjû. She was appreciative of their support.[13]

When , answering several questions raised by an interviewer in 1983, she recalled this same period, Shidzue was somewhat more frank and less idealistic. The interviewer questioned her bluntly about her relationship with Katô Kanjû during the mid-thirties. Hadn't she "kept company" with Kanjû in spite of the fact that her divorce plans could not be realized, and couldn't this be labeled "free love?" No, she responded, it could not be called free love. The two of them were "circumspect" in their relationship. The interviewer then asked whether Katô's wife was aware of this relationship, to which Shidzue responded that she was sure Kimi inferred what was going on, but was not sure she understood the extent of the companionship. "And didn't he have children?" "Yes." "And didn't it pain you to know that although you loved Katô he had a wife and children?" "No, I did not worry at all. In those days a man who worked in the labor movement simply, in truth, did not have any responsibilities toward women. He treated all women, whoever they were, the same." "Ah," retorted the interviewer, "In those days if men in the labor movement subjugated women...." She interrupted, "Ignored. They ignored the women....Yes all the men were like that. Men working in the labor movement were definitely not democratic in their relations with women. It's all very painful to talk about but women were ignored."

Not willing to let Shidzue off that easily the interviewer commented with a smile that she had disagreed intellectually with her husband, Ishimoto Keikichi, over issues of subjugation of women, and feudal standards for marriage, and had wanted a divorce. And yet, she loved Katô Kanjû without reserve and was not repelled by his apparent belief in the inferior role of women. "This is really incomprehensible," he concluded. Shidzue attempted to explain this contradiction, by saying, "Through me, for the first time, Katô met, a woman of intellect." She continued that since she had been "baptized in liberalism" she believed in and trusted the labor movement and she accepted the importance of the leaders and the necessity that they lead. Her admiration and respect made it possible for her to accept their interpretation of the role of women. This admiration and her affection became intertwined. " Ha ha. Love is blind," the interviewer blandly concluded.[14]

In spite of Shidzue's memories, her relationship with Kanjû was not without substantial intellectual contradiction. Love may not have been blind, but it certainly was forgiving. Kanjû filled the depressing void which had come into Shidzue's life. She was willing to follow him and learn from him and any elements of inequality in their relationship were irrelevant to her. Privately, she enjoyed his companionship and publicly she took advantage of the opportunity to share the speaker's podium with him. She loved him without reservation and believed that he returned her love to the best that he was capable. This was enough for her. She did not feel it necessary to work out the ideological inconsistencies in their relationship. And so Shidzue's love of Kanjû, and her sympathy with and overt support of his political activities, placed her alongside him on his political platform and consequently in jeopardy in December, 1937.

Opportunities from America

Shidzue's successful American lecture tour and her best selling book had only temporarily solved her financial problems. Her work in the birth control movement and other political activities did not help economically. Kanjû was not responsible for her or her sons. Money was always on her mind. Therefore, when Mary Beard contacted her in the fall of 1935 with a new writing project, Shidzue happily anticipated the possibility of further royalties. Fortunately she was enticed, as well, by the assignment for, not only would there be no future financial rewards, this project had the markings of "dangerous thoughts."

Mary Beard had been elated by the successful publication of *Facing Two Ways*, a book which was in fact her own inspiration, and now she had a new project. Although this one was the brain-child of Madame Anna Askanasy of Austria, it was on a topic of great intellectual significance to Beard. Askanasy wanted to bring out a multi-volume work on the history of women from the perspective of various women's liberation movements throughout the world, the *International Encyclopedia of Women's History*. Beard asked Shidzue to be responsible for the volume on Japanese women, and she accepted.

Shidzue wrote in 1948 that she saw the research as an opportunity to study women's roles in ancient Japanese history. She had a vague memory of hearing about an historical period when women had ruled Japan and power had passed through the female ancestral line. She wondered what that period had been like and what changes had led to the institution of male primogeniture. There was also, she believed, a later period when male heads of family had not meant automatic subjugation of women. Her vaguely formulated theory suggested that the historical point separating a more egalitarian role for women from one of outright oppression would prove to be the period when private property had become significant. As her research progressed she felt her hazy historical memory and her theoretical suppositions had been correct. She discovered that the institution of private property and the legal protection of inheritance by a male heir demanded that a wife's chastity be carefully guarded to insure purity of the ancestral line. This led to the concept of wives as chattel. It was to protect this system of private property that Confucian morals were imported from China and women were brought under the total control of men. The Japanese family system was established, she concluded, to assure male supremacy and, subjugate women. Shidzue's research showed clearly she believed, a connection between the economics of private property and the development of a family system which had enslaved her and led her into economic depression.[15]

Shidzue met Beard's new challenge with great excitement and immediate action. She asked four trusted friends to join.[16] Two were well known writers, and one was a social worker associated with Shidzue in the birth control movement. The fourth was Mitsui Reiko, the daughter of a descendent of the main branch of the House of Mitsui, married to a descendent of another branch. She not only agreed to join the group, but offered to help finance the project as well. In addition to the core of four researchers a few "liberal" men were invited to help. In fact it was a young professor[17] who borrowed the library books and secured the research room at Tokyo Imperial University, an option not available to women. As Shidzue explained, "When we started this work and wanted to go to the library, we were told that no woman could cross its sacred threshold, so when we wanted reference material we had to bow to the men and beg them to look up our references."[18]

Because of the increasingly repressive political atmosphere of the mid thirties, the group felt they could not meet openly. Fully convinced that their research was subversive, and that they could be prosecuted under the "dangerous thoughts" provision of the 1925 Peace Preservation Law, they devised ways to hide their project and disguise their meetings. Members would come to Shidzue's home as if on a casual visit and stay for research, discussion and writing. They would also meet at an appointed Japanese inn or would be alerted by a cryptic, brief announcement in the personal column of the newspaper.[19]

The group gathered data from all eras of Japanese history with the goal of selecting one hundred representative women. These were not selected to represent a particular political perspective but to show that women were significant at all times in Japanese history for better or worse.[20] Over the years from 1935 to 1939, the group became increasingly careful to conceal their activities, matching the government's paranoia. Shidzue believed wholeheartedly that the authorities were determined to prevent any historical research which might present information in a light other than that sanctioned in the national histories. As she said a decade later, "By the time we finished compiling the material, Japan was moving toward fascism and all history treating facts as such was against the national policy. Many prominent scholars were taken to court because well-indoctrinated associates accused them of writing and teaching the truth about Japanese history."[21] The research group was fully convinced that a project which sought to radically reconstruct the role of women in Japanese history would be suppressed and those involved jailed.

The Japanese research group worked diligently and finally in 1939 Shidzue wrote to Mary Beard saying, simply, "It is finished." Mary was delighted that a portion of the evidence she sought in support of her own theory was completed. She did not recognize that Shidzue had drawn conclusions from her research which were quite the opposite of Beard's. For the Japanese believed she had provided evidence of patriarchal oppression of women, while the American found the work anti-feminist in its support of women's enduring power. Practically, she had to write back that no other country had finished the project, and that Anna Askanasy herself had been forced to flee Austria after destroying all her papers. She placed the manuscript in her World Center for Women's Archives in Rockefeller Center.[22]

Far from bringing any additional funds to add to Shidzue's meager bank account, the women's history project consumed some of her pocket money as well as necessitating that she solicit a larger contribution from Mitsui Reiko. Fortunately in 1936 Feakins Lecture Bureau came to Shidzue's financial rescue once again. The first lecture tour had been so successful and *Facing Two Ways* had made such a hit that Feakins invited Shidzue to come once again, this time for a four month stint. She considered this trip a "financial necessity." Leaving her two grown sons, Arata now eighteen and Tamio seventeen, she set off for the West Coast arriving in Seattle on January 10, 1937. In the many prearranged host cities throughout the U.S. as well as places added as the tour progressed she offered a choice of four lecture topics: "The Mission of Women in Japanese Civilization," "The Conflict of the East and West in Present Day Japan," "The Classical Culture and Modern Civilization in Japan," and "Internationalism and Nationalism in Japan." The last topic recognized the political interests of her previous audiences, and the current state of affairs in Japan. It was a grueling tour for in addition to the constant lecturing in English and the drudgery of long distance travel, Shidzue was often on exhibit as the guest of honor at teas and dinner parties, and was asked to speak informally with members of the American birth control movement. This was not the romantic adventure of the first tour, it was hard work performed to earn desperately needed cash.

Newspaper articles and official Feakins publicity advertised Ishimoto Shidzue as: "The Margaret Sanger of Japan," a "modernized peeress," "a liberal and a feminist," and with a story "full of humor, vivid description and understanding." Her dress, always kimono, was carefully described and she was applauded for her "perfect" English and praised as "both charming and attractive." A typical description read, "Japan's leading woman liberal, Baroness Shidzue Ishimoto, wisely clings to the traditional kimono of her native land. On her arrival yesterday she wore a slim silken garment the color of wisteria. Seated demurely on a couch in her Biltmore sitting room, the Baroness might have been a feudal lady strayed from a seventeenth century print."[23] The article then praised her struggle for women's suffrage and spoke of her work in the birth control movement. A socially prominent American friend was quoted in the Feakins flyer, "I have never seen an audience pay more keen and rapt attention. What the Baroness said was extraordinarily interesting, much of it was moving in a deep human way, and it was all in excellent English."[24]

The social side of the tour began in earnest the week of January 20th in Los Angeles. The Baroness was a celebrity and Gladys DeLancey Smith, director of the California Birth Control Committee, planned an itinerary which included a formal dinner, a supper, a tea and a luncheon, all featuring the Baroness as guest of honor. The primary purpose, however, was to gather together prominent members of the community with an eye toward snaring unlikely future support for birth control. Shidzue was the bait.

Not every moment was crowded with strangers. One Sunday afternoon Smith and Shidzue motored "in state" viewing the countryside. As Smith explained, "Mr. Hori, Japanese consulate, sent his gorgeous, streamlined seven passenger limousine and chauffeur for the Baroness to use. I am happy the Baroness had this very friendly and courteous experience, since some of the Japanese Consulates have unfortunately been 'criticizing' her for some of the things she has been saying in her lecture. (this is confidential, please).... Baroness Ishimoto did appreciate the use of his lovely Packard Car."[25] This gesture, however, did not include a meeting with anyone in the consulate higher than the chauffeur. Smith spent many hours "motoring" with the Baroness here and there and helping her with her lectures, and, like all of the other people Shidzue met on her tour, was much taken with this "adorable" woman who was "just like a 'sweet breath of loveliness and inspiration' from Heaven."[26] It seemed difficult even for Shidzue's colleagues to take her completely seriously.

As she crossed the country presenting her prepared talks, she believed she was delivering important information and not merely entertaining her audience with a glimpse of the exotic East. In her speech contrasting the ways of East and West she would comment on modern Western ways in Japan, using her own life as an example. "In every aspect of life the modern Japanese finds himself leading a double life. It is important not to lose our beautiful old culture, yet we must adapt ourselves to the modern way of living. Some high-born Japanese have their houses in two sections, one old and one new, the one for festivity, and the other for business. As for me, I have given up Japanese clothing and Japanese household ways because I am too busy. Only the ladies of leisure who still devote themselves to tea ceremonies and flower arrangement can cling to the old costume. I find American dresses more comfortable, but I cannot get used to American shoes. Only when I am very dandy do I wear high heels. I still prefer to wear sandals, and warm socks."[27] The contrast between the charming and attractive Japanese Baroness attired in kimono speaking in such a westernized, modern fashion appeared lost on her audiences and even on her friends, for it was the "dainty" woman of old Japan that attracted and enthralled both the audiences in auditoriums and the elite members of upper class society who gathered to honor her.

On the serious issue of birth control Shidzue tried to balance her advocacy with her fear of further agitating her government which disapproved of limiting births. "There is no law against birth control in Japan, and no religious prejudice, but we do encounter political opposition from leaders who believe that strong soldiers are synonymous with a rich country. My answer is that soldiers are stronger if they have grown up in families which have been able to adjust their size to their incomes. Many of our soldier conscripts are suffering from tuberculosis. Birth control is the best remedy for that problem. Among the proud old families, too, there is the feeling that many children add to the family's glory. But thoughtful people of Japan now are anxious to give better education to their children and to provide other advantages possible only if the children are limited in number."[28]

On March 5th Shidzue arrived in New York City, where only two lectures were scheduled for her three week stay. This gave her more time for parties, teas and dinners, and for presentations off the Feakins lecture circuit. On March 19th a formal reception[29] was given in her honor by the Birth Control Clinic Research Bureau. In the absence of Margaret Sanger, who was making her own lecture tour on the West Coast, Dr. Hannah M. Stone, medical director at the bureau, welcomed Baroness Ishimoto declaring that the issue of birth control should be regarded as a problem of "the whole human race."

Dr. Robert L. Dickinson of the National Committee on Maternal Health, and a pioneer for birth control, provided the formal introduction. In his comments he expressed the hope that Japan would work rapidly toward the acclamation of birth control and toward its further development so that it might be a leader in the "art of the spread of well-being through care of motherhood, and in the art of peace." He then revealed an elitist side to his message. "You [Ishimoto] are being welcomed to a country which prides itself on common sense and uncommon science and yet refuses to apply either to the basic need of which you and Mrs. Sanger are focusing your attention; namely, the health and economic well-being which birth control can bring. With two million fertile couples on relief producing children more rapidly than if the head of the family were employed, the Government has not dared to act. With ten million unemployed, the bogy of a declining birth rate is still raised."

In striking contrast Shidzue told the assembled guests that the birth control movement in Japan was important to the well being of the masses of people. "While the military leaders of Japan are not sympathetic to the birth control movement for obvious reasons, nevertheless, birth control in Japan is legal and we are not handicapped by any religious problem. There is a great and growing demand from the masses for adequate and reliable information and any announcement of a birth control lecture is certain to draw a very large audience." Shidzue never equated the need for birth control with an attempt to breed out less economically fruitful or a less desirable class of people. Her political and social concerns demanded that she see limitation of family size as a positive good in itself for mothers and for children rather than as a class weapon.

She continued her presentation with comments on population control and world peace. While she recognized the economic consequences which resulted from an increase of people who cannot be properly cared for, she was not so naive as to equate successful population reduction with peace between nations. "I do not believe at all in the sentimental attitude toward world peace. I think women must study the fundamental reasons why nations go to war and realize that until we remove or remedy these fundamental causes, there can be no world peace."

During her stay in America Shidzue never drew back from criticism of Japan's 1930s policy toward population increase. At the same time she was careful to phrase her comments in such a way that she emphasized alternative solutions to problems of poor health, economic distress, and overpopulation rather than stating outright opposition to militarist policies. She pointed out that birth control, which was not illegal, could provide a better answer to the economic and demographic problems facing Japan than present government policies. Shidzue walked a fine line between advocating her position and not offending her government any more than she already had.

After leaving New York, Shidzue headed back to the West Coast lecturing on the way in the Midwest and the Southwest. She spent her last ten days in Portland recuperating from her exhausting tour, and buying gifts to take back to her sons. As she recalled a decade later, "There had been so many places on my itinerary that by the time I returned to California, I was suffering from tremendous fatigue, a ringing in my ears, and I couldn't hear what was said to me. Fortunately I was able to stay with my uncle's family in Portland for ten days while I recovered my health."[30]

Her final act in America was to initiate one last transaction to secure a little more cash. She wrote a friend, "I have asked Mrs. Tsurumi of Portland to send two kimono and a haori to you as I have written about in my former letter. I hope you like 'haori' and also hope that selling kimono may not be too bothersome to you."[31] After Shidzue returned home she would wear Western clothes almost exclusively. More importantly, as always, she needed money. Somewhat rested and eager to return home she sailed from Vancouver arriving at the port of Yokohama on May 7, 1937.

The Vagaries of Political Suppression

During Shidzue's absence in the winter and early spring of 1937, Katô Kanjû had been busy carving a new left-wing political party out of his Labor-Agrarian Proletarian Council, or Rôkyô, and campaigning for election of party members in the March 12th Tokyo Municipal election. The party held 357 meetings in support of their slate of candidates as they publicly presented their platform which criticized the effects of military expenditures on rising inflation, opposed increased taxation of the masses, and accused the sitting city administration of corruption.[32] Of the fifteen candidates backed by the party, four were successful, including Katô. One week later the Rôkyô changed its name to Japan Proletarian Party [Nihon Musantô]. The Seventieth Diet was dissolved at the end of March and the new party prepared to run candidates in the Diet election scheduled for April 30th. Katô, running in the left-wing district, number five, in Tokyo, which comprised a mixture of industrial and middle class residents, was the only Proletarian Party candidate elected.[33] He would take his seat in the lower house of the new Diet the next month.

Ishimoto Shidzue returned from her lecture tour in May, 1937 to find Katô Kanjû and other socialist friends elated over the results of the April 30th Diet elections. Although the Proletarian Party seated only one MP, Katô, the Social Masses Party more than doubled their membership with thirty-seven seats. Those who supported Katô Kanjû's platform could still hope for a future coalition under a "popular front." It seemed to Katô and others that many voters had responded positively to the year long campaign in the labor and socialist journals and from platforms against what they saw as the government's rapid progress toward fascism. Criticism of the liberal parties and government policy seemed to be bearing fruit, and the April election was seen as a positive turning point for the socialist movement in Japan. With 8.2% of the Diet Lower House seats the Social Masses Party became the most powerful socialist group.[34] The post-election excitement had not died down when Shidzue returned and she was eager to join in the celebration.

Shidzue was invited to mount the Proletarian Party's platform and speak in support of the successful representative, Katô Kanjû, and other local politicians in office under the party's banner. Concerned about a political system which increasingly pressured against women's liberation movements and her own family planning movement, Shidzue found hope in the only legal political party which held high its anti-war banner and provided room on its platform for speakers interested in women's issues. She used this opportunity to proclaim the right of women to plan the spacing and size of their families, and to speak out for full human rights for women. She saw women as part of the proletarian have-nots and felt they should receive their due from this party dedicated to the masses. This was not a dreary task for Shidzue, it was an exhilarating mission, and in all of these activities and associations she enjoyed herself immensely. What a contrast these activities posed against the lecture tour she had just completed! In America she need have no fear of the authorities, but found her reception tied closely to interest in her apparel and appearance and the exotic figure she cut. In Japan fear was ever present, but her cause was seriously accepted and the political goals were clearly vital.

During local elections as well as victory celebrations Shidzue entrusted herself to the cause of the Proletarian Party and "jumped into action giving supportive speeches." Because of the restrictions placed by the Home Ministry, the Peace Preservation Law, and the "special higher police's" concerns about "dangerous thoughts," all of these political meetings and rallies were attended by police "rattling their sabres." It was government policy to pressure the proletarian parties through careful attention to the wording of all public utterances.[35] When the police heard particular words or the expression of suspicious ideas they would stop the speakers and issue warnings, cut the speaker off entirely, or, finally, remove the speaker for questioning and possible arrest. Katô Kanjû had the dubious honor of being the second most interrupted candidate by the police during his run for office in Tokyo in May, 1937.[36]

Shidzue was a featured speaker at the election reception celebrating Kanjû's victory. After she had given her prepared remarks, she discovered that the next speaker had not yet arrived. She had no alternative but to continue speaking. This meant that she had to speak extemporaneously for an additional half hour. Consequently, her wording was not as carefully restrained as it had been in her prepared text. She began to state the issues in a manner unacceptable to the watching authorities. Her delivery became agitated, and it was obvious that she had gone beyond the accepted solemn manner of presentation. The watching police shouted at her to stop, and then led her away. They detained her at the local police station until late that night. Finally, admonishing her that a housewife should not be out so late, they told her to go home.

She returned to her house to be greeted by two very worried sons, frightened by her unexpectedly late absence. She could not think of a way to pacify their fears, for the social conditions of the day meant that dangers were obvious for those who participated in left-wing movements. Her sons did not like to see their mother pressured by the authorities, but they did not ask her to give up her activities. She felt that they understood how important propagation of her beliefs was for her own sense of personal freedom in a society which automatically oppressed women.[37]

This brush with the police should have forewarned Ishimoto Shidzue and her associates of difficult times ahead, but in May and June 1937 this was a minor reminder of government power. Generally speaking Kanjû, Shidzue, and their friends and associates felt that liberal ideas were winning the day and Japan could be swayed from its militarist ways. Optimism about a democratic future for their nation was high.

Notes

1. Rev. Francis J. McConnell, Methodist Bishop.

2. Kanda Fuhito, *Nihon no tôitsu senzen undô* [Japan's Popular Front Movement], 1979, p. 69.

3. Written and trans. by Inomata Tsunao, a socialist colleague and proletariat theoretician, who had been a member of Communist Party in twenties. Itoya Toshio, ed., *Nihon shakaishûgi undô shisôshi.* [An Intellectual History of Japan's Socialist Movement] Vol. III, 1982, p. 174.

4. Also speaking, Roger Baldwin, future founder of A.C.L.U. and acquaintance of Shidzue's through Sanger. Baldwin would seek Shidzue and Kanjû out after the war. See Chapter 9.

5. N.Y. Times, 6/25/35 and 6/30/35.

6. Kanda Fuhito, *Nihon no tôitsu senzen undô* [Japan's Popular Front Movement], 1979, pp. 69-70; Itoya Toshio, ed., *Nihon shakaishûgi undô shisôshi* [An Intellectual History of Japan's Socialist Movement], 1982, p. 174; and Takahashi Hikohiro, *Nihon no shakai minshûshûgi seitô* [Japan's Social-Democratic Parties], 1977, p. 162.

7. In the 60s and 70s two different versions of meeting were publicly admitted. Katô, the socialist, claimed he listened to Nosaka, but insisted that he, Katô, would judge how to conduct "popular front" movement in Japan. Nosaka, the communist, said he devised the mass based, anti-fascist "popular front" plan; Katô merely agreed to carry it out. Kanda Fuhito, *Nihon no tôitsu senzen undô* [Japan's Popular Front Movement], 1979, p. 69 and ff.; for Katô see Katô Kanjû's Hearing Sept. 19, 1972; for Nosaka, *Mainichi Shimbun,* Aug. 29, 1972. Nosaka told about secret meeting in his 1962 autobiography; Katô in a 1964 book.

8. *Chûô Kôran*, 9/36, trans., *Contemporary Japan*, 12/36, pp. 472-473.

9. Richard Mitchell, *Thought Control in Prewar Japan*, Cornell U. Press, 1976, p. 63.

10. Ishimoto to Florence Rose, 3/20/36, Reel 18, Sanger, LofC.

11. Memo from Sanger, Reel 18, Sanger, LofC.

12. Confidential Report on Japan, Reel 18, Sanger, LofC.

13. 1948, Chapter 4.

14. Endô Shûnsaku, "Meijijo no kyôkiyun; Katô Shidzue" [The Heart of a Meiji Woman], *Bungei Shunjû*, July, 1983, pp. 353-354.

15. 1948, pp. 100-101. Interestingly this interpretation of the role of women in Japanese history and the oppressive nature of the family system exists only in Ishimoto's thirties writings, 1948, and a few letters and comments of the 40s. No such radical ideas appear in later writings. She categorically refuted them in 1978 interview, when she stated that she was unhappy with some comments made in 30s

research papers. "[M]any were representative of a period of leftist thinking and not representative of my present ideas."

16. The four listed in 1948 were Yosano Akiko, Hasegawa Shigure, Okamoto Kanoko, all well known women writers, along with an unnamed benefactor. In 1981 Yosano and Okamoto were omitted and replaced by Hasegawa Shigure's husband, Mikami Otokichi, and the social worker, Niizumi Itoko. The benefactor, Mitsui Reiko, was now named.

17. Endo Motô, who became Professor of Women's History at Japan Women's University [Nihon Josei Daigaku] after the war.

18. Ethel Weed to Dorothy Brush, 1947 Interview, Smith.

19. A notice saying, "Mikami Otokichi, residence unknown Hasegawa Shigure," meant Mikami had finished writing a long section. 1981, p. 87.

20. In December, 1937, while addressing an Oberlin College luncheon, Mary Beard revealed a research project designed to rescue women from a present position as "a lost sex in history." Beard explained that the published results would support her interpretation of history, that women have always been a vital force, for both good and evil, in the development of civilization and culture. *Japan Times & Mail*, 12/30/37. For Beard's theory see *Mary Ritter Beard: A Sourcebook*, Ed. Ann J. Lane, Schocken Books, 1977, pp. 129-130, 138.

21. Ethel Weed to Dorothy Brush, 1947 Interview, Smith.

22. Papers were transferred to Smith College, where they are today.

23. *Los Angeles Times*, January 22, 1937.

24. Herbert Houston of New York City.

25. Memo to Bernice Wickham "1/20 - 1/26, 1937," Reel 38, Sanger, LofC.

26. Gladys DeLancey Smith's Memo, 1/23/37, Reel 38, Sanger, LofC.

27. *Herald Tribune*, undated, Smith.

28. See news clippings in Sanger, Box 235 Japan, Sanger, LofC.

29. Remarks from this event are in Smith.

30. Tsurumi [mother's] relatives, 1948, p. 104.

31. Ishimoto to Gladys Smith, 5/6/37, Reel 38, Sanger, LofC.

32. William D. Wray, "The Japanese Popular Front Movement; July 1936-February 1938," *Papers on Japan VI*, Harvard University, 1972, p. 118.

33. William D. Wray, "The Japanese Popular Front Movement," pp. 118-124; Andrew Gordon, *Labor and Imperial Democracy in Prewar Japan*, Univ. of Calif. Press, 1991, p. 305.

34. Stephen S. Large, *Organized Workers & Socialist Politics in Interwar Japan*, Cambridge U. Press, 1981, p. 199.

35. 1948, p. 110-111.

36. Andrew Gordon, *Labor and Imperial Democracy in Prewar Japan*, 1991, p. 319.

37. 1948, Chapter 4.

5

Discreet Activism (1937)

During the summer of 1937 the political left was surprised and alarmed, then put on guard by an "incident" between Japanese and Chinese troops which occurred near the Marco Polo Bridge just outside Beijing. At first the fighting seemed a minor clash which would be easily confined. In fact the "incident," which escalated quickly, threatened to become a full scale war. In July the Japanese occupied Tianjin and Beijing; in August they bombed Shanghai. Fighting raged on during the fall as several more cities fell, most notably Shanghai in November. The year ended with the infamous "rape of Nanjing" culminating in the capture of that city on December 13, 1937. In spite of all this carnage the "China Incident" was no closer to a solution on December 13th than it had been on July 7th.

The warning of the "Marco Polo Bridge Incident" was clearly heard by the left. By late July Katô Kanjû and his colleagues began to tone down references to their party's opposition to Japan's China policy. It was obvious to all in the Proletarian Party, and in Katô's labor union, that their freedom to criticize government action was on a short chain. Softening their election and post-election rhetoric, party spokesmen no longer used the term fascist, spoke of Japan's leaders as military and bureaucratic dictators, or stated direct disapproval of the government's China policy. Instead they began to talk about providing for the families of the soldiers at the front in the face of a declining standard of living for Japan's masses.

Prime Minister Konoe Fumimaro called a Special Diet Session[1] beginning July 22nd. Over the next two weeks, until adjournment on August 8th, this extraordinary session passed a number of bills affecting every facet of Japan's economic life. Primary objectives were provision for economic self-sufficiency and a strong financial base for military needs. The government hoped to effect a swift military end to what they characterized as an "incident" in China.[2] "The Diet's patriotic response to Konoe's appeal was total," according to one Japan scholar.

"Following the unanimous approval of a resolution condemning 'anti-Japanese forces in China who ignore the principles of international faith,' the Diet quickly approved thirty-four of the thirty-five bills..."[3]

Given such wholehearted political support for the military action, which included the Social Masses Party on the left, it is not surprising that the Proletarian Party leadership began to modify its public statements. In secret meetings held from July 22nd to July 26th party leaders stressed economic issues and did not speak about the government's policy of "fascist militarism" as they had. However, in the report made public on July 26th, item number five declared that the party would "support a settlement of the war by peaceful means and a policy of 'non-expansion'."[4] Though muted, opposition to the government's military driven foreign policy was not yet completely silenced. The day before the party's statement was released, the Imperial Army subdued the Beijing-Tianjin area. It seemed doubtful that a peaceful solution was being considered.

The fighting in China threatened to disrupt Shidzue's political activism as well. In May 1937, just before leaving America, Shidzue had learned that Margaret Sanger and several other friends would be stopping in Japan on their way to China. Though disappointed that the stopover would be brief and not the primary focus of this trip, Shidzue was pleased that Margaret had set aside a week to visit and lecture in Japan. Over the next few weeks the timing of this visit seemed even more propitious. In spite of the usual police monitoring of socialist political activities, and the few instances of substantial interference, Shidzue and her associates on the left experienced strong feelings of optimism. It was, she thought, an auspicious moment to open a new birth control clinic. She awaited Sanger's visit, anticipating with great pleasure the boost this would bring to her latest venture and to Japan's birth control movement in general.

After the Marco Polo Incident of July 7th Shidzue, like Kanjû, became apprehensive. During the rest of that month, as hostilities with China intensified, and the nationalists and militarists won the hour, opposition to Japan's imperialist adventure began to crumble. Both political and social activists became nervous, but Shidzue determined to go forward with her plans. She opened her birth control clinic on July 31st and continued her lecture arrangements for Sanger and her entourage. Most of the plans were formulated by mail exchanged with Sanger's secretary, Florence Rose, who was in Shanghai the summer of 1937, preparing for the more important China leg of Sanger's tour. Florence had assured Shidzue that much could be accomplished in a one week stopover if all were in readiness and so the two of them planned each moment of Sanger's trip with great care. Shidzue warned that "we are told that we better refrain from war talking," but aside from that there shouldn't be any difficulties.[5] The authorities were much too busy monitoring the "dangerous thoughts" of politically influential men to worry about the lecturing of a few women.

In China, however, things looked very unstable, and Florence Rose wrote to Shidzue on August 2nd, "...[C]onditions here are as uncertain as they were in your country; and I shall tell M.S. either by telephoning Honolulu or by cable, that all agree that it would not be possible to carry out any extensive program at this time...." She wrote again, however, on August 8th making further arrangements for the Japan visit. On August 9th the Japanese army in Shanghai began to make new demands on the Chinese, who responded by moving three divisions in place to attack the Japanese. The Japanese army and navy fought back; Chinese aircraft bombed the Japanese; in retaliation Japanese aircraft bombed Nanjing; and on August 13th the Japanese cabinet authorized bombs to be dropped on Shanghai.

Shidzue was frantic. She wrote Florence on August 16th, "Are you safe? It is really a heart breaking misfortune to hear about that fearful bombardment which took place in Shanghai. I noticed that your hotel was not one of the two attacked but it must be located pretty nearby. I hope nothing happened to you. Please come back here, don't stay in that dangerous zone any longer."[6] She went on to say how pessimistic she was, and that the Americans remained too optimistic under the circumstances. The whole situation had made her sick to her stomach and she had had to spend several days in bed. In the rest of the letter, however, she managed to lay out precise practical arrangements for the Sanger visit. The war news was tragic but it was across the sea and needn't interfere with birth control advocacy.

The business side of Shidzue's letters to Florence Rose included comments on policy conflicts between competing birth control organizations, lists of materials Sanger would need for her public and private meetings, groups which could be counted on to sponsor lectures, radio stations which would broadcast lectures, and names of people and groups which objected to Sanger's message or refused to participate "in view of the present emergency."[7] Shidzue and Florence also agreed upon a format for the eight formal lectures scheduled.

Meanwhile Sanger, Dorothy Brush, her son Charles and two other members of Sanger's organization had left Honolulu on August 7th, expecting to dock at Kobe on the 20th. Sanger described the group's initial feelings in a letter to friends.[8] "Needless to say, despite peaceful seas, there was not 'smooth sailing' in our minds, owing to the rumors of war, and the possibility of a major conflict involving the whole of Asia and perhaps the world. But, opposed to these fears was the faith, based on experience in the past, that the difficulty would be likely to blow over, and the Chinese 'incident', so-called by the Japanese, be of short duration. It was the general opinion that by the time of our arrival in China, peace negotiations would be under way. On August 1st, I wrote and wired the Secretary of State for advice, and was informed that the United States Government was not advising American citizens against going to China."

Sanger had prepared for her trip by reading everything available on such diverse subjects as Japan's population, medical facilities and physicians, military, raw materials, the Manchurian Incident and the current significance of Manchukuo, and on economic conditions in Japan and in her territories. After careful study she concluded that there was a demographic basis for the expansionist policies of the 30s, that Japan's level of medical knowledge and the attitudes of its physicians were "backward," and that the Japanese government was bent on war and the repression of its people.[9] Her evaluations, substantiated by her interpretation of the evidence as she examined it, happily coincided with her own ideology and program for birth control.

En route, rumors aboard ship heated up as daily reports on the radio suggested that the situation in Shanghai was deteriorating. Some said that the ship was carrying munitions for China and that it might be boarded and searched at any moment. Missionaries on board were cabled not to go on to China but to stay in Japan. Dorothy Brush wrote, "Then came word of the bombing of Shanghai. Miss Rose, MS's secretary was in Shanghai! For days we were terribly anxious - then came the news that she had escaped the ruins of her hotel by inches. We were worried...('Dangerous thoughts')." And again, "Japan had begun to chastise China - or so the Japanese newspapers called it. Soon it was evident there was neither any hope nor need of taking Birth Control to China. War, one of Nature's most favorite checks on population, had beaten us to it. We wondered how we would be received in Japan."[10]

Sanger continued the story of the bombing of Shanghai and Florence Rose's fate. "By August 14th communications with Shanghai were entirely cut off, and by the time we arrived at Kobe, no one knew what the actual conditions there might be. We were therefore relieved and delighted to see Miss Rose awaiting us on the pier at Kobe; and shocked to learn of the terrific bombardment of Shanghai, which had already been in progress for three days preceding her escape. Her account of the terror and horror that accompanied successive bombings of sections of Shanghai crowded with helpless refugees, including the heart of the International Settlement where she had gone for greater safety, made it evident that all plans for China at this time must be abandoned. We were met at Kobe also by Baroness Shidzue Ishimoto, who has bravely and gallantly led the birth control movement in Japan..."[11]

Birth Control Advocacy in a Time of Crisis

Shidzue traveled to Kobe to meet her friends. By August 20th, in spite of the escalation of the war in China, she was only mildly worried about the effect the government's tightened noose would have on Sanger's visit or on the activities of her new birth control clinic. The authorities did not have time, man-power or adequate interest in these women or their message to prevent their activities. In truth, the government officially did oppose limiting births but neither the dispensing of family planning information nor the establishment of birth control clinics were yet illegal. They might represent a form of "dangerous thoughts" but during the summer of 1937 the Home Ministry, and the "special higher police" were far too busy checking the more threatening activities of well-known public men whose political pronouncements might stir up opposition to the escalating hostilities in China to bother with these women. Katô Kanjû had to change the tone and content of his publicly proclaimed political platform, but Ishimoto Shidzue could proceed with her arrangements making only minor changes or adjustments to satisfy local police regulations or circumvent nervous lecture hall managers.

Shidzue met the ship and was shocked to see Sanger descend the gang plank sporting a sling on her arm.[12] It seems that a few days before, Sanger, dripping wet from a swim, had slipped on the stairs and broken her arm. The group went immediately to International Hospital where the doctors rebroke and reset the arm, a very painful ordeal, and told Sanger she would have to remain a few days in the hospital. Shidzue had arranged a lecture that very day at Ama-no-Hashidate, a small but celebrated town on the Japan Sea about five hours by train from Kobe. Sanger, determined not to disappoint the fifty doctors awaiting her visit, signed herself out of the hospital, and left for the train with her cast still damp. The pain proved too great, however, and she got off at Kyoto leaving Shidzue and Dorothy Brush to continue the journey alone.

Much to Dorothy's dismay she was designated Margaret's stand-in, a role which terrified her. On the other hand Dorothy enjoyed the chance to converse with Shidzue during the long train ride. For Dorothy "the Baroness" was "one of the truly great women of the earth."[13] The American commented on her companion's Western dress; in New York she had always worn a kimono. Shidzue explained that Western clothes were in vogue in Japan and any woman who could get them was envied. She continued that Japanese women rushed to dressmakers with pictures of the latest fashions, but when the dress was finished, it seldom looked like the picture. Undoubtedly a Westerner would laugh at the finished product. She then said, "Each time I go to America I buy myself everything. Then I wear the same things until I go again. Even when they are four or five years old, my friends think I am a fashion plate."

Though rickshaws lined the street outside the station at Ama-no-Hashidate, the women were taken by bus to a Japanese-style inn to spend the night. After "freshening up" they went to the local police station for the obligatory entry of their names into local government and military records. Dorothy Brush was also asked to show the speech she would deliver. To her surprise the police assured her that she could speak freely about birth control, but she was warned not to mention anything about "the little difficulty with China."

That evening the two women were brought to a large "100 mat" rectangular hall lined with individual knee high tables each set with tea and a fan. Seated behind each table on the tatami flooring was a kimono clad Japanese, only three or four of whom were women. The police lined the sliding doors. The guests of honor, which included Baroness Ishimoto, Brush, and Dr. Oota Takeo, a gynecologist, sat Japanese style at similar tables on a slightly raised platform at the front of the hall. When invited, Dorothy stood in stockinged feet to give her address and Shidzue interpreted for her. The presentation was given sentence by sentence, allowing Dorothy to think carefully before she spoke. Even so she found that differences in attitude meant that her audience seemed puzzled at statements she intended to be humorous and burst into unexpected laughter at others. Sanger had brought a few films showing the human biology of reproduction accompanied with explanations of the use of contraceptive devices. Before presenting these films Dorothy Brush requested that all those in the room who were not physicians please leave, a required procedure in America. She was taken aback when Shidzue, the police, and everyone else laughed heartily. Why should some adults be prevented from viewing an informational film? In America such shocking pictures were not permitted to be shown publicly to anyone outside the medical profession. In Japan they were shown to all.

The chance to spend time with Dorothy was important for Shidzue. As she wrote on September 18th, the time for exchange of attitudes about the "joy and sorrow of life" had brought her closer to Dorothy. Shidzue had developed a strong attachment for her American friends and appreciated their reciprocation of this emotional tie. There was a sympathy and understanding which she found lacking in thirties Japan. Her American experience and her dedication to Sanger's principles had given her a different perspective from most Japanese. Also, her growing concern over the militarist direction of Japan's political center, with its increasing commitment to war in China, separated her from many of her own neighbors and relatives. The feeling that she would always be of "one mind" with her American friends, though an ocean separated them, was essential to her emotional well-being. In the future these friends would actively support her through her imprisonment, emotionally sustain her during her war years, and eagerly seek her out after the war was over.

Once in Tokyo Sanger felt well enough to carry out her heavy schedule. Shidzue arranged formal lectures for physicians, birth control advocates, Tokyo municipal leaders, including the mayor and health department officials, and social activists. She also had an informal gathering to which she invited about fifty "progressive men and women writers, poets, Drs., labor leaders etc. women suffragets" as Sanger described them in her diary. Formal and informal meetings went well and many in attendance were interested as well as curious. Shidzue used this occasion to build her own movement and encourage contributions for the clinic she had opened the month before. It was difficult for her to raise money for women, in general, did not have their own money to spend and men were not as interested. She had deliberately refrained from seeking support from the foreign community in Japan, as she had wanted this to be a Japanese project.[14]

At no time did the group have difficulty with the police or the military. No one stopped Sanger from presenting her message and there was no suggestion that the governments, local or national, opposed the presentation of birth control information within Japan. Some individual officials did not agree with the message, or were not sure whether they agreed, but still they welcomed Sanger and feted her beyond the requirements of simple courtesy. She spoke freely at arranged lectures, formal and informal gatherings, in more intimate discussion groups arranged by the Baroness and attended by the social and economic upper classes. She was also interviewed for three hours by the editors of a syndicate representing fourteen newspapers who intended, then, to run articles for the next several months. The editor of a women's magazine spoke with her for four hours to gather material for a feature article to appear in a month or two. These print media events and her radio interviews and broadcasts gave her a wider, more general, if still relatively well off, audience. Sanger also felt free to speak to women on the streets, shopkeepers, geisha, and prostitutes, through the good offices of Shidzue's guidance and interpretation.[15] Dorothy Brush thought that the leniency of the authorities toward Sanger resulted from their concerns with military rejections of inductees because of poor health. She connected this with the large Japanese families, crowded living conditions and general economic deprivation attributed to too many mouths to feed.[16] In other words she thought that the militarists felt a need for Sanger's message. More likely the celebration of her permitted by the authorities reflected the government's evaluation of this level of "dangerous thoughts" as minor when compared with its obsessive concern about the China Incident, and its determination that truthful reports of the "chastisement" of China not reach the ears of the Japanese public. The women were permitted to say what they wanted about "women's issues" but were not even to speak privately about anything related to China. The influence of Sanger, which seemed so large to the Americans and so financially fruitful and spiritually rewarding to Shidzue and her supporters, seemed minuscule to the authorities and, therefore, could be ignored for the time being.

Geisha and Prostitutes

Although most days and evenings were filled with lectures, and discussions, there were moments for relaxation and some sightseeing. Interested and curious about all kinds of feminine roles in Japan, Sanger wanted to speak with a geisha. Shidzue arranged such an interview at an expensive tea house.[17] The young woman was in her twenties, and spoke English well. She told Sanger that she had graduated from a Kyoto girls college and had become a geisha in order to support her mother and grandmother. She expected to complete her four year contract in one more year and hoped to take up stenography and secure another job. She had been attracted to the geisha world by the artistic accomplishments which these women displayed. She seemed anxious to dispel the stereotype of geisha as lovers and prostitutes.

Next Sanger asked the Baroness to take her to the famed Yoshiwara district, as she had in 1922. This heavily taxed and policed section of Tokyo housed the licensed prostitutes. Shidzue was happy to accede to the request and commented that there was also an unlicensed quarter where women ended up who had failed the health examination or were otherwise unlicensable. Of course, the curious Americans asked to see that too. Apprehensively, Shidzue pointed out that this area would be risky to visit as it was not policed. Sanger replied, "What makes you think I want policemen around?"

The next evening Baroness Ishimoto picked up Sanger and Bush at their hotel in her chauffeur-driven car, and directed the driver to take them to the Yoshiwara district. Brush asked her what the chauffeur thought about being asked to take them to such a place. The Baroness replied with a smile that he was not paid to think. Shidzue then described the role of licensed prostitution in Japan. She emphasized the financial gain for the government from high taxes, frequent health examinations, and close police supervision. All of this was designed to protect the men. "'But what happens if they [the prostitutes] do contract venereal disease?' asked Margaret. 'They are thrown out - turned over to the unlicensed unregulated section. You'll see them there, if you still have the courage to go.'"

Dorothy Brush described these adventures in several drafts of her journal notes. One such version of the licensed quarters ran as follows. "The Yoshiwara runs along both sides of a broad long park-like area gaily lit with colored Japanese lanterns and hung with painted scrolls. At the opening is a police booth. A narrow pavement stretches on each side before the rows of houses. Each one has a long show case out in front, filled with photographs of the goods for sale within - very modest photographs we thought, since they showed only the head and nape of the neck. Shidzue explained that sexually this is the most exotic [sic] attraction. Most of the houses had two curtained doorways with a booth in front occupied by a 'barker' clad in a thin kimono sitting cross-legged, girls peeked out from the curtains, giggling, flirting but only two went further. One lifted her kimono above her knees and another allowed hers to fall open. There was nothing but girl beneath."

Margaret then asked to interview one of the young prostitutes, and Shidzue arranged with a "Madam" for such a meeting. The interview took place in the "Madam's" presence with Shidzue interpreting and was far from revealing as far as the American's were concerned. They did learn that the young girl earned, according to the "Madam," "not one yen until she has repaid all she has cost us," and that according to the rate card in the room her charge was "about seventy-five American cents for an hour, two dollars for an afternoon; four dollars for a whole night." The memory of this visit, as recorded and revised by Dorothy Brush, was both sad and romantic.[18]

Shidzue directed the chauffeur to drive from the Yoshiwara district to the unlicensed quarters. This visit turned out to be a harrowing and frightening experience, and does not seem to have served any purpose except to provide a view of the seamier side of Tokyo life. The group left the highway and drove down dark, winding, crowded streets which seemed like alleys to the Americans. Actually this was probably on more typical Tokyo streets than their previous drive.

There were no protective police here and it was an area which did not welcome foreign guests or seemingly wealthy Japanese women. The three women actually got out of the car expecting to survey the area on foot, but a shower of stones and angry shouts which the Americans assumed to be obscenities soon sent them scurrying back inside. A man grabbed Shidzue roughly by the arm and growled something at her. Within the safety of the car, which quickly sped off to the main road, Shidzue translated some of the remarks. The angry man who jostled her was asking how she, a Japanese, could show these horrible sights to Westerners? Others were calling out taunts of, "Is it me you want?," and, "Haven't we met before girlies?"

Dorothy Brush and Margaret Sanger saw their world as full of social and economic evils caused primarily by overpopulation and they saw birth control as the solution. The introduction to geisha, licensed prostitutes, and the squalid unlicensed areas reconfirmed their world view, and Shidzue's comments about the position of women in Japan added weight to their conclusions. It is interesting that although Shidzue drove them about in a chauffeured car (which they believed belonged to her), took them to wealthy homes where they were lavishly entertained, introduced them to the cream of the artistic and educated Tokyo society, and arranged discussions with socially and politically activist women, they still saw her and her associates as beleaguered women with no influence or independence.

The visits to the geisha and prostitute quarters, and a few random street interviews were really the only first-hand experiences Sanger and Brush had with non-elite Japanese. Sanger, however, did not write about these events in her private letters or public press releases. Rather she described the official receptions and interviews and exclusive social events. For example she highlighted a Japanese dinner held at a fine restaurant. "At the invitation of the Baroness, many old and new friends were present, including several distinguished physicians and two members of the famous Mitsui family, one of the five oldest families in Japan, noted for their widespread interests and their philanthropy. We were entertained the following day at a garden party in one of the Mitsui family estates, established and designed hundreds of years ago by feudal lords."[19] But the few encounters with the "ordinary" people did enter heavily into her analysis of the role of women in the society. "I was disappointed, although not surprised, to find that the progress of the women of Japan has been retarded. They have not been able to maintain the advances they had made as far back as in 1922. Then they were making rapid strides on the wings of enlightenment in education. Soon after the earthquake [1923], however, reactionary forces set up a strong, bureaucratic, militaristic government, and since then women have not been allowed the natural freedom of evolutionary progress."[20] Sanger was never shy about selectively remembering, compressing history, or drawing conclusions which fitted her personal ideology.

On the other hand Sanger was amazed at the freedom which she was allowed given the "reactionary forces" and "strong, bureaucratic, militaristic government" which was in charge in Japan. She was never prevented from presenting her controversial message completely uncensored. She was, then, given a freer platform than she could expect in her homeland. There were, of course, bureaucrats along the way who disagreed with some of her points, but their exceptions were always taken most politely. She knew from Shidzue that national policy opposed birth control, but that did not seem to affect her right to express the most radical ideas. She listened to Shidzue's stories of the struggle she was experiencing in disseminating information, raising funds, and opening her new clinic, but the aura of success which surrounded her tour could not be diminished. The well planned meetings lent "truth" to her growing belief that the aristocratic and educated groups which she addressed represented the response to her message of the Japanese society as a whole. She began to see Japan as the locus of potential fulfillment for her life's work, a feeling which grew as the years progressed. More than two decades later she would evaluate her campaigns in Japan as her finest hours.

Celebrating a New Clinic

Shidzue was elated with how well Margaret's visit was going. She decided that in spite of the politically dangerous times she would hold a reception which would both honor her guest and celebrate the establishment of her new private clinic. She realized that she would have to be circumspect about her plans for the grand opening, lest it alert the authorities to another pocket of "dangerous thoughts." At the same time, she felt she could not deny her cause the celebrity that the Sanger presence would bring. The opening could be a publicity event and financial success beyond her greatest dreams. The politically smooth progress of the Sanger visit so far with its benign acceptance by the police and local officials was reassuring. Just before the formal opening of her Birth Control Clinic of Tokyo, Shidzue took Margaret Sanger and her entourage for an on-site visit. Sanger wrote in her diary, "We all went to see it hidden away in a working class district. Joey, (Mrs. Joanne Parker) and Dorothy gave the Baroness $650 and I added $150 which made $800 almost the years expense."[21]

The festivities of August 30th began with a "welcome party" for Sanger, which was followed by the formal reception and speeches. Ishimoto Shidzue had invited everyone of note in activist women's circles, as well as those involved with her family planning movement and other birth control organizations. She included social workers, physicians, teachers, leaders of the women's suffrage movement, labor leaders, all of the people who might help her project succeed. At the same time she kept the gathering intimate enough not to attract too much attention outside her circle. Before Sanger's keynote speech Shidzue welcomed her guests and expressed appreciation for Sanger's visit pointing out that it had been only fifteen years since Sanger's first tour, a motivating factor for all birth control organizations since that time to form their own birth control movement and accept the challenge to meet Japan's social needs in this arena. She then praised her own group for their progress over just three short years and enumerated their successes. They had been consulted in person or by letter by more than 10,000 women. "The income of most of these women's husbands is 30 yen [about $10.00] a month, and they have families averaging 6 and 8 children." The desire for birth control information was strong but their ability to pay was minimal. Although it cost as little as one yen to be protected only about 700 out of the 10,000 could afford the protection and the information. She then made a veiled plea for funds for her clinic as she suggested that the "saddest part" for the birth control movement was that they had no way to solicit effectively for funds given the militarist acts and policies. "The public is not sympathetic with this movement, and at the present time a campaign of public education is not possible for us, and so we must fight harder than ever, and I hope you will encourage and help us in this time of difficulty."[22]

Perhaps it was somewhat inaccurate of Shidzue to emphasize that the actual acquisition of contraceptive devices and literature by her inquirers represented primarily an inability to pay. In fact the problem of education was an even greater obstacle, as many women faced the disinterest or refusal of their husbands to cooperate. Also, no mention was made of the many other sources of supply beyond Shidzue's home offices and now her clinic. There were other birth control organizations and clinics operating in Tokyo and Osaka and there were many stores on street corners which sold contraceptives called "SANGA" [Sanger] and "100 HAPPY NIGHTS," and newspapers advertised contraceptives, primarily condoms, which could be ordered by mail. But this was a celebration of Shidzue's accomplishments and the opening of her clinic, and so she could not be expected to mention competing organizations or detail other sources of contraceptives.

Margaret Sanger's remarks were brief, cordial, and particularly laudatory of her colleague and host, Ishimoto Shidzue. She placed her along side the names of Mary Wollstonecraft, Madame Curie, Susan B. Anthony, Olive Schreiner, and Ellen Key in an international pantheon of pioneer women. "Japan should be proud, and I believe her children's children will pay homage to one of the greatest women today, to Baroness Ishimoto, for Baroness Ishimoto is not only a pioneer in Japan, but also a Marco Polo of Japan, because through her lectures and speaking to thousand and thousands of people from East to West and North and South, [she] carries the message of Japan. I consider Baroness Ishimoto as really a bridge between Japan and the United States, bringing the message of what you are doing here, and what we are doing there." At this point Sanger stressed her belief about a division in society which determined that some people were superior and others inferior. This attitude separated her from other socialist feminists, showed her capitulation to the eugenicists' position,[23] and gave her message a conservative twist. She felt that population problems were at the root of all problems and certainly crucial to Japan's current "internal relations and international relations." Each nation, including Japan, must solve her population problems first. "And population does not involve only the question of food, of rice and wheat and other things we eat; it concerns itself with the quality and the kind of people that are being brought into the world to carry on the destiny of your nation. You are not going to bring up the highest intelligence if you will multiply too rapidly because a rapid multiplication has always demonstrated that as we multiply too quickly we level down, but as we control our numbers and our rate of growth, we evolve to a higher destiny." She closed with a plea for "spiritual" support for Shidzue's work using intelligence and ideals and, by implication, money to help in the national and international battle for birth control, a battle which involved the very essence of the survival of not only Japan but the civilization of the world.

Comments from the audience were then heard. Dr. Majima Kan, who headed a rival birth control organization, spoke, his invited presence softening the competitive discord which had entered into his relationship with Ishimoto Shidzue. He thanked Sanger and congratulated "Baroness Ishmoto for her courageous activity" in opening a birth control clinic. He then said that although he was prohibited by law from speaking in public about birth control, because this was a "closed meeting" he would speak out. He praised Sanger and assured her that many doctors in Japan favored the practice of birth control but that they were in a very difficult position because of the fear of breaking the law. He felt sad at the "problems we are facing at present" and hoped that "these difficulties will have passed" soon. In spite of the closed nature of the meeting Dr. Majima, like so many others, still felt he must speak in code.

At an earlier reception the commissioner of the Tokyo Health Department had tried to explain to Sanger that the "perpendicular" Japanese attitude of morality which extended downward from Emperor to head of the family with the wife always below the husband made it impossible for Japan to embrace birth control. His remarks were intended to be polite while supporting government policy. Sanger interpreted this essentially confusing explanation to mean that since control over reproduction would give women "more power, greater freedom, and a greater chance to develop her personality; and from this growth her economic dependence on man, and the male members of her family clan," would be lessened, a policy favorable to birth control could not be sanctioned.[24] During the testimonial remarks following Sanger's speech, Kaneko Shigeri, who was also an employee of the Health Department, spoke in opposition to her superior's remarks. She had been present at the Health Department reception and wanted to make clear that the commissioner had expressed a "personal point of view" only. She, on the other hand, advocated birth control. She, then continued, "Women have a right as well as a duty in having children, and I think we can assume that right as we wish."

Seven other guests spoke including the well-known leader of the women's suffrage movement, Ichikawa Fusae. She told of her visit to Sanger's New York clinic fifteen years earlier commenting that her observation at that time was that public opinion in America had not been favorable to Sanger's movement and that she, too, had experienced oppression by the government. Ichikawa, then, expressed admiration of Sanger and her followers who sold Sanger's *Birth Control Review* on busy street corners as they sought to get their message to the public. Ichikawa felt that she and her compatriots should work harder and take courage from Sanger's experiences. She also hoped that in her movement for political equality for women she could be "as brave and as faithful as Margaret Sanger was in carrying on her movement."

The reception was a great success and one of the more memorable occasions for Sanger. She wrote in a September 23rd public press release that "[M]ost encouraging was the gathering to celebrate the opening of the first modern birth control clinic in Japan.... We congratulate Baroness Ishimoto and her co-workers who have carried on birth control service and educational work under great difficulties." Sanger was impressed with the advances of her counterparts in Japan in spite of her conflicting remarks about the backward slide of women in that society. She went on to warn, however, "[O]ne can never foresee what may happen in a militaristic country, and so the future is still dark and over-clouded...," and then added somewhat self-congratulatorily, "with the cooperation offered on this trip by many of the outstanding medical men and the approaching inauguration of a public health program, I dare hope that the seeds planted may eventually bear fruit." The fearful atmosphere she described overshadowed the growth of the "seeds" she had planted. Within six months the government would force Shidzue to close her clinic.

The Americans departed on September 3rd aboard "the bombed and crippled" *S.S. President Hoover*. As Sanger wrote, "the riddled deck" and "shattered glass" were "echoes of the tragic and harrowing conditions in China." Shidzue was left with memories of the brief but exciting visit. She reminisced to Dorothy in her letter of September 18th.[25] "The summer was one of the most delightful ones for me having you and Mrs. Sanger and my English is not sufficient to express my gratitude and admiration to you who gave me and Arata such a joy in many ways." Shidzue singled out an overnight at Lake Chuzenji as a highlight of the visit. At that time the inn was crowded and she and Sanger shared a room. This became an opportunity to talk about future projects for the birth control movement and to express feelings of life long friendship. Shidzue said, "I felt that I heard a voice in the wilderness while I was listening to Mrs. Sanger in spite of this dreadful atmosphere of war." The feelings of friendship expressed during the visit and in these letters became especially important to Ishimoto over the next war filled years, a time she called her "winter years."

Notes

1. Seventy-first Diet.

2. Michael A. Barnhart, *Japan Prepares for Total War: The Search for Economic Security, 1919-1941*, Cornell U. Press, 1987, p. 94.

3. Gordon Mark Berger, *Parties Out of Power in Japan, 1931-1941*, Princeton U. Press, 1977, p. 140.

4. William D. Wray, "The Japanese Popular Front Movement, July 1936-February, 1938," in *Papers on Japan VI*, Harvard University, 1972, p. 125; Furuta Hikari, Sakuta Keiichi, Ikimatsu Keizô, eds., *Kindai Nihon shakai shisôshi* [A History of Social Thought in Modern Japan], 1971, p. 128.

5. Ishimoto to Florence Rose, 7/31/37, Reel 18, Sanger, LofC.

6. Florence Rose to Ishimoto 8/2/37, 8/8/37, Ishimoto to Rose, 8/16/37, Reel 19, Sanger, LofC.

7. Quote in letter from *Christian Science Monitor* correspondent, William Henry Chamberlain to Ishimoto 8/16/37, Reel 19, Sanger LofC.

8. 8/6/37, Reel 19, Sanger, LofC.

9. See "Diary of Japan Trip" in Sanger, Box 29, File #224, Smith

10. From Dorothy Brush's unpub ms. in Smith, and from Brush's journal notes, Box 29, File #218, Smith.

11. Sanger's letter 9/6/37, Reel 19, Sanger, LofC.

12. See Box 235 Japan, Sanger LofC, for a news clipping. *Osaka Mainichi*, 8/21/37, which shows a photo of Sanger, arm in a sling.

13. Dorothy Brush's notes, Box 44, File #363, Smith.

14. Box 29, File #224, and Box 29, File #218, Smith.

15. 9/9/37 Report to associates, Reel 19, Sanger, LofC, and Press Release, 9/23/37, Reel 56, Sanger, LofC.

16. Box 29, File #218, Smith.

17. Dorothy Brush describes this and the following events in her journal notes and versions of her unpub. ms., Box 29, File #218, Smith.

18. See Sheldon Garon, "The World's Oldest Debate? Prostitution and the State in Imperial Japan, 1900-1945," *American Historical Review*, 98:3, 1993, pp. 710-732, for historical context.

19. Sanger's Newsletter of 9/6/37, Reel 19, Sanger, LofC.

20. News Release, Reel 56, Sanger, LofC.

21. Box 29, #224, Smith. Contribution should be considered in light of Clinic's yearly expenses: rent, salaries of one secretary and one M.D., office expenses, publicity expenses, car fare, postage, miscellaneous, and reserve fund, 1,560 yen or $516 were estimated. "Monthly Budget," Reel 19, Sanger, LofC.

22. Transcripts of speeches in Box 29, #218, Smith; private letters of Sept.; Sanger's news releases and general letters and notes on event, Reels 56 and 19, Sanger, LofC. Shidzue does not mention Sanger's 1937 visit in any of her autobiographies. See also, Helen M. Hopper, "Shidzue Ishimoto and Margaret Sanger in Japan, August, 1937," *Phoebe: An Interdisciplinary Journal of Feminist Scholarship, Theory & Aesthetics*, 1:1, 1989, pp. 34-50.

23. See Ellen Chesler's less negative interpretation of Sanger and eugenics in Chesler's, *Woman of Valor: Margaret Sanger and the Birth control Movement in America*, Simon & Schuster, 1992.

24. See news from Sanger, Reel 19, Sanger, LofC.

25. Smith.

6

Political Suppression (1937–1938)

At six o'clock on the morning of December 15, 1937 Ishimoto Shidzue was awakened from a sound sleep by the excited voice of her maid, Sendai, who was yelling to someone outside. *"Dame desu, dame desu, Okusama* will not let you come in! You can't do this without my mistress' permission." Shidzue, who could not quite hear what the intruder was saying, got up, quickly wrapped something around her, and went to the front door. There she saw, just inside her door, a large man with two others behind him. Sendai turned to her and said, "Okusama, the police have forced their way in." Shidzue recalled that moment. "In the twinkling of an eye my sleepy head had cleared and my heart called out, 'they've come.'" In those few seconds she vacillated between thinking she should fight this intrusion and rejoicing that what she feared for so long had finally come to pass.

One of the men handed her a paper and another told her to hurry up and get dressed. She was under arrest. On her way to her room to dress she stopped to reassure her frightened elder son. She told Arata, not to worry, for she had done nothing illegal. Very worried indeed, her son lay down again to try to think this through. Meanwhile, Shidzue, who had heard many stories from Communist Party members about the stark, unheated jails, dressed in kimono, a wool sweater, and camel hair coat in preparation for the discomfort of a cell. She also packed as much warm, padded silk clothing, from long underwear to haori, that a small suitcase would hold. Then she combed her hair, washed, and put on her make-up in preparation for her ordeal to come. This took the twenty minutes she had requested from the police.

Thus, Shidzue prepared for what was to become a two week stay at her local police station. She was one of 2 women and 471 men rounded up that day in simultaneous raids throughout Japan. All were members of groups considered to be left-wing, and all were suspected of having communist sympathies, participating in anti-nationalist activities, and/or supporting a "popular front" movement. In short, the arrested harbored "dangerous thoughts." December 15, 1937 became a turning point in Shidzue's life as well as in the lives of all of the others who had in some way supported the legal left in Japan. The round-up became known as the "Popular Front Incident."[1]

From the moment of Shidzue's arrest the "special higher police"[2] showed interest in the books, and papers which she kept in her home. Later they would search her clinic office as well and listen carefully to her answers during interrogation sessions always seeking incriminating information about Kanjû and any possible connection with the "popular front" movement. Her association with this important left-wing leader and with his political party and labor activities was well documented. Shidzue had appeared on the political rostrum with Kanjû after his election to the Diet in 1937. Not only had she supported the socialists, but she had used their platform to deliver her own message about women's rights and family planning. Although these were not illegal activities, they made her an obvious target for police investigation as the government sought to destroy the political left.

Had the Home Ministry known just how intimately Shidzue was connected with Katô Kanjû, her interrogators might have been even more vigilant in their questioning. In fact, she was treated somewhat gingerly because of her relationship to others who were politically acceptable. After all, she was still the wife of Baron Ishimoto Keikichi, loyal supporter of government policy. One of her brothers, Hirota Yôji, was a member of the diplomatic corps. She was also the niece of Tsurumi Yûsuke, Popular Government Party [Minseitô] member of the House of Representatives. In the end it was undoubtedly Shidzue's relationship to the Ishimoto, Hirota, and Tsurumi clans, and her husband's tie to the Imperial Family, which outweighed her connection to Kanjû and protected her from harsh punishment.

Government Crackdown

By the end of the summer everyone associated with Katô Kanjû's Japan Proletarian Party feared a government crack-down on all left-wing socialists. Even while Shidzue had experienced elation over the opening of her clinic and the visit of her American friends, she, too, was aware that she was engaging in borderline activities that could invite government suppression momentarily. Intensified military build-up was accompanied by prohibition of anti-government speech. When Shidzue was escorting her American friends about, in late August, they observed a large military presence at all Tokyo train stations. Dorothy Brush described the scene. "We never boarded a train which did not take on a quota of soldiers or officers from every flag-bedecked village or town. As we drew in, all the inhabitants were down at the station to see them off. They were always in rigid formation; first a group in uniform; then a group of men in plain clothes; then the women; then the school children. All had flags, all shouted 'banzai'. But the waving and the shouting was as mechanical and as orderly as the toe-dancing of the Rockettes in Radio City. If there were tears on the faces of some of the women, they gave no other sign. If one or two soldiers, some so very young, blinked their eyes rapidly, there were no embraces. The trains drew in. The trains drew out. Over and over again it was the same." The Americans also commented that while they were free to speak about birth control talk of the "China Incident" was banned.

The war news worsened in September, as the government became even less tolerant of "dangerous thoughts." In spite of this Shidzue did not slow her efforts to provide birth control literature and contraceptives. She ran her clinic, requested and received various supplies from America, and spoke with doctors about experiments with new forms of contraceptives. She found the process of simply getting and distributing her supplies more complicated and expensive, and yet she managed to figure out ways to successfully ignore tightened rules, avoid payment or, if necessary, pay for added import taxes, and find substitute materials for those in scarce supply due to increased military requirements. She wrote to Florence Rose on December 2nd thanking her for some supplies, asking for others and generally carrying on her business. At that time she acknowledged the stress of the times but gave no indication that national or international events would affect her work. "Everything is depressing here as you suppose. We need courage to face this tragedy in the Orient. However, the money order for three yen is in my hand..." With this cheering gift Shidzue intended to provide a grand sukiyaki dinner for all her co-workers "to forget about our struggles" for a brief time.

Katô Kanjû, on the other hand, was essentially silenced by summer's end. On September 9th, the 72nd Diet was called into special session to legislate additional money for financing the war in China. The government continued to proclaim the myth that fighting constituted a quick clean-up effort and that the "Incident" would be solved with just a few more troops and the 2.2 billion yen appropriation which it was requesting. Political cooperation was expected and Prime Minister Konoe was pleased with the unanimous patriotic response. The special appropriations of the 71st (July) and 72nd (September) Diet sessions combined to almost double the budget for 1937-38. Nationalism and xenophobia seemed to catch hold of everyone in power; there was no room for public opposition to these wartime demands.

On October 9th Katô and four others met privately to discuss options for the Proletarian Party given the jingoistic climate of the day. Clearly any plan for a "popular front movement" was out of the question. Rather, the current concern was whether to cooperate fully with the government and publicly support the war effort in hopes of personal and party survival, or to continue to remain silent on the issue of China. Speaking against government policy was not an option. The consensus was that the proletarian movement could expect "bad results" in any case. It was finally decided that, while hoping for a quick settlement of the war, the Proletarian Party would not make a clear statement in support of government actions. Their internal statement concluded, however, that they might "slowly move in the direction of support."[3] In other words Katô and his associates capitulated to reality, but in an indecisive manner. As it turned out this response provided neither insurance against government suppression nor the satisfaction of a righteous act.

During the same October meeting Katô and all the other leaders firmly rejected party dissolution.[4] It was a futile and personally suicidal decision, but it underscored the last remnants of a moral commitment to socialist principles. Katô's labor union, Zempyô, was also silenced as a voice of opposition. The patriotic cries in favor of the government policies within the leadership of the individual unions which made up Zempyô's council as well as their rank and file showed signs of breaking with Katô. By the end of November several member unions had bolted and joined with their nationalistic union brothers.

By November 1st, if not before, public statements against government policy in China constituted "dangerous thoughts" and were punishable under the Peace Preservation Law. No one dared speak out. Furthermore, the legislation passed in the two special Diet sessions, and supported by all parties, left and right, had empowered the government to requisition all or parts of factories for war use, to order the distribution or supply of raw materials, and to make any other centralized decision deemed necessary by the government to carry out its national and international missions. A contemporary American political writer commented that Prime Minister Konoe's allies were the army's "young officers" and the socialists of the Social Masses' Party. He described these men as akin to the German National-Socialists, and their party as looking for a "totalitarian state with socialist slogans."[5] Katô's dream of a "popular front" was dead. By November 30th even his party, the furthest left on the socialist spectrum, had completely capitulated. A secret Home Ministry document of that date claimed that the China question was no longer an issue in either local or national branches of the Proletarian Party.[6]

As the only Proletarian Party member of the Diet and the chairman of the party, Katô Kanjû left on December 2nd for the obligatory trip to the troops as a "comfort officer."[7] The government expected someone in each political party and all other national organizations to perform this duty. Had Katô's Proletarian Party not sent someone to "console the troops" at the front, their patriotism would have been questioned and their already tenuous existence further jeopardized.

While to some Katô's willingness to support the war effort in this manner mocked any claim that he opposed the "China Incident," others interpret this trip as a cover. For example, one Japanese scholar claims, "Because Katô was known by the military police and the thought control police [special higher police], it was necessary for him to adopt a clever disguise. As a result, he inspected the troops in Central China in the role of an official Imperial Army Comfort Officer. He embarked on December 2nd, and, after arriving in China, inspected the troops up to the front line where they were readying to take Nanjing, but when he returned to Nagasaki on the 15th his disguise proved ineffective."[8] In other words this patriotic trip was simply a ruse designed to prolong the life of the proletarian movement. The trip might also be seen as a natural extension of the Proletarian Party policy established in late July, which called for "relief to families with soldiers at the front."[9] In support of this interpretation another historian comments that while on his official "Imperial Army Condolence Call" Katô exchanged conversations critical of the war with the wounded in field hospitals, and that he undertook to become a liaison between the soldiers and their hometowns.[10] Katô's required "comfort" trip, then, was a necessary wartime survival tactic to throw government watchdogs off the track. While continuation of a "popular front" movement and open criticism of the war effort were out of the question, if the party could simply remain free, there would be one group which secretly opposed the militarists. This would be more important morally than assuming a suicidal position. The ploy was ineffective and the party was destroyed upon Katô's return two weeks later.

On December 13th the Japanese forces capped two months of bloody fighting and bombing of soldiers and civilians with a victorious entry into the Chinese Nationalist government's capital city, Nanjing. On that day it seemed as if the Japanese army had finally achieved a victory which would force negotiations to end the war. Unfortunately the Konoe government discovered that it was no closer to an end to hostilities than just after the Marco Polo Incident in July. On December 14th a new Home Minister, Admiral Suetsugu Nobumasa, was appointed. Previously at work behind the scenes this new chief of the special higher police joined those on the right who had been agitating for eradication of "the root of evil - opposition within the country" and the unification of political parties on the "principle of emperor-centered politics."[11] Such an elimination of the last vestiges of a political left would mean that the regular session of the 73rd Diet, to begin on December 25th, would easily find consensus. In fact the called-for single party unanimity was still two years away, but elimination of the left-wing was only one day off.

On December 15th at the crack of dawn 473 people were rounded up and taken to local police stations for questioning. All received the fateful knock on the door at six a.m. as local police and "special higher police" from Admiral Suetsugu's Home Ministry converged simultaneously on residences and public inns in eighteen counties and Tokyo. At five p.m. Katô Kanjû, was arrested just as his ship docked at Nagasaki. The "clever disguise" as "comfort officer" was not clever enough. Once in custody Katô was immediately sent to Roppongi police station in Tokyo. The efficient execution of the operation meant the raids had been planned some time previously and the careful timing probably related to both the change in the leadership at the Home Ministry and Katô's return.

The public learned of these arrests after the police lifted a press ban on December 22nd. At that time articles featured Katô Kanjû, Suzuki Mosaburô and Inomata Tsunao all of the Proletarian Party, and Yamakawa Hitoshi of the Labor-Farmer Group as the most prominent leaders in custody. Front page coverage was also accorded the only two women arrested, Ishimoto Shidzue, identified as a propagandist for Margaret Sanger's birth control movement, and Hirabayashi Taiko[12] a well-known proletarian writer. The front page of *Asahi Newspaper* referred to the two women as "roses in the midst of thorns." Another newspaper called them "two red flowers of the Popular Front."[13] Baroness Ishimoto was featured in articles in the *New York Times* , the *New York Herald Tribune* and the *Christian Science Monitor* as well.

On the same day that the public announcement of the raids took place, Katô Kanjû had been required to sign the order for dissolution of his Proletarian Party and of his union, Zempyô. The government proclaimed the leaders, and their members of these organizations had defied the first article of the Peace Preservation Law, and thus accused them of advocating the alteration of the national polity, the *kokutai*, denying the system of private property, associating for the purpose of realizing a communist society based on the dictatorship of the proletariat, and building a united anti-fascist popular front.[14] The photo of Katô on the front page of the *Asahi Newspaper* on December 22nd showed him complying with the demand to sign the papers of dissolution and thus publicly admitting to harboring such "dangerous thoughts." This event was inextricably tied to an anti-communist sentiment which formed one element of the government's foreign and domestic policies. Those arrested were believed to be following the directions of the Soviet sponsored Seventh Comintern held in the summer of 1935 and following instructions from the Communist Party, USA. Official announcements accused those arrested of working for revolution and spreading anti-war propaganda.[15]

Many of those arrested, like Ishimoto Shidzue, were held for a brief time and then released with warnings not to participate in political activities, publish or speak publicly. Others were detained in local jails for lengthy periods of time, tried and released or sentenced to imprisonment. For those detained and/or sentenced average imprisonment was two to three years. Katô Kanjû was sentenced to three years and actually served two full years, after which he remained under surveillance until the end of the war. The longest sentences, five years each, were handed out to Suzuki Mosaburô, secretary of the Proletarian Party and member of the Tokyo Municipal Assembly, and Yamakawa Hitoshi, leader of the Farmer-Labor Group. Suzuki actually spent one year and nine months in detention at Suginami Police Station, was finally officially sentenced, and served an additional eleven months in jail.[16] Hirabayashi Taiko, received a sentence of several years. She was released after serving eight months because she had contracted tuberculosis which was aggravated by the damp, unheated prison cell.

The two month period in which Shidzue experienced arrest, two weeks of prison interrogation by both the local police and the "special higher police," and the mandated closing of her clinic represented a sad turning point in her life. They proved all the more depressing because of the imprisonment of her beloved Kanjû and the continued oppression of other activist associates. It is not surprising then that these events formed a primary focus of her letters to American friends beginning in January, 1938, her contemporary diary dedicated to her beloved Kanjû, and her post-war autobiographical writings.

Each contemporary document about Shidzue and her relationship with Kanjû and her later remembrances adds to our understanding of the political significance of the "Popular Front Incident" of December 15, 1937 for her, for Kanjû, and for others on the left. The detail which emerges in these private sources includes the physical circumstances of her police detention, her political and social priorities, her relationship with her family circle, her emotional dependence on Kanjû, and her will to thwart the authorities. In a larger sense the writings add a new dimension to public sources which focus on official Japan and on the male leaders in positions of political prominence. The case of Ishimoto Shidzue reveals a gap in the government's determination to close down all opposition to their policies, for this woman managed to continue privately her political and social activities in opposition to official demands. As a woman functioning in a private role, she found ways to circumvent the prohibitions of official Japan. She was confined and publicly silenced, but her freedom of thought and action continued on the margins of the society.

Jail and Interrogation

Shidzue's official ordeal began with her arrest at 6 a.m. on December 15th, and ended late at night on December 29th. Shidzue has recollected this in each of her post-war autobiographies, but the description which is closest in time to the actual event is recounted by her elder son, Arata, in a letter of January 2nd to Margaret Sanger, a letter written by one breathless with excitement over the recent "sensational occurrence." Arata wrote that he had been sleeping deeply that night after staying up late studying for his term examinations. At about 6:15 in the morning "suddenly the door was opened, someone dashed into my room." Thinking at first it must be the maid, he was surprised to see that it was his mother. She told him that the police were downstairs and that they were going to take her to the police station, but he shouldn't worry. After she rushed out again, he locked his door, lay back down on his bed and tried to think. "Oh! What an event! My mother arrested!" His mother had warned him of such a possibility, but the reality of it was shattering. While Arata struggled over just what he should do, the maid came to the door and asked just that question, "What will you do? Will you go downstairs? A party of policemen is searching all over the first floor, so I think you had better stay upstairs." Arata refused her offer to bring him breakfast, dressed in his school uniform and went downstairs.

There he found a policeman taking books out of his mother's bookcase in the dining room. Another was examining books and papers in her study. This intruder then entered his mother's bedroom, which was separated from the study by undrawn, thick green curtains. In the small adjoining dressing room he saw his mother, still in her kimono, eating breakfast. Standing beside her was a police detective, obviously the one in charge of the search. Arata "trembled from head to toe. What a humiliation! What a disgrace! There penetrated to the very bedroom of my dear mother, a stranger, a police detective who is by far under my mother at the point of culture or personality. An almost rank and file policeman, who <u>cannot read even English</u>. Looking at this sight

I cried to myself, 'Go to Damn!' 'Don't you realize what a shameful role you are playing, a role of suppresser of liberty and welfare of a fighter of humanism!' I could only prevent myself with difficulty from the impulse to strike him down and shatter him to pieces." Arata only said these things to himself. In fact he behaved quietly. His mother introduced him to the policeman who politely assured him, "There is no need to worry. Mr. Katô and Mr. Kuroda[17] were arrested upon charges of their alleged violence [sic.] of the peace preservation law. We should like to take your mother as a mere participant of this case." This could not be exactly what happened as Katô Kanjû was not arrested until later that evening. Just the same it is what Arata remembered on January 2nd.

Shidzue wrote her own memories of that day and the two weeks which followed as the first entry in her diary for Katô Kanjû. She began to write on January 3rd and, in a prologue, reflected about the fact that just one month had passed since her beloved Kanjû had left for his trip "to comfort" the soldiers in China. He had been at her house the night before his departure, and they talked about the brief two week separation to come. Counting each day before Katô would return, Shidzue awaited their reunion, which was not to be. Instead she had only her diary to console her. She filled its pages with descriptions of her ordeal interspersed with testimonials to her beloved of the strength his teachings provided during this period of great stress and loneliness. "You have said that a prime merit of mine is that I have hope," she wrote as she described her packing to leave for jail. This optimistic characterization carried her through the next two weeks, and then the next two lonely years.

After the police searched her house, they drove her to her local police station, at Ooi in Shinagawa. This was a great relief for, more than anything, she had feared she would be taken to one of the notorious larger jails or to the headquarters of the "special higher police." She believed this to be a political gesture which recognized the peripheral nature of her association with the proletarian movement. In fact there was no consistent pattern in the institutional choices the police made for rounded-up political prisoners. Even some of the leaders ended up at local stations.

The Ooi police station was a dreary place with bare floors, no heat, and cramped rooms. She was not taken immediately to a cell, but was ushered into an office in which three members of the "special higher police" were eating lunch. For more than three hours during this first afternoon's interrogation, Shidzue suffered "equal parts of pain and insult"; not physical pain, but the pain of humiliation and distress. The three seated "thought police" were eating bowls of rice topped with eel. As soon as she entered they stared up at her and began to "scrutinize their catch." The interrogation had started. They pulled out journals, and, from these, they displayed such articles as Katô's "America's Turning Point" and Inomata's "Answers to the Farm Question." Next they piled up literary works, labor newspapers, and magazines, and Katô's election addresses. Finally they produced some of Shidzue's own English writings and asked that she explain them.

The interrogation was interrupted by a phone call, and Shidzue heard one of the three say, "Ha - We don't have any proof yet, but we are investigating these communications one by one. Yes, yes - until 4 pm." This was the only hint she had about what was going on. "Then," she wrote in her diary, "they pulled out a letter from 'you' [Katô Kanjû] to Keikichi [Ishimoto] written at the time of the copper mine strike" [1923] and another dated about 1920-21 signed by Katô and an associate.[18] These letters did not seem to have any relationship with the formal articles. Shidzue could not figure out her inquisitors' motivation. Were they trying to establish a seventeen year "connection of friendship" between her and Kanjû? Much of what they said to her consisted of insults: such comments as; "These are either stupid or clever," in reference to the old letters; "I would rather a woman have seven pregnancies," in reference to her propagation of birth control education; and "Even if your husband were to return to Tokyo he would have to sleep in the Station Hotel because he couldn't get into your house," an apparent indication that Ishimoto Keikichi was no longer welcome in his wife's home. Shidzue was pained by their arrogant manner but did not reply.[19]

After several hours of interrogation she was taken to the cell area. Since this was a neighborhood jail it had few cells. A variety of criminals, some held for theft, some for fraud, and so forth, were all thrown in together. The first cell held about thirty men. They all stared at her. This, thankfully, was not where they would put her. She was to stay in a small three mat room (6' X 9') with barred windows, which was set aside for women prisoners. It was already occupied by another woman, whom, she later learned, was about twenty-eight and had been arrested for prostitution or some other sex related offense. She was a quiet sort of woman, and sat in a corner making herself very tiny. Only at mealtimes would she look somewhat lively as she ate the scanty, bland food as if it were tasty. Shidzue thought that she must live a most miserable life to react in this way.[20] At night these two women were joined by the jail's maid. Shidzue mused over the fact that even though the maid had committed no crime, she, too, was incarcerated.[21]

Shidzue was devastated by her circumstances, but, once again, she called upon Kanjû, her inner strength, to help her to endure the ordeal "as a soldier of humanity" so that "together with you [Kanjû] I will understand both suffering and joy."[22] Her first meal was brought to her in a dirty wooden bowl. Even though it smelled awful, and was served with just a cup of hot water as accompaniment, she ate it, for she realized that it was important for a fighter to fill her stomach. Her companion doubled over after eating the food, saying her belly ached and that she was cold. She then asked Shidzue if she played *mah jongg* and when she was told no, suggested that her cell mate was probably above such entertainment. The woman was shivering and blue in the face and Shidzue, feeling great pity for her, suggested that she get some sleep so that she would feel warmer. All night long Shidzue thought about Kanjû and wondered what he was experiencing.[23]

Shidzue was not permitted to have any books nor allowed to write. During her second day in prison she did nothing but think and fight determinedly against her urge to cry. On December 17th she was comforted by another prisoner, a political acquaintance, who was in the men's cell. This was Mr. Kuramochi, a young man of about thirty who was a member of the Tokyo Transport Worker's Union [Tokyo-shi kôtsû rôdô kumiai], one of the three largest unions affiliated with Katô's labor council, Zempyô. She hadn't recognized him when he had called out to her from the men's cell on that first day. Two days later, she suddenly remembered having met him. He was a thin, unhealthy looking man, appearing much older than he was, with a prominent gold tooth, thinning hair and a bald spot. He looked quite pathetic in his checkered plaid outfit with the gold buttoned coat of a streetcar conductor. "But because he was one of 'your' followers, a comrade, I had feelings of good will toward him," Shidzue wrote in her diary entry to Kanjû. He was loyally solicitous in his concern for Shidzue, and she could often see him through her barred windows. On the seventeenth he surreptitiously handed her a note which told her to "persevere" *[gambare]*, and that she should not worry about this "incident" for "there was no evidence." She should maintain her peace of mind. The two then talked about Kuramochi's own trials with his very ill four year old child, and thus began a friendship born in mutual distress.[24] Over the course of the next two weeks she was, also, cheered by visits from other followers of Katô, who had not been jailed.

Ishimoto Shidzue was formally interrogated on December 18th by three members of the "thought police" from headquarters. She was brought to a special room upstairs, where she was ordered first to stand and then sit. Her interrogators sat in front of her at a large table. Recognizing the significance of this meeting, she had dressed herself in *kimono* and *haori* and had taken great pains to comb her hair properly, a difficult task, for her jailers had taken away all of her hairpins on the first day.

"Do you know why you've been brought here and did you consent?" one began. The prisoner answered that she had been shown a summons which said it was because both Katô and Kuroda were under suspicion of violation of the Peace Preservation Law. Inspector Anzai Suekichi, First Service Division, Metropolitan Police Headquarters, Special Higher Police, then lectured her for about twenty minutes. The other two spoke on occasion, as well. The substance of the diatribe was to describe Katô's "popular front" movement and its efforts to undermine the foundations of government authority. The police linked her to this group through her proven association with Katô and scolded her, "a woman of high social standing," for joining such people. It was even more shameful, they said, that she had criticized her own government in a foreign country (the United States). She replied that a people to people exchange, such as her lecture tours represented, signified strength for all humanity. She thought to herself, "Your [Kanjû's] words streamed through my breast." Her victory would be like that of a sumo wrestler who, though lighter in weight, would use spiritual strength to overcome the heavier opponent.[25]

Her interrogations, though frequent, were not continuous. The content ran the gamut of topics from politics; the "popular front" movement, the Proletarian Party, Katô Kanju; to her own social activism; the birth control movement, women's liberation. Shidzue was obviously more in control when the discussion centered on her own activities. Her interrogators asked her if she advocated birth control for anti-militarist reasons. She explained that "it was for the sake of poor Japanese mothers who could not afford to have more children."[26] They criticized her work in this movement saying it was contrary to national requirements during the present emergency. She argued for birth control education in order to protect mothers and to reduce the high rate of infant mortality. These points seemed to receive some sympathy, but beyond health issues the inquisitors were concerned about the danger of her movement to the national polity [kokutai].[27] By associating her movement with the words "dangerous to the *kokutai*," the police appeared to be laying the groundwork for her imprisonment under the Peace Preservation Law. She reminded them, "Aren't thoughts about women's liberation and birth control legal? Please instruct me in the ways in which these can be considered crimes....If I have made a mistake I will admit it. Just tell me my mistake, what I have done wrong."[28]

The police questioned her many times about the government's China policy and her attitudes toward government military actions and the effect these might have on the home front. They asked her what would happen when the soldiers who were fighting in China returned to their homes. She responded that "the war is costing a lot of money and the people will be very poor."[29] She concluded that the economic consequences of the war would be devastating for all citizens regardless of the morality of the China Incident. This line of questioning was directed at two "dangerous" issues. First, Shidzue seemed to link large numbers of children with the problems of poverty and suggested that birth control, a practice currently opposed by the government, was the solution. Secondly, the focus on the impoverishment of the working class grew out of the Proletarian Party's July public policy statement, which emphasized the party's concern about the welfare of military families and the party's intention to assist soldiers returning home. The authorities were leading Shidzue toward admissions which would firmly tie the proletarian movement to an anti-war position. The platform of economic concern for soldiers and their families was deliberately posited so that the party would not appear to be anti-government and thus violate the Peace Preservation Law. In fact this policy was seen by the authorities as a shibboleth for opposition to the war, and, therefore, an attempt to "alter the national polity [kokutai]." She was asked repeatedly about any relationship between Katô or his associates and communism. As she wrote Sanger a few weeks later, "The whole plot" [the popular front incident] was conjured up by the thought control police. "According to them, liberal and trade union workers who have been organized into the 'Nippon Proletariat Party' were trying to violate peace in this country under Marxian doctrine, so they had to crush this movement at its roots."[30]

The regimentation of jail life impressed Shidzue. She was told when to eat, when to go to bed, when to get up. She was ordered to and from interrogation sessions at which she was told when and where to stand or sit. Her meals were served three times a day at exact hours in a corner of the women's cell. For the most part they consisted of foreign [bad] rice, two *takuwan* (radish pickles), and scraps of boiled vegetables for lunch, the same for dinner plus *misô* soup and, on occasion, a small chop. She could not have books or writing materials and was prohibited from talking with her prison mate or the maid. When she was not eating, sleeping, or being interrogated, she had little to do but think.

Once, the routine was broken by a visit from two doctors. They arrived on December 24th to make routine examinations of all the prisoners. Prison officials were concerned about "cement illnesses," such as kidney problems, scabby skin, and other skin diseases. After looking at the men in the neighboring cell, they came to her, "without even washing their hands," and expected her to disrobe and let them examine her body while the crowd of men looked on. To even suggest such a thing in that cold, damp, unclean and public atmosphere was "contemptuous," she exclaimed to her diary, and so she "adamantly refused" to comply. In the end the "soft-spoken" one merely looked at her face while not touching her body at all, and said, "That's fine."[31]

She was permitted to have visitors with the police present. After her third day in jail, members of her family came regularly. One of Shidzue's most welcome early visitors was her uncle, Tsurumi Yûsuke. When Shidzue was first arrested, she had telephoned another uncle, Tsurumi Sadao, who lived next door. He was not home, but his wife came over immediately after phoning her brother-in-law, Yûsuke, who took charge. He immediately contacted government officials to try to determine the reason for his niece's arrest. Since Tsurumi was a respected member of the centrist Popular Government Party, he was given immediate answers to his questions. To nobody's particular surprise, he was informed that her association with the "popular front" had made her suspect. In the days to come her close relationship with someone trusted by the government undoubtedly helped to balance Shidzue's associations with politicians on the left. On the other hand, it must have been inconvenient, at the least, for Tsurumi to have a relative in a round-up of political suspects at the very moment he and his daughter, Kazuko, were about to leave on a friendship tour of the United States.

On December 29th late at night Shidzue was released and returned home. She was tired and chilled but had remained healthy, catching only one cold throughout her ordeal. Arata commented that his mother could smile and seemed cheerful. Shidzue believed that the timing of her release was related to her New Year's obligations. As the wife of the Baron Ishimoto Keikichi, she was expected to pay her respects to the Emperor and Empress at the Imperial Palace on New Year's Day. In fact she did not attend the festivities.[32] Shidzue's American friends thought that it was their intervention which secured her release. When the first news of her arrest reached American newspapers on December 23rd some of her friends began an extensive private and then public, letter writing campaign on her behalf.[33] As one friend wrote Sanger upon hearing of Shidzue's release, "I have no doubt that the telegrams and letters of protest sent to the Japanese Ambassador in Washington by her American friends had much to do with obtaining the release. Perhaps they may have been surprised to find how many friends and admirers she has in this country."[34] Though Shidzue did not believe the letter writing campaign nor favorable newspaper articles had any effect, she was gratified by the concern and affection it represented. She also remarked that the commentary on her case was good publicity for the birth control movement.

Much of the information which her American friends received came from an interview she gave to her good friend, *New York Times* journalist, Hugh Byas.[35] Shidzue was amused that he actually detailed her prison fare, "rice, pickles and bean soup for breakfast, rice pickles and vegetables for midday dinner, and rice, pickles and vegetables for supper - these were the short and simple menus..." The article went on to quote Shidzue on her experience and on her interpretation of the reasons for her arrest. "I came out tired cold and hungry, but the experience was very interesting. I had a small room six by nine. It was unheated, but I had put on plenty of clothes. Writing and reading were forbidden. Luckily I do not smoke and do not mind healthful food such as our farmers eat the year round, but when you have said it's healthful you have said it all." Her tone was jovial and hearty. Neither this article nor any of the many others which came out in the American press revealed the loneliness, stress, or fear which gripped Shidzue during the two weeks. Her reference to Katô suggested that he was merely representative of the many "intelligent working people interested in social progress," who ."..would be correctly described as liberals of the Left wing, perhaps, but certainly neither as Communists nor as revolutionaries." Katô's importance to her survival remained concealed. Shidzue sounded brave, almost flippant, in these reports. This contrasts dramatically with her diary entries which reveal worry, personal distress, fear, and family pressures.

Her ordeal over, she wrote Sanger a more personal account of the arrest in early January. For the first time, she hinted at a longer, though professional, relationship with the leader of the proletarian movement. "Mr. Katô has been one of my close friends and co-workers since I became interested in birth control work." She continued that she had "joined his election campaign to use his platform for birth control propaganda" in order to reach the masses. She then lauded his character emphasizing that he was one recognized leader who had "never surrendered to the military or fascistic forces" and that he holds a "deep-rooted confidence among the intelligentsia" and, yet, is "also popular among the labor class." She felt that by associating with him and with his party the birth control movement would not be used for wrong purposes but would provide information to the class that really needed it. She claimed that government officials had sought her out as a "witness in the case" who might help to link Katô to communism, but "the anticipation of the police was betrayed," for their search uncovered "nothing to back up this allegation of unlawful relation with communists."[36] It is no wonder that Shidzue's American friends remained in the dark about the intimate nature of her relationship with Katô, or that they formed such a benign picture of her confrontation with the police. While her courage and determination came through in her letters to America, her loneliness and pain, and her fear of the loss of her independence did not.

The Pressures Continue

On December 17th, while the Baroness was being interrogated at the local police station, five police detectives conducted a thorough search of her clinic. The young doctor who was present told Shidzue that the raiders had taken away patient records, receipts, cash books, hundreds of letters from women, and her mail register book which listed mailings of contraceptives, in sum, all of the records essential to the work of the clinic. Consequently, a few days after her release, Shidzue closed her clinic for what she hoped would be a brief reorganization period. Under the conditions of her release, she was prohibited from all public speaking, attendance at public gatherings, and all publication. The January issue of *The Scientist's Pen* contained her article, "A Profile of Margaret Sanger" as well as articles by others who had been arrested. The whole issue was banned. One of the "special higher police" told Shidzue that her article was a bad influence and that he could see "'a distinctive tendency of marxist ideology'" in its content. Stunned and angered, she wrote Sanger, "Can you imagine how one can write a short article about Margaret Sanger and her work [in] relation [to] Marxism? No argument, no public opinion, but 'thought control' in the country under fascistic regime." In spite of the official prohibitions, on January 20th, feeling the importance of family planning education so urgently, Shidzue spoke publicly at Union Church in Tokyo. Her audience was a women's organization and her speech, given in English, was on the subject, "The Birth Control Movement in Japan." She received 15 yen.[37] Shidzue was reluctant to give up her activities, regardless of police warnings, for she needed the intellectual and emotional focus and the money.

In spite of the brave front which she put on in her letters to her friends, and the strength which radiates in the pages of her postwar autobiographies, the winter of 1938 was a time of great sadness and worry for Shidzue. She had lost her primary emotional support, Kanjû, and was being pressured to make unwanted choices by her older brother and her mother, and by the husband she thought she was rid of. Her elder son, Arata, stood resolutely by her, but he did not have the control over her livelihood that the others did. Ishimoto Keikichi, who was very much in evidence after the arrest and jailing, wrote a letter which Shidzue received January 7th reminding her that she was still his wife. She had long before ceased to think of him as her husband and was dumbfounded by this declaration. During January he came to Tokyo several times to discuss her future with her, her elder brother, her mother and Arata. Although Keikichi stayed at a hotel on each of these occasions, he spoke with her at her home, in the hotel, and over meals in restaurants. They primarily discussed Shidzue's impoverished economic circumstances and her financial liabilities. Keikichi also lectured her on her responsibilities to his family and the danger she had brought to the Ishimotos by her choice of companions and her social activism. Shidzue presented her world view, her attitudes toward the social issues of the day, and her great need for independence. She also made clear that she had no intention of returning to him or to his family, nor would she give up her allegiance to Kanjû and his cause. She commented to her diary [to Kanjû] after one such meeting that "it was not possible for me to be charmed by my separated husband for one minute," and that she was absolutely determined to lead her own life.[38]

During January, arrangements were worked out to insure Shidzue's livelihood and the education of her sons. In all of this Shidzue's mother sided entirely with Keikichi and expressed continual dismay that her daughter would not embrace her responsibilities as a member of the Ishimoto family. Far from comforting Shidzue over her stressful experiences, her mother, "who was from a different era" which interpreted the role of wives in a subservient fashion, "could offer only criticism."[39] Her elder brother was sympathetic, but he was also realistic, and saw that it would be impossible for Shidzue to live independently. She reluctantly agreed to move in with her mother temporarily, an arrangement which did not last long. She calculated her living expenses at about 325 yen a month including her sons' tuition of 85 yen. Keikichi agreed to send her 100 yen a month and her family pledged the rest.

Keikichi further informed Shidzue that she must carefully refrain from further "dangerous" activities. He had secured an interview with the undersecretary of the Imperial Household Agency and been told that this agency had not received a report from the Metropolitan Police Department, and consequently they would not have to issue Shidzue a "reprimand." Any future problems, however, would surely cause a reconsideration of this position and would result in serious repercussions, including the revocation of Keikichi's peerage. Shidzue's family was shocked and worried as they listened mutely to Keikichi's words. It was clear to everyone that the Imperial Household Agency was aware of the police reports and that they simply had chosen to ignore Shidzue's involvement at that time.[40]

Shidzue was dejected and filled with melancholy. She was trapped physically and emotionally and "yearned for" Kanjû, as she cried herself to sleep. Even the realization that Kanjû would "scold" her and demand that she pull herself together did not blot out her depression. Attempting, however, to respond to his phantom scolding, she determined to survive her residence under her mother's roof by leaving the house early each day and not returning until late. She simply could not "understand her mother's heart." This unsympathetic member of her own Hirota household seemed indistinguishable from the opposition, the Ishimotos. These were the sorts of things she "told" her diary, the worries she cried over, and the feelings she put on paper for Kanjû. The contrast with her brave letters to America and her brief, matter-of-fact, statements in her post-war autobiographies is striking.

On January 31st Shidzue was summoned to the Metropolitan Police Board in Tokyo,[41] where she expected to learn when she could reopen her clinic. Such optimism was unfounded. She was told by the police that recent developments had altered the government's analysis of rapid population increase. Whereas this had seemed a serious problem in the past, it was now believed that population growth was necessary for national expansion and development. Her view, therefore, contradicted official policy. In sum, she was not to be permitted to propagate birth control.[42] While the police admitted that her work was still "not unlawful," as someone connected with the December 15th arrests she was prohibited from participating in any public activities of a partisan social or political nature. She must close her clinic. She received a warning from the Imperial Household Agency as well, stating she was to stay out of trouble with the police. Once again her status as a Baron's wife had brought her to the attention of the legal arm of the Imperial advisors. Her lawyer persuaded her that she could not fight the power of Japan's autocratic authorities. Accordingly she closed her clinic on February 8th.[43]

In response to a newspaper article announcing the closing of the clinic a rush of people called or dropped by to ask frantically where they would be able to obtain contraceptives in the future. Shidzue continued to receive a stream of letters from rural women, as well, who had not heard of the closing. She answered these letters and sent what supplies she had available from her own home under her personal name. This was in direct contradiction of the demands and orders of the Metropolitan Police Board, the Imperial Household Agency, and members of her family. Certainly her public activities had to be curtailed, and, perhaps, halted altogether. Just the same as a woman, and therefore a person whose political past could soon be forgotten, she continued to advocate birth control and supply necessary contraceptives and literature, though she did it quietly from the privacy of her home.

Notes

1. Descriptions of Ishimoto's arrest and imprisonment are composites from 1948, 1981, and 1988b; 1/and 2/37 letters from Shidzue and Arata to American friends, Smith, and Sanger, LofC; from contemporary newspapers, and from 1978 interview. When there is substantial disagreement I favor the contemporary diary, 1988b.

2. For information on special higher police: Elise Tipton, *Japanese Police State: Tokkô in Interwar Japan*, U. of Hawaii Press, 1990; and Richard H. Mitchell, *Thought Control in Prewar Japan*, Cornell U. Press, 1976.

3. From files of the Police Board at the Home Ministry as quoted in William D. Wray, "The Japanese Popular Front Movement, July 1936-February 1938," in *Papers on Japan VI*, Harvard University, 1972, pp. 127-128.

4. Suzuki Mosaburô, a major party figure, not present at this meeting, later rejected dissolution.

5. Gunther Stein, "'Totalitarian' Japan," *Foreign Affairs*, January, 1938, p. 305.

6. William D. Wray, "The Japanese Popular Front Movement," p. 128.

7. See William D. Wray, "The Japanese Popular Front Movement," p. 127; Furuta Hikari, Sakuta Keiichi, Ikimatsu Keizô, eds., *Kindai nihon shakai shisôshi* [An Intellectual History of Modern Japanese Socialists], 1971. p.128; George O. Totten III, *The Social Democratic Movement in Prewar Japan*, Yale University Press, 1966, p. 172.

8. Mori Shôzô, *Fusetsu no hi shôwa junnansha retsudan* [A Storm Memorial: Biographies of Martyrs in the Shôwa Period], 1946, p. 111.

9. William D. Wray, "The Japanese Popular Front Movement," p. 127.

10. Kanda Fuhito, *Nihon no tôitsu senzen undô* [Japan's Popular Front Movement], p.111.

11. As quoted in Gordon Mark Berger, *Parties Out of Power in Japan 1931-1941*, Princeton U. Press, 1977, p. 142.

12. Her husband, Kobori Jinji, writer and critic, who was arrested with her was a member of Proletarian Party and strong supporter of Kanjû.

13. *Asahi Shimbun*, 12/22/37; 1981, p.101.

14. Itoya Toshio, *Nihon shakaishûgi undô shisôshi* [An Intellectual History of Japan's Socialist Movement], Vol. III, p. 254; see Richard H. Mitchell, *Thought Control in Prewar Japan*, for Peace Preservation Law.

15. *Asahi Shimbun* 12/21/37.

16. Richard H. Mitchell, *Janus-Faced Justice*, U. of Hawaii Press, 1992, p. 97.

17. Kuroda Hisao, member of the Labor Farmer Group, and Representative from Social Masses' Party. He strongly supported a popular front and was expelled from the party due to his arrest. See George O. Totten, *The Social Democratic Movement in Prewar Japan*, p. 100. Arata's letter in Smith, underlining added by Sanger.

18. Asô Hisashi.

19. 1988b, pp. 10-12.

20. 1981, p. 100.

21. 1948, p. 117-120; 1981, pp. 97-98; 1988b, pp. 15-18.

22. 1988b, p. 15.

23. 1988b, p. 17.

24. 1988b, p. 21; in 1948, p. 122, Shidzue speaks of an "Executive" of the union and of "an exchange" of letters, without going into detail.

25. 1988b, pp. 26-27.

26. *New York Times*, 1/1/38

27. Ishimoto to Sanger, 1/11/38, Smith.

28. 1981, p. 98.

29. *New York Times*, 1/1/38.

30. Ishimoto to Sanger 1/11/38, Smith.

31. 1988b, p. 39-40; See Richard H. Mitchell, *Janus-Faced Justice*, p. 91-92 for comparative comments about the jail conditions, specifically skin disease.

32. Interview, 1978.

33. See Sanger' to Japanese Ambassador Hiroshi Saito, 12/24/37; to Ishimoto, 1/2/38; and enclosed letters; also, see quoted letter from Antoinette Peterson, Sanger, LofC; Shidzue expresses her gratification for the efforts of her friends in 1988b entry of 1/26/38. See also Florence Rose's letters to friends, especially Mary Beard, 12/23/37, and Gladys Smith, 1/4/38, Sanger, LofC.

34. Enclosed with letters from Sanger and friends to Ishimoto 1/2/38, Sanger, LofC.

35. *New York Times*, 1/1/38. 1948, 1988b, entry 1/22/38.

36. Ishimoto to Sanger, 1/11/38, Smith.

37. Ishimoto to Sanger, 1/11/38, Smith; 1988b, p. 69.

38. 1988b, p. 76.

39. 1988b, p. 79.

40. 1988b, p. 80.

41. 1988b, p. 85.

42. *Japan Times*, 2/1/38.

43. Ishimoto to Sanger 2/3/38; Ishimoto to Florence Rose, 2/23/38 Smith and Sanger, LofC.

7

Quiet Disapproval (1938–1939)

From the beginning of 1938 until the end of the war Shidzue lived first for her beloved Kanjû's release from jail and then for the war to end. She called these years her "winter period" and, although in the beginning she continued her political crusades, sometimes openly but primarily covertly, she saw the entire period as one of marking time, sadness, and grief. After the forced closing of her clinic she continued, privately, to help women obtain information and contraceptives. Though she lamented in a letter to America, "Birth control is a forgotten word here," she added that quiet activities were not interfered with.[1] She kept mentally alert and intellectually stimulated by reading, and writing, and by discussion, especially with foreign friends. Her research and translation projects produced: first the sketches of Japanese women for Beard's encyclopedia; then a war novel for publication in America; and finally, drafts of articles for a journalist friend. Until the last allied journalist, diplomat, or missionary was jailed or repatriated in 1942, she sought friendship, uncensored news, and international camaraderie among Japan's foreign community. In quiet moments at home she read a variety of Western and Japanese thinkers, novelists and poets. Personally, she managed with help from her estranged husband and her family to support herself and her college student sons, in spite of the ever increasing hardships brought about by Japan's wartime economy.

Ishimoto, forced to spend only two weeks in jail, suffered for her many friends who were less fortunate. On February 1, 1938, the authorities rounded up thirty-eight new suspects in connection with the "popular front movement." All were intellectuals from such institutions as Tokyo Imperial University and Waseda, and all were charged with harboring "dangerous thoughts" and crimes against the Peace Preservation Law. As Ishimoto wrote to Margaret Sanger two days later, "[the arrested are] well known and distinguished people in our intellectual society....Thus the fascistic storm is sweeping the way, and we are really frightened [about] what will happen next." Ten days later eleven more people were arrested, thus completing the destruction of the legal left-wing, the proletarian movement. In March, 1939, Shidzue learned that yet another friend, her colleague in the birth control movement, Dr. Oota Takeo, had been arrested secretly in the fall of 1938. His crime had been sympathizing with the anti-war movement, as the "popular front" was labeled. A "questionable" political contribution, most probably to Katô's Proletarian Party, had put him at risk. In a letter to America Shidzue summed up the series of "popular front" arrests. "Like Germany, our jails have been crowded with liberals. So many friends of mine are being shut behind bars. Japan is labouring to give birth to a New Japan and under this process so many fine people are forced to sacrifice their lives."[2]

Shidzue felt she was out of step with her country. The underlying cause of this estrangement was the ever intensifying, ever widening war in China. In spite of the hardships of opposition to this war policy, Shidzue and Kanjû never wavered in their rejection of the government's China policy nor, later, the fully involved war in the Pacific. Both had declared from 1931 that Japan's foreign policy was fundamentally imperialistic. During the mid-thirties they had spoken against the war in China sometimes publicly and often privately, depending upon the intensity of the government's control over dissent. After December, 1937, when public commentary opposed to government policy was impossible, Shidzue continued to criticize her government privately. Neither Shidzue nor Kanjû ever recanted their previous statements and beliefs. This set them apart from many other left-wing associates who performed *tenkô,* that is, accepted government policy and expressed publicly a change of political direction, a change of heart.[3] In her communication with foreign friends, which continued uncensored until 1942, Shidzue explicitly criticized her country's belligerent actions characterizing them as fascist. This did not merely constitute "dangerous thoughts," a crime in itself, it was clearly treasonable. She was never, however, arrested again. The Japanese bureaucrats, from the feared "special higher police" to the local censors, were far too busy with more dangerous male opponents to examine the private sphere of a woman's correspondence or to reconnoiter her social movements within the international community.

Shidzue followed Japan's military actions in China carefully through regular reading of foreign newspapers. She had access to *The New York Times* and *The Christian Science Monitor* through friendships with their respective foreign correspondents, Hugh Byas and William Chamberlin. She also received clippings and news from missionary friends such as Dr. and Mrs. Theodore T. Walser.

Consequently, her knowledge of the war was far broader than most of her neighbors. A reading of *Japan's Feet of Clay,* Freda Utley's[4] diatribe against Japan's economic and military policies, further prejudiced Shidzue in favor of Western interpretations of her nation's imperialist policies.

Shidzue wrote a friend, "The war with China which appeared a local conflict at first has stayed so long and developed endlessly. The result is that the people of both countries are to suffer bitterly. We are sorry for the Chinese people but we too have to suffer much. It is one of the outcomes of the war that our government began to suppress all liberal thought and activities.......I believe that all the victims are the most faithful Japanese patriots, but when one country becomes fascistic these things happen. It is, indeed, a shame from the sense of civilization."[5] She feared the political and economic consequences of the war for Japan, and she mourned the tragedies of human loss in China. Unlike most of her compatriots she knew the war in China was not merely a "chastisement" but a blood bath. Her foreign friends eagerly showed her new articles from home, which countered the statements made in the Japanese press. At dinners and lunches, which she was privileged to enjoy with Western diplomats, missionaries, correspondents, and businessmen and/or their wives, she had direct access to uncensored news.[6] She treasured this window of truth even though it was terrifying in its tragic detail.

One lasting impression provided independently by both a minister and a journalist, concerned the vicious atrocities performed by Japanese troops during the taking of Nanjing, December 13, 1937. Shidzue recalled the clippings of this event, and the shocking pictures of executions and other barbarous actions which her friends passed along to her. She was one of few Japanese who could compare battlefield photographs which appeared in the American press with the joyous and benign front page photographs in Japanese newspapers and theater newsreels, which depicted jubilant, but disciplined, soldiers riding triumphantly between rows of cheering, welcoming crowds of Chinese, as the conquerors passed through the Nanjing gates. It was not until long after the war ended that these atrocities were acknowledged by her compatriots.[7]

Undoubtedly some of Shidzue's anti-war feelings were colored by the terrifying anticipation of Arata's and Tamio's inevitable induction into the army. The brief postponement each received under the continued deferment of college students in the late thirties and early forties would last for just the years of schooling. Just the same, when both sons matriculated for baccalaureate degrees in 1939, Shidzue breathed easier. As she wrote Dorothy Brush, "It would be many a patriotic mother's prayer to dedicate her sons to the country for constructive purposes, not for destructive. Arata and Tamio have four more years ahead to be spent in studying and I hope we can restore peace by that time."[8] Besides an understandable interest in self preservation, both sons appeared to echo their mother's feelings that the war in China represented a fundamental injustice. Tamio even suggested anti-fascist books and articles for his mother to read.[9]

Wartime Shortages

In a February letter to America Arata commented that he and his compatriots were experiencing a "rapid increase in the price of commodities, ever increasing taxation, frequent suppression of magazine articles, and the persecution of pacifists and liberals." He then related a story he had heard about students who were caught spending their time "idly in coffee shops or in the front of the movie houses." The government arrested these young men and announced that students should not be frittering away their time during a national crisis. Derisively, Arata compared these student activities with those of government officials, military officers, and businessmen who spent time and money in geisha houses. "Why do not the authorities restrain or arrest them? That is my question."[10]

As the war in China continued Shidzue found it more difficult to obtain necessary birth control supplies than to circumvent police on the look-out for "thought criminals." Her first problem was finding rubber to make pessaries.[11] Rubber and metal, needed to make contraceptives, were scarce and their distribution was closely monitored by the government. Given the opposition to propagation of birth control education, there was no legal supply for Shidzue to tap; she had to rely on the small amounts of materials sent from America. The fact that she received any supplies from abroad and that, from her home, she continued to provide literature and contraceptives bore witness to the low profile which a female social activist could maintain even in the repressive political environment of 1938.

By July, Shidzue had only four to six months worth of supplies left. To continue her work, she would need more materials from America. About one hundred old and new clients continued to contact her each month. How could she smuggle contraceptive materials past the officials? One ingenious, if risky, route, which she instituted for a short time, was to have people in Sanger's organization send supplies to her brother, Hirota Yôji, who was serving at that time as a member of the Consul General's staff in San Francisco. He would then distribute this contraband to other officials who were willing to transport it home in diplomatic luggage. Unfortunately, Hirota was promoted and returned to Tokyo at the end of 1938, closing this mail service.

More frequently, Shidzue asked Sanger to send literature and contraceptives directly to her home address. These would automatically end up at the customs house in Yokohama, where she would be required to collect them in person. Had the boxes, contents deliberately mislabeled, been checked, the smallest penalty would have been confiscation of the goods. Happily, none of them were ever opened. Sanger also sent items with friends passing through Japan, missionaries returning from home leave, or members of the U.S. diplomatic corps. Shidzue paid for most of the contraceptives with her own funds plus contributions she had received. She then charged her customers the cost plus a small profit, thus providing a service while realizing a small source of independent income. She continued her private propagation of birth control in direct opposition to the orders given her by both the Metropolitan Police Board and the Imperial Household Agency until the end of 1939, after which it became impossible to obtain supplies.[12]

Though Shidzue and Arata admitted that life in Tokyo was "tranquil" compared with the war zone, they still complained about national and personal economic deficiencies. The shortages which affected them before 1940 seem more inconvenient than drastic. Just the same, commodity scarcities did decrease their already modest standard of living. Shidzue wrote that food and material shortages were making them anxious. "Arata and Tamio must go to school with 'geta' when the three pairs of shoes they now possess are worn out. This month the amount of gasoline for a private car was cut to 1.3 gallons a day." In July she said resolvedly, "Fortunately we do not feel so bad with food, though the prices are going up rapidly. Japanese are a thrifty nation anyway, so perhaps we can stand this though I personally miss American dishes!" In a less light-hearted manner Shidzue wrote in her diary entry of August 1st that her maid Sendai complained that each time she went out to buy bread the yen had been reduced in value, and, to add further insult, she was confronted by rude soldiers in the local store. Commenting on gasoline rationing, Shidzue objected heatedly to the scoffers and cheaters who selfishly used illegal means to insure their own full tanks. Arata also gave details on the shortages. "Recently the Authority made several codes to limit the production of cotton cloth, shoes, metal apparatus, rubber, etc., owing to the shortage of materials. So I bought a pair of shoes and over-shoes hastily."[13] Apparently, he was not short of ready cash. At this point the family's circumstances were difficult in comparison with their pre-war, upper class life, rather than with the real suffering which was yet to come. After all, they still had shoes to wear out, cash to purchase available goods, and they owned a car, which made gasoline rationing of interest.

Like most middle and upper class urban Japanese during the late thirties, shortages and rationing for the Ishimotos was more an aggravation than a severe hardship. In fact Japan, unlike the United States and Europe, had, for the most part, recovered from the depression by the mid-thirties and, as a nation, had enjoyed substantial economic improvement during second half of the decade. This is not to say that individuals and certain groups within the nation, particularly the urban working class and farmers, were not suffering, but urban industrial and financial capitalists were doing quite well indeed. In fact Japan's economic isolation encouraged both by American and European policies and Japan's own search for economic independence, provided an opportunity for internal growth which worked to her advantage in the late thirties. Just the same, the war with China was beginning to take an economic toll especially in rising inflation and selective shortages of goods needed by the military.

Since the future was unreadable, bureaucratic officials and cabinet members under the leadership of Prime Minister Konoe felt it necessary from both a psychological and economic standpoint to enact a general mobilization policy, which would insure that public sacrifices could be easily and quickly commanded whenever needed. In spite of heated opposition by many representatives in Diet debates, the National General Mobilization Bill was passed in March, 1938. This law was necessarily quite broad, covering an inordinate array of public activities, and, theoretically providing for total mobilization of human and material resources. With a simple directive the government could institute price controls, regulate all commerce, declare items to be rationed, regulate wages, dismiss or hire workers, outlaw strikes, regulate financial institutions, place vital industries under government control, censor the press and radio, levy wartime taxes, require and regulate savings, and more, all without recourse to further legislation.

The rationing and induced shortages which Shidzue and her family experienced in 1938 and 1939, represented a psychological preparation of the people for future all out mobilization, rather than providing essential materiel for the current war. It was not until Prime Minister Konoe formed his second cabinet, July, 1940, that the Mobilization Law of 1938 began to cause real hardships. At that time Konoe's new Minister of War, Tôjô Hideki, insisted upon the development of an overall mobilization plan complete with tightened government economic and social controls. Conditions during 1938 and 1939 only hinted at a life to come.

While economically things were not too squeezed, emotionally, Shidzue was on edge and lonely because of the separation from her beloved Kanjû. She was not, however, alone. She kept an active social exchange with a few like-minded Japanese friends and with members of the foreign community. She also met with her husband, Keikichi, who showed up at regular intervals to discuss family business, see his sons, or simply exchange news with Shidzue. After all, he was still legally the head of the family. Although he made benign suggestions on how she should run her house, he did not object strenuously to any of her activities. Other members of the Ishimoto household were less reserved, though not particularly critical. Intermittently she was contacted by two of Keikichi's younger brothers, one a Lieutenant General, and the other a Major General attached to the Army's General Staff Headquarters. While she wrote in her diary that she found the visits of her brothers-in-law and their comments sometimes unwelcome, she did not record any objections from them about her family planning activities or her social engagements with foreign friends. Surely, had there been public or private concern about her birth control activities or her frequent interaction with members of the press and others in the foreign community, she would have been reprimanded by the family.

A Dangerous Alliance

At one particularly notable international party, on March 10, 1938, Shidzue was introduced to an Associated Press reporter, Relman "Pat" Morin, at a dinner given by her dear friend, Sophie Trosten Chamberlin, wife of William Chamberlin. Recording the event in her diary, Shidzue highlighted a particular conversation because she knew Kanjû would be interested in any uncensored political speculation when he returned home. "Both Chamberlin and Morin believe," she wrote, "that Japan's national strength is not as brittle as the Americans noise about. Furthermore, they think that the Japanese intelligentsia, who say simply 'we will fight if war comes' are making a statement that is simplistic and based on an uncritical attitude. As for the politics in the Diet, they think it is far superior to that of other fascist countries. Given all of this they don't believe that unrest of a revolutionary scale is on the way. The British Ambassador's private secretary agrees."[14] The social event, sanctioned as it was by the Chamberlins, and the intriguing political analysis which suggested that Shidzue's class might not, in the end, support full scale war, made both the evening and the meeting with Morin memorable. Consequently, when, shortly after, he asked her to help him sift through and decipher Japanese information for his dispatches, she was eager to assist. Thus began an emotionally confusing friendship and a successful literary collaboration.

After their initial meeting Morin relied on Shidzue to translate news releases. Later the two decided to translate *Wheat and Soldiers* , written by the well known novelist, Tamai Katsunori, under the pseudonym, Corporal Hinô Ashihei. Tamai, a prize winning novelist and a conscripted foot soldier, participated in the Tenth Army's landing at Hangzhou Bay, south of Shanghai, on November 5, 1937. Later he was assigned to an intelligence unit in occupied Shanghai and then sent to the front lines at Suzhou. Like so many of her compatriots Shidzue had found Hinô's descriptions of Japanese troops very moving. She believed the book spoke to the spirit of the common soldier and of all mankind. She saw it as a protest against the cruelty of war, which expressed the common humanity of both the Japanese and Chinese, a cry against the destruction of any human life. Though the translation was a joint effort, the publication came out under the Baroness Ishimoto's name alone. As she commented in a letter, "for some reason my American collaborator" did not want to be acknowledged and so she had to act as if it were her "sole work."[15]. The book, as it appeared in America, included an abridged version of *Wheat and Soldiers*, a view of the army in Suzhou, preceded by a complete translation of Hinô's shorter, earlier work, *Earth and Soldiers*, [Tsuchi to heitai] which chronicled events in Hangzhou.

The project became more complex than expected, because Morin was apparently sexually as well as intellectually attracted to Shidzue and his modest advances distressed her. Although she would decry it, she seemed, at first, to be attracted to Morin. In truth, she had to employ a strong measure of discipline, reinforced by the spirit of her absent Kanjû, to retain her composure and remain steadfast to her "one true love." On July 21st, Shidzue found herself explaining to Kanjû, through her diary, the previous night's events which had taken an unexpected turn along a potentially dangerous path.

July 20th had been cool and refreshing, and she had enjoyed an evening outside at a rooftop restaurant, and then, though it was quite late, she had gone to Morin's hotel room to do some manuscript revision. "At that time, even though he did not know me very well, he revealed that he had amorous feelings toward me," she wrote. She obviously had some mixed feelings herself for she admitted that she was then and continued to be "emotionally moved" by Morin. Yet, the next day she wanted to make absolutely clear to her "beloved Kanjû" that her behavior the previous evening had been proper in every respect, and that no one could replace him in her heart. She "explained to him" that "in spite of the fact that I have a great capacity for love, I also have a character flaw which does not permit me to love more than once in a lifetime. And so, when he [Morin] drew near to me in friendliness, I yearned for you even more. I'm sure you will understand my feelings of that moment." She was not only reassuring the absent Kanjû, but finding the moral strength within herself to resist Morin's advances.

On July 29th she wrote that she had gone once again to Morin's hotel to work on the manuscript. While she waited patiently, he worked for two hours "revising my prose into beautiful sentences....He is the only man who has drawn close to me in friendliness. And he has offered to help me with a most important project. I have offered him no more than my appreciation. My actions have never been seductive. But such things do happen. It is difficult to express this, but I must admit that I was at my wits' end. It's not that I don't like Mr. Morin. If it weren't for you I don't believe I would have been able to resist him. It is not my fate to walk a comfortable road. It is my fate to love someone who embraces an extraordinary mission, someone more extraordinary than anyone else in Japan. You are that most extraordinary person. Sometimes it is painful to follow such a person, but one has no choice when that person demonstrates a strength so powerful that it must be emulated. And so, every day I exercise an overflowing spiritual strength in pursuit of my beloved who is confined to prison."[16]

Shidzue treated her diary as if it were a personification of Kanjû, and as if she were accountable for her actions to a super human being who was with her in that very room. She willed Kanjû's spirit to transfer to her the strength and discipline which she imagined he possessed, as she continued to intertwine their personal relationship with his superior political mission. She saw any show of human sexual response to another man as a betrayal of the most perfect relationship she could ever experience. Writing her feelings into her diary conjured up her beloved before her eyes as both the manifestation of her own strength and that of a power over her own actions. She seemed to feel it necessary to explain all of her personal actions to Kanjû, to be sure that he would find her worthy of his love. This was not the case just with Morin, who apparently represented a real threat to her sublimated sexual life; it was true with her husband, Keikichi, as well, who never aroused any passion in her. Keikichi often occasioned several sentences of commentary about the very fact that she had not the least residue of love for him. Such statements inevitably were followed by declarations of love and admiration for Kanjû.

On July 30th Shidzue sent Morin a letter. She had worked through her bewildered feelings, and she had recognized the seriousness and potential danger in their relationship. The letter was written "while I was wide awake, with a transformed mind and without the 'forbidden fruit' around." Though the letter is not quoted, it was clearly meant to halt any future intimacy with Morin. At the same time she intended to continue the professional association. Once again, she used the diary to clarify her feelings to Kanjû. She confessed that while "nothing had happened, even this non-event was an offense" to him. She now felt that she must analyze her true heart, which she assured him, had not changed one bit toward him. He continued to be the foundation of her spirit. By way of an excuse for her perceived misstep, though she "had not sinned in any way," she commented that this was the longest they had been apart since her American tour in 1932-33.

Morin must have been quite amazed by the letter he received. Although Shidzue never mentioned a response, her few comments about the personal nature of their relationship over the next year suggest that he had been, at the least, perplexed, and more probably, annoyed, by her actions. While he had been friendly and warm initially, as well as professionally helpful, he became more and more abrupt and domineering. In the end Shidzue did not seem to like him at all. She became quite insulted by his continuous correction of her literary interpretations and English translations. He seemed to imply that she did not have the ability to do more than substitute for a dictionary in support of his superior intellect and splendid prose. In January, 1939, after completion of the first section of the book, she protested his statement, "I am really proud of you," as the sort of comment a teacher would make to a pupil, a superior to an inferior. As she pointed out to Kanjû , "I have my own style and ability and definitely do not need the constant supervision of this person." Her tirade finished, she calmed herself sufficiently to reassure Kanjû of his continued powerful influence over her life.

Shidzue was an independent, free woman, to be sure, but not when it came to her relationship with Kanjû. She wrote in her diary, on January 12, 1939, "What is this strength which has carried me through from my 'instant trouble' [the July 21st evening with Morin] to this moment? It is the application of my good sense and my triumph over obstacles by skillful cultivation of my strength. It is totally directing my love and emotions toward you."[17] Her courage was derived from Kanjû's strength and from his love. Like many politically emancipated women of this era, Shidzue's liberation was not complete. She constantly reminded herself that she was, in fact, purposefully and deliberately tied to a man, who, so she believed, was more able and more significant to the progress of liberal politics than she was. Though absent and imprisoned, he was more in control of her sexual and emotional fate than she was. In those days she spent many nights reading romantic novels, such as *Lady Chatterly's Lover* and *Gone With the Wind,* and she agreed enthusiastically with what she understood to be sexual freedom for women as portrayed in those books. She read philosophy, politics and history and embraced new ideas about the human condition and world events. As she applied this knowledge to her own life, however, she was fated to hobble herself to what Kanjû would think or how such readings would influence him. The fact that he was not available to actually interpret meanings for her or to approve or disapprove of her thoughts and actions, was irrelevant. Her independence was restricted by a ghost.

A Publication Debacle

Shidzue's anticipation of success with the publication of *Wheat and Soldiers* cannot be overestimated. She hoped for foreign sales which would compare favorably with the book's best seller status in Japan, accompanied by royalties which would ease her economically pinched life. Perhaps of greater importance, however, was the political rapprochement which this might bring between the people of her country, more and more maligned abroad, and those of her adopted culture. She was convinced the American public would empathize with the conscripted soldier who wrote with such feeling and honesty about the pointless absurdity of slogging through a rain of bullets seeing nothing but tragic death all around him. No one could help but hear the soldier's cry for all humanity. Her belief in the communality of understanding between Americans and Japanese was bolstered when her good friend, William Chamberlin, actively promoted the translation with letters and telegrams and agreed to write a forward. He too saw the book as a humanistic portrayal of every people.[18]

Shidzue worked steadily on this project and in January, 1939, she commented that, though it was an especially cold winter and typing hurt her finger tips, she continued to work from morning until night. She was warm only when she finally went to bed after enjoying a portion of a special Hiroshima *sake*. From January until the manuscript was sent off the end of February, she did little else than translate and rework her versions with Morin. Upon completion she wrote excitedly in her diary, "Hinô Ashihei advocates for the heart of the soldier, and I can't say how many times I have grieved for this....[H]is gentleness captures the heart of the people." This project, she insisted to "Kanjû," is as important as advocating women's issues, discussing social problems, or arguing about women's roles and sexuality. The translation, in other words, could be politically justified, though for Shidzue it was a matter of the heart.

When *Wheat and Soldiers* appeared in American book stores the beginning of May, Shidzue felt proud of her accomplishment. Chamberlin's generous forward thrilled her, for he testified, "*Wheat and Soldiers* is, to the best of my knowledge, the first deeply significant book to come out of the Sino-Japanese conflict. The author, Corporal Ashihei Hinô, is a soldier in the ranks of the Japanese army; but the first quality that lifts his work far above the general run of 'war books' is the complete absence of any propagandist element.....he endeavors...to show himself and his fellow-soldiers not as legendary heroes but as credible men, their moments of despair and weakness blending with acts of great courage and devotion." Chamberlin went on to compare this work to Remarque's *All Quiet on the Western Front* from World War I. In conclusion he exclaimed, "Hinô is telling what war really is, with all the elements of pain and terror that are systematically omitted from censored newspaper correspondence and official military publications."[19]

Viewing the relationship between the U. S. and Japan from the distant shores of a closed Japan at war, neither Shidzue nor Chamberlin realized that American reviewers and the public would see this book as "propagandist." Most reviewers would ignore Chamberlin's kind words, and chastise the "Baroness" for flaunting her government's twisted vision of its army engaged in an innocuous romp through China. As of May, 1939, the foreign community in Japan still believed that the "China Incident" would be diplomatically resolved and relations between Japan and the U.S. would be normalized. In fact, by this time, the American public's hostility toward Japan was rapidly intensifying while its sympathy for a ravished China was increasing in even greater measure. At the time that *Wheat and Soldiers* went on sale, Americans had no taste for evenhandedness when it came to judging Japan's war in China. Even though the foreign community in Japan, and through them, Shidzue, as well, knew about the atrocities the Japanese had committed in China, they did not realize that shocked Americans had hardened their hearts toward both the Japanese army and the Japanese people.

With great excitement Shidzue wrote in her diary on June 1st that Keikichi had call her from his hotel to report that the May 31st issue of the *Tokyo Nichi Nichi Newspaper* included an article about the positive reception of her translation by the American public. The article was captioned with big headlines and included a photo each of Shidzue and the book's author. The work was heralded as "critically acclaimed in America." Shidzue was excited and pleased. Soon after the *Tokyo Asahi Newspaper* excerpted a supportive critique of the book by Pearl Buck, an author of great repute in Japan. According to the paper, Pearl Buck had praised the work for its "truth, credibility, and simplicity" and stated that its "delicate consciousness toward beauty and even greater depth of understanding of humanity completely overpowers." The article went on to quote Buck, "In this work there is not the least preaching or assertions of propaganda or self-importance." On a personal note Buck remarked, "Hangzhou and Suzhou are longed for memories of home for me for these are the locations for *The Good Earth*. It is in these peaceful places that the war goes on. I was carried away by the sadness and could barely finish the book."[20]

Although Shidzue was well aware of the censorship rampant in war reporting, it did not occur to her that a review of her book would be anything other than a word for word translation. In fact the review, as published originally in *The New Republic* [21], was quite different in both content and intent from these excerpts. The review was a reproval of Japan's inhumanity. The *Asahi* had taken single words and phrases out of order and reconfigured them to create a favorable picture. Shidzue would have agreed with Buck's actual review for it captured exactly the image she had hoped for; the sensitive view of an actual foot soldier juxtaposed against the benign bureaucratic explanations of the government's China policy intended to camouflage the barbaric actions of the army at the front. She had expressed similar sentiments in letters to her American friends.

The problem was not the content of this review, one of the less vindictive, but the overall reception of the book by the public after reviewers, like Buck, had had their say. Few copies sold; most were returned to the publishers. As Shidzue said later, her intention had been to acquaint the American public with a soldier whose feelings were in contradiction with the militarists. She wanted to elicit from her readers an understanding of the tragedy faced by the Japanese soldier and the humanity which remained a part of him. Unfortunately, "there was no tolerance for this soldier's story....Public [American] opinion interpreted my translation as no more than an attempt to give the actions of the Japanese militarists a rational appearance, and so my translation encountered a boycott and sales did not go well."[22]

The most damaging review, both personally for Shidzue, and commercially was T. A. Bisson's. [23] Although he called the work "an unforgettable little masterpiece," he meant this to be both a literary compliment and ironic praise of its nasty propagandistic nature. Bisson went out of his way to damn the translator personally. He wrote, "The translation by Baroness Ishimoto, clothing the direct, concrete sentences of the original in common American idiom, is itself a literary achievement of unusual merit, and should go far to mitigate the suspected anti-war proclivities for which she was jailed in December, 1937." Bisson saw the Baroness as an apologist for the government who had committed *tenkô*, that is, had converted to a pro-militarist position, to atone for previous anti-government activities which she now recanted. In other words, he accused her of the one action she had zealously resisted. Bisson concluded his review with a scathing critique of the manner in which the book glossed over the evil and horror perpetrated by the Japanese against the Chinese and commented that "Corporal Hinô and Baroness Ishimoto have, in fact, done their bit" to spread the militarist's illusionary propaganda.

Shidzue was devastated.[24] She believed reviewers had distorted her message. So used to working with metaphor and searching for grains of truth in censored and twisted information, she had seen visions of compassion and hope in the author's smallest desire for peace, or his slightest dismay over the trauma of battle. Given the government's prohibition of "dangerous thoughts" it seemed amazing to her that any "truths" of battle were expressed in the stories. In her excerpted translation of *Wheat and Soldiers*, about a quarter of the original book, Shidzue had carefully selected the vignettes of soldiers slogging through mud surrounded by bloody, dead bodies, over the many less dramatic descriptions of quiet patriots serving their emperor, with all the terror and death carefully sanitized out. Neither the American literary elite, nor the general reading public, was conversant with the subtlety with which any opposition to government policy had to be handled in the Japan of 1939. The reviewer for *The New York Times* came closest to such understanding when, after quoting a particularly sensitive passage about "indignation against war," he commented that these words "seem to be preciously close to 'dangerous thoughts'." Perhaps he would have been surprised to learn that it was the translators, not the author, who courted danger for they had added this deliberate outcry against war which was not in the original.[25]

In July and August Shidzue received reactions to the book from American friends. While Dorothy Brush made "generous comments" on the translation, she did not mention the content. It was left to the outspoken Mary Beard to turn the knife in Shidzue's heart. Mary Beard wrote, "I don't know whether you know this or not, but when you were imprisoned, I initiated a liberation movement on your behalf, and I inspired celebrities throughout the nation to reason with Japanese envoys. And now, I have received the diary of a soldier which you have translated into English. I have read the book and I am concerned about your introduction.... Ah, has such a day come to pass?" Here she meant Shidzue's complicity in apologies on Japan's behalf for their aggressive actions in China. "And if it has, I can never again turn my face to the East. And I can never again meet you."[26]

In her August 6th diary entry Shidzue described for "Kanjû" the immense hurt she felt at Beard's remarks. She explained how hard she had tried to maintain her equilibrium in the face of a Japan "carried away by its enthusiasm for imperialism and nationalism." How she had sought to hold onto the internationalism which she valued so highly and focus on a world which permitted "co-existence and co-prosperity." Distraught by the discord within her own environment she continued to "rebuke" her society while attempting to guard her own position. It was a difficult tightrope to walk. And then, at this moment of trial a brief letter "breaking off relations" had arrived from Mary Beard, the woman she embraced with affection and respect as her intellectual foremother. Shidzue's sadness was so great that she could not eat or drink as she wept for the loss of a beloved friend.

Why, she asked, did Beard find this publication a "betrayal of her confidence?" She continued, "Must individuals living in a Japan which has given way to the destructive power of the military authorities completely cut themselves off from individuals in other countries? Has that day come?" She then directed her anger and sadness specifically at Beard saying, "How can someone make a snap judgement that the soldiers of an aggressor nation inevitably sympathize with that nation's aggression?" As Shidzue continued her defense, she underscored her abhorrence of her government's actions and revealed how much she knew about the real events occurring in China. "Our soldiers have committed atrocities, but it is not they who are responsible. Until this is over, I will live in this insane Japan and mix with these insane Japanese, while I await the return of law and order." Shidzue did not intend, she protested, to excuse herself either. As a member of the Japanese society she could not "feign innocence," but she did believe that "by introducing the human spirit of a soldier to America I acted correctly. This is definitely not a betrayal of Mrs. Beard's confidence." Shidzue rested her case, "Mrs. Beard has intertwined Japan's destructive authorities with all of Eastern culture and has made us all responsible provocateurs for a Second World War....[It seems] my translation is also responsible for these terrible events....Mrs. Beard has strong reasons and I can understand her fears, but, even so, she seems severely lacking in human feelings." She then concluded, "I am a Japanese. Even though I detest the present day Japan and the Japanese of this Japan, I am Japanese."

The demoralization caused by Beard's letter colored the rest of the day's diary entry as she tied her own indignation to Kanjû, as well.

Since he was confined to jail for anti-government activities, he should be even more deeply offended by Beard's abrupt remarks. Shidzue reasoned that if Japan succeeded in becoming the supreme ruler of East Asia, the subjugation of the captive peoples both abroad and within Japan would weigh heavily on Kanjû's own conscience because of his failure to prevent this. His own life would be like "merely existing in a pack of homeless of dogs...,for if Japan can be hated you, Kanjû, can be hated too." Beard's remarks, and by extension the attitude of all Americans, undermined both Shidzue's political position, and more importantly, that of her beloved Kanjû, who had fought valiantly against the government.

Apparently Mary Beard dashed off her letter as a minor reprimand with no idea of the effect it would have on her isolated friend. Intellectually Beard knew Japan was fascist, and yet she still imagined Shidzue was able to think and act freely. About a month after the brief but traumatic letter arrived, Shidzue received a package from Beard containing two books. Undoubtedly these were meant to entice Shidzue away from dabbling with Japan's fascist line. Though concerned about Shidzue's politics, Mary Beard had not cut her friend off.[27]

Publication of *Wheat and Soldiers* had been a disaster. It brought neither the political praise nor economic relief Shidzue had expected. Although she wanted to continue "enlightened activities," she found it difficult to do so publicly, and so, she decided to take the advice of one of her foreign journalist friends and "hold her tongue." However, she said, "I will continue to think about the issues of women's liberation and birth control." Her friend responded, "Even the government cannot control what goes on in your mind."[28] On the few occasions she tried to break this resolve, she discovered again the wisdom of her friend's advice. She tried, for example, to discuss the war with a liberal friend known as an intellectual interested in social issues. This patriotic woman excused Japan's actions in China with the comment that in wartime excesses could not be helped. Shidzue was shocked. She felt that she "absolutely could not" keep company with someone who thought that way. Of course, this had been an intellectual discussion based on hypothetical circumstances for the other woman did not have access to the foreign new reports of atrocities which Shidzue was privy to. After the war Shidzue commented that in the late thirties many "progressive intellectuals and cultured people" recanted their past beliefs (committed *tenkô*) and affirmed the militaristic way which was revolutionizing the manner in which Japanese authorities ruled the nation. She concluded sadly, "The intellect is fragile."[29]

Women and the Militarist Cause

There were few liberal women actively promoting progressive causes by the late thirties. For example, the most well known socialist, Yamakawa Kikue, had retired to a farm outside Tokyo several years earlier and was quietly raising ducks. Others struggled on, but had to compromise their principles more and more. One last political push occurred in December, 1938. At that time Shidzue joined a group of women representing the Women's Suffrage League to make one last attempt to address the issue of women's participation in politics. They failed once again. Soon all women's organizations were either forced to dissolve or to fall in line with government views through reorganization into approved women's groups. Most women joined the two primary government sponsored organizations, The Greater Japan Defense Women's Association and the Patriotic Women's Association. Shidzue's liberal friends and associates, who continued to work for organized groups, tended to join a third, much smaller, umbrella group, the Japan League of Women's Organizations [Nihon fujin dantai renmei], or formed subgroups which were loosely connected with one of the other larger groups.[30] Women tried to advance issues important to women such as child care, health care, livelihood, sanitation, working conditions, social services, and "enhancement of national spirit" by working with the government.[31]

The two umbrella women's organizations, the Greater Japan Defense Women's Association and the Patriotic Women's Association grew in the late thirties to memberships of about eight million and three million respectively. The army dominated The Greater Japan Defense Women's Organization under the patronage of the Ministry of Defense, and ran it at the local level through groups sponsored by local army administrative units. The grass-roots based power structure of this organization primarily composed of the wives of soldiers, laborers, farmers, and lower level merchants made it more powerful than its middle and upper class competitor, the Patriotic Women's Association, sponsored by the Home Ministry. These two reorganized national women's groups were pledged to militarist policies, and the women wore either a white or khaki apron to show their unanimous patriotic endorsement of government policies. The women members supported the war effort by lecturing, leading patriotic ceremonies, organizing funerals for the war dead, helping families of active duty military and, in sum, waving the banner for national goals on the home front.[32] These organizations were not concerned with women's problems, women's freedom, or the improvement of women's position in society. Their leadership was dominated by men who directed the membership on how they could aid the militarist cause. These organizations were fully compatible with the traditional feudal structure of the family system and declared absolute loyalty to the Emperor.

From Shidzue's perspective neither of the two ultra-patriotic organizations, nor any of the smaller groups which her friends had chosen reflected the values or concerns which she had espoused, and, consequently, she withdrew from public organizations entirely. As she commented after the war, "Figuratively speaking, in those days it seemed as if I were riding on a passenger liner of life propelled by a harmonious spiritual warmth, while outside unhappy conditions made the vessel rage and storm as if on wild seas." She could read and write at home and be content with the fact that her sons were settled in college. But even home was not a total haven. She was saddened by continual battles with her younger brother, who "championed the opinions of the fascist bureaucracy."[33] By the turn of the decade Shidzue sought calm and solace in her reading and writing and the freedom of her own mind, as well as some continued conversations with trusted Japanese and foreign friends.

Notes

1. Ishimoto to Dorothy Brush, 6/26/38, Smith.

2. First letter: Ishimoto to Sanger, 2/3/38, Smith. New arrests described in Itoya Toshio, ed., *Nihon shakaishûgi undô shisôshi* [An Intellectual History of Japan's Socialist Movement], Vol. III, p. 254. Second letter: Ishimoto to Dorothy Brush, 4/3/39, Smith

3. Patricia Steinhoff, *Tenkô: Ideology and Societal Integration in Prewar Japan*, Garland, 1991, and Steinhoff, "Tenkô and Thought Control" in *Japan and the World*, Gail Lee Bernstein and Haruhiro Fukui, eds, St. Martin's Press, 1988, pp. 78-94.

4. Florence Rose had sent this in 1937.

5. Ishimoto to Gladys Smith, 2/23/38, Reel 19, Sanger, LofC.

6. See diary entries, 1988b.

7. 1981, p. 104-105; see diary, 1988b for references to war in China. No specific reference to atrocities. Even today the atrocities are glossed over in textbooks and debated away. See pp. 78-79 of "The Emperor and the Militarists: Reexamining the Prewar Record" by Watanabe Shoichi, reprinted in trans. in *Echo*, XVIII:2, 1991.

8. Ishimoto to Dorothy Brush, 6/26/38, Smith.

9. 1988b throughout.

10. Ishimoto Arata to Brush, 2/25/38, Smith.

11. A diaphragm-like device invented in the 19th century inserted into vagina to block sperm. In 1930, Majima Kan made significant technical improvements to this Western invention.

12. The courier service and other methods of obtaining supplies described in letters between 1/and 7/38, especially between Ishimoto and Florence Rose in Sanger, LofC and Smith.

13. Ishimoto to Dorothy Brush, 6/26/38, Smith; to Florence Rose, 7/5/38, Sanger, LofC; 1988b, p. 188-189; Arata to Brush, 7/14/38, Smith.

14. 1988b, p. 117. Curiously, Kanjû's older brother, Taiichi, was a Minseitô Diet Representative then, like Tsurumi Yûsuke

15. Ishimoto to Dorothy Brush, 8/4/39, Smith. In an October, 1992, International House lecture, Donald Keene noted this as the only contemporary Japanese novel available in the U.S. just before the war.

16. 1988b, p. 185.

17. 1988b, p. 252.

18. 1988b, p. 216 & 233.

19. *Wheat and Soldiers*, Trans. Baroness Shidzue Ishimoto, Farrar & Rinehart, 1939, vii-viii.

20. As quoted in 1988b, p. 298.

21. June 7, 1939, pp. 134-135.

22. 1948, pp. 136-137. Highly negative reviews included: Clifton Fadiman, *The New Yorker*, May 27, 1939; one in the *Nation*, 8/5/39, p. 154, and T. A. Bisson, "Japanese Soldier," *Saturday Review of Literature* 6/3/39. One positive review was by Shidzue's friend, Bradford Smith, then in Kobe, *Books*, 5/28/39, p. 4.

23. T. A. Bisson, "Japanese Soldier," p. 5.

24. On July 6th she spent five hours producing a response to criticisms for August publication in the magazine, *Kaizô*.

25. *NY Times reviewe*r, S. T. Williamson, "A Japanese Soldier Comes Home From the China War," *New York Times Book Review*, 6/4/39, p. 3. Since Morin could not read Japanese, Shidzue was responsible for selection of passages. This passage appears on p. 181 in Ishimoto trans. For original see "Mugi to Heitai" in *Hinô Ashihei shû; Nihon bungaku zenshû*, Vol. 67, 1972, p. 115. For comparison see pp. 129-130 of Lewis Bush trans., *Barley and Soldiers*, Kenyûsha, also published in 1939. In this more literal translation there is no "indignation against war," rather a desire "to shoot and cut down those Chinese who were killing my comrades and who threatened my own life..." which is, in fact, in the original. See also, Donald Keene, *Dawn to the West*, Holt Rinehart & Winston, 1984, pp. 916-926 for comments on Hinô and Keene's trans. of parts of this same passage. Keene finds Hinô to be a strong pro-militarist.

26. Ishimoto to Dorothy Brush, 8/4/39, Smith. Beard's letter is quoted in 1988b, p. 306. In an apparent attempt to excuse the supportive preface, Beard explained that Chamberlin had telegraphed a local newspaper suggesting that Japan's actions abroad had "completely severed the life-blood of China's resistance." Beard implied that Chamberlin thereby revoked his support for the book. Shidzue told the editor of her diary, Funabashi Kuniko, that Chamberlin did not telegraph any such message. See the whole of entry for 8/6/39, pp. 303-309.

27. In 1947 Shidzue commented offhandedly that Mary Beard "scolded me for attempting to write such a story [*Wheat and Soldiers*] -- one which she said made it look as if I was cooperating with the militarists." Lt. Weed to Brush, June or July, 1947, Smith.

28. 1981, p. 103; not referred to in her diary, 1988b.

29. 1981, p. 106.

30. Japan League, presided over by Gauntlett Tsuneko. Ichikawa Fusae, Kaneko Shigeri, Gauntlett Tsuneko, Hani Motoko, Dr. Takeuchi Shigeyo, and Dr. Yoshioka Yayoi, for example, formed the Women's Group to Study the Current Emergency [Fujin jikyoku kenkyûkai] in March, 1939. Yamada Waka, considered a government lackey, founded the Mother's Protection Society [Bosei hogo renmei].

31. See Mitsui Reiko, *Gendai fujin undôshi nenpyô* [A Chronological History of the Women's Movement], , 1963, p. 163; Sheldon Garon, "Women's Groups and the State," *Journal of Japanese Studies*, 19:1, p. 38; "Women's Groups to Map Out Long-Term Plan," *The Japan Times & Mail*, 3/24/39, p. 2; Oohama Hideko, "Japanese Women Take Active Part in China Incident," *Japan Times & Mail*, 3/27/39, p. 4..

32. Aprons were white for Defense Women and khaki for Patriotic Women and were worn over kimono and work clothes. In the forties the general uniform for all patriotic women was the loose fitting trousers and shirt of the farm women, or *mompei*. See Richard J. Smethurst, "The Army, Youth, and Women," in Edward R. Beauchamp Ed., *Learning To Be Japanese*, Linnet Books, 1978, pp. 157-162 for women's groups; Sheldon Garon, "Women's Groups and the State," Journal of Japanese Studies, 19:1, pp. 37-39.

33. 1948, p. 130.

8

"The Winter Years" (1939–1945)

On January 23, 1941, Shidzue wrote Dorothy Brush expressing gratitude for the "unchangeable friendship" which she had warmly extended. She told Dorothy that she would "cherish" their friendship even more "when the water on the Pacific is rough." She had just finished reading *The Tragedy of France* by André Maurois, and in sympathy with this writer's words, she told Dorothy, should war come between Japan and America, she would "feel the same grief which this French author felt toward his English friends. What a pity! How ridiculous, unbelievable that our nations should have to fight after a hundred years of contribution to each other! However reality is cruel. The political air has been so intense, that it makes me fear that this may become my last chance to write you until peace comes back on the Pacific." Until then she had refused to admit to herself that war with America was possible, but finally she had "realized that no individual can attempt to stop this tide [from sweeping] our shore....Indeed, my heart is aching from what I witness and hear everyday, and also I feel the very earth on which I am footing [sic] has begun trembling."

With sadness she noted that Japan was in the midst of a revolution in which the old order was being overthrown but no one yet knew what might replace it. She believed that the people anticipated this revolution with a thrill based on a misunderstanding of the "disagreeable experience" they would have to endure. "After long mental sufferings, disappointments and re-thinking," she had come to the conclusion that she must try to get "through these days of war" by maintaining "an infinite faith in the future."

In a lighter vein Shidzue attached a postscript telling Dorothy how far her gift of five dollars had stretched in those economically trying times. She took her "almighty American dollars" to a "Thrift shop" run by American and Japanese ladies of charity. The shop sold used items which Americans were disposing of before leaving Japan. Dorothy's gift bought a blanket, eight linen sheets, and two towels.

Shidzue commented how fortunate she was to find such items for no Japanese store had sold "pure woolen and linen goods" for the last three years. Shidzue remained in contact with American friends throughout 1941, but both sides acknowledged that communication would eventually be cut off. In April Florence Rose wrote, "we must depend to a great extent on thought waves to carry all that one wishes to say."[1]

In late May, 1941, Shidzue wrote her friends about meetings with Madame Kamaladevi, of India's family planning movement. "Madame Kamaladevi has been popular here since she is being introduced as 'anti-British'." She then went on to say that the audience did not seem to understand that their interpretation of "anti-British" and that of the woman from India differed. The Japanese women assumed that Kamaladevi supported the Axis cause and, therefore, like the Japanese, opposed the enemy, Great Britain. Ishimoto construed the speaker's words differently and was concerned that Kamaladevi's words were not being faithfully translated and that some "paragraphs have been swallowed up by her tactful interpreters."[2]

At a tea given by a group of her friends Shidzue was the interpreter. She found the audience hostile when she faithfully rendered Kamaladevi's comments on Japan's war. "My stupid honesty could not soften her words when she frankly said that she had no sympathy for Japan's 'holy war' against China. To my shock and disappointment, all the women there expressed their disapproval of her criticisms. However, to me, this was a rare chance in knowing where the Japanese people's feelings are, in spite of my sorrow in finding myself alone in my analysis of this war."[3] In another letter Shidzue added that Madame Kamaladevi had confided in her that she was willing to speak in a country whose militaristic actions she abhorred because she hoped she might "convince the jingoists of Japan" of the error of their international actions. Shidzue was particularly frank in these letters because she was bypassing the mail system and sending the letters out with someone sailing to America.

Although Kamaladevi was a family planning activist, she had come to Japan to speak only about India. The Japanese government, which had cautiously permitted her visit, had specified that she was not to discuss birth control, which by that time had been outlawed. In 1940 the Ministry of Welfare had promulgated and the Diet had passed the National Eugenics Law [Kokumin yûsei hô] which stipulated that all young people would be required to undergo physical examinations to determine whether they had any of a number of specified debilitating mental or physical diseases designated as cause for forced sterilization. On the other hand no person found healthy would be permitted to be sterilized. In 1941 a policy statement on population growth was promulgated. Of particular interest to Shidzue and others engaged in family planning was the stipulation in the accompanying "Outline for Population Policy" that "Artificial methods of birth control, such as contraception and abortion, should be prohibited...." The set of regulations which comprised the total policy elevated a woman's reproductive role above any productive role within society, formalized interference in a woman's private home life and sexual activities, glorified the traditional family system by threatening against "unsound thoughts" which might compromise the male dominated household, and provided economic rewards for procreation.[4] It is not surprising, therefore, that in April, 1941, the government would watch nervously over the visit of a well-known birth control advocate. It is equally understandable that Shidzue would rejoice in even a brief exchange with someone of a similar mind.

Shidzue received her last communication from Mary Beard shortly before the December 7th bombing of Pearl Harbor. In it Beard wrote that even if the relationship between Japan and the United States worsens "our friendship will not change." Reflecting several decades later on this final pre-war letter from America, Shidzue commented that when the reality of war had settled in after the bombing of Pearl Harbor, Beard's words became even more important to her, as she hoped that all her American friendships would withstand this ultimate horror.[5]

From 1942 until the fall of 1945 Shidzue's friends received no word of her. Their last contact had been through Gladys Walser,[6] missionary resident of Japan, who had returned home in 1942. Like all other Americans caught in Japan on December 7, 1941, Walser and her husband had been immediately confined as internees at a camp on the grounds of a Catholic school located between Tokyo and Yokohama. After several weeks of negotiations between the US, and Japan, through Swiss mediation in the spring of 1942, those in the camp, diplomats and staff held at the American Embassy, and journalists who had been imprisoned in local jails, were advised they would ship out on June 17th. These detainees would be exchanged mid-voyage for returning Japanese nationals who had been residing in America.[7]

Detainees who had homes in Tokyo were permitted to return to pack a few belongings and sell everything else before sailing for home. Mrs. Walser wrote for her alumnae notes of November, 1942, that the evening before she was to leave and the morning of the departure friends came to call, "filling the dismantled rooms [of her home] with warmth and fellowship." Others met her at the police station where she had to register before taking the train to her ship. Among her well-wishers were "two women writers, friends of mine for many years..."

The two were Baroness Ishimoto and Sumie Seo Mishima, the author of *My Narrow Isle*. "Both these writers speak from the depths of their own experience, and by reading them we are given an insight into the brave hearts and fine courage of the modern Japanese woman." She continued with an expression of "high regard for those friends whom I have left behind, whose high hopes for mankind must remain unexpressed for a time. They, like many thousands of others, are weary and discouraged."[8]

A few months after Ambassador Joseph C. Grew returned to Washington on the same exchange ship as the Walsers, Florence Rose wrote him hoping to learn more about Shidzue. In a brief note Grew explained that he and all of his embassy staff had been held "incommunicado" until the June evacuation and thus he did not have any word of the "present situation of Baroness Ishimoto."[9] This ended attempts by Shidzue's friends to contact her until after the war.

For Shidzue the years of war between Japan and America were painful because of her lost communication with American and other foreign friends, her feeling of political isolation within her own land, and her loss of social focus; but it was her family tragedies above all else which made her characterize this as her "winter period." In September, 1942, Shidzue's elder son, Arata, graduated from Kyoto Imperial University only to be drafted immediately into the army, and in April, 1943, he shipped out to the Southeast Asian battle front. Her second son, Tamio, who lived with her in Tokyo, had cut back on his rigorous academic schedule at Tokyo University in 1940, but could not fight off the debilitating effects of the tuberculosis which he had contracted earlier. He died in June, 1943. As she said in *Remembrances*, an autobiography filled with many of her saddest experiences, "during the war everyone had days of sadness and there were many times for floods of tears."[10] In 1943 Shidzue's personal grief knew no bounds.

A Proud Mother

In March, 1939, a good life was still possible. That month she rejoiced in her sons' educational achievements. Arata graduated in science (biology) from Tokyo's aristocratic Gakushuin, the Peers' School. Following the pattern set forward in the "University Ordinance of 1918," by the time he entered this higher school, or, more accurately, university preparatory program, he would have completed at least eight years of elementary training and four years of middle school, that is, secondary education. Even though Gakushuin was in a special category without connection to the bureaucratic authorities of the national education ministry, it followed this program. Under the exclusive control of the Imperial Household, it was the school of choice for the Imperial family, members of the old nobility, and selected others who were educated there by the will of His Imperial Majesty. Shidzue had attended the girls' division of the elementary school in the first decade of the century. In April, one month following his Gakushuin graduation, Arata entered the faculty of science at Kyoto Imperial University. He would be twenty-two the following June.[11]

On March 13th Shidzue and Arata went to the Kansai area to make living arrangements for his three years of study in Kyoto. They stayed briefly in Kobe with American friends, the Bradford Smiths. He was a professor of English and a graduate of Columbia University, and would write one of the few positive reviews of the *Wheat and Soldiers* translation later that summer. In nearby Kyoto they also met with Mrs. Thomas, who would provide a room for Arata while he studied physics at the university. These associations with Americans, Shidzue believed, would give her son an opportunity to improve his English, and a more comfortable physical environment than that afforded in most student housing. While visiting the Smiths Arata enjoyed "his first opportunity to dance with an American lady. It was a remarkable experience for a shy boy like Arata." Mother and son returned to Tokyo so that Arata could pack for the April beginning of classes. For the next three years Arata studied physics and biology, practiced English, and was tutored in Russian, apparently living a quiet and studious life which culminated in a university degree by September, 1942.[12]

Tamio had also graduated from higher school in March 1939; he would be twenty-one in October. He had concentrated in literature at Daiichi, First Higher School of Tokyo. This prestigious public school, the oldest higher school in Japan, was founded in 1875. Two years later it was named preparatory higher school for Tokyo Imperial University and placed under the university's direction. Completion of the three year preparatory course almost guaranteed placement at that premier national university. On March 21st, when the list of successful entrants was posted, Tamio's name was among them. He did not see the list himself, for he had left four days earlier with a group of school friends to travel in Manchuria, Northern China, and Inner Mongolia.[13]

During his higher school years Tamio had trained like an athlete; "his body had matured beautifully as he gained weight, developed sturdy muscles, a broad chest, and a thick neck." He was especially strong in rowing, a sport excelled in by his grandfather Ishimoto, and, hoping to follow in his grandfather's footsteps, Tamio aspired to join the university rowing team. In Daiichi he had been very popular with other students, and made a dashing figure as he rushed about Tokyo in his black school cape and cap with a white stripe designating his high student office. He greeted everyone and was greeted in return looking like a "superior species in a pack of mongrel dogs. In the student world, Tamio's value was high." His relatives admired him and his father was filled with a new pride which manifested itself in even greater parental indulgence.[14] Shidzue felt very close to her son, for he shared the excitement and enthusiasm of his activities with her, providing her with a window on the world which brought a fresh breeze to her stifled existence. She rejoiced as she watched him grow in physical stature, intellect, and humanity. At the same time Tamio indulged himself in his independence, enjoying the freedom of living away from home and the joy of peer admiration. His health, however, began to take a turn that Shidzue failed, at first, to notice.

When Tamio entered the Daiichi Higher School he was "bewitched" by the atmosphere and insisted upon experiencing all aspects of student life. Consequently, he begged his mother to permit him to live in the dormitory, and in his final year before college she acquiesced. A characteristic feature of higher school dormitories throughout Japan was the emphasis on student self-government. Naturally, Tamio was elated when in his last year of higher school he was chosen chairman of his dormitory. Enthusiastically he devoted most of his energy to this respected role, though he did continue to spend some time on his studies as well.

The elected office of dormitory chairman represented the pinnacle within the public school hierarchy of the Education Ministry's enforced self-government activities. Beginning in elementary school these exercises were designed to produce students who exhibited the desired qualities of self-discipline and social cooperation, and would become adults who served society with appropriate civic attitudes and beliefs. The few students who progressed through the upper ranks of the education system became more independent and carried out more elaborate and time consuming duties within the broadened realization of self-government. Everything at the higher school dormitories pertaining to student life was left to the students. The chairman was expected to work with and oversee all committees, which were in charge of meals, books, student activities, the school newspaper, and auditing all of the expenses for these services. Tamio, therefore, had an especially arduous role, for he chaired all business which was transacted for the more than 250 students in the dormitory, coordinated the elected committees in his own dormitory, and met, as well, with the chairmen and committee heads of the other dormitories. In all of this he had only one supervisor, a professor assigned to provide some general direction.

Tamio's election as chairman must have been exhilarating, but the work was exhausting and by the time he entered university he was already, at the very least, physically run down. Unfortunately this last year at Daiichi coincided with a health crisis, a steady increase in the numbers of tuberculosis victims. Although in principle TB victims were mostly the elderly and people living in unsanitary conditions, young students were also exposed to this disease in heavily increasing numbers. Dormitory life with its crowded conditions was acknowledged as a breeding ground for the disease. Extrapolating from statistics of 1937 it would appear that Tamio's dormitory had as many as 260 students in about thirty rooms. Years later Shidzue commented that "people said that a dormitory was an incubator for the tuberculin bacteria. It was common for first year students to get sick and even die of tuberculosis. A good friend of Tamio's, a first year student, died that very year."[15] In retrospect Shidzue has commented that she tried, to no avail, to prevent Tamio from living in the dormitory. There is, however, no contemporary corroboration of this memory. It would seem from the 1939 diary entries that everyone, including Shidzue, was much too impressed with Tamio's accomplishments to dwell on any negative aspects of dormitory life during that final year in higher school.

With Tamio living in the dormitory for 1938-39 and Arata involved in his studies at Gakushuin, Shidzue had the luxury of concentrating almost exclusively on her own life. In many ways she must have enjoyed the time to herself, in spite of her longing for Kanjû's return and government curtailment of her clinic work. During this period she especially related to the dark writings of the Russians, Dostoevsky and Tolstoy, and to works by writers like D. H. Lawrence whose *Lady Chatterly's Lover* suited her loveless life. She also kept up with the world's political events, attended several lectures, enjoyed Hollywood movies, and met friends for lunches, dinners, and teas. She must have been thankful for the opportunity, for the first time, to follow her own will without checking first to see that her family responsibilities were taken care of. This was a conflicted time with emotional lows mixed with some intellectual highs.

Many times during each day Shidzue's thoughts turned to her beloved Kanjû. She remained close to him silently through her private diary. Actual communication with him was also possible through letters and news transmitted between them by his lawyer and others. On November 28, 1939, their first meeting since December, 1937, was arranged. Kanjû had been permitted to leave his cell briefly to visit his wife, who was in the hospital undergoing an operation for uterine cancer. Kanjû's lawyer, who was charged with taking the prisoner from his cell to the hospital, arranged a meeting at his Marunouchi office between his client and Shidzue. "Though it was only one hour," her joy knew no bounds.[16] One month later, on December 28th, Tamio burst into the house to tell Shidzue some very good news, "Mother, Mr. Katô has returned." He told her he had read this report in the morning *Nichi Nichi Newspaper*. Shidzue's joy was unbounded. The most vital part of her life would begin again, she believed. From 1938 to early 1940, then, Shidzue had much more on her mind than her sons. It is not surprising that she may have missed the onset of Tamio's illness.

The beginning months of Tamio's university life must have been exhilarating for him. One of his comrades, Fujisaki Akiyo, remembered Tamio warmly as an enthusiastic first-year student, and described their meeting on the first day of classes.[17] Tamio had a boyish face and an imposing physique, "a handsome young man," but was wearing shabby clothes and an old hat. This disheveled appearance contrasted strikingly with his correct and elegant bearing, which revealed that he obviously hailed from a good family. "I thought, here is a man capable of shouldering the fate of the Japan of these days....This was how I met the outstanding talent, Ishimoto Tamio, who went prematurely to his death." Fujisaki went on to tell about Tamio's youth and energy, and the way he threw himself into everything from rowing to studying. "He was a regular guy, who could be trusted, depended upon." He could joke with his comrades, assuming airs by using Imperial language in the gossipy atmosphere of the rowers locker room, bearing the flavor of the aristocracy while simultaneously retaining the affability of a local "regular guy." In academics his specialty was political history within the faculty of law where he particularly admired his professor, Oka Yoshitake. He confided proudly to Fujisaki that Professor Oka had praised his paper, "The Labor Movement in the Meiji Period." Tamio wasn't just a playboy. He was a young man of great talent who was well liked by his peers.

Despair and Tragedy

At some point, probably in early 1940, Tamio began visibly to change. His mother could not help but notice that he appeared less robust, his healthy appearance of higher school years much diminished. Shidzue reflected in 1948, that as early as 1938, the dormitory year, she began to see some changes.[18] In those days Tamio acted like a "happy demon," overtaxing himself and conspicuously endangering his health. She remembered that she tried to get him to slow down, but then she was the "only parent" at home and did not seem to have any influence; he would not listen to her. "Belatedly," she became truly alarmed and insisted that he go with her to a doctor. He did so and agreed, as well, to get x-rays at the university hospital. These examinations confirmed that he had become infected with tuberculosis. The symptoms appeared to be advanced; however, even this medical confirmation of his condition did not prevent him from continuing his activities against doctor's orders and his mother's wishes. The scientific evaluation, though validating her fears, cast up a barrier up between Shidzue and her son, for they could not agree on his treatment. Sometime, perhaps shortly after his first year at the university, mid-1940, Tamio was forced to withdraw from classes and rely on tutoring. Not too long after that, he had to withdraw from his university studies altogether. Shidzue wrote in a May, 1941 letter to America, "Tami has not been well for sometime. Like most of the 'grade-A' university students, he became thin and pale which made me quite worried. Now he promised me to consider his health problem first and studying second."[19] In fact he was no longer on campus.

Although it is not certain exactly how Tamio contracted his fatal disease Shidzue blamed his death on the unhealthy conditions of dormitory life combined with lack of nutritious food during his years of illness and inadequate access to penicillin. Another factor which she suggests only in her 1948 remembrances was his trip to Japanese controlled lands in China in March, 1939. She remembers that even though Tamio had been diagnosed with TB he insisted upon following through with his travel plans to Manchuria and Inner Mongolia. Shidzue begged him to cancel the trip and enter a sanitarium. In spite of the scarcity of available beds in those days, she had managed to find one for him.[20] Although, in hindsight, it is far from convincing that the prognosis for the infected patient was any better under sanitarium care, Shidzue believed, at the time, that this was Tamio's best hope. He refused her appeal saying that he would find such confinement equivalent to a "neck tether"; it would mean imprisonment. His heart was set on the trip abroad. In the end, though very much against this scheme, Shidzue gave in.

A trip to the Japanese controlled lands of Manchuria, Mongolia and Northern China was not out of the ordinary for young men of Tamio's age. By 1939, in fact, it was becoming a goal for both school leavers and university students. There were private tours, like Tamio's, and the government was active in forming groups of students, especially teenagers, to visit or migrate to these new territories. For instance, in March, 1939, the Overseas Affairs Ministry announced its intention to send 32,000 youth volunteers to "Manchukuo" to settle. This government agency would initially "train" the young men at home for two months and then send them off to camps in different parts of Manchuria for three more years of training. Two thousand were set to leave in April, 10,000 in May and the rest were to be sent at intervals through February, 1940. In April, 1939, the Education Ministry in cooperation with the War Ministry and the China Affairs Board, announced that in July they would send 500 students from various colleges and universities to North China with the purpose of observation and inspection as well as to engage for about one week in "pacification works," or labor in mines, factories, or hospitals, according to their specialties at college. Also in April, the Japan Young Men's Society in cooperation with the Youth Training Institute for the Development of Manchukuo announced that it would try to recruit upwards of 100,000 young men to go in groups to farm during the summer season. The three-fold purpose of this project was to give "a better understanding of the new state to the Japanese young men," promote "friendly feeling between the Japanese and peoples in Manchukuo" and to render "assistance to agricultural colonies in that country."[21] It was government policy to encourage young men to visit this newest portion of Japan's growing Empire.

From early 1940, not long after his trip to northern China, Tamio was confined to home. His only change of scene came when he sought the curative powers of a hot springs mountain resort, probably during the summer of 1942, where he improved enough to walk around outside for an hour at a time. Over New Year's, 1942, he spent a brief time at another hot springs, a little more than two hours by train from Tokyo. Shidzue was able to pay for these health trips because she had received "a generous payment from America for a manuscript." She found it more difficult, however, to provide adequate nutrition, penicillin, and other medicines. Due to shortages and rationing, providing nourishing food at any price was next to impossible. Sometimes she was successful in adding protein to Tamio's diet, "of course, things like eel could not be obtained. I hunted high and low in desperation for eggs and meat."[22] Nothing, however, slowed the progress of the disease. By mid-1942 it was difficult to coax Tamio to eat any of the food she was able to scavenge. Most probably by that time recovery would have been impossible under the best dietary and medical conditions. In those days, even in well-off America, diagnosis of TB was received as a death sentence.

Arata returned home in September, 1942. Shidzue, consumed with anxiety and exhausted over Tamio's care, was overjoyed to have him home, even though she knew that soon he would have to leave for military service. Since he had a college degree he could qualify to take the examination for the officers' training corps; a career as an army officer would have been fitting considering the distinguished military career of his grandfather Ishimoto and the fact that two of his father's brothers currently served as army generals. Writing in 1981 Shidzue explained that, because Arata resolutely opposed the war, he had refused to join the officers' corps. Instead, she claimed, he decided to wait for his draft notice and serve as a foot soldier. He did not wait long. About ten days after his return in September he received the dreaded "red letter."[23] The military-affairs clerks throughout Japan, who kept records of every eligible draftee, were very efficient and their counter-parts in the military draft offices delivered the list of draft notifications without a break.[24] Arata, in fact, described the incident a little differently. He said that about ten days after graduation in September, 1942, he was drafted and that three months after that he took an officer candidate examination, but failed, so he was "obliged to remain a private in the army."[25]

On the day of Arata's induction he took his sandwiches and tea and joined the others who had just received their "red letters." They all ate and talked together "without regard for family status,"[26] as they waited to receive their active duty papers. Although Arata did not train for the officer corps, he still avoided the life of a rifle bearing foot soldier. Since he had learned to drive a car while in higher school, he had no trouble getting assigned to the transportation corps as a truck driver. His orders were to report for duty immediately, and on October 1st he entered the army and was posted to Setagaya-ku in Tokyo as part of the transportation corps of the Awajima Imperial Guards. Shidzue despaired over the loss of her recently returned son, and once again was alone with the gravely ill Tamio.

After the outbreak of war with the United States, Shidzue had found it more and more difficult to obtain the food and help she needed to care for Tamio. She had had to let her beloved maid, Sendai, go, which left her alone to take care of the house and look after Tamio. It was very difficult for her to leave the house to search for food and medicine. Tamio did not like to be left alone, for at any moment some member of the *tonarigumi* [Neighborhood Association] might call out from the front *genkan* [entry way] and disturb his rest.

Order Number Seventeen entitled "Essentials of Providing for Community Councils" had been issued by the Home Ministry on September 11, 1940. This directive formed the basis of the wartime *tonarigumi* which required that every household within a given area of about ten families be organized into a small governmental unit run by a council which would then direct each neighbor's participation in the "moral training," "spiritual unity" and economic stability of the community.[27] The activities of each *tonarigumi* were extensive and participation mandatory. Essentially, it was up to the council and its chairman to administer the rationing system. They would have to determine distribution of scarce goods according to size and needs of families under their jurisdiction. As early as the winter of 1940-1941, *tonarigumi* were responsible for distributing charcoal for the cold months ahead and making sure that the neighborhood and then each family received its appropriate share of staples such as rice, sugar, and match sticks which by June 1940 had been rationed. Small shop owners were also assisted by the *tonarigumi* in their acquisition of tools and stock, and fair distribution was monitored on a daily and monthly basis. Every day someone delivered a circular to each household which might contain vital information about foodstuffs, but would also announce deaths in the neighborhood, deaths of neighbors' sons fighting abroad, names of sons returning from a tour of duty or about to leave. In this way neighbors learned about available rations and were alerted to their obligation to show solidarity with others by offering sympathy and assistance to a bereaved family or, "armed with blazing sun flags," joyously sending a new recruit off to the front.

By April, 1941, a ration book system was in place and the list of rationed items increased. After war with the U.S. began, it was obvious to everyone that the allotment of rice per person per day was lower than that required by a healthy adult. Shortages had become severe. By February, *misô,* soy sauce, potatoes, bread, cooking oil, and vegetables, among other food items, were added to the list of rationed foods, and the protein rich produce, fish, eggs, and tofu, as well as the grains which housewives had used to augment the reduced rice servings, required ration coupons.[28] Clothing was also placed on a rationing system, with each person receiving a coupon book of 100 points to be used for everything bought during the year—socks (2 points), coats (50 points), blouses (8 points), etc. Everything manufactured, from dry goods to finished products, had a point equivalent and was supposed to be carefully monitored. In response to the impoverished legal market in all foodstuffs and commodities, black markets sprang up simultaneously with each new regulation. At the same time, all food and material necessary for the military effort was diverted away from the civilian population.[29] It was the responsibility of the *tonarigumi* to administer the rationing system and to make sure that the rules of distribution and usage were fairly administered. Sometimes this was efficiently accomplished and sometimes chairmen and councils took advantage of their positions of power for their own gain, or favored neighbors, and relatives.

Shidzue remembered her *tonarigumi* as thoughtful and kind, and said that they recognized the special burden of her family circumstances. They compassionately shortened, as far as possible, her participation in required air raid exercises and her contribution to the community's labor services. They did not refrain, however, from bringing around announcements or making deliveries when she was out trying to procure, often through the black market, additional protein rich food or medicine for Tamio. While she was gone a member of the *tonarigumi* might bring around a circular. The neighbor would open the sliding front door and call out in a loud voice from the entry way expecting someone inside to come read and stamp the letter. Consequently, Tamio was always filled with apprehension when his mother left; he would become nervous and his sleep was disturbed. There was no way his mother could both stay at home and search for the food and medicine he needed. In this distressful manner, mother and son painfully existed into the spring of 1943.[30]

Just before Arata left for the war zone in April, he telephoned his mother and inquired after Tamio's health. This had to serve as the brothers' final farewell. During that conversation his mother gave Arata urgent instructions. She told her elder son that, no matter what happened, his first duty was to survive. Shidzue told him that should the situation arise he must allow himself to be taken prisoner, and, if he became a prisoner, he should be cooperative. She told him that his ability to speak English would be an advantage if captured and, therefore, an ally for survival. "No matter what, his goal should be to live."[31] This, of course, was directly contrary to army orders which demanded that, as a loyal subject of his Imperial Majesty, he should fight to the death, and never surrender to the enemy.

On April 22nd Arata left Shinagawa station on the 7:29 a.m. train to join his troop ship. His mother wrote him in her first letter of that same date, that "while fixing Tamio's breakfast I listened to the radio announce the exact time of 7:29 and my heart was full to breaking. I prayed for your safe return." In her second letter, written late at night on that same day, she asked, "How did you spend your day? Your mother's day, from morning to night, has been devoted to Tamio's care. In the intervals between nursing duties I thought of you. Then I gazed at the sky in a westward direction and called out into the distance, 'be strong, be strong'. And I heard you call the same back to me." She recalled this event a little differently in 1981. At that time she told how the train ran nearby her house, and that she had gone to a hill which overlooked the tracks so that she could watch the troop train as it passed by. Sadly she could not see anything because the train window shades were drawn. In 1984, she elaborated further explaining that she could not go to the train to see Arata off for that would alert the *tonarigumi*. "I had to keep [the date of departure] a secret. If I told anyone in the *tonarigumi* then one by one they would come by, flags waving. When my son shipped out I would be very sad and might cry. A tearful face in front of these important people would be embarrassing." She did not want her neighbors to see Arata off, and she knew that, if she went, the contemporary culture would demand that as a mother she exhibit courage and even joy at the departure of her soldier son.[32] Her heart was much too full to behave properly, so she stayed away from the railroad station altogether.

On April 26th Shidzue wrote again to Arata "I wonder what sea the ship will set off for today and how far it will get by tonight." Arata's destination was Sumatra.[33] Exactly one month later, on June 26, 1943, Arata's 26th birthday, Tamio died.

Tamio was one of many Japanese who suffered from TB. From 1937 to 1943 deaths from TB increased from the already high rate of 203 per 100,000 population to 225.[34] Coincidentally with Tamio's trip to North China, the Welfare Ministry, in cooperation with the Education Ministry, stepped up its fight against the disease. Again, in April, 1941, as part of a general health crusade, the Welfare Ministry encouraged specific behaviors which would prevent tuberculosis. Included was an emphasis on improving nutrition, a somewhat ironic suggestion considering that the number of food items controlled by rationing had escalated regularly. In fact, rice rationing in major cities coincided with this announcement. Perhaps the Welfare Ministry considered they had resolved this paradox with their slogan, "Don't take too much rice, but eat more sardines." A general campaign to educate the people about the causes of TB was led by physicians, government officials, and neighborhood associations and included lectures, discussion meetings, and movies which emphasized proper hygiene, physical exercise, clear ventilation, and sun baths. None of these efforts appeared to slow the advance of the rampant disease. As the war widened and more and more money, products, and energy had to be diverted from civilian to military use, there was no possibility that the TB epidemic could be stopped. In 1943, the same year that Tamio died, and the last year during the war for which statistics are available, about 200,000 Japanese succumbed to tuberculosis.[35] The sad statistics of TB within Japan as a whole, however, did not lessen each family's tragedy.

On June 30, 1943, Shidzue wrote Arata about his brother's death. "At 8:55 in the evening of June 26th, after a courageous final three month battle against his illness, his last moment was announced. With his father holding his left hand and his mother holding his right hand, our beloved Tamio, quietly and peacefully, slipped into an everlasting sleep." She then described the funeral and told Arata that the memorial address was read by Tamio's revered Professor Oka

Yoshitake. She told about Tamio's last days with special emphasis on his reflections about Arata. Realizing that Tamio would not last much longer she had asked him if he wanted to send a message to his brother. In a very faint voice he asked her to please tell Arata that he had entered the Catholic faith, that he was extremely weak, but that he was improving little by little, and that Arata shouldn't worry. With a contented expression he wished his brother good health and begged him to continue his studies. Shidzue's letter was long and detailed, a pouring out of sad events.

In the 1974 reflection on his friend, Tamio's university classmate, Fujisaki Akiyo, mused about the turn their lives had taken in 1943. Fujisaki, like Arata and many of Tamio's classmates, left for the battlefield soon after graduation. At the time of parting Fujisaki expressed sympathy to his friend who had the misfortune to be confined to his bed. Tamio responded with his "usual smile," saying, "You are very talented. Even though the war has begun and you have to leave, do not feel defeated." Fujisaki then traced his own wartime career in one sentence, moving from the joy of early victory to the "beginning of night" at Midway, and then to the sickness of the "Manila heart." He was cheered by a note from Tamio which finally reached him on the battlefield after his friend had passed away. Tamio's last words were, "You are my dear friend and must not forget to live for me." To the soldier in the battlefield this encouragement, from one who had escaped the war in the most terrible of ways, exuded a spirit of hope. Fujisaki concluded, "In the Fall of 1943, not too long after his death, I felt a breath of fresh air penetrate the battlefields of New Guinea." Tamio was not forgotten.

On July 3rd Shidzue wrote to Kanjû informing him of the sad event. She began the letter similarly to the one she had written Arata, but with one important descriptive change. "On June 26th, at 8:55 p.m., Tamio, enveloped in his mother's arms, peacefully passed away....Just before he died I whispered in his ear, 'Tami-chan, 'Go to sleep, sleep peacefully.'" Ishimoto Keikichi had disappeared from this version of the final scene of his son's life. Shidzue went on to tell Kanjû about the funeral and then included a more intimate and detailed commentary on her own grief. She spoke of having endured a terrible ordeal. She had not stepped foot outside her door from April 19th until the day of the funeral, and had not been able to meet with anyone, speak to anyone or write letters. The awesome responsibility of caring for Tamio had forced her to live a life she would not have chosen "the life of a Catholic nun.." Now she was drawing a line, cutting off her past from her future. What did he think of this new plan? In conclusion she asked him to call at his earliest opportunity.[36]

Shidzue was completely alone; both sons were gone, one to the war and the other to the grave. Ishimoto Keikichi, "the shame of the family," remained her husband but they were bound only by the family register. She thought of herself as a "widow."[37] Just before New Year's Day, 1944, she moved from her home in Ooi to a small house in nearby Setagaya. Sadly, she said good-bye to her memories, and left carrying a basket with Chibi, her cat, the only remaining link to her life with Arata and Tamio. It was after this move, she recalled, that she felt free to "think of her own life as a woman." Now that her responsibilities to her sons were ended, she could concentrate on her own needs. Shidzue reflected, "Though I had passed the period of a young woman's passions, I had feelings which must find a home."[38] It was from this time that Kanjû began to regularly visit once again .

Personal Joy Amidst Bombs of Destruction

Before Arata left for the war zone she consulted with him about her future and the possibility of remarriage. Of course, she was not yet single, but Kanjû, whose wife had died of cancer in 1941, was, and a marriage seemed more promising. Arata approved.[39] By 1944, she felt free to follow her heart. It would not be simple, for she must once again contend with the feudal family system. At this time, Kanjû was also living alone in Tokyo. As a released political prisoner, he continued to be watched by the "special higher police," and could not participate in any political or labor organization. He made a slim living, according to Shidzue, as a newspaper columnist for the *Tokyo Mainichi Newspaper*. At this time his teenage daughter and son lived with relatives.

Kanjû proposed, after a fashion. "After a while he asked me to marry him. It was a totally awkward proposal. His manner of proposing was to say, 'My comrades are searching for a second wife for me and I cannot fight against them. If you can't marry me I will have to marry someone else.'"[40] Shidzue accepted and began the process of securing papers of permission from the Imperial Household Agency to show to officials at the civil office who could then grant the divorce. She had talked about divorce with the Ishimoto family and her own relatives many times before, but with no success. This time she would persist until she won. According to aristocratic family tradition she must gain support from two male members of her family before the Imperial Household Agency would consider the matter. Finally she convinced her elder brother, Hirota Kôichi, and her brother-in-law, Ichikawa Yoshitaro, at that time a member of the Foreign Affairs Ministry, to support her petition. They justified their action to other family members saying that, since she no longer had sons at home, her responsibilities to the Ishimoto family had been fulfilled.[41]

The divorce was granted in November, 1944, and her name was stricken from the Ishimoto family register. Shidzue, now 47, and Kanjû, 52, planned to be married immediately in spite of continued opposition from some of her family. Her mother and her mother's younger brother, Tsurumi Sadao, in particular, continued to grumble. They felt it was degrading for someone of Shidzue's status to marry a labor organizer with a proletarian class background. Uncle Sadao, an officer in the army, found it especially embarrassing that he would have to acknowledge a member of the family who had ties to the left-wing.[42] The wedding was not to be stopped, but the ceremony would take place in Kyoto away from the site of family conflict, and away from the first severe American bombing raids over Tokyo. The mayor of Kyoto acted as their go-between and the chief of the *Mainichi Newspaper*, who had a large, beautiful home and garden in Kyoto, offered the couple a place to stay. The ceremony itself took place at the Kyoto's Heian Shrine. For those few moments Shidzue was able to forget her recent personal tragedies and ignore the escalating terror of a war brought home.

Upon their return to Tokyo, Kanjû and Shidzue rented a newly built house in Koyama, Shinagawa which had been abandoned by its owner who sought peace in the countryside. At the time of the move they discussed what to do about Shidzue's extensive trousseau of clothing and furnishings which she had brought to her first marriage. Kanjû told her that all she need bring this time was herself; and so it was decided that her accumulated property of thirty years would be left behind, and she moved only the few things which could be put in a small cart. Kanjû's two children joined their father and step-mother. The following winter, March 30, 1945, the family grew to five with the birth of a new baby, Shidzue's "miracle" child, Takiko, "great joy."

Shidzue wrote jubilantly about this miracle. "The impossible became possible. Yes, something that one as worldly as myself would call unimaginable actually happened. The child I had long desired was born..... I was quite old to became pregnant. Twenty eight years had passed since my last pregnancy. I had to seize this last chance.... Just the same it was impossible for me to believe that in fact after so long a time I was indeed pregnant. What a miracle! When finally I believed that this miracle was true, I experienced great joy. I also experienced a consolation from this joyous event for the loss of my beloved son Tamio. I believed that the new life sleeping in my womb was given me in exchange for the life of my lost son."[43]

She was overjoyed to be carrying a child and not at all concerned that the child would be born just four months after her official marriage to Kanju. Writing publicly about this fact for the first time in her ninetieth year, she dispensed with the issue in two simple sentences. After describing details of her marriage, she continued, "A short time afterwards I was blessed with a daughter, Takiko. I was 48 years old. She was born on March 30, 1945. Since my marriage ceremony was performed in November of the previous year, there were people who made much of the trivial fact that the months did not add up. But from our perspective our real marriage had taken place when we began living together in March, 1944."[44]

Despite her age and the deprivations caused by the war and intensified bombing of Tokyo, Shidzue maintained good health throughout her pregnancy. Kanjû searched about and found nourishing food and made her eat it, and she felt as strong as she had in her twenties. The pressures from war meant that she had to do everything to prepare for the baby by herself. Making do with what was available she sewed baby clothes and prepared for the birth. Her husband arranged a place for her at a hospital, and so she went there to await the birth. She spoke with the obstetrician, who was obviously anxious and could only mutter such things as "I'm worried because of your advanced age," and "It's troublesome, isn't it?" Finally, she, simply left, returning home by a bicycle-drawn rickshaw. This was all for the best, she said later, because, "after all, the hospital could have been bombed during an air raid."

Shidzue had reason to fear the worst for the hospital, her home, and her family. Shortly before she was to give birth, the most severe bombing raid of the war occurred over Tokyo. This single raid of March 9-10, is said to have killed over 200,000 people. General Curtis B. LeMay, who directed the firebombing, called it a "diller." Radio Tokyo called it "slaughter bombing" telling of the "sea of flame which enclosed the residential and commercial sections of Tokyo." During the rest of March, throughout April and on into May, General LeMay followed up with intensive bombing, delivered by low flying B-29s, over Tokyo and throughout Japan.[45]

In spite of this public terror, Shidzue's private miracle continued. Unlike every other night, March 30th, the night of Takiko's birth, was calm. "There were no shrill, ear piercing sounds of the sirens, no electric failures, and no water stoppages. My midwife said this was a blessing given by the gods." Shidzue was delivered of her baby that night at home. Four nights later the skies were once again filled with death, but while others ran out to find shelter, Shidzue stayed home, and covered her new baby with a blanket to shut out the sounds of the planes, explosions, and wailing sirens. The baby slept, and the house remained intact. "It's a miracle," she cried out.

On the evening of May 23rd, the bombing finally came to the Katô's section of Tokyo. Putting the baby in a basket, they left the house. First they went to the shelter which Kanjû had dug, carrying with them just two bottles of milk for Takiko. The bombs fell nearby and the fires were less than a mile away, coming toward them like the lava which swept down the mountain at Pompeii. A house just a few yards away burned down. With the help of a young couple they managed to extinguish the flames which threatened their own home. Finally, beneath a sky ablaze with lights of "B-san," they had to flee. Not knowing where to go they simply wandered about searching for water, keeping to the narrow streets. Worn out, they sheltered under a bridge, about two train stops from their home, and prayed. For the next twenty to thirty minutes they watched what seemed like a typhoon of fire. Tired, discouraged, and without direction, they decided to return home. The first sight they saw was the burned out rubble of their neighbor's house. The houses all around theirs were razed to the ground. Their house remained untouched. As Shidzue entered her home, she called out "Kamisama (god), thank you."

Over the next few months they survived. Kanjû suffered from acute inflammation of the kidney, a condition brought on by fatigue and lack of adequate nourishment. Hearing of his illness, friends within his old labor union and associates among the intelligentsia brought the family food. They brought pumpkins, the new staple, and, most importantly, milk for Takiko which they had purchased on the black market. With help, miraculous luck, their own determination, and Shidzue's trips to the countryside to find food, the family all survived to experience the surrender and with it the end of hostilities.[46]

Notes

1. Brush, 1/23/41, Smith; Rose , 4/11/41, Reel 19, Sanger, LofC.

2. See Kamaladevi to Sanger, 5/26/41; to Florence Rose 7/7/41 (Box 6 - Rose), Ishimoto to Sanger and Rose; all in Smith, and 1948, p. 134.

3. Ishimoto to Sanger, 5/24/41, Reel 19, Sanger, LofC; a second letter, Ishimoto to Sanger, 5/24/41, Smith; Ishimoto to Rose, 5/23/41, Smith. For Kamaladevi's long evaluation of visit see letter to Sanger, 5/26/41 in Smith.

4. Yoshiko Miyake, "Doubling Expectations: Motherhood and Women's Factory Work Under State Management in Japan in the 1930s and 1940s," in Gail Lee Bernstein, ed., *Recreating Japanese Women*, U. of California Press, 1991, pp. 278-279; quote from Miyake, p. 279.

5. 1981, p. 113. Beard seems to have forgotten her harsh remarks of 8/39.

6. Wife of Presbyterian minister, Theodore T. Walser. Shidzue mentions a tea with Walser on 9/22/39, 1988b, p. 318, at which they discussed war in China and US-Japan relations. It was probably Walser's foreign group who ran the "Thrift Shop" where Shidzue bought the linens etc. with Sanger's money, beginning of chapter.

7. See Otto D. Tolischus, *Tokyo Record,* Reynal and Hitchcock, 1943, pp. 377-397.

8. *Smith Alumnae Quarterly,* 11/42, Smith.

9. Joseph Grew to Florence Rose, 1/13/42, Reel 19, Sanger, LofC.

10. 1984, p. 109. References to Arata's army service and Tamio's death are in: 1948, pp. 139-179; 1981, pp. 107-111; 1984, pp. 109-122; 1988a, pp. 113-117. There are three letters to Arata dated the end of April, one letter to Arata dated June 30th, and a letter to Katô Kanjû dated July 3, describing Tamio's death, 1988b, pp. 341-351.

11. Higher school information for Arata's and Taimio's schools in, *Education in Japan,* Tokyo Municipal Office, July, 1937. See Donald T. Roden, *Schooldays in Imperial Japan,* for descriptions of dormitory life, ceremony, self-government, etc. Although the emphasis of this book is on Meiji, the descriptions fit those described by Shidzue. Also, there are several specific references to Tsurumi Yûsuke's activities at same school early in century.

12. Ishimoto to Dorothy Brush, 4/3/39 & 8/4/39, Smith; 1988b, p. 274.

13. 1988b, p. 274.

14. 1948, p. 140. 1988b, p. 276.

15. 1981, p. 109

16. 1988b, p. 327.

17. Fujisaki Akiyo, *Nihon Keizai Shimbun,* 1/26/74 as quoted by Funabashi Kuniko in commentary, 1988b, p. 380-381.

18. This may reflect the wish she had seen the onset of ill health earlier. There is no contemporary corroboration, no reference in the 1938-1939 diary, 1988b, and earliest mention of Tamio's illness in a letter is to Florence Rose, 5/23/41, Smith.

19. Ishimoto to Florence Rose, 5/23/41, Smith.

20. *Japan Times & Mail* 4/29/39 states at the beginning of 1937 there were just 32 public sanatoriums with 6,000 beds and in that year a ten year plan called for increase to 40,000 beds. Thomas R. H. Havens, *Valley of Darkness, The Japanese People and World War Two,* University Press of America, 1978, p. 144 puts the number of beds available in 1938 at 10,000 and number of TB patients at 1.5 million.

21. *Nippon Times,* 3/7/39. 4/11/39, 4/15/29.

22. 1948, p. 145. Perhaps money was that advanced for the ill-fated *Wheat and Soldiers* trans. 1948, p. 110.

23. 1981, p. 109. 1984, p. 111.

24. See Haruko Taya Cook and Theodore F. Cook, *Japan at War: An Oral History,* The New Press, 1992, pp. 121-127 for an interview with a military-affairs clerk.

25. Arata to Sanger, 4/7/48, Smith.

26. 1984, p.111.

27. Thomas R. H. Havens, *Valley of Darkness*, p. 75.

28. Margaret A. McKean, "Japan's Rationing Economy in War: Cheating vs. Cooperation in Adversity," Association for Asian Studies, 1987, pp. 9-10.

29. See interviews by Haruko Taya Cook and Theodore F. Cook, in *Japan at War, An Oral History*, Part III.

30. 1948, pp. 145-146.

31. Interview, 1978; 1984, p.112; also alluded to in less detail in 1981.

32. See Haruko Taya Cook and Theodore F. Cook, *Japan at War*, pp. 178-179 for a compassionate recollection sympathetic to Shidzue's feelings.

33. These three letters, two of April 22nd and one of April 26th, are reproduced in 1988b, pp. 341-343.

34. Thomas R. H. Havens, *Valley of Darkness*, p. 144. *Nippon Times*, 12/29/46 gives 215 per 100,000 as the figure.

35. *Nippon Times*, 12/29/46, p. 1. Havens concludes, "Crowded city living after 1937 created conditions that spread the disease faster than the health officials could contain it, and reduced nourishment alone was probably less responsible for the rise in TB rates than poor housing, long work hours in dank factories, and bad sanitation." *Valley of Darkness*, p. 144. While perhaps correct for the population in general, this does not accurately portray the reasons for Tamio's death. As startling as the 1943 statistics are, the deaths from TB were considerably higher after the war with 1945 showing 283 per 100,000 people vs. the US figure of 42.

36. 1988b, pp. 349-351.

37. 1948, p. 174.

38. 1948, pp. 174-176. This 1948 reconstruction of events probably dates her decision to focus on her personal relationship with Kanjû about six months later than was the actual case.

39. 1948, p. 174.

40. 1981, p. 114.

41. 1981, p. 114; 1984, p. 123-124.

42. Interview, 1978.

43. 1988b, p. 352. Although this description has been included in 1988b, Funabashi, volume's editor, has told me that this entry post-dates the event.

44. 1988, p. 122.

45. Edwin P. Hoyt, *Japan's War*, McGraw-Hill, 1986, pp. 385-387.

46. 1988b, p. 357.

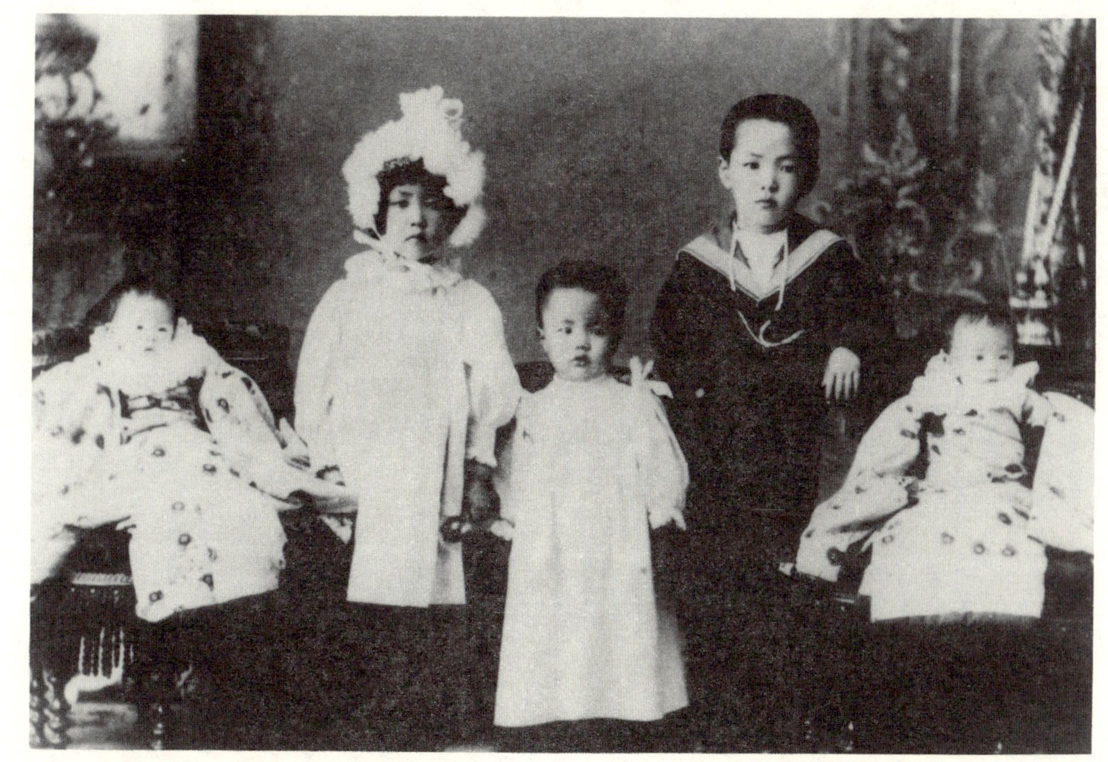

Hirota Shidzue (second from left) at 5 years old with her brothers and sisters Kiyo, Yôji, Kôichi, and Kayo (left to right), 1902. The three older children are wearing Western clothing their father brought home from Europe. Hirô, the youngest sibling, was not yet born. Courtesy of Katô Shidzue.

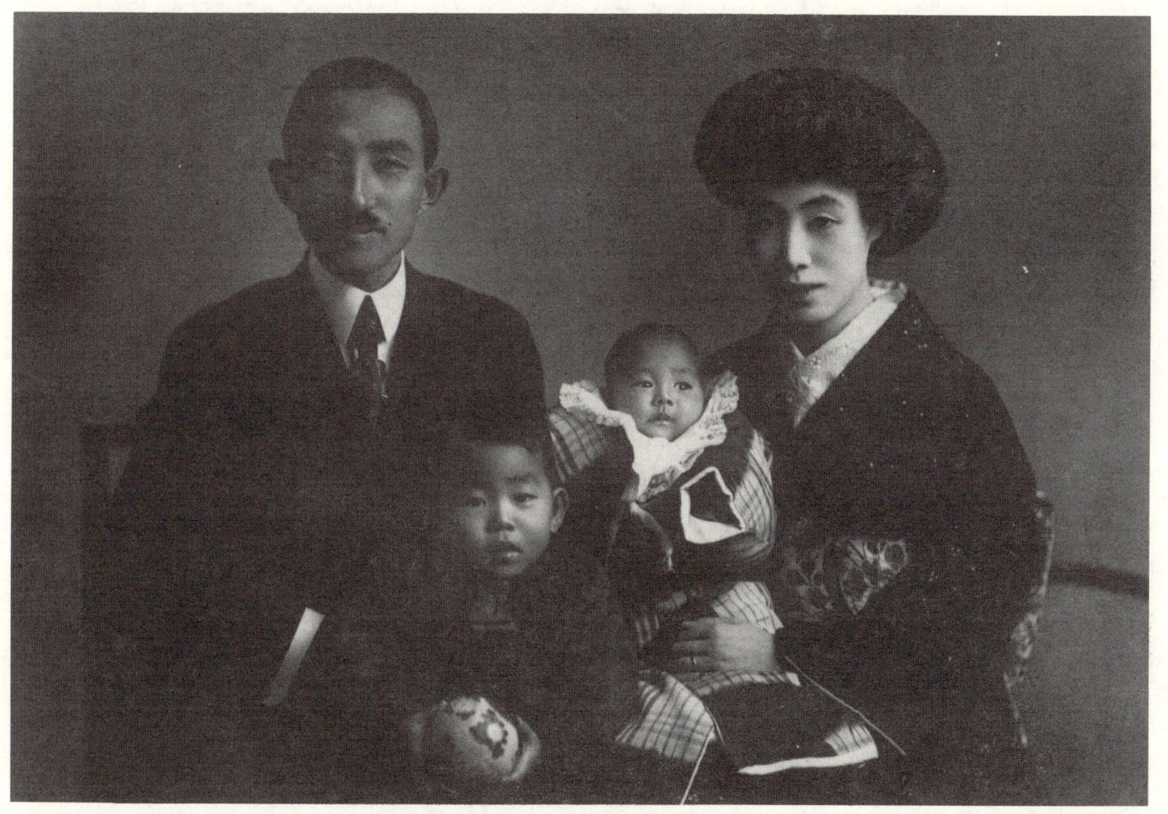

Baron Ishimoto Keikichi and Baroness Ishimoto Shidzue with their sons Arata and Tamio, 1920. Courtesy of Katô Shidzue.

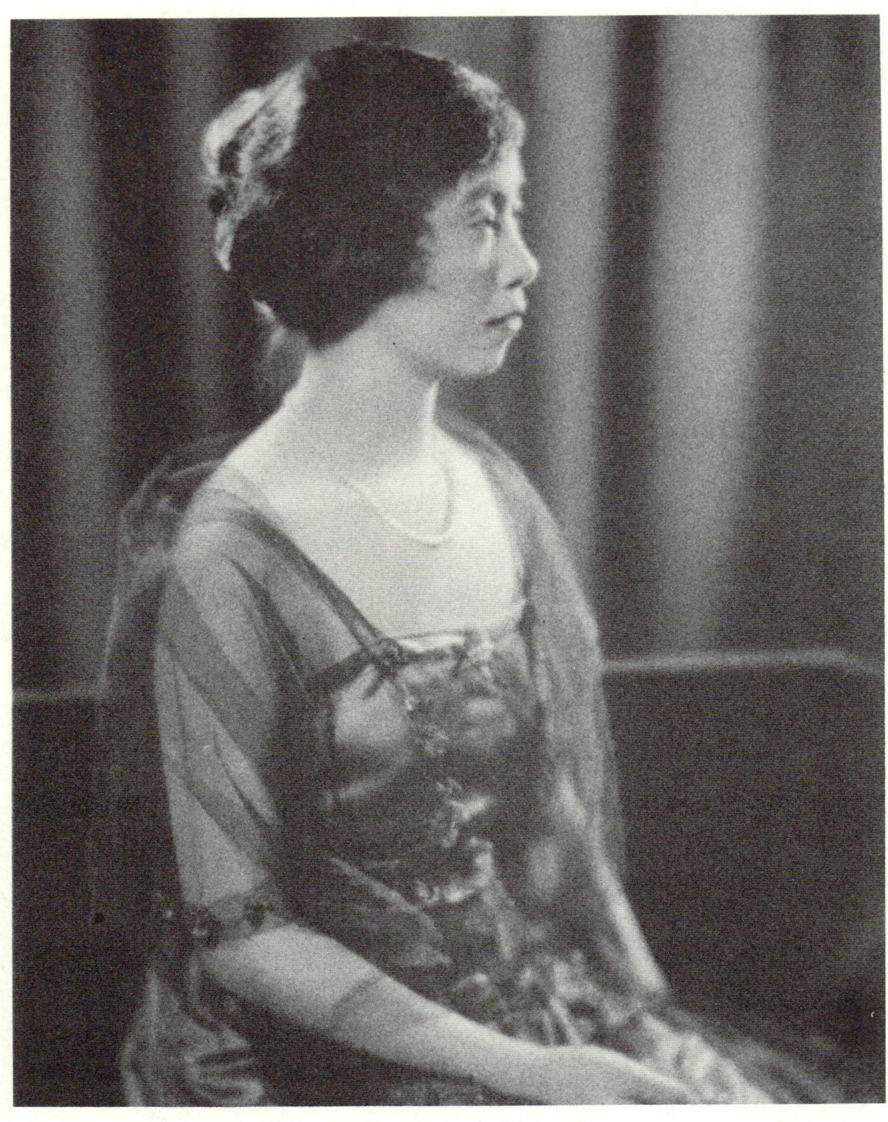

Baroness Ishimoto Shidzue after her graduation from the Ballard School, 1920. Courtesy of Katô Shidzue.

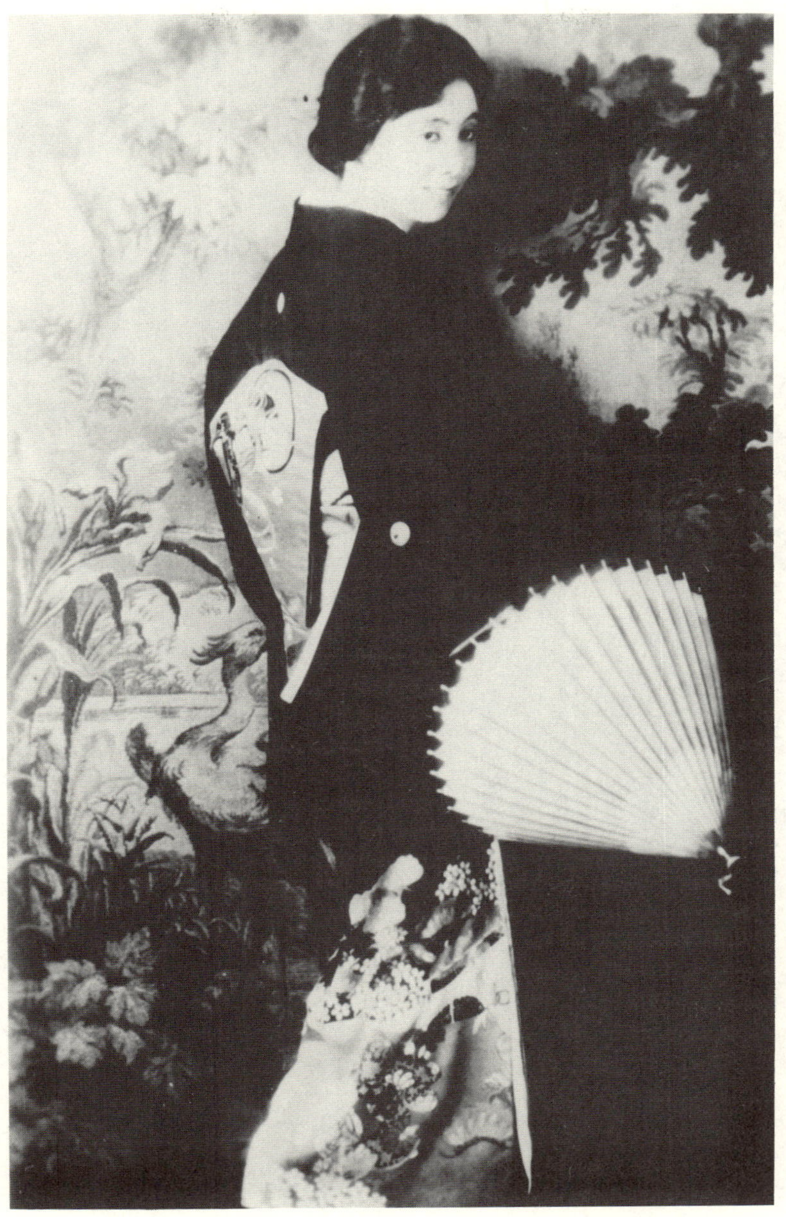

Baroness Ishimoto Shidzue (photo taken in a New York studio), 1924. Courtesy of the Sophia Smith Collection, Smith College. Reprinted with permission.

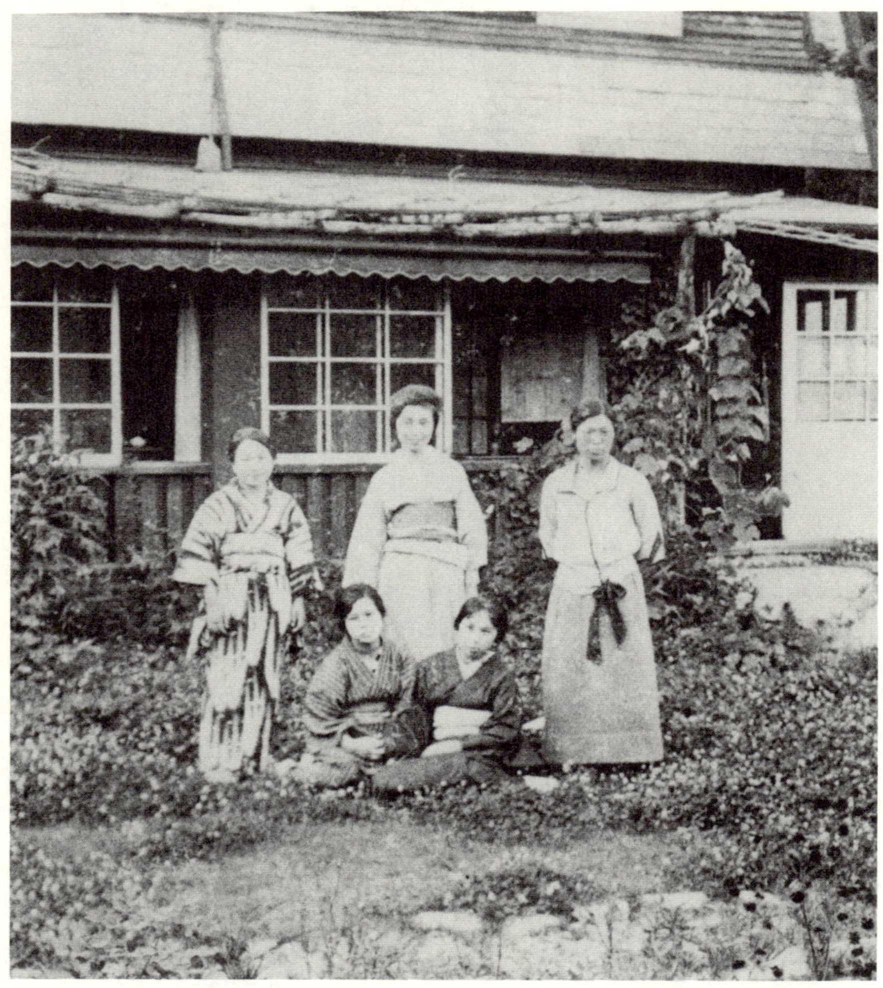

Women of the Japanese suffrage movement at the Ishimoto Kamakura villa in the mid-1920s. Standing left to right, Yamataka Shigeri, Katô Shidzue, and Ichikawa Fusae. Courtesy of Katô Shidzue.

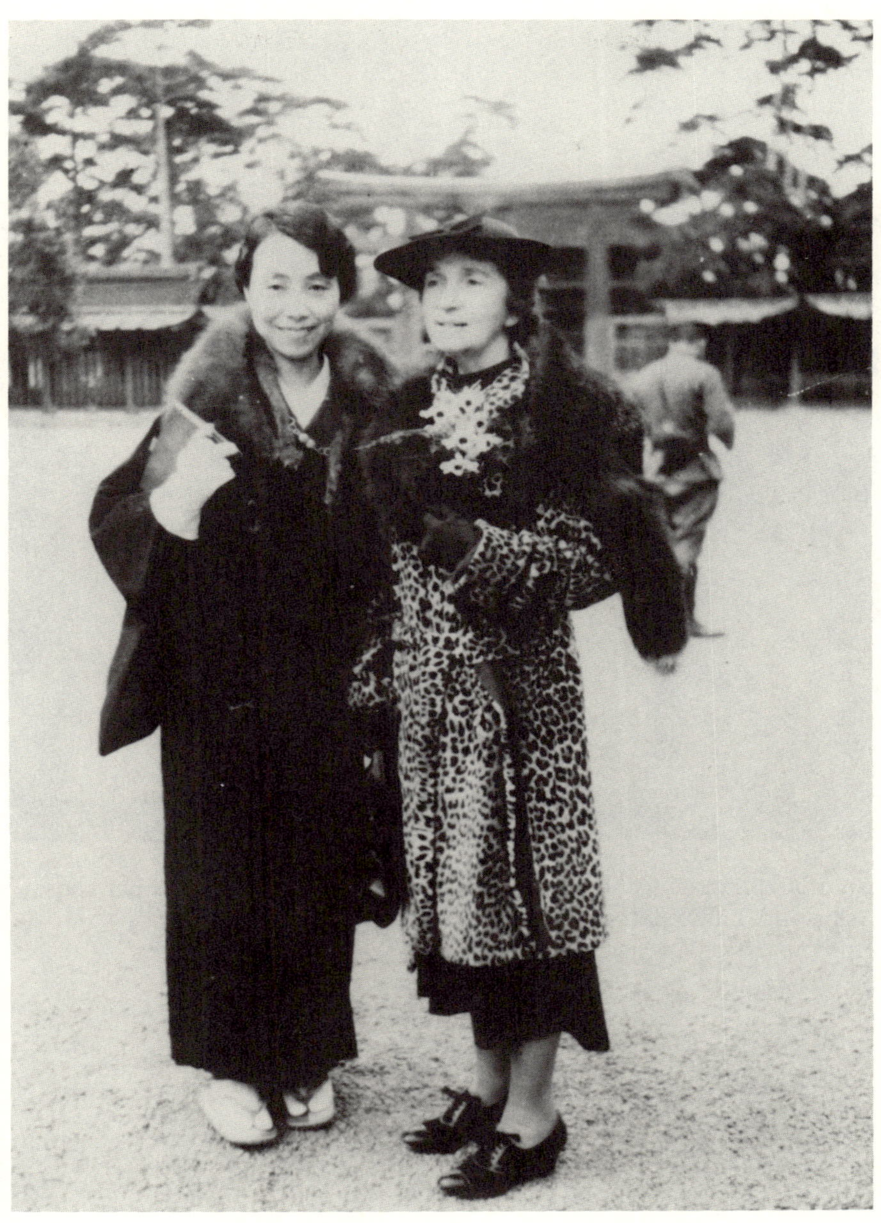

Ishimoto Shidzue and Margaret Sanger in Tokyo just after the January declaration of martial law, 1936. Courtesy of the Sophia Smith Collection, Smith College. Reprinted with permission.

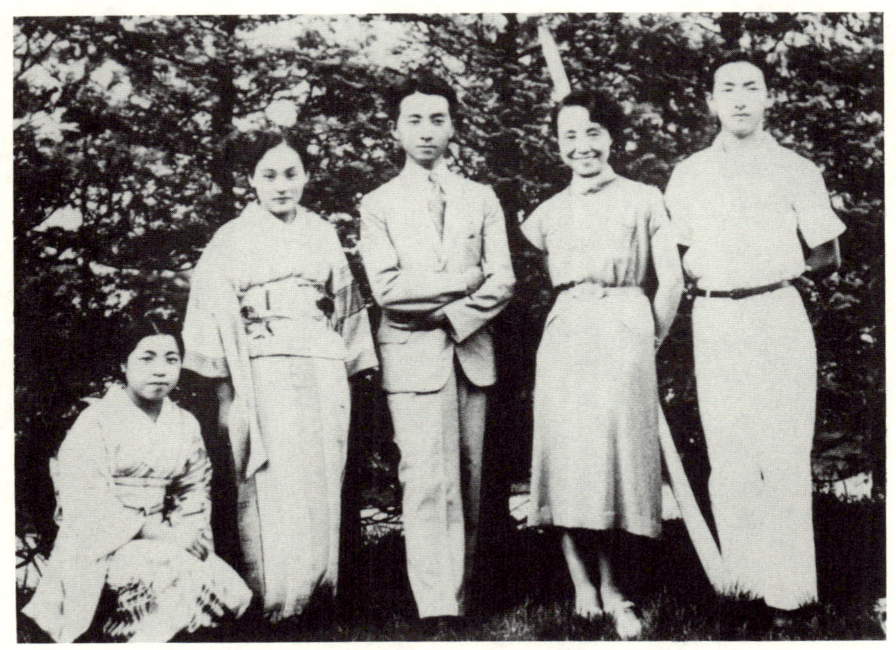

Ishimoto Shidzue (center) with a maid, the maid Sendai, and her sons Arata and Tamio (left to right) in her garden, 1937. Courtesy of Katô Shidzue.

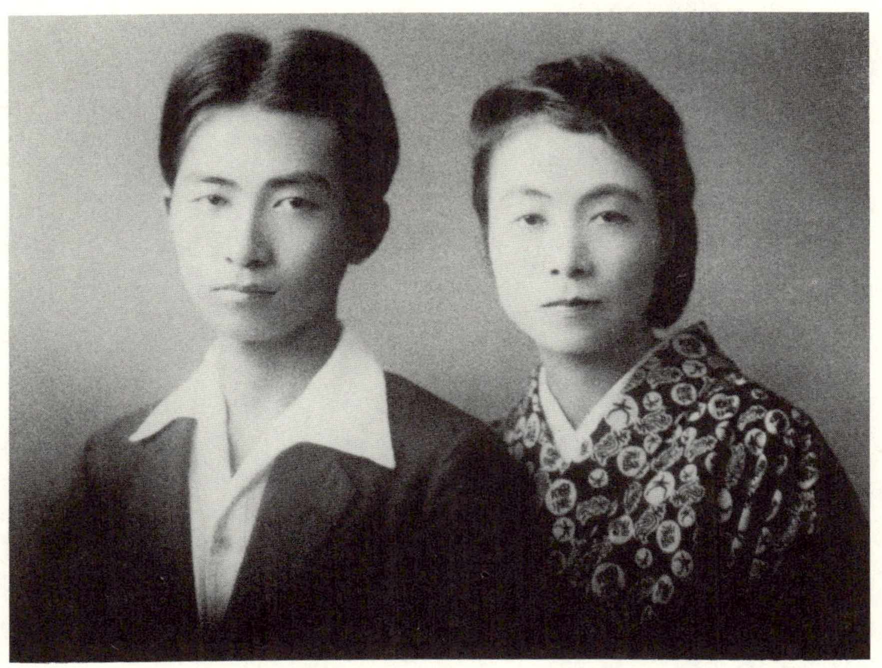

Ishimoto Shidzue with her son Ishimoto Arata upon his graduation from Kyoto University, 1942. Courtesy of Katô Shidzue.

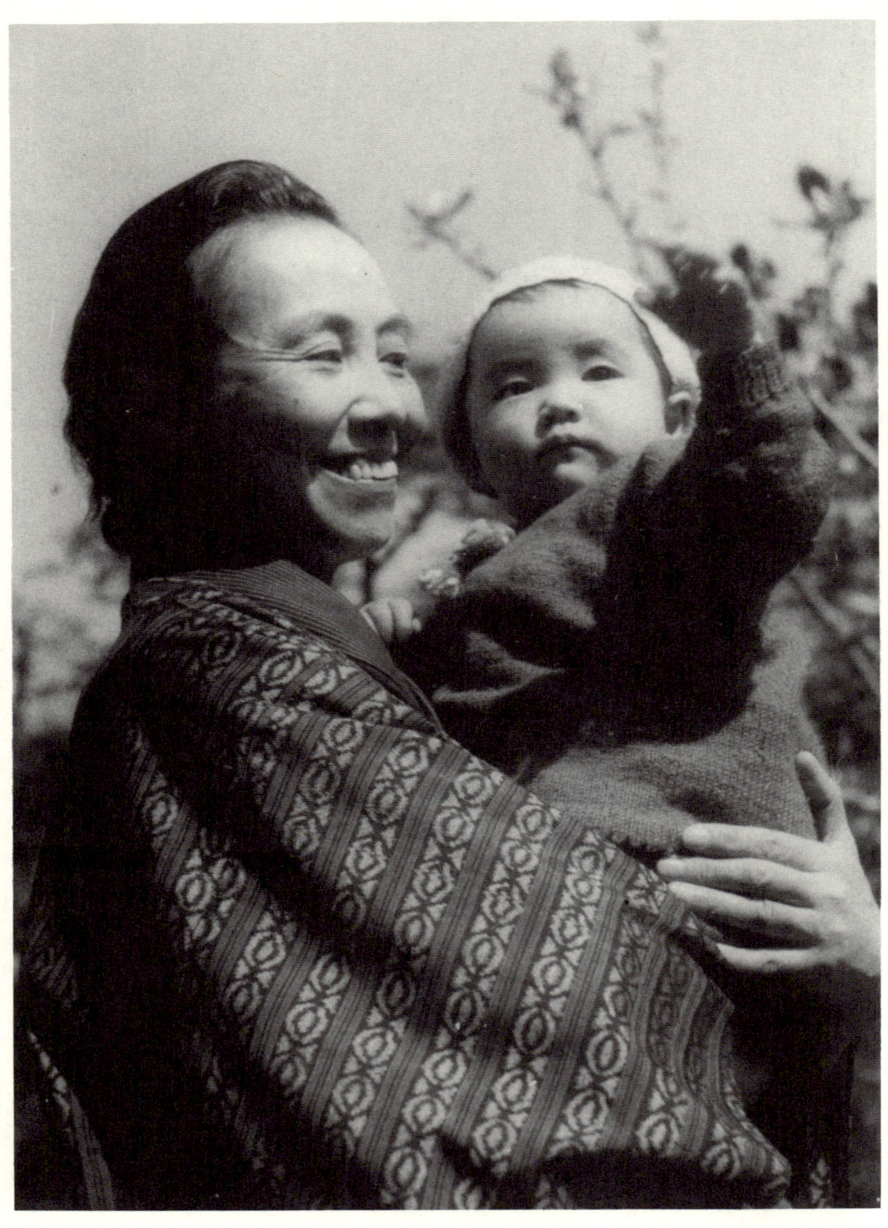

Katô Shidzue, accompanied by her daughter Taki, on her way to vote in the first democratic election, April 1946. Katô Shidzue won election to the Diet. Courtesy of Katô Shidzue.

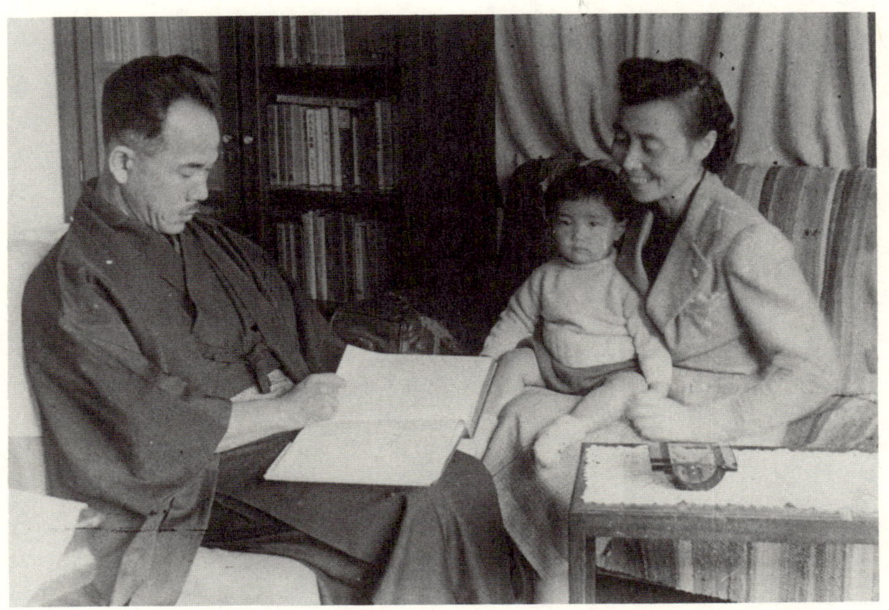

Katô Kanjû and Katô Shidzue at home with their daughter Taki, 1947. Courtesy of Katô Shidzue.

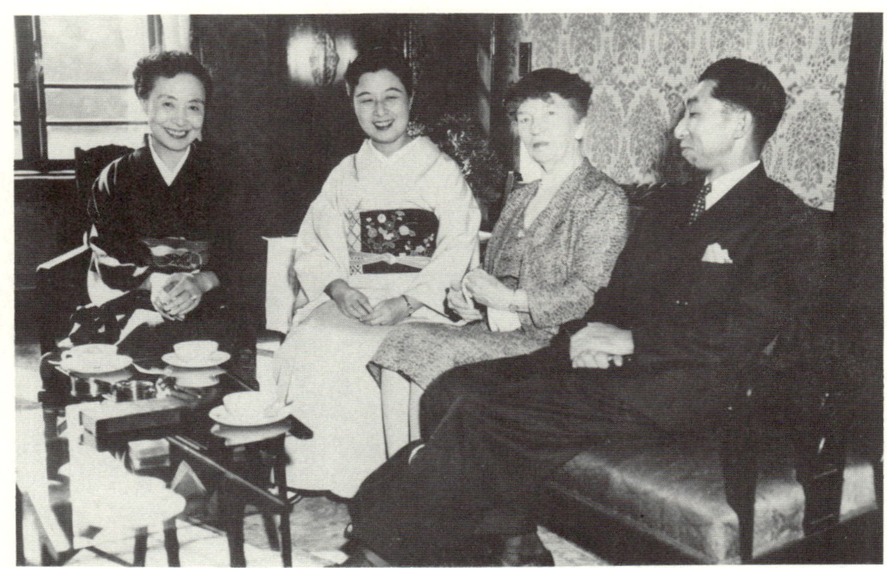

Senator Katô Shidzue and Margaret Sanger visit Prince and Princess Takamatsu at their Royal Highness's residence in Tokyo, 1955. Courtesy of the Sophia Smith Collection, Smith College. Reprinted by permission.

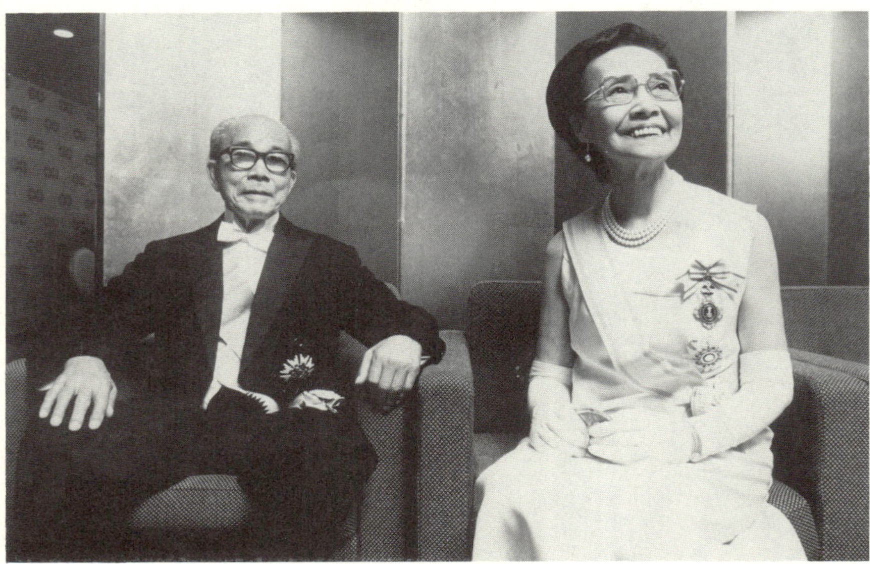

Senator Katô Shidzue and her husband Katô Kanjû, upon their receiving First Order of Merit awards from the Japanese government, 1972. Courtesy of Katô Shidzue.

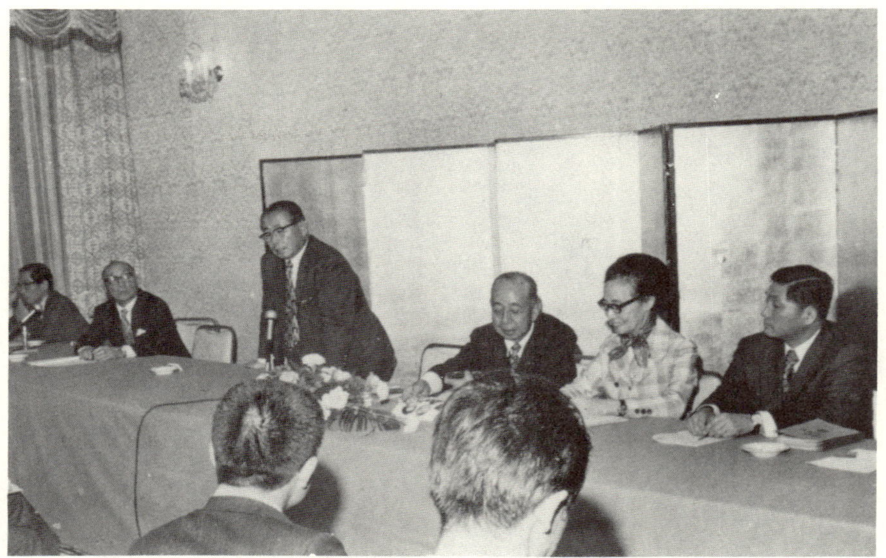

Senator Katô Shidzue and colleagues hold a press conference regarding their study of Asian population growth and family planning, 1973. On Katô's right is ex-prime minister Kishi Nobusuke. Courtesy of Ashino Yuriko and the Family Planning Federation of Japan. Reprinted by permission.

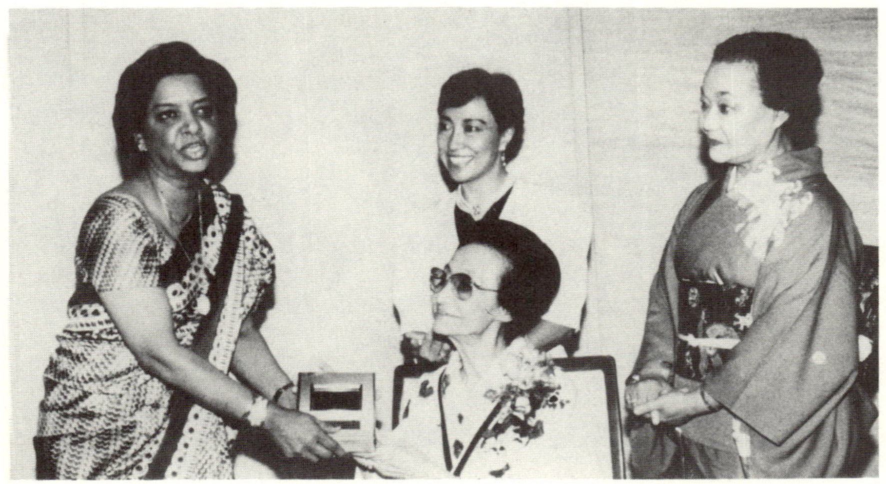

Katô Shidzue, with daughter Taki and stepdaughter Ohmori (Katô) Sumiko, receives a United Nations Population Award from Dr. Nafis Sadik, Executive Director of the United Nations Family Planning Agency, 1988. Courtesy of Katô Shidzue.

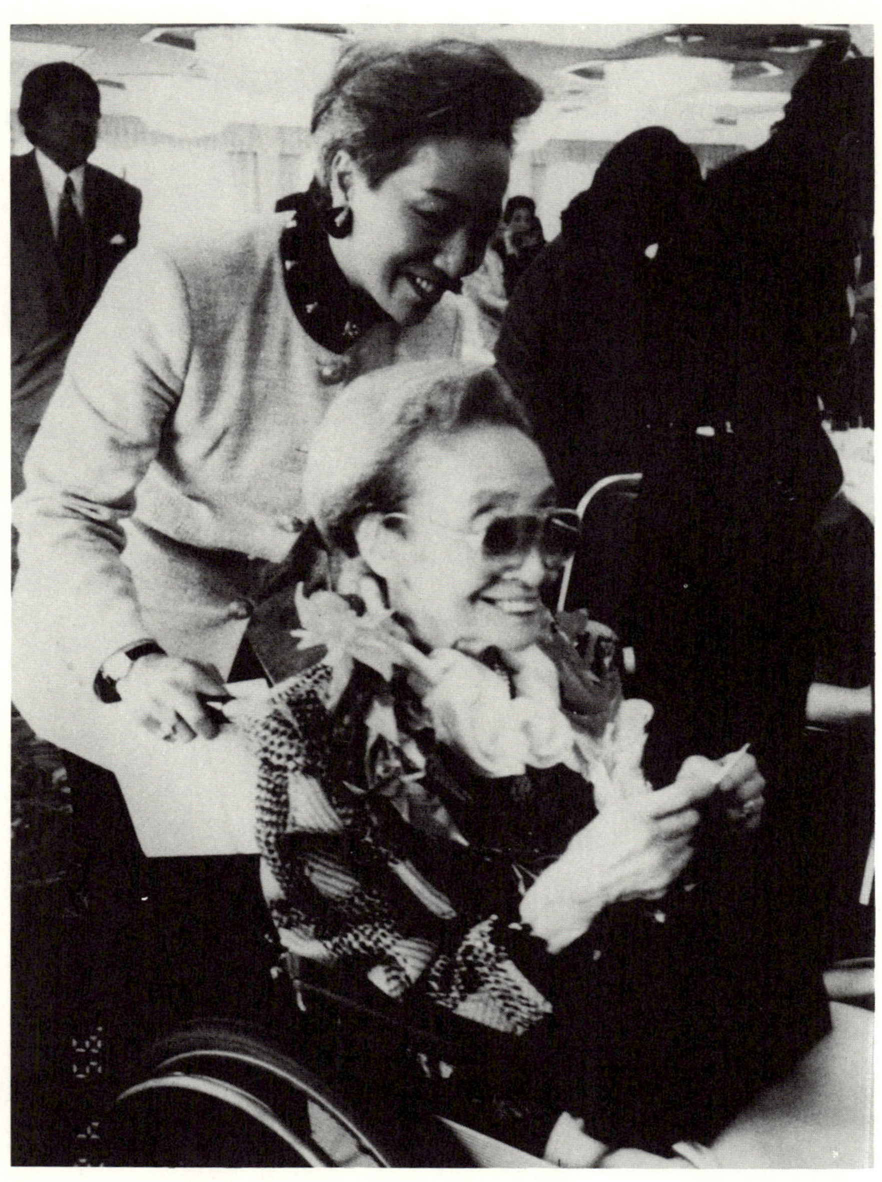

Katô Shidzue, with daughter Taki, at celebration of her long life, April, 1995. Courtesy of Katô Shidzue.

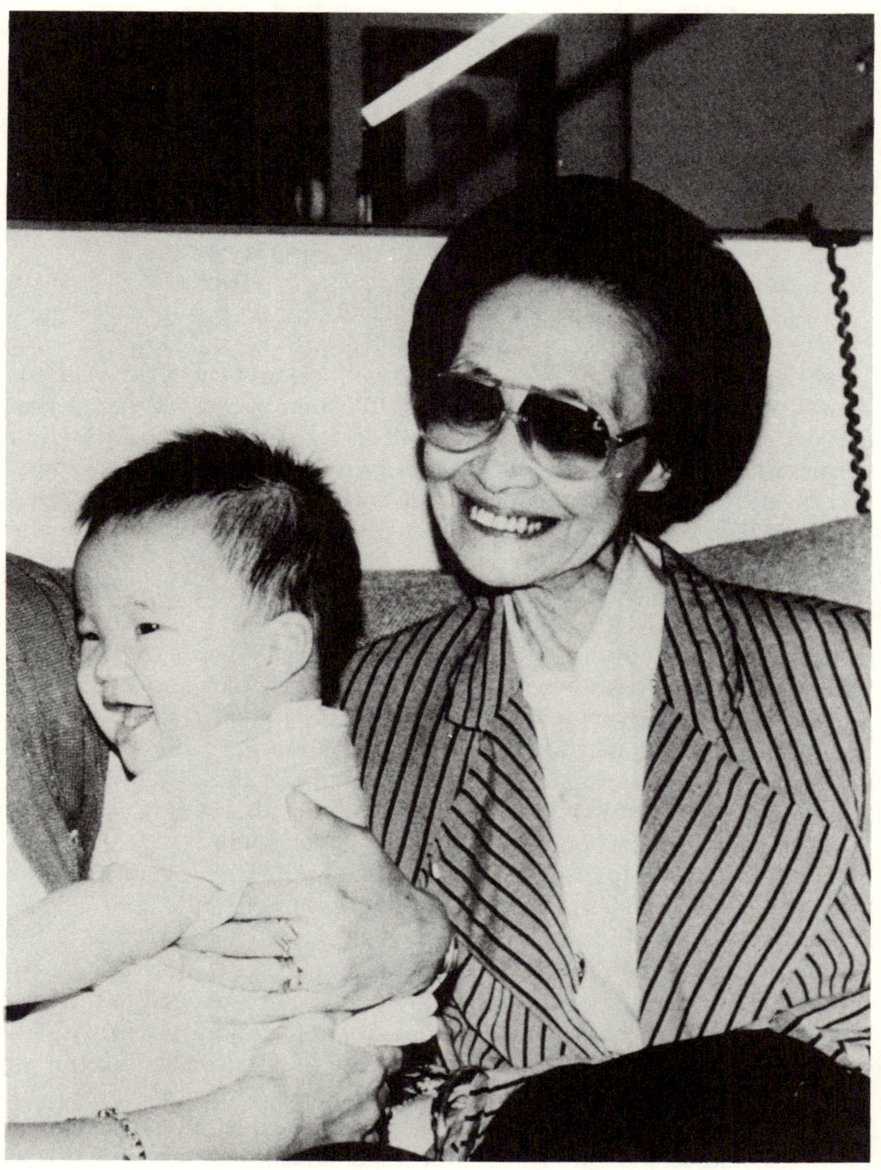

Katô Shidzue with her grandson (Taki's son), Sho, 1987. Courtesy of Katô Shidzue.

9

Rising from the Ashes (1945–1946)

The end of the war meant a return to political and social activism for both Katô Shidzue and her husband. Katô Kanjû began his changeover from a political pariah to leader within the first weeks following surrender as he plotted the renaissance of the socialist left-wing which had been destroyed in the arrests and party dissolution of December, 1937. Shidzue had not yet worked out her own role but knew that she would be publicly active in the new Japan. She saw the defeat of Japan's militarist leaders by the allies as an inevitable outcome, and she decried the sacrifice of "many invaluable lives and [the] formidable consumption of materials" which was Japan's tragedy. The time had finally come when "deep-rooted feudalism and militarism would be swept away," and she, together with others "who [had] adamantly resisted the militaristic policy of the government" would experience "a revolutionary change of social position." Kanjû would reenter elective party politics and Shidzue would work toward the "dream from [her] girlhood days," a life in government.[1]

The Allied Occupation began officially with the signing of the documents of surrender on the battleship *Missouri* on September 2, 1945. A short time later Shidzue and her husband were visited by one of the American servicemen stationed in Japan. Shidzue explained. "On my return from the country where I had gone in search of food, a difficult journey on trains crowded beyond imagination - a journey in which I carried on my back a large rucksack filled with potatoes, so heavy that I fell many times as I walked along the bomb-torn street from the station to my house - I was astonished to see a jeep standing in front of the house and beside it a visitor from General Headquarters of SCAP. It [a jeep parked outside] was quite exciting for a Japanese home at that time and I could not imagine what was going to happen. The visitor was Lt. Tom Tsukahara who had come to confirm that we [Kanjû and Shidzue] had no trace of war crimes in our background and some time later both Mr. Katô and myself were invited to see Capt. Arthur

Behrstock who asked our cooperation in securing information about the labor situation."[2]

In fact the U.S. government had previously gathered evidence which cleared both Katôs of any support of the defeated militarists. From 1941 to 1944 the intelligence department in Washington, known then as the Office of Strategic Services, had collected information on Japanese nationals. One such file, labeled "Friendly Persons" and containing just a few cards, included a report on "Baroness Shidzue (Hirota) Ishimoto," dating from 1941. In it an informant, a former missionary to Japan, testified based on hearsay, that "Baroness Ishimoto is reported as being anti-militaristic, and pro-American." Additional information was drawn from a 1938 *Who's Who,* and Shidzue's own *Facing Two Ways.* [3]

Information on Kanjû came primarily from a June 22, 1945, report[4] which the Director of Security and Intelligence in Washington had obtained in an interview with Darley Downs, a Congregational missionary, who had lived and taught in Japan from 1919-1941. He had been interned in the Philippines in 1942, and resided in the U.S. upon his release in February, 1945. Downs was considered by the interviewer to be "intelligent and observant" and his information "reliable." He described thirty-nine Japanese whom he believed would be useful to occupying forces. Both Katô Kanjû and Shidzue's Uncle, Tsurumi Yûsuke, were among those "personalities who, in his [Downs] opinion possess liberal attitudes on political, economic or religious matters...," were probably anti-militarist and could be expected to help the Americans.

Downs reported that Katô Kanjû had "headed the most radical Socialist Party in Japan," had been a member of the Japanese Diet, and had been jailed under charges of communist activity. "He is intellectually brilliant and has ample grievances against the old militarily dominated government." Downs believed that Katô would deny being a communist but would admit to the label of radical socialist. Downs had even more recent knowledge of Uncle Yûsuke, for he had been the first commandant of the Manila internment camp, Santo Tomas, and had been considered "reasonable and liberal in his administration" by the inmates. Tsurumi was characterized as one who could "certainly be counted on the liberal side among pre-war politicians." In addition, he had an excellent command of English and had published articles in the *Saturday Evening Post,* and other American magazines, before the war. Apparently, neither the fact that Katô was a radical socialist, nor that Tsurumi had commanded an internment camp, which included American civilian internees, barred these men, in Downs' mind, from consideration as potentially helpful to a triumphant American authority.

It is not surprising then, that Mr. and Mrs. Katô were taken to the offices of the Civil Information and Education Section [CIE] at the General Headquarters [GHQ] of the Supreme Commander of the Allied Powers [SCAP] for discussion during that first harried month of the Allied Occupation. Positive intelligence reports on Kanjû combined with the American authorities' interest in labor reform, labor union development, trust busting, and promotion of opposition political parties assured that he would be a fruitful informant for SCAP. Shidzue's strong pro-American reputation, good command of English, and knowledge of women's issues, a high priority at CIE, guaranteed an immediate interest in her as well.

During the September interview Shidzue was asked what Japanese women would most want to achieve in the post-war era. She replied broadly that they would want to see their rights as human beings assured. When asked to be more specific, she educated her questioners with a brief history of the pre-war women's movements which had purposefully sought to secure political and social liberation for women. At this point the interviewers expressed astonishment over the extent to which Japanese women had already made democratic demands, and the fact that these women were not "in the dark" about civil rights. Her interviewers next asked for suggestions of particular women who had been active in the past and might want to join with her to press once again for women's concerns. Using as her guide the names of leaders who had joined together in December, 1938, in the Organization for the Acquisition of Women's Suffrage, she suggested six women. Kubushiro Ochimi was general secretary of the 1938 suffrage organization, had been active from the early twenties in suffrage activities, was the Christian daughter of a minister who had been pastor of a Congregational Church in Oakland, California, and was active in Japan's Women's Christian Temperance Society [WCTU]. Ichikawa Fusae was a recognized leader of the suffrage movement, a member of the legislative section of the 1938 organization, and, independently of any American sponsorship, had already begun to reactivate the League of Women Voters. Kawasaki Natsu was in charge of petitions to the Diet in 1938. Kaneko Shigeri had been a Health Department employee in Tokyo before the war, and had worked with Shidzue on family planning issues. She was in charge of publicity for the 1938 attempt to gain voting rights. Yamataka Shigeri had been a member of Shidzue's Women's Birth Control League of Japan, and had worked on publicity for the franchise issue. Finally, Shidzue suggested Gauntlett Tsuneko , who had been in charge of finances in 1938. Born Yamada, she had married a British teacher, who had become a naturalized Japanese citizen before the end of the war. She was active in the WCTU and the Women's Peace Association. After bringing the names of these prominent women to the attention of CIE officials, Shidzue emphasized her unalterable position that the creation of a democratic Japan without full political rights for women would be meaningless.[5]

During the same interview Kanjû was questioned about the pre-war labor movement and about labor issues which could be expected to arise in these first few months.[6] Shidzue remembered this interview as unthreatening and characterized the atmosphere as one of mutual respect. This meeting marked the beginning of Shidzue's intimate relationship with officials at GHQ. The experience also generated her first real thoughts about resurrecting a life of social activism and inaugurating political activities. For Kanjû the meeting was merely an interesting side trip on his journey back to political power.

Resurrection of Socialist Politics

The Emperor's broadcast announcing the end of the war had motivated several prewar socialist leaders, right, center, and left, to leave their sanctuaries and gather together to plan for a socialist position in the new Japan. Within ten days of surrender Katô Kanjû had arranged a Tokyo meeting for about a dozen leftists who had belonged to his Proletarian Party, the Social Masses Party and the Labor-Farmer Group. While those gathered at the meeting clearly wanted to establish one socialist party, there was disagreement over just who should be invited to join. Even the inclusion of Katô and his close associate Suzuki Mosaburô was objected to by some right and center socialists because of their far left philosophy.[7] Discussion did not extend, however, to the issue of inviting women to join. The left remained unanimously imbued with its prewar sense of inequality.

On September 22nd leaders of the prewar proletarian parties called a meeting which included members of each faction of the non-communist left.[8] The twelve sitting Diet members associated with the pre-war left were included even though they had publicly supported the war. After all, as one Dietman commented, unlike representatives in the British Parliament, members of the Diet could be arrested for criticizing the war, and British prisons were like smart apartments compared to the jails in Japan. Support for the war, then, was not cause for automatic rejection. On the other hand the group decided to exclude titled nobility like Prince Tokugawa because the "social masses" would not be able to identify with such people. Those assembled determined that they would adopt a flexible policy toward the right, that is the Liberal Party [Jiyûtô] and Progressive Party [Shinpotô], and toward the left, the Communist Party [Kyôsantô].

This new party core met again in early October so that a preparatory committee of nineteen could hammer out a platform. The committee, heavily weighted toward the right with Katô and Suzuki the primary representatives on the left, experienced great difficulty agreeing. By October 20th they finally proclaimed socialist policies on economic, financial, labor, agricultural, cultural, and women's affairs which were submitted to the membership as a whole. More substantively, the party would push for a labor ministry and campaign for recognition of labor unions, minimum wage laws, a 48 hour week, and unemployment insurance. A vague statement on land reform contained a demand for "fundamental revision of the present system relative to the treatment of arable land," and there were demands involving mechanization, state control of fertilizers, and organizations for farmers and fishermen. Social insurance and relief measures for the war wounded and for civilians who had suffered from the air-raids were proposed. They also advocated scientific research, increased years of compulsory education and adoption of Esperanto as an international language. Its plank on women included a demand for equal rights for women in employment, politics, and education.[9] This plank, like all the others, were decided without the participation of any women.

A political advisor at SCAP observed, "From the point of view of personnel and program, the Socialist Party at present seems to offer the most hope for political and economic reforms in Japan. Its weakness is its disunity; there is a vast difference for example, between the right wing represented by Toyohiko Kagawa and the left of Kanjû Katô. It remains to be seen whether the party can hold its various components together. If so, it may attain considerable political power."[10] Indeed the difference proved continuously contentious and finally too great. The party split just before the American overlords left and full control over its own affairs was returned to Japan in 1952.

Communist Party political prisoners were released from Fûchû Prison on October 10th. On October 19th a JCP representative, met with a few Socialist Party leaders to discuss the possibility of a "popular front," but since the socialists could not agree with communist demands for the abolition of the emperor system or for government confiscation of private property, there was no possibility of uniting these left-wing parties. Just the same those on the right lumped the JSP and JCP together and complained that the Americans at SCAP were paying altogether too much attention to the Japanese left-wing. As one contemporary noted, "The Prince [Konoe] lamented that the situation is heading directly towards communism,....Also, it is as if they are planning 'communization.' The likes of Katô Kanjû frequent headquarters."[11] The Japanese right believed Kanjû had achieved the status of a much too "friendly person" at SCAP.

On the morning of November 2nd, the official inauguration of the Japan Socialist Party [Nippon shakaitô] took place at Hibiya Hall, which was filled with a capacity crowd of about 2600 people. After eight speakers, including Katô Kanjû, addressed the crowd a seventeen member Executive Committee headed by Secretary-General Katayama Tetsu, was installed. Four seats on the committee were assigned to the left and included the two old friends from the Proletarian Party, Katô and Suzuki. Katô was also appointed Chief of the Labor Organization Liaison Section and a third left-wing member, Kuroda Hisao, was made Chief of the Women's Section, since no women had yet been invited to join the party.[12]

Women, however, did not wait for invitations from men to begin their political activity. At exactly the same moment socialist men held their August organizational meeting, a group of women gathered to discuss their role in the postwar era. On August 25th seventy-two women joined to form the Women's Committee on Postwar Countermeasures [Sengo taisaku fujin iinkai]. The women gathered had been prominent in a variety of prewar and wartime activities extending from early protests against the militarists to full support for the war effort. Although they represented a broad spectrum of viewpoints, all were agreed on their determination to achieve equality with men including full political rights.[13]

It took Katô Shidzue a few weeks longer than the August Women's Committee to find her role in the "new Japan." But then, she had a six month old baby to care for and a husband too busy with national politics to help out at home. Finding food and other life sustaining necessities in the midst of the rubble of destruction was a full time job for Shidzue and the other Tokyo citizens in the fall of 1945. Although the Katôs were more fortunate than most, for their house had withstood the bombing, Shidzue still had to make arduous trips to the countryside in search of food. Elation over a new political era did not provide nourishment for her daughter. Even so, early contact with SCAP officials and observation of her husband and other socialists generated a political excitement that she could not resist.

When Lt. Ethel B. Weed joined the staff at CIE in October her job as Women's Information Officer in the Women's Affairs Branch was to formulate policy in areas affecting Japanese women and to develop "programs for the dissemination of information pertinent to the reorientation and democratization of Japanese women in [the] political, economic, and social fields."[14] To effectively carry out her assignment Lt. Weed began immediately assembling a group of Japanese women who had been active in suffrage and social movements before the war. Katô Shidzue became a prominent member as did the women she had named in her September CIE interview. The mutual respect and friendship which developed between Weed and Katô in their first weeks of contact is readily evident from the many meetings, and phone calls which are logged in Occupation documents. The extraordinary warmth of the relationship is further attested to in admiring references to Katô in letters to Margaret Sanger, Mary Beard, and other Americans. In addition Weed gave Katô the special privilege of using her name and office address as a mail box for letters, educational materials, and an occasional gift from friends in America, during the period when Japanese were not permitted international postal rights. There are no comparable references in the archival material or in Weed's personal correspondence of similar privileges extended to any one else during these early days of Occupation. The resultant influence of Katô Shidzue on the Women's Affairs Branch in general and Weed in particular is striking and this positive American connection forms a significant feature of Katô's own political and social attitudes.[15]

Rediscovered by American Friends

By the end of October, 1945, Shidzue's American friends had received the news through intermediary sources that their dear Baroness Ishimoto had survived the war. Roger Baldwin of the ACLU heard through private correspondence from a military friend serving in Japan. On September 20th Lt. Col. P. F. "Mac" McLamb wrote Baldwin a long letter describing his first impressions of defeated and occupied Japan. He also offered to try to locate anyone Baldwin might want to find. Baldwin wrote back immediately thanking Mac for a "close-up unobtainable in the press" and asked for information on "two Japanese liberals.... One of them is the well-known trade union leader, Kosiju Cato [sic] who has been in prison. The other is Baroness Ishimoto, the leader of the women's rights movement and in the birth control campaign. She, too has been in prison during the war but was paroled to her distinguished family." He enclosed a letter to the Baroness offering to help her establish a civil liberties union in Japan. Baldwin had been on the same New York platform with Kanjû in 1935 and had met Shidzue through their mutual friend, Margaret Sanger.[16]

By late October MacLamb could describe for Baldwin his successful search. He began his efforts with inquiries "through the proper people in GHQ" who told him that "records" for the two Japanese in question "were favorable and they were glad to have me deliver your letter." Following advice given at GHQ, Mac went to Metropolitan Police Headquarters where he found a civilian employee who "turned out to be a friendly and accommodating fellow and an excellent interpreter." He agreed to accompany the colonel and a major friend on their continuing search. Although the search proved difficult, the Japanese was a "never-say-uncle man" and eventually they found the Ishimoto residence. To their surprise, the woman who came to the door told them that "the lady in question now lives at the home of Kanji [sic] Kato San." Recalling that that was the other name Baldwin had mentioned, Mac determined that they "were on the right trail."

Later that evening they found the Katô house, knocked, asked for the Baroness, and were "invited to remove our shoes and come into the library (I guess you would call it that). Presently a very fine lady, doubtless with much charm, poise, culture, and education entered the room. I asked if she were the Baroness and she explained (before I could introduce myself) that she was formerly the Baroness but was now married 'with' Mr. Kanji [sic] Kato. She was reserved and very serious. She read your letter slowly and with much apparent thought. Finally she smiled for the first time, made excuses for her English which has suffered from lack of use these past years, and relaxed considerably. She seemed ever so grateful for your letter and for my having delivered it. She wanted to know how she could write you, and, knowing that there are yet no civil mail services out of Japan, I offered to send any letter she wanted to you through the Army postal service."

This meeting led to an invitation to meet with both Kanjû and Shidzue at Radio Tokyo on October 23rd. There they were "joined by some of their wealthy Japanese friends." From the radio station they went to the home of one of their "wealthy" friends who lived "next door to Prince Konoye [sic], a former Premier of Japan and now coming back into something of his own unless real liberalism blooms from the start!" He did not have much opportunity to converse with the former Baroness, and her husband spoke no English, but he did learn that Mr. Katô was "thinking of a political party for his labor followers." Obviously McLamb was not familiar with Socialist Party developments and Kanjû's active role. On the same evening Mrs. Katô expressed to McLamb her interest in taking Baldwin up on his offer to help start a civil liberties union in Japan. She was either being polite, keeping her options open, or had not yet determined the precise nature of the activist role she would play in the postwar era, for this never came to anything. On the whole, however, politics was not a major theme of the evening, for this was a party to entertain the American.

The assembled group, undoubtedly chosen by Shidzue, wanted to show Mac "something of Japanese life, customs, food, etc. in the top families; and to get acquainted." At the end of the evening Shidzue "urgently begged me to join her and her husband on a visit to other wealthy friends in the nearby city of Atami next Sunday."

Writing Baldwin on October 29th, McLamb described his visit to Atami "with the Katos and some of their wealthy friends. They went 'all out' to honor and entertain me and a few other officers.... Have noted that the Katos live well above the level of Japanese masses and laborers. Their wealthy friend in Atami was represented as being in sympathy with Kanju Kato's 'movement'. With my limited knowledge of Japan and age-old conditions here, I do not readily understand these well-to-do liberals and their intentions to better the conditions and opportunities of Japanese, real improvement cannot come about overnight. Some start, however, must be made - and the sooner the better." McLamb enclosed a note from Shidzue expressing how delighted she was to receive Baldwin's letter, the "first news from friends in America." She continued, "Mr. Kanjû Katô and I were married during the war, so we are ready to work together for our convictions. We are very interested in establishing a union to defend civil liberties in Japan." She closed with kind words for General MacArthur's team at GHQ and commented, also, that "intellectual Japanese are looking forward to establishing a better country for ourselves although conditions of food and transportation are very critical now."

This last remark stands in striking contrast with McLamb's continued emphasis on the "wealth" he saw exhibited by the Katôs and their friends amidst devastated Tokyo. His observations were perhaps influenced by the houses which he visited, dwellings of the elite which had survived amidst the general destruction. Also, he was no doubt overwhelmed by traditional Japanese hospitality which, even in the face of disaster, demands that guests be treated with the best and the most expensive. Just who owned the homes he visited is not certain, but they were surely a part of the prewar upper class; just how they got the food and drink to entertain, is also unknown, but the black market comes to mind. A little money, regardless of how hard it was to come by, entertaining an American military officer attached to GHQ was not a bad investment. As for the Katôs in particular, there is no doubt they enjoyed a house above the level of most of their burnt out neighbors, but that they had substantial material well-being beyond that seems far-fetched given the descriptions by other observers. It is noteworthy that McLamb had concluded that the Katôs lived well, primarily based what their "friends" possessed.

Campaigning for the Diet

Katô Shidzue had never seriously considered devoting her political energies to organizing a civil liberties union, but she benefited from the association with Col. McLamb and other American officials which he introduced her to.[17] By November, 1945, Shidzue had decided that her future contribution to the "new Japan" would be elective politics. She had not yet determined a party affiliation, in fact, no women had been invited to join any postwar party, and it was not yet legal for women to vote or run for office. It was her trust in the American promise of equal political rights for women, that gave her the vision to project a professional future which was not yet possible.

On October 10th MacArthur ordered the new Prime Minister, Shidehara Kijûrô, to facilitate Diet enactment of five basic principles, the first of which demanded passage of an election law providing women the right to vote and run for office. The Diet which was to legislate this change consisted of sitting wartime members primarily from established parties on the right. After much debate and foot dragging, this wartime Diet passed MacArthur's demanded equal rights elective law on December 15th. A month before this dramatic legislative action, on November 14th, Katô Shidzue became the first woman to announce her intention to run for a seat in the House of Representatives at such time as new election laws permitted.

Everyone expected January elections. SCAP, however, wanted time to institute a purge of public officials deemed responsible for the war, before elections took place. This purge directive effectively removed at least 83% of the incumbent representatives. Hardest hit were the members of what had become the Progressive Party, which lost 260 of its 274 founding members including Secretary-General Tsurumi Yûsuke, Shidzue's favorite uncle. Even the JSP was decimated. Of the original seventeen founders ten were purged, representing ten of twelve sitting Diet members.[18] Elections were set for April 10th, and the newly reconstituted parties scrambled for candidates. Kanjû announced for the Socialist Party, Shidzue, who began her campaign as an independent, eventually joined the Socialist ranks as well.

Newspapers highlighted Shidzue as the first woman to seek government office, identifying her as the former Baroness Ishimoto. Her prewar role in Japan's birth control movement and association with the famous American birth control advocate, Margaret Sanger, was restated in each article. In interviews she always spoke first about her 1937 arrest, and then enumerated the issues stressed in her campaign: democratization of women's lives and promotion of family planning.

For her control of family size was inextricably intertwined with improved quality of life, and both were essential if women were to enjoy civil rights and equality with men.[19]

Shidzue credited "a general," Brig. Gen. Kermit "Ken" R. Dyke,[20] chief of CIE, for suggesting that she run. He had summoned her to his office and asked why she had not announced her candidacy. She protested that her husband was campaigning, and they couldn't both run. The general chastised her saying, "Haven't you heard that women have received the franchise? Wouldn't it be good if a prewar leader in the women's movement continued her work?" Her arguments against running went something like this; Kanjû would definitely run and two candidates from one household would be too expensive; there was no possibility that she could finance her own campaign, and it was unlikely that the Socialist Party or any other group would come to her aid; and, finally, someone had to maintain the household with its two teen-aged children (Kanjû's son and daughter) and an infant not yet one. On top of everything else, her husband, who would run from his "home" district of Nagoya, a distance of a little over 200 miles from Tokyo, would be out of town a lot and would need much support. Shidzue's responsibilities were great, and her time was not her own. She did, however, agree to consider General Dyke's suggestion. After she received unexpected financing from a factory owner friend of Kanjû's, husband and wife agreed that she should run. The money was repayment of a debt from the thirties, and her underwriter was the man who had invested Shidzue's royalties from *Facing Two Ways* in an endeavor which went bankrupt and then skipped off to Manchuria. In 1945 he reappeared and offered money for her campaign.[21]

She began her campaign immediately. Her response was so quick, in fact, that, in spite of Shidzue's autobiographical protestations, it is difficult to believe this had not been her intention all along; perhaps she felt that she should hide, to some extent, her eagerness to step out of the home and onto the political stage. Since no women had yet been invited to join parties, she sought support as an independent. She was frugal with her money, seeking votes with her voice and a megaphone as she walked all over Tokyo's large second district. Whenever she could, she gave lectures, spoke at schools, put up posters, and gave speeches on street corners. It was a truly populist campaign. Admitting that her political statements were not brilliant, or theoretical, but, rather, practical, she would tell her constituents, "If I am elected I will ask for increases in rations of rice, sugar and tobacco." She recognized that Japan, a defeated nation, had to ask its conquerors for everything and so she urged the people to go to GHQ and ask for staples, for meat, to ask that Japanese soldiers be returned home immediately, but, in any event, to speak up, raising their voices in protest.

From the beginning Shidzue recognized the usefulness of radio for educating her constituents about issues. Fortunately, her associations with CIE afforded her substantial radio access both on the air and behind the scenes, and she became adroit at building support through frequent use of air time. She would hitchhike rides in GI jeeps, saying, "I am electioneering and I need to get from here to NHK [BCJ] radio to make a political announcement. Could you take me?"[22] This campaign method reached more people in less time than leg power and megaphones. Radio was critical to Shidzue's success.

On a much larger scale radio was crucial to SCAP's plans to democratize the country as a whole. Consequently, one of its first actions had been to take "advisory" control of radio broadcasting, and Occupation officials continued to direct and censor this medium throughout its tenure of power. Declaring that the American goal was minimum interference in Japanese engineered and programmed broadcasting, SCAP set up a Japanese supervisory committee which would work with a designated group of Americans to make sure that SCAP's basic regulations were met while the Japanese would be permitted to provide day to day radio programming and management. The American overseers did insist that the news component of programming be "truthful," that nothing broadcast "interfere with domestic tranquillity," or express "destructive criticism of the Occupation." Of course, SCAP officials retained the right to censor programming in accord with their interpretation of these regulations.

SCAP established a division at CIE to oversee and monitor four types of programming: providing for 1) complete information about Occupation objectives and directives; 2) accurate and well-balanced news; 3) comments by qualified observers on matters of national interest; and 4) educational, cultural, and entertainment which responded to listener suggestions. Radio was expected to advance concepts of peace and security, aid the establishment of a democratic government, and protect the rights and freedoms of the people as defined by Occupation directives. To assure these goals SCAP controlled over 10% of all programming and retained the right to censor the rest.[23]

Given the fact that Shidzue agreed with SCAP's evaluation of radio's potential for generating political and social change, it is not surprising that she participated eagerly in Occupation sponsored programming, and, accepted an invitation to join the Japanese committee created by SCAP to advise the Broadcasting Corporation of Japan [BCJ]. In this way she gained access to radio broadcasting for her own political campaign, could help Lt. Weed's Women's Affairs

Branch launch various educational programs for women, and had a new medium through which to propagate family planning.

One of the most successful daytime programs, was the "Women's Hour." This was a daily show which encouraged women to exchange ideas on social and political issues and highlighted women's new political rights and the April elections. In the evening a variety of forums[24] encouraged women to form organizations, publish magazines, and participate in other activities related to women's issues. Evening programming was especially useful for political candidates, and Shidzue gained further exposure through regular participation. For example, in December she was a guest on "Round Table of the Air." The featured topic that evening was "Women's Place in Japanese Democracy," a controversial issue given the strong opinions generated by the new law which enfranchised women. During the discussion Katô and Home Minister Horikiri Zenjirô, the first highly placed government official to appear on such a program, squared off on the general question of women's participation in politics versus women's performance of traditional roles in the home. This was probably the first serious public debate of public vs. private roles for women. The nature of the discussion called into question substantial sections of Japan's family system as embodied in the Meiji Civil Code of 1898. The Home Minister was a perfect foil for Katô, ˜ who displayed a feminist attitude as she took the "radical side in defense of womanhood." This was also her first opportunity to speak against the traditional family system and the way in which it imprisoned and oppressed women, a theme she would continue to emphasize in the Diet after her election. She also used this national platform to discuss birth control issues, a topic which stirred considerable interest in her radio audience. Americans who commented on this successful program were strongly biased in Katô's favor. One commented that the "forum in which Mrs. Katô quizzed the Home Minister on his position regarding women was a major triumph in so far as women were concerned. He has been reactionary at every turn, and women have resented it." Shidzue returned to the air on January 31st to moderate the program "Should Birth Control Be Legalized." This time the forum included a social worker, a doctor, a midwife, and a mother discussing the effects that use of contraceptives might have on the health and welfare of mothers and children. The issue was particularly daring since eugenic laws passed in the early 40s still prohibited the use of contraceptives.[25]

The chief of SCAP's information operations during the first few months of the Occupation was Bradford Smith, who "made several crucial recommendations for immediate and long-range goals, set in motion many media projects, and devised information and democratization themes. Smith also had extensive prewar experience in Japan and helped Dyke find cooperative Japanese."[26] It will be remembered that Bradford Smith was a good friend of Shidzue's in the 30s and that he and his wife entertained Shidzue and Arata in Kobe in 1939. It is not surprising, then, that in January, 1946, when SCAP created a committee to advise BCJ, Katô Shidzue was asked to join. The new committee was mandated to "draft a reorganization of the Broadcasting Corporation of Japan, to establish a screening system to remove both purgeable and ultra-radical personnel, to amend employment, pay and promotion methods, to establish a labor management committee, and to recommend three candidates for the position of president." There were seventeen appointed to this committee including three women, Katô, Miyamoto Yuriko, and Maki Yuko, one Socialist and two Communist Party members. Baba Tsunego, President of *Yomiuri Newspaper,* was appointed interim chairman.[27]

The committee met initially with General Dyke, who lectured them: "Radio belongs to the people. Radio should be a mirror of all opinion on all controversial subjects. Facilities of radio should be made available to all parties. Radio does not take sides with any party or Government in power." He did not include any comment on the need to refrain from criticism of Occupation personnel or policies. The newspaper recounting the event did not remark on the hypocrisy of Dyke's statements considering the censorship role of SCAP for no such criticism could be made because of that unmentioned self censorship rule. A second speaker emphasized that the committee "should meet in an atmosphere of free, open and purposeful deliberation. Only under such circumstances would the needs and desires of the people of Japan be fully met."[28]

At the very first meeting the committee discovered that "free" and "open" discussion was not necessarily "purposeful deliberation," but could in fact lead to conflict and deadlock. Ideology came into play during the group's first assignment, which was to appoint a permanent chair. Baba, who wanted to remain as chair, complained to SCAP officials later that the committee was dominated by communists who were closely linked with the broadcasting company's employees union. He asked SCAP to request resignations from everyone on the committee and then appoint more conciliatory, less radical, committee members. In an attempt to gain a clearer picture of the cause of the conflict, CIE Radio Division representatives met with Katô Shidzue, and two men. The three Japanese agreed that if requested the committee would resign en masse, but they suggested that this might indicate to the public that GHQ lacked confidence in their own appointees. Shidzue argued that no single faction dominated the committee, but she did admit that it was she who had recommended Miyamoto Yuriko for the post of chair. On February 15th Baba resigned. Later he was purged.[29]

Admired by Americans

By the last two months of 1945 Katô Shidzue was thoroughly caught up in working for the "new Japan." She was hard to catch, busy with her campaign, her media engagements, and her intensified interest in family planning. Her few moments of private life were spent with her family and new baby. She did not even have time to write to her American friends, who had to be content with letters written on her behalf by Ethel Weed. In November Weed wrote Margaret Sanger bringing her up to date about Shidzue'. Weed then requested the latest information about "the birth control movement in the United States and other countries.....Women who are actively behind the new era here are starved for information about what is happening and has happened in the outside world over the past few years. Anything you send about organization, type of program, pamphlets, reading materials, etc. will reach untold numbers of women who desperately need help."

Sanger wrote back immediately enclosing an emotion filled letter to "My dear Shidzue." "No words can tell you what joy and Thanksgiving we all felt getting news in the press that you are alive out of prison and best of all married and happy." She then offered to send Shidzue, through Weed's office, "some small size diaphragms for mothers & some foam powder & sponges for others. As these are also scarce I do not want them to be confiscated & wish to get word from Miss Weed if I can send them before doing so."[30] If Shidzue had had any thought that she could not take on yet another project, Sanger's enthusiasm and offer pushed her toward taking up again the practical side of birth control advocacy. Weed's willingness to permit her office to be a post box for educational materials and contraceptives in direct defiance of Japanese law assured availability of needed supplies.

Shidzue did not have time to write letters. On January 31st Ethel Weed replied for her, thanking Sanger for her interest and assuring her that Shidzue "was deeply moved at receiving your letter, and you'll be hearing from her shortly, I know." Weed continued with a list of Shidzue's activities. "There are at the moment a thousand and one demands on her time. She's running for the Diet, serving as a member of our women's advisory committee, organizing a new democratic women's club—the first really new organization to come out of the occupation—and, in short, has her hand in everything that is happening in Japan today." Thus, she began a thick file of letters apologizing for Shidzue's negligence, while providing news and expressing appreciation for favors rendered. Weed assured Sanger that her packages of material were welcomed by all of the women, who would need every bit of help they could get as they worked for a "new Japan." As if to prove her point, she added that Mrs. Katô would be including the latest Holland-Rantos material on contraceptives in an article she was writing.

Ethel Weed solicited personal advice from her new American contacts discovered through Shidzue. In January, she asked Mary Beard for suggestions of American women she might invite to Japan to help give "new impetus to the women's movement after the election." Beard wrote back quite derisively about her compatriots calling them "mental children" on the topic of women's rights and public responsibilities. In further disparagement she commented, "[American women] are so strongly bourgeois that they cannot even conceive rural women as powerful women today or in the long past. So you really need more adult minds to aid in the Japanese women's movement... What I think the Japanese women's movement needs is the erection of a structure of feminine force on the basis of its historic force there—a structure of creative intelligence for the contemporary age.... I'd rather have Mrs. Katô unfettered by light-minded Westerners of a doctrinaire type than be a party myself to the dispatch of Western women who would, I fear, merely try to put over their urban and shallow notions of women in politics." Adding a specific criticism, Beard preempted any thought Weed might have to bring Sanger to Japan. She believed that "[Sanger] and Shidzue Katô had different perspectives, somewhat, on the objectives of birth control, reflecting their different backgrounds. Mrs. Katô is the greater statesman in my opinion; she realizes better what a working class means in society." Beard was a firm Katô supporter and a less than enthusiastic fan of Sanger. In a letter to a personal friend a few months later, Beard offered an even more frank evaluation of Sanger vis-a-vis Katô. "This is it as to my opinion: that courageous and steadfast as Mrs. Sanger is with respect to her birth control philosophy, her vision is narrower than that of Shidzue Ishimoto Katô. Mrs. Sanger looks to the elimination of 'the lower class'. Mrs. Katô looks to the improvement of labor conditions so that no class need be deprived of the right to have children and give them the advantages of a civilized way of life."[31]

There is no doubt that the frequent correspondence between Weed and Katô's noted American friends elevated and solidified Katô's already liberal entree to Weed's office. In addition, as early as January, 1946, she was readily welcomed by other officials at SCAP, particularly those attached to the Government and CIE sections. The support of these power centers gave her added confidence and energy to carry out her multiplying projects and to run her successful campaign for a Diet seat. The opportunity to use Occupation controlled facilities, from airwaves to paper, from mail service to thumbed jeep rides, gave her advantages that other women invited to GHQ (often through Katô's endorsement) could not begin to compete with. She used these resources well. She did not merely parrot "democracy" as taught by the Occupation, for she had her own version of socialism, women's rights, and political democracy drawn from her aristocratic roots of noblesse oblige, instruction by influential and politically liberal men, her practical work with different prewar women's organizations, and her experiences in America. Attached to this roughly formed, multifaceted philosophy she also had a personal vision of internationalism based on a naive belief in the value of peaceful cooperation. These attitudes, formed more by experience and stubborn belief than by theory, would tie her closer to a world view than a strictly national one, and this would immerse her, as time went by, in conflicts with other activist women, and the Socialist Party. On the other hand, at SCAP she was never without a sympathetic audience, if not always unequivocal support.

Notes

1. Shidzue to Sanger, 12/23/46, Shidzue to Brush, 12/10/49, Smith.

2. Interview with Lt. Weed, Summer, 1947, Smith. See also 1948, 1981. Tsukahara is Tsukamoto Taro in 1981, p. 122.

3. National Archives, classified in Friendly Persons Section of OSS File, #138764. Informants were Isabelle MacCausland and Elizabeth K. McKinnon.

4. National Archives, OSS Confidential File #11553, Intelligence Report, Declassified #VND750140. Downs was interned at Los Baños.

5. These women are listed in 1981, p. 123. Kubushiro and Gauntlett appear on Darley Downs' list. See 1988a, p. 131, 1988a, chapter 8 and 1981, pp. 121-130. I have found no text of this meeting in the Occupation archives.

6. 1981, pp. 121-130. Kanjû was asked specifically about Suzuki Bunji, labor movement and pre-war Socialist Party [Shakai taishutô] Diet member; Matsuoka Komakichi, future president of the All Japan Federation of Trade Union [Sôdômei]; and Nishio Suehiro, a founder of postwar JSP.

7. Junnosuke Masumi, *Postwar Politics in Japan, 1945-1955*, U. of California Press, 1985, pp. 85-87. "There was a hard-line view regarding those associated with the leftist procommunist Japan Proletarian party (Nihon musan to)-that is, that if Katô, Suzuki, and those associated with them were allowed to join, there would eventually be trouble, and therefore it would be better not to let them in."

8. This meeting and its outcome recorded in National Archives, Record Group [RG] 331, Government Section, Box 2243 - Misc. files which include a 1945 report on the JSP.

9. RG331, Govt. Section, Box 2243, and *Nippon Times*, 10/23/45.

10. RG331, Report of the Office of the U.S. Political Advisor, Week Ending 10/18/45.

11. The JCP representative was Shiga Yoshio, a pre-war JCP executive. Quote from Hosokawa Morisada's Diaries in Junnosuke Masumi, *Postwar Politics in Japan*, p. 90. At the Cabinet meeting of 8/17/45 Konoe Fumimaro, Prime Minister, late 30s and 1940 to October, 1941, became Minister of State.

12. There was vigorous discussion over the name. Finally Nippon shakaitô was chosen, awkwardly translated Social Democratic Party of Japan, later shortened to the Japan Socialist Party, or JSP. I have chosen to use JSP or Socialist Party throughout to avoid confusion. See RG331 Govt. Sect., Office of U.S. Political Advisor, Reports for Weeks ending Nov. 3 and 10 for details of meeting. (Masumi gives the crowd count as 1000.) See RG331, Box 2243, Political Parties in Japan, Reports from October, 1945 through 1946 for elected officials.

13. The executive committee included Ichikawa Fusae, Akamatsu Tsuneko, Muraoka Hanako and three others. For details a complete listing of the women, see Kodama Katsuko, *Senko no Ichikawa Fusae [The Postwar Ichikawa Fusae]*, 1985, pp. 8-13. For a translation of the *Asahi Shimbun*'s incomplete version see Occasional Papers of Research Publications & Translations #29, *Women's Movements in Postwar Japan*, ed. and pub., Institute for Advanced Projects, East-West Center 1968, pp. 1-3.

14. As quoted in Susan J. Pharr, "Ethel B. Weed" in Barbara Sicherman and Carol Hurd, eds, *Notable American Women, The Modern Period*, Harvard University Press, p, 721.

15. This contrasts quite dramatically with the sparse mention of Katô Shidzue in either the secondary Japanese sources on postwar women's activities or the autobiographies of other activist women. Katô's own autobiographies are the primary Japanese source for her actions. Without the English archival material and letters and a few contemporary newspaper articles there would be no real corroboration of her own words. In fact English archives present a far richer picture of Katô's activities than do her own writings.

16. The Baldwin letters are in the Roger N. Baldwin Papers Collection, [Baldwin Papers] Box 12, Princeton U. Library, Princeton, N.J.

17. After McLamb returned to the U.S., December, 1945, he turned Katô "post box" to Major Charles M. Prosser. Prosser in turn introduced the Katôs to another Baldwin friend, Lt. John W. Orton. While this did not result in the Katôs establishing a civil liberties union in Japan it helped enhance their already close relationships at GHQ.

18. Masumi states there were 14 or 15 founding members, *Postwar Politics in Japan*, p. 85. RG331, Box 2243, "Report on the Japan Socialist Party" lists 19 including the names of 12 sitting Diet members.

19. "Vote Aims Revealed by Baroness Ishimoto," *Nippon Times*, 11/15/45, p. 2.

20. Katô told Dorothy Robins-Mowry Gen Van [sic] Dyke suggested she run, *The Hidden Sun*, Westview Press, 1983, p. 93. See Shidzue's detailed description in 1981, p. 131.

21. 1981, p. 131; Lt. Weed interview, summer, 1947, Smith.

22. 1981, p. 133.

23. RG331, SCAP, *History of the Nonmilitary Activities of the Occupation of Japan, 1945-1951, Vol. 11, Social, Monograph 33,* "Radio Broadcasting, 1945-1951." See Marlene Mayo, "The War of Words Continues: American Radio Guidance in Occupied Japan" in Thomas W. Burkman, ed., *The Occupation of Japan: Arts and Culture,* General Douglas MacArthur Foundation, 1988, pp. 45-83, for detailed description of SCAP's radio role.

24. RG331, Box 5246, File #19.

25. 12/19/45; RG331, Box 5116, CIE Weekly Reports, 12/29-1/4, 1946. A Japanese Public Opinion Investigation Institute survey conducted among 180 listeners reported that 114 respondees favored birth control and 62 opposed. See RG331, Box 5246, File #19 for quote about Home Minister, and CIE Weekly Reports for information about other broadcasts.

26. Marlene Mayo, "The War of Words Continues," p. 55.

27. See RG331, *History of the Nonmilitary Activities of the Occupation of Japan, Volume 11, Social Monograph 33,* "Radio Broadcasting, 1945-1951," p. 31 for committee mandate, and "17 Advisors Named to Supervise Radio," *Nippon Times,* 1/31/46, p. 2, for names of all appointees.

28. Colonel Gilbert Hayden, acting chief signal officer of the Civil Communications Section of GHQ. Both are quoted in *Nippon Times,* 1/31/46, p. 2.

29. The two male Japanese were Iwanami Shigeo, and Shimigami Zengoro. See RG331, Box 5116, SCAP, CIE Weekly Reports. The Committee members selected Takano Iwasaburô, president of the Ohara Institute of Social Problems, president. RG331 *History of the Nonmilitary Activities of the Occupation of Japan, Volume 11, Social Monograph 33,* "Radio Broadcasting," p. 32.

30. Sanger to Weed and Katô, 11/30/45, Sanger Box 118, #1194, Smith.

31. Beard to Weed, 2/8/46, first two quotes. Letters are in Beard folder, Smith. For comparison of Sanger and Katô see Beard to Margaret Grierson, 6/2/46, Grierson file, Smith.

10

Political Triumph (1946)

Katô Shidzue believed that a democratic revolution would bring about the new Japan. On this point she was in agreement with Kanjû, their associates in the Socialist Party and their political competitors to the left, the Japan Communist Party; however, the definition of these two words, "democratic revolution," were different for all who embraced them.[1] For Shidzue these words meant realization of an "American-style" democracy imbued with equality for men and women brought about through peaceful elections. She believed that Occupation officials would support people like herself in their quest for adequate economic welfare for women and children, protection of families in which husband and wife were equal, and individual social and political freedom with justice for all. When she spoke more concretely she specified a national health program, particularly protective of women and children, a basic level of livelihood protection, nationalization of the communications and transportation systems, and the nationalization of primary heavy industry. In fact her vision for society was more closely akin to Britain's postwar Labor Party program than anything she had seen in America. It was, however an idealized image of "American democracy" that packaged her vision. She most decidedly opposed the ideology of the Communist Party and the abandonment of economic capitalism in general to a communist state. She assumed that the Socialists would grow in strength, and, with the help of newly liberated women, would bring this democratic revolution about peacefully, without Communist Party assistance. The reactionary and conservative right would pose no problem. The counterweight to this old guard would come from the Occupation officials and their purge of prewar militarist sympathizers. In her first few months of working with CIE and SCAP's government section, she had become convinced that the Americans agreed with her perspective, and that they would help create the "revolution" which would bring about this "new Japan."

All signs seemed to support Shidzue's analysis. The Socialists, in spite of their divisions, had designed a platform which would improve the lives of all members of their natural constituency from farmers to workers, from returned servicemen to women and families, indeed the great majority of the population. Officials at SCAP appeared to be backing the Socialists. The communist opposition was small, and a purge of the conservatives promised to decimate their strength. Economically, Japan in 1945 and early 1946 was worse off than it had been in the last days of the war. Something had to be done if the people were merely to survive, let alone rise from the ashes. Some form of social democracy seemed to be the answer. Given SCAP's interest in constitutional reform which would assure universal suffrage for all adults, freedom to organize for labor, land reform for farmers, and basic economic livelihood for everyone, the democratic revolution seemed assured. Since Shidzue forced her idealization of democracy to fit with her experiences in America, it is not surprising that she believed the Americans at SCAP were like-minded and would help save her country. She would soon discover that neither SCAP's goals and motivations, nor those of her countrymen in power agreed with her definitions or her interpretation of what should constitute the "new Japan." She would further discover that automatic support from the Americans for socialist causes should not be assumed and that she and the Socialist Party should not have counted out the old right guard so soon.

A Women's Club for Democratic Activism

The first months of 1946, however, were euphoric. Shidzue sensed a meeting of minds with her CIE mentor, Ethel Weed, and with her associates from pre-war women's movements on the question of democracy. The evolution of the Women's Democratic Club [Fujin minshû kurabu], beginning in late January met both Weed's and Katô's criteria for social democratic activism. Weed saw in her mandate to engage women in democratic activities encouragement of organizations which would be both activist and educational and would spread throughout the nation growing in membership, numbers, and sophistication. She began sharing this vision with individual women who came to her office. Prominent among these was Katô and in a January 31st letter to Sanger, Weed credited Katô with "organizing a new democratic women's club—the first really new organization to come out of the occupation...."[2]

The core of the Women's Democratic Club consisted of Katô Shidzue, Matsuoka Yôko, and Hani Setsuko, all well known at CIE. Matsuoka often served as an interpreter, and Weed frequently called upon Hani and Katô for advice and information. Five more influential women were then added to the group. Hani suggested Miyamoto Yuriko and Sata Ineko, and Katô suggested Yamamoto Sugi, Akamatsu Tsuneko and Yamamuro Tamiko. The preparatory committee of eight drew in fifteen more women with varied backgrounds and interests. Next, a still larger organizational meeting was planned for March 16th. At this inaugural meeting Hani proposed the organization's name; Miyamoto presented a proclamation along with three guiding principles suggested primarily by Sata; and Matsuoka was named the first chair. Members of the newly formed national organization then fanned out throughout the nation developing regional affiliates.[3]

The original eight participants were women who had known one another before the war and who were united in their determination to motivate women to work for a democratic Japan. Matsuoka Yôko, a journalist and interpreter, had lived in the United States in the thirties, graduating from Swarthmore College in 1939.[4] Hani Setsuko, also descended from the elite Matsuoka family, was Yôko's cousin. Her mother, Hani Motoko, a Christian, was a noted prewar journalist and educator. During the thirties and early forties both mother and daughter "assisted the wartime government in urging women to economize and 'rationalize' their daily lives,"[5] and Setsuko ran a school in Beijing for Japanese children during the thirties. After the war she advocated women's suffrage and other liberal causes.

Both Miyamoto Yuriko and Sata Ineko were writers with prewar and postwar ties to the Communist Party. Miyamoto was married to the well-known JCP member, Miyamoto Kenji, who served twelve years in jail for his communist activities and after the war became a significant force in the JCP, rising to the position of Party Secretary. Yuriko was in and out of jail half dozen times during the thirties and forties, severely injuring her health. (She died in 1951 at the age of 52.) In the forties, like so many writers, she joined a literary organization approved by the militarists. Although she claimed that she refused to renounce her political views [tenkô], she did associate willingly with pro-government writers such as Hinô Ashihei of *Wheat and Soldiers* fame. After the war she worked with various women's organizations, and the Communist Party, and wrote her most highly praised works. She was welcomed at CIE, as were several communists during those early months, and was, along with Katô, one of the three women members of the BCJ Advisory Committee on radio broadcasting. Miyamoto represented the most left-wing perspective within the Women's Democratic Club, and she and Katô locked ideological horns early on. Sata, a longtime close friend of Miyamoto, was also a writer and active in both communist politics and proletarian literary groups in the twenties and thirties. She capitulated to the demands of the militarist government after her arrest in the thirties and admittedly committed "*tenkô*," recanting her previous anti-government thoughts and actions. She showed her loyalty to the wartime government during the early forties by joining "comfort" groups which traveled to China, Korea and Southeast Asia to boost troop morale. After the war she rejoined the Communist Party but, much to her amazement, was expelled in 1951. She continued her literary endeavors during the postwar era, writing about her wartime experiences including her collaboration with the fascist government.[6]

Akamatsu Tsuneko was a founding member of the first post-war Women's Committee created in August, 1945. She had a long history of labor and feminist interests, joined the JSP as soon as women were invited, and in September, 1946, became the first female chief of the JSP Women's Section. She also headed the women's section of the All Japan Labor Union [Sôdômei]. In 1947 she was elected to the Diet in the first postwar House of Councillors election. Akamatsu and Katô served on a number of committees together in the JSP and worked together on legislation both while Katô was in the House of Representatives and after she, too, was elected to the House of Councillors in 1950. Yamamoto Sugi was a physician and had been a member of Katô's Birth Control League in the thirties. She was much admired by Katô for the fact that she was both an activist and a "knowledgeable scientist." Katô believed that Yamamoto's pointed refusal to collaborate with the wartime government, illustrated by her rejection of a high position in the Imperial Rule Assistance Association, showed great courage. Yamamuro Tamiko, a Christian, was the daughter of Yamamuro Gumpei, the founder of the Salvation Army in Japan.

The first general meeting of the Women's Democratic Club was held March 16th, with about a thousand people attending. Miyamoto read the organization's three founding principles: 1) We must fight for liberation from the feudal ideas and customs which women have been forced to uphold; 2) We must pull together from the workplace to the family to develop new and independent perspectives on our way of life; 3) We must advance and illuminate Japan's new democratic achievements in anticipation of the exhibition of all capabilities of women which have been heretofore suppressed.[7] She then read her proclamation[8] in which she condemned the wartime government for mobilizing women in support of a war which created the devastating economic circumstances under which the women were now forced to suffer. She further criticized the peacetime holdover government which failed to generate new women's groups dedicated to solving their chaotic postwar problems. "We Japanese women do not react to all these matters with indifference, as if they were someone else's affairs. In order that the new Japan might walk the path of international justice when women suffrage is attained...every woman must bury her oppressive past and rise up with courage and prudence and with wisdom befitting a woman who devotes herself to the building of a bright and healthy Japan." She continued with a description of women's sad prewar life. "[W]e were driven like a herd of cattle and when exhausted had only a single lamp and a small fireplace under a tiny roof by which to rest our hearts and bodies. Do you not think that such a life was too miserable a lot for Japanese women? We must come to a self-realization of the life-potential that rests in women and of its importance in the building of a happy society." In her concluding sentences Miyamoto spoke of the business of the day. "The Fujin Minshu Kurabu shall be founded as an organization composed of women who hold such views and aspirations [to build a new, democratic Japan]. Although the idea of having such an organization was conceived initially in the minds of just a few people, the club shall stand as an organization for all women in the whole of Japan."

The contemporary Japanese historian, Maruoka Hideko states that for Miyamoto "Japan's feudalistic foundation was the source which had created the war and its hunger." She further claims that in the spring of 1946 Miyamoto and others "were intent upon creating a modern democracy based on the realities of urban society." They wanted to replace the "torn up dikes" (the feudalistic supports) with "a firm foundation which would come from the power of the masses of people..." They believed "the workers must shoulder the power. The Women's Democratic Club would lead the way, but they would be supported by a broad based mobilization of masses of women." According to Maruoka, then, Miyamoto saw this organization as part of a class movement born on the tide of historical determinism which could not be turned back. Consequently, Miyamoto could be forgiven, according to this contemporary analyst, for not recognizing other perspectives, or the possibilities inherent in other types of women's groups.[9] One of the other perspectives which she could not countenance was that of Katô Shidzue.

An enthusiastic CIE report of March 23rd commented that the Women's Democratic Club was the "first large New Democratic group for women to grow out of the Occupation." The report continued, "sponsors for the organization are members of the GHQ advisory committee. At present 'acting leaders' are self-appointed; at an early date a democratic election will be held. At the discussion period following the speeches members of the audience expressed their opinions quite freely."[10] CIE was not concerned about Miyamoto's communist ideas, nor aware that an ideological split existed among the original eight founders. All important was that the general meeting had been a resounding success. The next step was establishment of local clubs throughout Japan. CIE officials and Japanese club members met to discuss the shape which local organizations should take. Katô, intimately involved with this process, later traveled throughout Japan to help women start up their own branches. The new local clubs became centers for discussion of women's issues and sponsors of formal conferences and lectures. The ideological conflict between Katô and Miyamoto, which had the potential to split the organization, was glossed over temporarily in the excitement of the moment and the anticipation of the upcoming April election.

Election to the Diet

The first postwar election took place on April 10, 1946. There were 2,624 candidates, including 97 women, vying for 466 seats in the House of Representatives.[11] It had been an extraordinarily long campaign, and Katô Shidzue, the first announced woman to run for office, had spent five months seeking votes. She had made effective use of both traditional campaign methods and the informal channels provided by her American connections. Her platform pressed for further extension of women's rights based on "humanism," positive advocacy for the "Margaret Sanger School" of family planning, and general improvement of women's miserable economic circumstances. An interested public, led by the media, followed her campaign and those of other candidates closely. There was particular curiosity about candidates associated with left-wing parties because communists, like women, were running in their first election and socialists, running in greater numbers than ever before, could conceivably win enough seats to form a government. The purge had resulted in deep cuts in the experienced ranks of politicians and over 80% of all candidates were running for the first time.

Speculation about the role of women in elective politics ran the gamut in newspaper editorials and celebrity quotations. Conservative writers mistrusted the women's participation while radicals generally applauded it, though writers in all camps felt that women's influence, at least at first, would be unprogressive.[12] A typical news writer's conclusion read, "Although they can become good wives and virtuous mothers, they have not been educated for public or social living." A radical journalist conceded that women would probably vote for conservative candidates this time, because they were "weak in political knowledge." Expecting positive change in the future, he concluded that any participation in politics would indicate women had taken steps toward "improvement and development." And so, "We must do everything to free women from militaristic and feudalistic bonds."

Many well-known women commented on the potential of women in politics. The newswoman, Kamichika Ichiko, known in the twenties for her love affair with the anarchist, Oosugi Sakae, wrote, "Women's suffrage means progress and is a weapon of which we must make the greatest possible use." Kamichika would become a JSP Diet Representative herself in the fifties. Hani Setsuko, "the well-known suffragette," and a founding member of the Women's Democratic Club declared, "Women believe in growth and progress. I know that there are many who claim that women's vote will favor the right wing. This is a conspiracy aiming to use women's sensitivity for reactionary purposes....I know Japanese women are ignorant; give them freedom and they will begin to learn. We have had enough of politicians who do not trust the people and of educators who do not trust the pupils!" She further exclaimed, "Japanese women shed blood and tears during the war" and only the current fight for freedom "can console the broken hearts of the women who were humiliated and beaten by the demonic war." Hirabayashi Taiko, the other woman arrested with Shidzue in 1937, said "I have heard some people say that they [women] would rather choose a pound of sweet potatoes than women's suffrage, which you can neither eat nor drink." This conclusion was foolish, Hirabayashi believed, since politicized women could work to improve the food distribution system and the education system, and thereby ensure that Japan never again initiates a "tragedy." On the other hand, Ichikawa Fusae, the leading spokeswoman for women's suffrage, admitted that given the choice women would choose sugar over suffrage, that is, food over political rights. But she envisioned a bright future through education and growth which would result from participation in the new political system. Ironically on April 10th poll watchers would not allow her to vote claiming she had not registered. Later, purged by the Americans, she was prevented from running for elective office until her purge was canceled in 1950.[13]

Questions about how many eligible voters would vote, whether any women would actually be elected, how the parties and the previously inexperienced candidates would fair in the election were answered on April 10th. A little over 72% of the eligible electorate voted, a few percentage points higher for men than women. Out of the 466 seats up for election 381 were filled by candidates running for the first time and of these 39 were women. Each of the three largest parties (Liberal,

Progressive, and Socialist) elected eight women, one Communist Party member, Karasawa Toshiko, was elected, and 14 women running with smaller parties or as Independents were successful. Katô Shidzue was elected from the traditionally socialist Tokyo second district.[14] Katô Kanjû, elected from Nagoya, was one of the few Diet members with previous experience as a national legislator. The elected husband and wife were christened *"oshidori giin,"*[15] a pair of love bird representatives, a take-off on *oshidori fûfu,* happily married love birds. Katô Shidzue joined the first postwar Diet with energy and optimism, excited to be involved in the legislative process. She saw her election as a watershed between preparatory activities publicizing her causes and formal action which would convert her ideas into law. In a show of solidarity she joined the other seven elected JSP women in a public statement declaring that socialism was the best instrument for solving the problems of mothers, children and working women.

Organization of the lower house in this ninetieth Diet focused on committee assignments with appointments effectively determined by the party leadership. Each committee was composed of members from the ruling coalition and from the largest minority party, the JSP. Since women had still not been integrated into the any of the parties, they did not have a say in this selection process and were placed on committees at the whim of their party's leadership. Katô Shidzue, undoubtedly in part due to her marriage to one of the most powerful Socialist leaders, was appointed to two important committees, Budget and Constitution Revision. She took these assignments seriously and determined to make herself heard under extremely difficult circumstances. As a woman she was not only ignored, but physically isolated with other elected women at the back of the chambers. Also, as a member of the opposition party Shidzue was without power to originate legislation or speak directly in the Diet. Finally, she was relegated to the JSP's subordinate division, the Women's Affairs Division, a subgroup headed by a man until the next fall. Speaking her mind at committee meetings or in general Diet sessions would be difficult, at best.

In spite of these legislative hurdles Shidzue had an agenda. She campaigned in the media for legislative reinstatement of the war widows and orphans pension fund. Due to general discrediting of all who served the war effort these innocent women and children had become impoverished and appeared to be without hope of public support. In a visit to an orphanage on May 4th, Shidzue promised to obtain government financing for destitute children. She saw the Budget Committee as a platform for this cause and for widows' pensions. She had an equally important agenda for the Committee for Constitution

Revision. If women were to become fully equal with men in all aspects of their political and social lives both the Constitution and the Civil Code of 1898 would have to be substantially changed. Although these tasks would prove monumental, and Shidzue's influence problematic, in those heady early days nothing seemed impossible.

Rallying for Change

Katô Shidzue and her colleagues recognized immediately that any hope of achieving their political goals would necessitate using informal political methods which enlisted public and media support. Accordingly, on April 22nd the women held their first "women only" solidarity rally in Tokyo. Over two thousand women attended. Billed as a meeting of the Women's Democratic Club, it was primarily a celebration of the election of women to the Diet. Katô, Yamaguchi Shizue, also a JSP Representative, and Yoshida Sei of the New Japan Women's Party delivered speeches which focused on solving the urgent problem of inadequate food supplies. Katô also raised the issue of birth control for she believed women's economic distress was increased according to the number of unplanned children.

Shidzue's demand for more food for women and children represented one part of a multifaceted campaign to protest the government's maldistribution of economic resources in general. Citizens used public protest to criticize the resigned Shidehara Kijûrô government, warn the new Yoshida Shigeru government, and, by implication, reprove SCAP for the inadequate attention to this vital issue. While living had certainly been difficult during the last two years of the war, it became even more arduous after surrender. Food shortages, already critical, increased daily. Women who had worked during the war had been dismissed by fall, 1945, and now found it impossible to maintain even a modest living for themselves and their children. Tokyo was a pressure cooker with the burner turned up high.

On Sunday, May 12th, women and men joined together and, about one thousand strong, followed a Communist Party led protest through the Imperial Palace Gates demanding more rice . The following Sunday a much larger and more politically varied group gathered to demonstrate at the Imperial Palace for a "Food May Day." The crowd, estimated at 250,000, demanded distribution of more food. After marching to the Imperial Palace, entering the grounds, and parading through the nearby streets, many participated in a several hour sit-down strike at the prime minister's residence. The next day General Douglas MacArthur personally issued a directive prohibiting mass demonstrations which could lead to "mob violence." He said nothing about the food crisis which gripped the city. Prime Minister Yoshida, startled by the seriousness of the situation, negotiated "behind the curtain" with MacArthur, who promised that no one would starve under the Occupation. Yoshida tried to mollify the opposition by appointing a socialist as his Minister of Agriculture.[16] The food problem, however, did not lessen in the face of these political machinations.

Could the Diet act to solve the worsening economic crisis? Could the women acting in unison play a role? One politically active woman, Ichikawa Fusae, not yet a member of the Diet, dreamed of women representatives acting in concert as a voting bloc and thereby multiplying their power to fight for women's economic and political needs. To this end, with guidance from CIE and the cooperation of Representatives Katô and Takeuchi Shigeyo, Ichikawa inaugurated the Women's Diet Club (Fujin giin kurabu)[17] shortly after the election. The organization's first public meeting took place on April 29th under Ichikawa's sponsorship and with Katô as one of the primary speakers. At the end of May, under the Diet Club's auspices, Katô, Ichikawa, Hirabayashi Taiko, and Fukao Sumako planned a gathering at CIE to honor the newly elected Diet women. At that moment a voting bloc of Dietwomen seemed a congenial and efficient way of gathering public support for women's issues.

The Diet Club's most dramatic and heavily publicized event took place on June 20th, the opening day of the Diet, when the newly elected women were invited to meet with General MacArthur at his office. At that time the Diet Club's spokeswoman, Katô Shidzue, addressed the Commander directly on the crucial issue of food shortages and the distressing effect this was having on the health and welfare of women and children. Katô, bowing low in apparent obeisance, began by thanking MacArthur "very much for granting us suffrage and educating us as to the use of it to establish democracy in Japan." Continuing with a few more suitably subservient phrases, she then spoke more frankly about the Dietwomen's legislative agenda and the enormous material needs of Japanese women. "[We Dietwomen] have agreed that we should try our best to study the draft of our new constitution and we shall particularly emphasize the article for the permanent abolishment of war....Then secondly, we are ready to work for various legislation protecting women and children. However, we are sure that all our efforts shall be stressed to eliminate feudalistic family systems. In this we are united. We also believe civil liberties must be safeguarded." And then, quite deferentially she put forward her most important issue of that moment as she sought his "Excellency's" favor for the women's "greedy" petition. "We would like to ask your favor for importing more wheat and soya beans for our people and milk for the babies. We are fully aware that the amount of food we have already been allowed to import has been secured only through your special consideration, however, our daily concern with food has made us forget our traditional training not to say we're hungry in the presence of an honorable person. We are all hungry in Japan now. Thank you very much General for your generosity and patience in hearing us."[18] What mass protest and behind the scenes political maneuvering had not succeeded in securing perhaps obeisance, flattery and obsequious language might achieve. Katô's words were carefully chosen, her meaning clear, and her English excellent.

When Katô had finished speaking MacArthur addressed the women. He sympathized with their expressed causes and declared support for their new democratic rights. He urged the women to work as legislators and not as a women's bloc, but rather that they "meet men on the [Diet] floor in complete equality, giving particular attention to the vital issues confronting the nation and accepting a full share of responsibility for their solution." Thus he praised the women for their "capacity for intellectual achievement and civil responsibility" and highlighted their "increasing interest in political, social and economic affairs" which was brought about by SCAP and for which he eagerly accepted credit. He ignored, however, the severe economic issues which the Diet women pressed, confining himself to high sounding phrases about the spirit of democracy, and, thus, he underscored his own power and their powerlessness.

Ichikawa Fusae, who was not in attendance at the meeting, expressed public displeasure over what had been said. She told the press that the "women," that is Katô, had been wrong to thank MacArthur for giving them the vote. She emphasized that political rights had been fought for by Japanese women since 1920 and that any suggestion that MacArthur had handed women civil equality belied a long and arduous historical process, which should be acknowledged and celebrated. This was, perhaps, the first public indication of a discordant rivalry between Katô and Ichikawa which would continue throughout their public lives.

In fact the MacArthur meeting was the only united action which the Diet Club sponsored. It soon became evident that the elected women, who spanned the political spectrum from far left to right, would never find common cause. On August 22nd, Katô Shidzue and the seven other Socialist Party members resigned stating that the Diet Club was not an effective means of accomplishing their aims. This announcement formally recognized the impossibility of creating a voting bloc of women which disregarded party policies. One month later, at a loss without the strong leadership of the JSP women, the Diet Club disbanded. Ichikawa was understandably disappointed that women legislators would not work together for the benefit all women. The action of the Socialist women, which Ichikawa saw as obstructive, and caused further disagreement with Katô.

Katô Shidzue's Diet membership had formalized her role in politics but it provided only one of several bases for her activities. She pursued her goal of social reform in several arenas, as Lt. Weed explained in a letter to Sanger in June. "She stopped in the office late yesterday afternoon [June 28th] with her husband and we chatted about the new constitution; a proposed welfare bill; the radio advisory committee to Radio Tokyo, of which Mrs. Katô is a member; the financial backing for a newspaper which the Women's Democratic Club is sponsoring; and the meeting which the Diet women had recently with General MacArthur. Finally Mrs. Katô sighed and said, 'I never imagined that being a member of the Diet would mean so much work.' She's constantly occupied, this despite the fact that almost everyone here is suffering from malnutrition and the consequent lack of energy." Indeed one thing which Katô had not found time to do was to write a letter to Sanger herself. In fact Weed had, in a sense, become Katô's secretary keeping track of her activities and relating those of interest to each American friend. As chief correspondent Weed made sure that Katô's contacts in America were kept current, and offered her office as a post box for receipt of needed materials for Katô's renewed family planning campaign and for public writings and speeches. This was a mutually beneficial effort, however, for Katô's activities fell within the parameters of Weed's goal to encourage women's active participation in political and social reforms, and their equal involvement in the new democracy as outlined in administrative directives.

Deliberating in the Diet

It was not easy for Katô and the other Diet women to successfully pursue their roles as legislators. None of them had power within their parties and most did not have the political education to operate effectively from the Diet floor, since rules for speaking in committee or in the general assembly inhibited women from active participation. Under constant scrutiny, the elected women were criticized by many as incompetent, by some as making slow progress, while a few excused them because of their lack of major party affiliation or the undemocratic nature of their male counterparts. In October the *Daiichi Newspaper* rated the effectiveness of the new Dietwomen, assigning them a percentage score for attitude and achievement. Katô Shidzue and Yoneyama Hisako, both with the JSP, and the JCP Representative, Karasawa Toshiko received the highest ratings, of 85% each.

Katô earned the respect of the journalists and public during that first summer as one of the few Dietwomen who tried to penetrate the legislative barriers of old political ties, ruling party power, and male domination. On July 6th, she became the first woman on the Constitution Revision Committee to speak publicly. Her concern was the feudal family system, an issue of great controversy. She urged that the Meiji Civil Code of 1898, which governed the rights of family members, be replaced with a democratic family system. Because of the convoluted manner of gaining the floor both in committee and in the general assembly she had to present her views using the required indirect method of interpellation. In other words, she had to speak through questions directed to the appropriate government minister as he presented legislation formulated in bureaucratic sessions open only to members of the ruling coalition. Only in this manner could she, a minority committee member, speak out. Her attitudes, criticisms, and legislative goals had to be properly phrased within the bounds of this deliberative approach which substituted for debate. Such an indirect method of legislative discussion was especially complicated for Katô, who suffered doubly because she lacked both the political savvy of the more outspoken men and any party power. It is no wonder that Katô was one of few women who braved this process to be heard publicly.

In this round about manner Katô spoke to constitutional issues of civil rights. She charged that there was insufficient attention to equal rights for men and women in the draft constitution under deliberation; she pointed out that the ignored 1898 Civil Code did not recognize the rights of wives. Her formal question rested on the issue of whether the government would recognize the feudal legal issues which were embedded in the Civil Code and the manner in which these conflicted with the democratic changes anticipated in the new constitution, or whether these would be passed off under the guise of traditional customs which, by accepted definition, were positive. With the convoluted rhetoric stripped away from the government's argument, it became apparent that Katô was fighting an oppressive system which necessarily subordinated female to male members of a family and male citizens of the nation.

Katô Shidzue refused to permit either Kanamori Tokujirô, the State Minister, or Kimura Tokutarô, the Justice Minister, to evade these issues. Putting her concerns in the appropriate format, she stated:[19]

> At the plenary session the other day, a Representative said that this article specifies equal rights for men and women, and asked the Prime

> Minister whether [the new article] would not destroy the beautiful customs of the traditional Japanese family. I recall Prime Minister Yoshida saying that those customs have to be respected and maintained. Did the Prime Minister mean by beautiful customs the traditional ethical virtues of the Japanese family system, such as members of the family protecting their family honor, cultivating harmony, manners, industrious habits, and the like? That was my understanding, but did he mean to say that the legal aspect of family life represented in the current Civil Code on family relations and succession as head of a household are also beautiful customs and must be preserved? I would like a clarification on this matter.

Katô was only too aware that the new equal rights article of the Constitution conflicted with the legal rights given the household head in the Civil Code of 1898. This was the import of her "question." Without waiting for a response she went on to describe what she believed Japanese family law ought to reflect:

> The life of a family must be where a man and woman engage in lawful and orderly sexual life, serving, at the same time, the function of maintaining and regulating the population of the race. It must also be the place where the members can serve the function of protecting children until they mature, and fostering their moral and emotional growth. Home must be the place where all the members can live happily and freely, develop their respective unique personalities and envelop maturity of character. I believe family life must be understood properly and protected amply so that it will serve those functions.
>
> I understand Article 22 [Article 24] of the draft as a welcome basis for dramatically democratizing our family life. But I see that the current Civil Code...which has been the legal basis of the family life so far, is in extreme contradiction with the clauses in Article 22. The current family system not only does not recognize husband and wife as legally equal, but it also considers the wife legally incompetent. Furthermore, there are many legal actions of family members that require the permission of the house head. I think those violate the rights of the individual family members to grow as free individuals, and pursue happiness. I take Article 22 of the draft to be proposing the legal standard according to which the feudal family system must be changed into a new and democratic one. I would like Minster Kanamori's response.

State Minister Kanamori responded to Katô's questions by explaining that Article 22 [Article 24 in the final version] of the new constitution would provide for basic equality of men and women and that the existing Civil Code would be revised separately. Ruling party spokesman, Justice Minister Kimura, agreed that established rights as protected by the Civil Code provided too much power for the heads of households and that the feudal elements of the family system should be abolished while leaving the good customs which underpinned positive ethical values in place. Far from answering Katô's questions, these comments brought forward new arguments over just what were "good customs" and positive ethical values, and when would the Civil Code be revised.

Katô then tried to place her concerns about this Article and its contradiction with the retained Civil Code in the perspective of specific social welfare issues which she felt might not be adequately dealt with if the traditional "good custom" of house head power remained. She felt that the state should be concerned for the welfare of women and children, and of orphans and widows, who had particularly suffered from the war, and who could not count on the "good customs" of the traditional feudal household to protect and provide for them. She tried to show that the continued acceptance of the Civil Code threatened the success of any democratic equality written into the constitution and that this, in turn, threatened the future economic welfare of women and children. Article 22 [Article 24] created a continuing problem for the Constitution Committee, for it went to the heart of the traditional feudal system. This was not lost on the male members of the Diet any more than it was on Katô Shidzue: there were nineteen interpellators questioning this article, second only in number to the article on universal education, which had twenty.

Katô's comments and questions in the Constitution Committee meeting were the focus of the next day's news reporting. Describing her performance, a provincial journalist wrote, "The way in which she [Katô] logically interpellated proved her real sagacity in statesmanship. By so displaying her education and qualifications, she, as a novice, showed that she is not inferior to the male Diet members. Generally speaking, female Diet members must develop further, but the spirit shown by Mrs. Katô promises a bright future for women's political activities."[20] It would seem that the greatest impression which Katô made was that she, a woman, was able to function within a man's arena. The import of her argument was second to the skill of her interpellation. In another quarter a "high male official" on MacArthur's staff, who was working on an American version of a new constitution, also praised Katô's remarks.[21]

While a new constitution was successfully passed in November, 1946, revision of the Civil Code continued to be hotly debated throughout much of 1947, and a revised Civil Code did not become effective until January 1, 1948. Katô would continue to press the issues of inequality under the family law as it existed in the 1898 Civil Code but would find that she could do so more effectively and openly on radio and in newspapers than in the Diet. During the rest of 1946 and throughout 1947 she insisted in the media that revision of the Civil Code was as important for the future of women as the rewriting of the constitution. She had not been fooled by the apparent agreement of the ruling parties in the summer of 1946 over her concern about the feudal family system. Prime Minister Yoshida had shown his support for the continuation of the 1898 Civil Code in June when he stated before the House of Representatives that the new constitution "does not negate such things as the rights of the head of a House, the family, or inheritance.... Japan's inheritance of house headship, etc., is one of the 'good ways and beautiful customs' peculiar to Japan."[22] In February, 1947, Katô recalled the Prime Minister's statement as she criticized the "conservative attitude of male delegates" to democratization of the feudal family system. She quoted Yoshida's comment that the feudal family system was a "fine old custom" and stated that conservative representatives who listened "withdrew with a relieved expression." Katô then called for "a change to good sense. To destroy a feudalistic family system does not mean to destroy all good aspects of home life, or to live a loose or selfish life. It means rather, that one's individuality should not be sacrificed for the sake of one's family."[23]

The final revision of the 1898 Civil Code did reflect the attitudes of Katô Shidzue and others who supported more clearly defined rights for women. The revised code did away with the legally superior position of men and the subjugation of women within a male dominated family system. This was what Katô and other activist women had discussed in legal and illegal political gatherings during the 20s and 30s and had worked for from 1946 through all kinds public forums; political rallies, magazine and newspaper articles, interviews, radio programs, and political debates. It was a goal sanctioned and supported by the Socialist and Communist Parties and some members of the Liberal and Progressive Parties and by the authorities at SCAP, most prominently Ethel Weed's Women's Affairs Section at CIE. Of less importance, it seems, was the work of elected women on the Diet floor.

Life Outside the Diet

At the time of her election Katô expected that one of her first efforts in the Diet would be to sponsor family planning legislation which would replace the 1940 Eugenics Protection Law, a measure enacted to carry out Japan's wartime policy of population increase. As a follower of Margaret Sanger, Katô favored legislation which would permit clinics and mid-wives to disseminate birth control information, contraceptives and safe medicines. She supported legal abortions performed at licensed medical facilities when the health of the mother required it or the fetus was abnormal; she did not believe that abortion should be used as a method of birth control. Her overall expectation was for government backing for a policy of family planning aimed at bettering the lives of women, but with recognition that this necessitated population planning for the nation as a whole.[24] Surely, she thought, the circumstances of poverty created by the devastation of war, the drain on meager Japanese resources escalated by the returning émigrés, the relief demands made on American charity, the new interest of women in social questions and their encouragement by SCAP, and the new power of the political left would assure a fair hearing for the sort of legislation which she envisioned.

Soon after its opening on June 20th, the ninetieth Diet became preoccupied with the important work of constitutional revision, budget questions, and specific legislation responsive to SCAP directives and suggestions. There seemed no opportunity at that time for Katô to begin the intricate process of securing sponsorship for family planning legislation. Outside the Diet, however, she continued to lecture frequently on birth control and to work with those interested in family planning. Her pamphlet, *Birth Control and Women,* was released by *Yomiuri Newspaper* in the summer of 1946. In September the JSP named a woman, Akamatsu Tsuneko, to replace, Kuroda Hisao, as chief of its Women's Division giving women greater recognition. In November the JSP Women's Division devised independent plans to establish birth control consultation clinics operated by physicians, nurses, and midwives. They knew they had no hope for formal legislation because the Yoshida coalition government would oppose it. Hope for informal support from SCAP officials was abandoned when no American with influence appeared interested in the issue. SCAP maintained neutrality toward any issue which might diffuse its pressures on the government to legislate in more urgent areas.

In spite of road blocks preventing birth control legislation Katô remained optimistic about the future of family planning, for she anticipated a steady growth in power for women in the new democracy. Katô's enthusiasm was not to be dampened by postponement of her legislative agenda. She was an energetic woman, soon to be fifty years old, married to a powerful Socialist leader. She was filled with ideas, contacts, determination and apparently unbounded vigor in spite of her multiple public and private responsibilities and the universal difficulties of providing for her family's daily material needs.

In September, 1946, a Red Cross worker, Robbie Buchman, summed up a few of Shidzue's difficulties in a personal letter to American associates.[25] Carrying a letter of introduction from mutual friends, Buchman arrived at the dining room of the Diet Building for an initial meeting. Recounting this event she wrote, "I came with a meager lunch because [Katô] had previously told me that she carries her lunch to the sessions. But today she had no food. She explained that she 'had had a late breakfast and so was skipping lunch.' So we shared my crackers and cheese and the tea which she purchased." One of the first topics which Katô wanted to hear about was food developments which had emerged in America from the war. "I told her about dehydrated foods, frozen foods, and the chemical nourishment of vegetables - a method which is being inaugurated here in Japan to provide fresh vegetables to the Occupation forces. When I commented on the problems which Diet members from other prefectures face in finding food and lodging in Tokyo, she said that some of them had arrived carrying bags of rice on their backs....! And transportation...! She has to travel one hour each way on horribly dirty, rickety overcrowded trolleys. People just hang to those cars like flies and the stench of body odor, fish, straw matting etc. is terrific. She says quite simply, 'It almost makes me sick.' I should think so! No taxi service is available and therefore when she has to go to any office at SCAP she must walk from the Diet Building - a distance of one mile. And to complicate matters, she has a skin infection on one of her legs 'brought on' she says 'because I haven't had time to take proper care of myself. We get very tired. Sometimes we work 16 hours a day, never less than 10.'"

After the lunch Buchman gave Katô a ride to Radio Tokyo where both women had appointments at CIE. During that ride Katô told her that even one year after surrender her son, Arata, was held at a prisoner of war camp in Sumatra, where he was an interpreter for the Allies. In contrast with his mother's conditions in Tokyo, he had written that he was being well fed with excellent food and that his treatment, also, was good. He expected to be repatriated soon. (He returned home in November.) Attempting some descriptive detail Buchman then said, "Despite all that she has been through, she looks reasonably well although I suspect that her American friends would find her much affected by these last years. That is only natural. She was in Tokyo during all the bombings. On the worst raid, fire bombs dropped on the whole area, beginning with the house next to hers. Everything was burnt round about, but her house was spared. 'It seems almost like a miracle', she says. I believe it was. A life like hers is of incomparable value in Japan today. What a blessing she survived."

In a practical attempt to help Buchman offered to get Katô one of the greatest luxuries affordable to a Japanese, cigarettes. She declined saying that neither she nor her husband smoked, but added, "my husband says that chocolates are his cigarettes." Later Buchman got a couple of candy bars and some grapefruit juice which she presented to Katô during the ride back to the Diet. "I shall see that she receives other things from time to time," she wrote in the letter. This comment generated a train of private "care packages" sent by American friends which included chocolate as well as other treats and staples for Katô and her family. According to Lt. Weed's instructions "Parcel post gift packages for Japan, not to exceed 11 pounds, may contain only essential relief items such as non-perishable foods, soap, clothing and mailable medicines. Japanese customs officials advise such parcels will be admitted free of duty." By the end of September Mary Beard had sent off a box with the apology that "the delay was caused by a search for chocolate bars and the kinds of desserts you had suggested. Dorothy Brush sent a "great cake of chocolate," and Margaret Sanger, Florence Rose, and other friends provided some extra rations. In October Weed wrote Beard, "It does my heart good to know that Mrs. Katô's friends are busy now preparing boxes for her. Worry about her health has constantly gnawed at the innermost recesses of my mind."[26]

Finally, on December 23, 1946, Katô wrote her first letter to Margaret Sanger in which she summed up the eventful sixteen months which had passed since the war had ended. She told Sanger that the "deep-rooted feudalism and militarism" were being "swept away" by the new democracy. "What does this mean for me? It just means a revolutionary change of social positions of those including me who adamantly resisted the militaristic policy of the [wartime] government. During the war I used to live under the custody of police and was deprived of every freedom of thought and expression. But now I am a member of the House of Commons and enjoy full liberty to discuss birth-control problems sometimes in lectures and sometimes through radio without considering the interference from the police. Even now I wonder sometimes whether I might be dreaming when I find myself in such a changed position." She did complain that the Yoshida government was not adequately enlightened to push vigorously for voluntary birth-control nation-wide. On the other hand she was pleased to report that a recent in-house report recognized that consideration of birth control might be necessary in formulating policies designed to stem the severe problem of population increase. She assured her friend that in time victory would be secured for a Sanger-style family planning policy. "I hope that you will share my delight in seeing the tree of birth control growing up to a thick and deep-rooted one from the seedlings which you transplanted to this country twenty years ago."

At the end of 1946 Katô still had a firm belief in her eventual effectiveness as a legislator and faith in both the importance of her political and social commitments and their eventual triumph. She believed wholeheartedly in the eventual success of a democratic revolution. She thought her own power would expand through her relationships with the Socialist Party and with Americans at SCAP. Although particularly interested in family planning, she had found other political causes of importance to women and children which she could champion. In her public life she continued to act vigorously and enthusiastically racing about crowded, confused post-war Tokyo hour after hour, day after day as she searched for ways to make the lives of women and children more bearable. In the few hours she spared for her own family she managed on slight rations to keep her household running. Although she had begun to discover informal channels of power proved more malleable, she still believed that her ultimate success lay in perfecting her ability to manipulate the political processes of the Diet. During her frustrating next few years, she would find that she had been wrong.

Notes

1. For discussion of intellectuals and democratic revolution, 1945-1955, see J. Victor Koschmann, "Intellectuals and Politics" in Andrew Gordon, ed., *Postwar Japan as History*, U. of California Press, 1993, pp. 395-423.

2. CIE Weekly Reports, RG331, Box 5117; Weed to Sanger, 1/31/46, Smith.

3. Ooe Shinobu, *Nihon no rekishi: Sengo henkaku, Vol. 31,* [History of Japan: Postwar Reform], p. 133. According to Miyamoto, proclamation was written 12/45,

4. *The Saturday Evening Post* published Matsuoka's article, "Japanese Women Try a New Puzzle," 6/46. It featured Katô and other successful women politicians. Matsuoka's autobiography, *Daughter of the Pacific,* New York, Harper and Brothers, 1952, makes no mention of her political role.

5. Sheldon Garon, "Women's Groups and the Japanese State" in *Journal of Japanese Studies*, 19:1, 1993, p. 38.

6. See Noriko Mizuta Lippet and Kyoko Iriye Selden, *Japanese Women Writers*, M. E.. Sharpe, 1991, and Yukiko Tanaka, *To Live and To Write*, The Seal Press, 1987 for more on these women their writings.

7. These appear in *Fujin minshu shimbun*,, p. 1, 9/26/46; reprinted verbatim in Itoya Toshio and Esashi Akiko, *Sengoshi to josei no kaihô* [Postwar History and Women's Liberation], Tokyo, 1977, p. 23.

8. All but one paragraph of proclamation is reprinted in Maruoka Hideko, *Fujin shisô keiseishi nôtô* [Notes on the History of the Formation of Women's Ideas], Tokyo, 1982, p. 20, dated 12/45 Trans. with additional paragraph in *Women's Movements in Postwar Japan*, Trans. Wake A. Fujioka, Occasional Papers, No. 29, East/West Center, 1968, dated 2/16/46, a more likely date. I have used the East/West Center translation and have included reference to prewar life, omitted by Maruoka.

9. Maruoka Hideko, *Fujin shisô keiseishi nôtô* [Notes on the History of the Formation of Women's Ideas], p. 21.

10. RG331, Box 5117, Weekly Reports, CIE, 3/16/46.

11. Figures for 1946 election are readily available, and sometimes vary slightly. I use Masumi Junnosuke's figures unless otherwise noted. *Postwar Politics in Japan*, U. of California Press, 1985, pp. 96-98.

12. Quotes from RG331, Publications Analyses, SCAP, CIE, Box 5167.

13. Ichikawa suspected Katô Shidzue engineered her purge. This accounted for the permanent rift with Katô. Neither Barbara Molony, biographer of Ichikawa, nor I have found corroboration for this in Occupation files.

14. In this first postwar election only, voters could choose three candidates. Shidzue felt she and other women benefited from this system, for, she believed, women often represented the third choice.

15. Kanda Fuhito, *Shôwa no rekishi*, [A History of Shôwa: Occupation and Democracy], Vol. 8, 1983, p. 148, one of many sources which refer to this title.

16. See newspaper accounts for "Food May Day" and MacArthur's public response. See Junnosuke Masumi, *Postwar Politics in Japan*, pp. 108-113 for details about political maneuverings and MacArthur's private response.

17. Ichikawa's and Katô's roles in the Diet Women's Club and full text of JSP departure statement, Kodama Katsuko, *Senko no Ichikawa Fusae* [The Postwar Ichikawa Fusae], 1985, pp. 37-39. RG331, CIE Weekly Reports 4-9/46.

18. *Nippon Times*, 6/22/46.

19. The quotations and summary if Japan's Constitutional debates, Kyoko Inoue, *MacArthur's Japanese Constitution: A Linguistic and Cultural Study of Its Making*, University of Chicago Press, 1991, pp. 241-242; see whole section on Article 22 [24], pp. 235-265. Koseki Shôichi tells me that public access to transcripts of constitutional debates is carefully limited.

20. *Nishi Nippon Shimbun* (Fukuoka), trans. in CIE offices, Smith.

21. Mary Beard to Margaret Grierson 7/10/46, Beard files, Smith.

22. Yoshida quoted by Yozo Watanabe, "The Family and the Law" in Arthur Taylor von Mehren, ed., *Law in Japan*, Harvard U. Press, 1963, p. 373.

23. Quoted in, *Fujin Asahi*, circulation about 100,000, trans. RG331, CIE, Box 5167, Publications Analysis #95.

24. 1978 Interview; autobiographies. See 1956 for articles on B.C.

25. From Buchman to Rose and others 9/19/46, Box 118, #1194, Smith.

26. See correspondence for Sept.-Dec., 1946, Beard files, Smith.

11

Populist Politics (1946–1947)

Election to the Diet had been exhilarating, but Katô Shidzue found that she exercised power more successfully by working outside this male dominated, conservative institution. In the company of other women she was instrumental in forming political and social action groups, petitioning and rallying the public in support of women's causes, and using the media to publicize women's issues. She also found time to write articles, pamphlets and her first autobiography in Japanese, all in the service of political goals she hoped to achieve. She was not always successful in her endeavors, but her viewpoints were continuously before the Japanese public and the Americans at SCAP.

Debating Democracy

One major success of 1946, attributable in large measure to Shidzue, was the establishment of an official newspaper for the Women's Democratic Club, *The Women's Democratic Newspaper [Fujin minshû shimbun]*. The first issue, launched on August 14, 1946, was four pages long, reported national and international issues of interest to women, and featured local club news. Over the next two years the paper's circulation grew to about sixty-eight thousand, considerably less than the 200 - 250 thousand circulation of the immensely popular and long established *Josei [Young Woman]* and *Shufu no tomo [The Housewife's Friend]*, but more than many women's magazines which printed in the range of ten to twenty thousand.[1] All newspapers and magazines were limited in both length and distribution by paper shortages, but they were all passed along to neighbors and so reached many more women than the official print count would indicate.

Katô Shidzue's name was joined on the editorial banner with the other seven founding members of the Women's Democratic Club and three additional women.[2] The first issue included articles by both Katô and Miyamoto Yuriko and future issues intermittently featured members of the editorial board. In issue No. 10, October 31, 1946, Katô presented her views on the equality of men and women as set forth in the new constitution. While she clearly believed that the new constitution was a substantial improvement over the old one, and that women had improved their status through the democratization process, she expressed grave concern that the changes had not gone far enough. She insisted that, if women were to truly experience protection of their equal rights in the family and in the community as stipulated in Article 24 of the constitution, the Civil Code of 1898 must be substantially revised. She wanted to alert women to those who would thwart real equality and would, thereby, maintain feudal, anti-democratic relationships which had made prewar men legally superior to women. This was to be her theme for the next year.

One would expect Katô's article to be applauded by all members of the Women's Democratic Club as an appropriately liberal interpretation of democracy. It was, however, precisely upon this liberalism and the issue of democracy, as Katô defined it, that her long association with Miyamoto Yuriko, and also with the club they both helped to found, was sundered. During the twenties, Katô had met regularly with Miyamoto in different discussion and political groups.[3] At that time they seemed like-minded on issues of women's rights. After Yuriko had traveled to the Soviet Union in 1927, however, her political ideas changed. Becoming inspired by the participation of women in what she viewed as a successful social revolution, she returned to Japan committed to a communist vision and joined the proletarian writers group, Alliance of Leftist Writers. In 1932 she met and married, Miyamoto Kenji, a leader in the illegal Japan Communist Party. They were together only a few months before Yuriko was arrested and Kenji went underground to hide from the police. Soon he, too, was jailed, not to be released until the Americans freed political prisoners in 1945. Yuriko spent several short periods in jail, but was finally released permanently in the late thirties due to deteriorating health. Shidzue recorded in her diary that she met Yuriko again on February 6, 1939, when both women attended a lecture given by a noted wartime economist on Japan's current economic status. This event made a strong impression on Shidzue who commented that it was not the lecture, but Miyamoto Yuriko's questions afterward, which had caught her attention. She went on to exclaim that of the women of that time Miyamoto was the one who deserved the greatest respect.[4] After the war the two obviously retained positive feelings for one another, for it was Shidzue who suggested Yuriko for the chair of the Broadcasting Corporation of Japan,[5] and, probably, Shidzue who first introduced

Yuriko to her own admirers at CIE. By fall, 1946, however, it was obvious that their political perspectives had become incompatible and that their friendship would not survive beyond the first postwar year.

Katô wrote briefly about her rift with Miyamoto in her autobiographies and explained her position further at other opportunities.[6] Their primary conflict centered on different interpretations of "democracy." Katô drew on her experiences in America and defined democracy [minshushugi] in a liberal fashion endorsing a definition which provided for freedom and equality for all members of a society. Miyamoto drew on what she called a "new democracy," saying that Katô's vision was old-fashioned and bourgeois. The "new democracy" drew life from the pragmatic experiences of the revolutionaries in the USSR and the Communist Chinese, not from the anachronistic interpretations heard in the U.S. and Europe. The division was deep, sides were taken, and by the summer of 1948 Katô, Akamatsu, Yamamuro, and Yamamoto, along with others, withdrew from the Women's Democratic Club.

Katô recapitulated her conflict with Miyamoto in an interview in 1983. "My concept of democracy is based on humanism. I believe this involves a sense of equality. Miyamoto Yuriko, however, called this old-fashioned thinking and, therefore, bad. Today's democracy, she insisted, was not so bourgeois. She said that from now [1946] on China's People's Democracy would serve as the model. I could not understand such a limiting view of democracy. After all it can't really be called democracy if only certain classes lead and are in control, at least, if one is thinking of equal rights. I completely lost this argument to Miyamoto Yuriko, however, who said that my thinking was archaic. Although in those days Yuriko exerted a tremendous influence with her ideas about China, before the war when she and Yusasa Yoshiko traveled to the Soviet Union she wrote upon their return that the USSR wasn't such a good place."[7] In 1985 Funabashi Kuniko explained Katô's ideas further. "Shidzue did not believe in a democracy which was based on one particular ideology. I think that her personality was strongly influenced by her experiences in America." Funabashi then pointed out that Japanese feminism had been influenced both by marxist thinking (as represented by Miyamoto) and by such European writers as Ellen Key, with her emphasis on the importance of motherhood and protection of mothers and children. Katô stood in the midst of these influences but drew her conclusions from a quite different line of thinking. She felt that people should be liberated from all dogmatic positions, from any particular ideology, for these would end up imprisoning the individual by dictating the way she must think. She drew her strength and her interpretations from a respect for fundamental human rights. This was her position in 1946 and continued to serve as her foundation the rest of her life.[8]

In fact, Katô's attitude did represent an ideological position, one founded in European liberalism, but dressed in an idiosyncratic interpretation of "democracy," which turned on international humanism. There is no doubt that Katô's definition, rather than Miyamoto's, represented a better fit with American thinking and the lessons in democracy provided in Ethel Weed's educational pamphlets. It is easy to see why Katô could not remain in an organization dominated more and more by its marxist thinkers. This included both the theoretician, Miyamoto, and the editor of the *Women's Democratic Newspaper*, Matsuoka Yôko, who agreed with Miyamoto's perspective. As Katô reflected in 1981, the compromise agreed upon in early 1946, that democracy meant equal freedom for all to express private opinions and to fight for individual opinions, resulted in battle after battle and a continual atmosphere of confrontation. After two years she simply withdrew from both the club and the newspaper.

Assaults on the Rights of Women

Before her days with the club waned, Katô became an important participant with other club members, Diet representatives, and labor union members in an astonishing example of women's solidarity. On November 15, 1946, two women members of the Japan Cinema and Theater Labor Union [Nihon eiga engeki rôdô kumiai] attended an early evening union meeting in Tokyo. At its conclusion the women returned briefly to their office and then walked to the nearby Ikebukuro train station. It was about seven in the evening. As soon as they passed through the ticket turnstile, they were accosted by American MPs while a couple of young railway employees, looked on. The women pleaded with the Japanese men to help them explain their presence to the MPs, but to no avail, and the MPs forcibly escorted them to a nearby police box. In spite of the attempts of the women to identify themselves as union workers, including showing their membership cards, the Japanese police and the MPs assumed them to be prostitutes and took them to Itabashi police station where they joined sixty-eight other women who had been similarly rounded-up. Different women were then asked such questions as "How often have been brought here? You must have had intercourse with several men. How old are you? It is amazing that you have not had any intercourse until now." (The youngest female brought in was fifteen years old.) Next, all of the women were trucked against their will to Yoshihara Hospital, where they joined others rounded-up throughout Tokyo, thus forming a group of 270. All of the women were forced to undergo venereal disease examinations for which they were required to pay a five yen[9] fee. By the time the two Cinema & Theater Union women were released it was one o'clock in the morning and, since the last trains had stopped for the night, they were permitted to stay until dawn in an unheated room chilled by the night air blowing through the broken windows.[10]

Although this was not the only such incident reported to union leadership and Dietwomen, it was the most vigorously publicized. Over the next few days detailed articles appeared in women's newspapers, while it was all but ignored in national newspapers. A most particularly detailed and damning story was written up in the *Women's Democratic Newspaper*, under the headline, "A Virgin Protests the Round-up of Girls on the Street." In this story one of the union victims emphasized the pain she and other "innocent virgins" felt at the treatment they experienced at the hands of the police. The official excuse, that the police could not be expected to treat prostitutes as human beings, and could hardly determine on the spot just who was and who was not, in fact, a prostitute, seemed a form of "barbaric logic" to this young woman. The article did not mention the role of the MPs for it was against SCAP policy to permit any negative reference to the army of occupation in a public forum. The outcry of this young union member against a consolidated effort to deprive her of her "fundamental human rights" was heard loud and clear by Lt. Weed, who was among those who had interviewed her at CIE, and Representative Katô, who was one of the Dietwomen notified by the union as it attempted to redress the wrongs done to the women.

Immediately upon learning of the complaint union representatives, Socialist Representatives Katô, Sakakibara Chiyo, Yamazaki Michiko and Yoneyama Hisako, and the Diet's lone female Communist Representative, Karasawa Toshiko, with some help from a few SCAP officials, most particularly Ethel Weed and Maryellen Glerum of CIE, began to carefully investigate the incident, and consider what might be done to prevent a recurrence.

In an interview at the Government Section of SCAP on November 29th, one of the victims stated that "a Reign of Terror for Japanese women had come." In further investigations the Dietwomen discovered that of seventy women taken to the hospital from Itabashi police station fewer than ten were found to be identifiable as prostitutes. Union women and men who interviewed the MP troops involved were treated contemptuously, as the MPs declared "you have no right to lodge a protest with us." When the Japanese asked whether their own police should have the right to question the MPs or determine the manner in which women on the streets should be treated, they were told, "The Police are practically incompetent at present. They should follow our orders absolutely....It is up to us to decide how to treat women rounded up. You have no right to say anything about it."[11]

Katô and the other concerned women worked vigorously over a two week period as they investigated the issues and questioned hospital authorities, local police, MPs, Metropolitan Police Board officials and others. Their research was detailed and thorough, and they sought assistance from anyone they felt was in a position to redress their grievances and influence policy changes. Katô in particular exerted her influence with Weed and CIE as she called on the telephone and in person frequently over this period of time attempting to bolster the women's cause. In addition she and Yoneyama drew up a letter which, after discussing the contents with Maryellen Glerum at CIE and A. R. Hussey, Jr., chief of the Government Powers Division, they sent to General MacArthur. Katô also met with Dr. O. M. Elkins of the Public Health and Welfare Division and with others to discuss educational programs about VD, and met with the Policy and Planning Unit of CIE to further discuss the entire issue of VD, and what might be done to solve the health problem without undermining human rights. In the end Katô, and the many other women investigating this travesty against women's rights, evaluated their attempts to redress a grievance and alter a policy as unsatisfactory. Their unanimous discovery was that no one at any of the Japanese or American institutions contacted accepted responsibility for the policy which led to indiscriminate rounding up of women for VD examinations. The police claimed that the MPs required the Japanese take this action. The hospital spokesman declared he was merely following police orders. SCAP (Provost Marshall, Public Health and Welfare, Government, Public Safety and G-1 Sections) disclaimed responsibility saying that there were "no written orders" for such a round-up.

Once again it was brought home to Katô and other activist women that when they attempted to secure women's rights either by formal methods in bureaucratic or legislative forums, or by informal methods through the offices of SCAP, they could not expect success unless the respective officials approached were in agreement with their goals. Gaining elective office might have given women pride but it had not given them power. Easy entree at SCAP might give the appearance of influence, but it only produced results if powerful officials sanctioned the specific activity or policy. As they had in the past the women determined to use another democratic weapon.

On December 15, 1946, about two thousand women gathered at Dai Ichi Elementary School in Tokyo for a "mass meeting" called by a coalition of sponsors to "demand a halt to alleged indiscriminate rounding up of 'clean working women as well as virgins' in periodic drives against 'street girls...[and] to demand police recognition of [women's] civil rights in 'new democratic Japan.'"[12] This "Rally To Protect Women" [Josei o mamoru kai] was sponsored by Katô, Yoneyama, Yamazaki, Sakakibara, and their associates at JSP, Karasawa and her JCP colleagues, the Women's Democratic Club, the large umbrella unions of Sôdômei [Nihon Rôdô Kumiai Sôdômei, Federation of Labor] and JCIU Congress of Industrial Unions [Sambetsu Kaigi], the New Japan Women's League, the Federation of Cooperative Unions, the Working Women's Union, the National Railway Workers' Union, the All Japan Farmers' Union, the Japan Women's Christian Temperance Union [WCTU] and the Young Communist League.[13]

This rally addressed larger questions than the particular incidents of forced VD examinations; the featured slogan was "down with the Yoshida government." Speeches, reports and comments placed blame for the policy of indiscriminately rounding-up women with the conservative coalition government headed by Yoshida Shigeru, and on the Japanese police. In accordance with SCAP rules prohibiting criticism of any actions taken by the army of occupation, the Americans and the MPs did not come under fire. The rally became an opportunity for speakers from each organization to decry the discriminatory nature of this specific grievance, the general lack of equality for women which it represented, and the travesty this policy made of democracy. Speakers emphasized that actions taken by the police were daily occurrences and that compulsory examinations ignored the human rights of women.[14] Equally important, the speeches emphasized more general problems: the lack of adequate food, rampant inflation, undemocratic actions against village women, the poverty of the working class, the inferior and unequal wage scale for women, generally undemocratic actions of the police, and so forth.[15]

The "Rally to Protect Women" preceded by two days a larger and more threatening rally sponsored by the Socialist Party in cooperation with twenty-two unions and the Cooperative Democratic Party, which sought to bring about the dissolution of the Diet and the downfall of the conservative Yoshida government. This rally, much larger and more aggressive than that of the women, brought angry reactions from Japanese conservative politicians and journalists and created a climate of grave concern within SCAP. It is not surprising that the women's efforts to gain support within a public forum, tied, as it was, so closely in time and theme to this more threatening rally, did not bring about the sympathetic response or the immediate policy changes which the women had anticipated. Just the same, the Japanese marxist historian,

Yoneda Sayoko praises the fruitless efforts of the women stating that "this was not the feigned 'democratization' of the army of occupation, but rather the women themselves fighting to protect women's rights. Without regard to intellectual or class differences these women spoke of their resolution to be united."[16]

According to the written record Katô Shidzue was vigorously involved at each juncture. The documents record that she pressured continuously at her most influential power centers, CIE and the Government Section of SCAP, to solve this human rights and policy question. And yet, she does not refer to this incident in any of her several autobiographies, nor does she mention it in any of her letters abroad. Perhaps the rally took the issue further than she had wanted to see it go; perhaps she was more at home dealing with other issues at SCAP which formed a part of her own account of her accomplishments in future documents; or perhaps she was too involved in assisting her husband with the larger rally of December 17th and helping him plan other actions, the most threatening of which was a general strike, to bring down the Yoshida government.

"Reverse Course"

The cancellation by MacArthur of a planned general strike for February 1, 1947, has been considered pivotal to the so-called "reverse course" of the trajectory of the American Occupation, which turned back the forward progress of Japan's labor, Socialist Party, and Communist Party movements. By the end of 1946 Japan's economy appeared to be making little headway against the devastation wrought by war and defeat. Inflation continued to rise, living costs increased, wages were held down, and what goods were available, were primarily exchanged through the black market. At the beginning of this second postwar winter housing was inadequate, availability of coal for heat was uncertain or it was too expensive, and warm clothing and adequate health care was out of the question for many workers. Although union demands for wage increases were fairly modest under the circumstances, they were unacceptable to the government or other employers. The JCP in cooperation with labor union leadership, and, later, the Socialists, determined that the answer was to call a general strike. It would be a strike involving thirty-three unions with a combined membership of six million workers, and it would bring Japan to a halt.[17] This strike, the 2/1 Strike, as it is often referred to, is mentioned in every labor, political, and women's history on the Occupation period. Perhaps it has become the most famous "non-event" of the postwar period.

Katô Kanjû was in the thick of the planning and of the last minute decision to call off this massive strike. He chaired the joint planning conference of the National Labor Union Joint Struggle Committee and the Action Committee to Overthrow the Cabinet which planned this event. As a member of the left-wing of the Socialist Party and a labor leader he was active in most discussions concerning the strike, and he favored the action unequivocally. Even when three-quarters of the JSP Central Executive Committee voted on January 23rd to avoid a general strike, Kanjû joined the five left-wing members who determined to go ahead. He remained solidly with the Joint Struggle Committee until the end. As he told the Government Section labor official at SCAP, Theodore Cohen, in 1973, the planned strike was "the logical culmination of the proletarian movement in response to the economic pressures on the working class."[18]

During this event Katô Shidzue, more than likely in her capacity as Kanjû's wife rather than as a JSP member, played a supporting role within the most subordinating definition of that term. On January 30th, after word had been verbally delivered that SCAP would not tolerate such a strike, Kanjû and other JSP, JCP and union leaders gathered to discuss how they would respond. In the midst of the meeting, at which they were trying to gage the seriousness of SCAP's opposition, Shidzue "entered wearing a kimono and carrying a *janome* (bull's eye design) umbrella in one hand. She tiptoed to muffle the sound of her high *geta* and whispered to Kanjû: 'It was no use.' She had just contacted a high-level GHQ official. 'They are saying that a cancellation of the general strike cannot be avoided. But there will definitely be no before-the-fact suppression. They will have the Japanese government take responsibility.' Katô and Suzuki Mosaburô began moving to recoup the situation."[19] On January 31, at 2:30 pm GHQ released MacArthur's directive prohibiting the strike. The planning of the past month and a half, accelerated in the final two weeks, was to be scrapped. After much discussion, at 9:11 pm the strike committee broadcast a statement entitled "Report on the Acceptance of the Strike Cancellation Order" which called off the following day's events. MacArthur, other SCAP officials, the Yoshida government, and much of the Japanese population breathed a sigh of relief. Japanese labor leaders, left-wing Socialists, and Communist Party leaders looked forward to different tactics to bring down the Yoshida government and secure a better livelihood for their constituencies.

To some this intensification of previous rulings by MacArthur to prevent mass meetings appeared to block labor's social advances which the Americans had seemed to be fostering in Japan. There was no doubt that it severely reduced labor's power, but it also had an adverse effect on women. As the "Rally to Protect Women" illustrated, women found that in difficult times, when they could not affect policy through either formal or informal power channels, the democratic right to assemble, or in this case to strike, was an important method for gathering support to address grievances and pressure for social change. The suppression of the general strike and the anti-"mass meeting" policy which it represented can be seen as a set-back for "grassroots" democratic actions by women as well as for the overall labor movement. In later comments Katô Shidzue would refer to MacArthur's action as oppressive and, like others, single it out as a primary cause of the demise of Socialist Party influence.

A Separate Department for Women's Affairs

On April 25, 1947, the second postwar elections for the Diet were held. Both Kanjû and Shidzue ran again and were reelected. This was particularly satisfying for Shidzue as most women elected the previous year lost. Out of eighty-six women candidates only fifteen were elected, three each for the Liberal Party and the Democratic Party, the latter newly formed from a large section of a dying Progressive Party, and nine, an increase of one, for the Socialist Party. The lone JCP woman Karasawa lost her seat. Out of twelve Socialists elected from Tokyo, Shidzue came in fifth, and out of six Socialists elected from Aichi Province (Nagoya) Kanjû was fifth. At the same time the House of Councillors held its first postwar election and the JSP won forty-seven of 111 seats. Two of the nine women elected were Socialists, including Akamatsu Tsuneko. The Socialist Party, which had gained a plurality in both Houses of the Diet, were asked to form a coalition government. There was some question at first whether Katô Kanjû and other leaders of the JSP left-wing, would join in the coalition or would stand with the JCP in opposition. Once these men had agreed to cooperate the way was open for JSP leader, Katayama Tetsu, to become Prime Minister and appoint a coalition cabinet.

Although this government, which lasted for only ten months, proved fairly ineffectual, the fact that the Socialists were in positions of importance during the last half of 1947 was helpful to Katô Shidzue, and her female JSP colleagues, as they fought for a separate national women's bureau. Beginning at least the first week in March, 1946, Katô met frequently with SCAP officials, most particularly Weed at CIE and Ruth Ellerman of the Government Section, over the next eighteen months to discuss and pressure for a cabinet level bureau for women's affairs. Though not the only woman working with SCAP officials on this issue, Katô was certainly the most frequent and persistent lobbyist, and, judging from the meeting invitations and phone calls placed specifically about this topic, she was both welcome and effective. Undoubtedly this was partly because the issue was of primary concern to the JSP Women's Section and so was pressed unceasingly after the 1946 election by Katô, in cooperation with Akamatsu, and JSP Representative Yoneyama Hisako. But perhaps of greater importance was the fact that Katô had the ability to carry on discussions with Weed and Ellerman directly in English, and could, therefore, interact comfortably with the Americans.

After the first postwar election in 1946, JSP women drafted a position paper describing the form which they thought a national bureau for women should take and presented this to CIE for discussion. During the second week in September American officials from the Government Section and from CIE met with Diet Representatives Katô and Yoneyama, with two male JSP Diet members, and with Akamatsu, the new chief of the JSP Women's Affairs Section, to discuss the issue. At this time a general outline was agreed upon including the possibility of housing such a bureau in the promised Labor Ministry, or, as they later suggested as "an independent Cabinet Board."[20]

At the end of September the Socialist Party took up the women's bureau in its annual meeting where Shidzue presented a draft describing what she and her colleagues saw as the purpose and function of the bureau. This was also submitted to SCAP officials for review. Shidzue introduced her plan with a preamble of justification. "It is absolutely necessary for the establishment of a democratic Japan to emancipate women from feudalistic bondage and raise their social status," she began. To accomplish this, she believed, the nation must not only revise the constitution but must extensively revise the civil and criminal codes and any other legal statutes which inhibit the full emancipation of women and thus undermine their equal status in society. Consequently there was "a pressing need to set up, at this moment, a strong institute" which would promote women's interests and formulate fundamental policies, provide appropriate facilities, and conduct research into questions affecting women in areas of education, labor, family, law, and nutrition.[21]

According to her plan the bureau, which could be a part of a new Labor Ministry or the Home Ministry or a separate cabinet division, should conduct studies and make recommendations. Shidzue made a few vague administrative suggestions, which would insure the bureau's independence, but the primary focus of her draft was to propose in detail the service to women which this bureau would be expected to perform. She was less clear on how these goals would be achieved. Her assumption seemed to be that laws and enforcement would naturally follow. Shidzue stressed issues of education, both social education and formal schooling, and included the supervision of women's medical colleges and nursing schools among the bureau's mandate. She did not concern herself with the fact that this would trespass on the prerogatives of the Ministry of Education. She saw the bureau as the supervisor for women laborers, specifically mentioning women in government enterprises such as transportation, communication and the tobacco industry, as well as women working in farming and fishing. Perhaps her strongest and longest description involved the general health and welfare of women and children and included medical care and education for women during pregnancy and childbirth, and medical care for infants and young children as well as management and supervision of hospitals and sanitariums for women and child care institutes. In conjunction with this she emphasized research and education about diet and nutrition, and adequate distribution of food, still an issue two years after surrender. For her, nationally funded health care was a given. Finally she hoped the bureau would actively protect women through a more sensitive judicial system, a women's police force, and a family court which would deliberate on the basis of revised statutes guaranteeing women's equal rights. In fact everything mentioned invaded the turf of other cabinet ministries and, consequently, had little hope of being written into law. This document of late September, 1946, however, underscores Shidzue's continued anticipation of a democratic social revolution for women and children.

The idea of a women's bureau was not unanimously favored by women leaders, and was adamantly opposed by the Yoshida government which remained in power until May, 1947. One influential woman who needed to be won over was Tanino Setsu, a labor specialist. She argued against the need for a separate bureaucratic institution to supervise and administer questions related to working women. She felt that since it was difficult to separate the needs of women workers from those of men, the establishment of a women's bureau might actually prolong the problems experienced by working women and equality of men and women might never be realized. Moreover, she felt it would be difficult to establish the jurisdiction of such an organization, and doubted whether there would be enough business for it in any case. Finally, in January, 1947, she conceded that a women's agency to investigate questions and devise plans might be useful.[22]

The combination of opposition from likely and unlikely places meant that from the time of the planning meetings within the Socialist Party and at SCAP in late summer, 1946, until the formal establishment of the Bureau in September, 1947, women who favored such an institution had to pressure relentlessly to realize their goal.[23] The issue became a topic for radio discussions and public lectures. The women lobbied in public forums, and in offices of SCAP's Government and CIE sections, where they met with sympathy from Lt. Weed and other women officials and were often ignored by more powerful men. They were not granted much opportunity to debate within government circles or in the Diet, although Katô was a sponsor of enactment legislation in the House of Representatives, and Akamatsu, after her election, was a sponsor in the House of Councillors.

By late spring and early summer of 1947, however, a women's bureau seemed achievable. At SCAP a few men, previously disinterested, had joined Weed and Ellerman in support of the project. On May 2, 1947, a Labor Standards Bureau was established within the Welfare Ministry and one of its seven sections was devoted to women and children. Tanino Setsu became its first chief, the first woman section chief within a cabinet ministry. From then on Tanino worked fervently for a separate bureau within the planned Labor Ministry and helped to determine the bureau's organization through involvement with drafting the Labor Ministry Law.[24] Also in May the Socialist Party leader, Katayama Tetsu, became the Prime Minister, and he agreed to support a women's bureau. Success was near.

The Women's and Minors' Bureau established on September 1, 1947, did not begin to incorporate the ideas specified in Katô Shidzue's draft. This reflected the Occupation's changed social agenda for Japan, as well as the continued power of Japanese conservatives even in the face of a coalition government headed by a Socialist. Also, since the bureau was housed in the new Labor Ministry, it became defined by articles five and nine of the Labor Establishment Law and consequently focused primarily on women in the labor force. Article nine, paragraph six declared predictable limits to the Bureau's scope: "Research, liaison and coordination of the problem of the promotion of women's status and all other women's problems, except that such liaison and coordination shall not preclude other Ministries from carrying out such affairs as are placed thereunder by law."[25] The Ministry of Labor had to be careful not to overstep the boundaries of other ministries.

The next question was who would head the new Women's Bureau. Lt. Weed at CIE was responsible, apparently, for insuring that a woman would be its chief,[26] and Katô Shidzue was influential in determining the woman selected for that position. On August 9, 1947, Katô wrote a letter to Weed explaining why she, in agreement with Senator Akamatsu, recommended Dr. Yamamoto Sugi, a physician and researcher on new treatments of TB, to direct the bureau. Katô stated that she was seeking Weed's support because "a certain group of women

[had] started a movement against the appointment of Dr. Yamamoto, recommending instead Mrs. Tanino Setsu, a section chief of the Welfare Ministry." In fact, it was Katô's rival, Ichikawa Fusae, who had put forward Tanino's name.[27] Katô and others objected to Tanino's selection, citing her less than outstanding record as Labor Standards Bureau Chief.

Katô's letter listed four reasons why Yamamoto would be the better choice. Though Yamamoto was not an expert on labor problems, she possessed "the most exceptional knowledge of the woman question in general." More importantly she was a scientist with political ability, had vast experience in Japan's women's movement, and was an enthusiastic supporter of women in the union movement. Finally, as a courageous supporter of democracy, she had not collaborated with the military during the war. The last statement pointedly contrasted her with the purged Ichikawa, Tanino's champion. Katô closed her letter, "Hoping that our urgent request may be granted by you," thus underscoring Weed's power in the matter.

Before Weed could act on this request, Katô revoked her recommendation of Yamamoto and, in a second letter, suggested Yamakawa Kikue instead. This letter, supported by Akamatsu Tsuneko, outlined the need for someone who was not only knowledgeable on women's issues but one who could "discuss with the Ministers of the other competent Departments on equal terms...[a woman] who is supported by women of all social strata." Katô praised Yamakawa as the most qualified person for the job, saying that she was the "daughter of a noted scholar of Chinese classics, graduate from the Tsuda Women's College, edited formerly, together with her husband Yamakawa Hitoshi, a monthly magazine, *The Study of Socialism*." She then added that the Yamakawas had never been communists and were upstanding members of the JSP. Those who opposed Yamakawa as too "radical" were themselves reactionaries and their suggestion that she possessed "dangerous thought" was "totally groundless."[28]

The recommendation was honored. The fact that Tanino was more conservative and conciliatory, and the highest female bureaucrat in the government, whereas her successful opponent, Yamakawa, held policy positions which coincided with the left-wing of the Socialist Party, would appear to speak volumes about the strong influence of both Ethel Weed and Katô Shidzue in the informal power structure which these women had devised. On the other hand, the change of government to a coalition headed by a Socialist was not without significance as well.

Reviewing Civil Liberties in the New Japan

The year 1947 was a busy one for Shidzue. In May she and her husband were visited by an old acquaintance, Roger Baldwin, who became the first American civilian without Occupation connections to be permitted to visit Japan.[29] His purpose as Director of the American Civil Liberties Union (ACLU) was to consult with Japanese leaders on the state of civil liberties in Japan. He was invited to freely interview any American at SCAP and any Japanese who would speak with him. Of course, he was limited in the latter instance to the use of interpreters or to speaking with the few Japanese who knew English. Needless to say the Katôs, most especially Shidzue, who could converse easily in English, came immediately to his mind.

Baldwin found that both Shidzue and Kanjû had good words to say for SCAP, though both were willing to criticize certain American sponsored activities which they felt interfered with civil rights. Kanjû, for example, complained that SCAP required five days notice of meetings and insisted that American MPs and SCAP interpreters be present at all left-wing Socialist meetings. He noted that during the militarist past even the Japanese police had required but a few hours notice. Kanjû continued by denying any adherence to communist ideology and dismissed any growing influence from the Communist Party on Japan's future course. "Only a conservative regime incapable of solving Japan's problems would make the growth of Communism likely," he believed.[30] In subsequent interviews Prime Minister Katayama and Cabinet Minister Nishio Suehiro, both JSP leaders, agreed in substance with Katô's conclusions, but added that they had been pleased that MacArthur had halted the general strike called for February 1st, because it was a "Communist adventure." This conflicted absolutely with Kanjû's evaluation of the strike ban, and should have instructed Baldwin about the vast differences in analysis and practice between Katayama's right-wing and Kanjû's left-wing in the JSP.

Baldwin spoke at greater length and more frequently with Katô Shidzue, who talked freely, venting some of her frustration over political injustices she felt keenly as a member of the minority in both the Socialist Party and the Diet. Overall, she identified bureaucratic arrogance and economic inflation as the two most pressing issues facing Japan. The tenor of her remarks suggested that the bureaucracy was corrupt and that it, as well as all of the political parties, had not been adequately purged of fascist wartime leadership. As to rampant inflation and other impoverishing economic issues, she believed "the time [was] ripe for nationalization of key industries, banking first, then coal and fertilizer." She found the twin goals of democratization of unions and political parties still elusive and, yet, their realization essential if the heralded democratic changes were to be achieved. Although she spoke favorably about SCAP's attempts to secure these ends, she found, for example, that the suppression of the February 1st General Strike "unduly intimidated" the unions and their leadership, and set-back the socialist cause. That said, she applauded the action's exposure of the anti-democratic Communists. Her solution to the union problem was to eliminate their political control and permit them to work as "an organic unity."

She was scathing about the autocratic internal workings of the Socialist Party, which she said was "dominated by an executive committee elected annually at a convention, and deaf to the voice of the membership, who [were] never consulted on policy or program." She believed that with the premiership in the hands of the Socialists it was even more important that "Party rank and file be consulted," but that there was, in fact, "no freedom of speech for Party members; they [were] dominated by a machine led by Nishio [Suehiro], Party Secretary, who [did] most of the thinking for its nominal head, Katayama [Tetsu]." She also blamed the "anti-communist policy of SCAP" for the Americans' determined support of "reactionaries" and the right-wing of the JSP. This, she believed, brought about a coalition cabinet drawn only from the conservative parties and JSP "right-wing extremists." This analysis might have been a reaction to Kanjû's frustrations as a leader of the left-wing, and his own opposition to many of the policies of those in control of his party. Considering, however, that Kanjû was a member of the JSP Central Committee and chief of the Labor Union Committee, he was not exempt from her criticisms either. She included the entire leadership in her scathing remarks, and implied that these men were determined to ignore women who, regardless of visibility, remained categorized with the "rank and file."

Shidzue continued, saying "some of the [Socialist] Party leaders should be purged as militarists" and that even in the JSP "there are leaders in collusion with the bureaucrats to get money by graft in the sale of hidden assets." Some JSP leaders, she asserted, maintained "connections with big business men" in order to "get in on their improper relations with government officials." Baldwin then specifically asked her opinion of the JSP leadership. She told him that Katayama was weak and manipulated by the right-wing of the party, particularly Nishio. "Mr. Katayama is a gentle Christian gentleman, timidly fearful of the responsibilities of power, and needing constant pushing by the left to keep his positions." She believed Nishio, whom she obviously disliked, to be the real head of the JSP.

Later Baldwin interviewed Katayama and Nishio together. Interestingly, his "own" impression of these two men was suspiciously similar to Shidzue's characterization. "Mr. Katayama struck me as a very sensitive, gentle character, lacking in force or resolution, but as a lawyer, with powers of conciliation and negotiation. Mr. Nishio is tougher, like an American trade union leader of the good old school...." Both in this instance and others Shidzue had obviously exerted significant influence on Baldwin's thinking. In 1961, during interviews for the Columbia oral history project, Baldwin had an opportunity to review the 1947 Socialist Party leadership once again. At that time he correctly placed Katô Kanjû on the left, but suggested that Katô Shidzue would "probably be counted on the right," in the moderate camp with Katayama Tetsu. And it is with the latter two that he sympathized.[31] Before the early 1950s Shidzue would have been unhappy to have been placed on the right with Katayama.

In other interviews with Baldwin, Shidzue discussed infringements on the rights of GIs and Japanese women who broke the rules of non-fraternization. The fact that SCAP prevented GIs from marrying Japanese women troubled her, because this policy resulted in many fatherless, poor children. Furthermore, she expressed a general concern about the lack of birth control education in Japan, and spoke more specifically about the tragic effect this had on the "hundreds of girls pregnant from US GIs" who got abortions. This dismayed her very much, for she was opposed to abortion, in general, and certainly did not find it appropriate as a birth control method. She explained that she was in the midst of trying to replace the wartime Eugenic Protection Laws with legislation which would emphasize education and the use of contraceptives and consequently make abortion less necessary.

Another issue raised by Katô and observed by Baldwin was the indiscriminate rounding up of women for VD examinations. He was appalled by this official transgression against human rights, and believed he might be able to do something about it. His reception at SCAP had been good, and he remarked positively on his warm initial meeting with MacArthur and the General's open availability to him throughout his stay. In fact he had found MacArthur "quite opposite to what I had understood him to be — autocrat who didn't listen, who didn't consult. At least as far as I was concerned he did."[32] Consequently, Baldwin felt certain that the memorandum which he sent on June 5th would be received personally by this sympathetic leader, who had "a driving faith in democracy and in the Japanese people."[33] Much of Baldwin's short document criticized the VD examination policy.

> Japanese women walking with Americans in the public streets have been frequently picked up by the Japanese police and taken to police stations for VD examinations. No regulation prohibits Japanese women from walking with Americans on the streets, and the police are quite indiscriminate in picking up Japanese anywhere for a VD examination.
>
> VD examinations should be made only of persons arrested for soliciting or otherwise apprehended as prostitutes.
>
> All of these operations are carried on without search warrants.
>
> There is no *habeas corpus* available in Provost Court Cases.
>
> There is no possibility of getting civilian counsel in any case except as they may volunteer for friends."[34]

There is no record of MacArthur's reaction to Baldwin's memorandum, but it certainly had no more effect than Shidzue's mobilized women had had in late 1946. When officials wanted to listen and act, they did, when the issue did not catch their interest or was in opposition to their ideology, they ignored, suppressed, or avoided it, as Shidzue had learned during her year as a legislator.

Katô Shidzue had found her political life of 1946 and 1947 both exciting and frustrating. Her greatest successes emanated from her associations with admiring American women at CIE, and she found satisfaction working with the Women's Section of the JSP. Her experiences in the Diet, on the other hand, and with the male leadership of the Socialist Party, proved to her that elective office and party affiliation had definite limitations, and the disappointments could be stultifying. Outside the political arena she was pleased with her new organization to foster a Margaret Sanger style educational program for birth control. At home she experienced the pleasures of watching her little baby, Takko, grow to two, three and then four years old, and endured both joys and trials with her stepdaughter, Sumiko, who was about to enter her twenties. She was relieved and happy by the return of her soldier son, Arata, now in his late twenties. He, too, lived at home and worked at CIE, a job secured through his mother's influence. In her spare time Shidzue wrote an autobiography, published in 1948; translated and then published some of Sanger's birth control pamphlets; wrote the occasional article; continued to appear on radio and respond to interview requests; and supported her husband in his work. Kanjû, for his part, worked exclusively with the JSP, immersed in left-wing socialist ideology, and was considered by the press, all parties, and SCAP to be an influential political and labor leader who had to be reckoned with. His participation in the lives of his family at home appears to have been minimal, but his needs and demands heavy. After the Katayama Cabinet resigned en masse in February, 1948, and a new coalition cabinet was formed by Ashida Hitoshi of the Democratic Party, Kanjû was named Labor Minister, in partial payment for his willingness to once again bring the JSP left-wing into the coalition. At this point, his political activities took even more of his time, and, if such were possible, more time from his already harried wife.

Notes

1. U. of Maryland's, Gordon Prange Collection, has most issues of Occupation Period's *Fujin Minshu Shimbun*. I am indebted to Frank Joseph Shulman for access to these materials. Circulation information; RG331, Pub. Analyses, SCAP, CIE.

2. Matsuoka Yôko, Hani Setsuko, Miyamoto Yuriko, Sata Ineko, Yamamoto Sugi, Akamatsu Tsuneko, Yamamuro Tamiko. The second wave additions were Kushida Fukiko, Tanno Setsuko, and Sagara Kazuko.

3. See Chapter 2.

4. 1988b, p. 266.

5. See Chapter 9.

6. 1981, p. 125-129 and 1988a, p. 129; and Funabashi Kuniko, "Yakusha atogaki" [Translator's Afterword], in *Futatsu no bunka no wa hazu kara*, 1985 (Trans. of *Facing Two Ways*), pp. 290-301.

7. Funabashi Kuniko, "Yakusha atogaki"[Translator's Afterword], p. 294, quoted from interview with Nishi Kyoko, *Fujin Tembô*, Nov./Dec., 1983.

8. Funabashi, Kuniko, "Yakusha atogaki" [Translator's Afterword], p. 294.

9. About 7 cents. Yen to dollar conversions, 1945-1949 are from equivalency table, p. 465 in Theodore Cohen, *Remaking Japan: The American Occupation As New Deal*, The Free Press, 1987. Cohen states, there were no currency exchanges in these years, so rates are highly theoretical, approximations based on monthly retail consumer price indexes. December, 1946=71 yen per dollar. A salary of 800 to 1500 yen a month would be $11 to $15.

10. Incident is most detailed publicly in 11/21/46, *Fujin Minshu Shimbun*. It is most complete in RG331, Box 5250 which includes interviews with victims and others. For detailed discussion see Helen M. Hopper, "A Case Study in Democratic Activism: Women Protest Indiscriminate, Forced Examinations for Venereal Disease (November-December, 1946)," presented Mid-West Japan Seminar, 10/30/93.

11. RG 331 Box 5250.

12. *Nippon Times*, December 14, 1946, p. 3.

13. Yoneda Sayoko, *Kindai nihon joseishi* [A History of Women in Modern Japan], Vol. 2, 1972, pp. 118-129 details some aspects of incident rally. Japanese research on this incident is thin because of American censorship of contemporary public sources. A full account requires Occupation documents. Other Japanese sources: women's newspapers, most particularly *Fujin Minshu Shimbun* [Women's Democratic Newspaper]. Briefly mentioned in Mitsui Reiko, *Gendai fujin undôshi nenpyô* [Chronological History of the Modern Women's Movement] 1963, p. 181, and in *Shôwa nimannichi no zenkiroku* [A Record of Shôwa, Day by Day], 1945-1946, p. 328.

14. Yoneda Sayoko, *Kindai nihon joseishi* [A History of Women in Modern Japan], Vol. 2. pp. 122-123; Mitsui Reiko, *Gendai fujin undôshi nenpyô* [Chronological History of the Modern Women's Movement], p. 181.

15. RG331, Box 5250.

16. Yoneda Sayoko, *Kindai nihon joseishi* [A History of Women in Modern Japan], Vol. 2., p. 125.

17. See Junnusuke Masumi, *Postwar Politics in Japan*, U. of California Press, 1985, pp. 112-132; Theodore Cohen, *Remaking Japan*, Chapt. 15; Richard B. Finn, *Winners in Peace: MacArthur, Yoshida, and Postwar Japan*, U. of California Press, 1992, Chapt. 10.

18. Theodore Cohen, *Remaking Japan*, p. 278.

19. Masumi Junnosuke, *Postwar Politics in Japan*, pp. 125-126; pp. 112-130 for planning of strike.

20. From SCAP Memorandum, Susan J. Pharr, "The Politics of Women's Rights" in Robert E. Ward and Yoshikazu Sakamoto, eds, *Democratizing Japan: The Allied Occupation*, U. of Hawaii Press, 1987, p. 243.

21. RG331, Box 5247.

22. RG331, Box 5247.

23. Susan Pharr calls the SCAP women a "policy subsystem" and credits that subsystem, in alliance with the policy subsystem of Japanese women, with successful establishment of this bureau in spite of opposition by American and Japanese primary policy makers. See Pharr's entire chapter, "The Politics of Women's Rights."

24. Gail M. Nomura, *The Allied Occupation of Japan: Reform of Japanese Government Labor Policy on Women*, Ph.D. Dissertation, U. of Hawaii, 1978, Chapt. 6.

25. Gail M. Nomura, *The Allied Occupation of Japan*, p. 172-73.

26. Susan J. Pharr, "The Politics of Women's Rights" p. 244. Pharr states, "Yamakawa Kikue appears to credit Katô Shidzue with having had a hand in her appointment," ff. 62.

27. RG 331, Box 5248, File: "Japanese Women, Individuals," comments about Ichikawa and criticism of Tanino.

28. RG331, Box 5247, File #4, for Katô's letters. Katô was determined to see her candidate selected over Ichikawa's. Akamatsu, then Tanino followed Yamakawa as chief.

29. Trip notes and interviews, Roger N. Baldwin Papers at the Princeton University Library. Additional information in "The Japanese Reminiscence of Roger Baldwin," Columbia Oral History Project - Occupation of Japan, LofC, microfilm #5107.

30. Baldwin Papers, Box 11, Album 10, Political Parties Section, "notes."

31. Microfilm, "Japanese Reminiscence of Roger Baldwin," p. 103.

32. 1961 Columbia Oral History Project, p.16.

33. Baldwin papers, "New Liberties in Old Japan" in *Survey Graphic*, August, 1947, p. 421.

34. Baldwin papers, File #24. Also next quote.

12

Discord (1947–1949)

There were times during these first post-war years that Katô Shidzue had to turn her attention away from politics toward extraordinary family matters. Certainly, at all times she had to look after her young daughter, now a toddler, find adequate clothing for the family, make sure there was food to eat, and provide any support her husband needed. These were the minimum duties expected of a Japanese wife and mother. Sometimes, however, as in the fall of 1947, even more was expected. Shidzue's step-daughter, Sumiko, had turned nineteen in April of that year. Impressed by her parents' associations with Americans and the welcoming manner in which they interacted with members of SCAP, Sumiko did not think it amiss to follow suit. In accordance with her age and interests she began to entertain an American GI.

As Shidzue recounted in 1988, in spite of her own close association with American officials and her longtime affection for America, having a GI hanging around her house was not what she wanted for Sumiko. She believed her step-daughter had picked up the wrong signals. "Katô and I were continuously going back and forth to GHQ, and even though I was a woman, I spoke on equal terms with those in the army of occupation. From Sumiko's point of view this seemed wonderful." She thought her step-mother glamorous because she spoke English and met easily with foreigners; she admired this international ambiance. Sumiko's own manner of entering that world, however, upset Shidzue very much.

One day Shidzue came back to the house and discovered Sumiko and a GI lounging on the sofa together. Shocked, she asked the young man for his superior's name. Her daughter was surprised and hurt. The GI left immediately and Shidzue explained to Sumiko that, while the GI was undoubtedly a "good person," he was "not interesting." She meant he was not the sort of person Sumiko should keep company with. She explained further that the elder Katôs' association with the army of occupation was a matter of business. Sumiko might think of her relationship with the GI in a similarly distant manner, but, in fact, outsiders would not be so benevolent. There would be gossip; people would speculate about marriage; and Sumiko might make a hasty decision, might act rashly. Shidzue concluded by suggesting that Sumiko was an emotionally inexperienced girl, and a romantic alliance was new and must seem exciting to her, but she must understand her duty and break off this relationship. Shidzue remembered this as a mutually respectful exchange which ended the issue according to the parents' wishes.[1]

Writing a life story, especially about emotionally entangling events reconsidered some forty years after the event, is a risky matter at best. It is certainly tempting to make sure that all loose ends are tied up and that everyone appears in the best light. Shidzue was writing about a delicate situation from several complex perspectives; her relations with her step-daughter, her own ability to handle an awkward family situation, her views on fraternization between GIs and Japanese women, her ideas on social class, and her attitudes toward the army of occupation in general. It is not surprising, then, that she would gloss over the rough edges of this incident. There is, however, a differently remembered description of this specific event or a similar one, which places it in a more probing light. This version is probably misremembered to some extent, as well. Certainly the quoted dialogue, which was in some cases second hand, could not be exact, but it was written for publication in 1951, just four years after the confrontation.

The second account is provided by the wife of an army colonel, who joined her husband in Tokyo in August, 1947. That fall she met Katô Shidzue personally, and a short time later heard her as the featured speaker at a University Club meeting. Shidzue, "Mrs. S." in the text, "was a slim, straight woman in a blue kimono, with good eyes and a determined chin. She'd spoken about her experience as one of the first women elected to the Diet....Throughout the evening, she'd shown much intelligence but little warmth of personality. That might well be her public manner, I thought. When she came to our house I found that Mrs. S.'s private manner was just the same. She sat very erect in our living room, her social mask carefully adjusted." The military wife was not sympathetic to Shidzue's public or private demeanor.

The meeting at the colonel's house was officially related to quelling noise from a nearby dance club, the "Bombshell"; but Shidzue had something more important on her mind. She asked if the colonel might intercede for her on a personal matter. She then told about a GI who was coming to her house every night, walking on the *tatami* mats in his shoes and making a general nuisance of himself. Her daughter had the idea that this young man was going to marry her. Shidzue is quoted as saying, "One night I came home late from a meeting, and there he was, lying on the mats with his bottle of Suntory [whiskey]. I asked him not to come so often. He said he'd come any time he chose. *Who* won the war? *Who* attacked Pearl Harbor? His language was very abusive." She then asked for help. She did not want public attention drawn to this situation; her name already appeared frequently in the newspapers. She asked the colonel to speak privately with the young man's commanding officer, which he did. The commanding officer, in turn, spoke with the GI who assured him that he would never go back there. Speaking quite rudely about Shidzue he added, "Most of the time she's out gadding around. I told her once she oughta stay home and take better care of her daughter." He then admitted that he had been drinking too much lately. "Ordinarily, I'm the quiet kind. But as soon as I take a drink, my brain starts buzzing and I lose my inhibitions." Then, after assuring the commanding officer that he had not compromised the daughter, the soldier was admonished to stay away from this girl and the matter was ended.[2]

This was a more serious incident than Shidzue wanted to admit, and yet so important to her life in those postwar days that she felt compelled to include it in her 1988 autobiography, though in a carefully sanitized fashion. Even her version shows a personal, if abbreviated, look at the emotional conflicts which necessarily accompanied private interactions with the army of occupation. There is also some indication of Shidzue's attitudes about social class in both versions of the event. She was all in favor of GI marriages with Japanese girlfriends when she discussed the subject dispassionately with Roger Baldwin, but she was much too savvy about the realities of young impressionable, well-bred Japanese girls dazzled by the apparent wealth and sophistication of American GIs to let such a romantic encounter ruin her own step-daughter's life. This illustrious family must be protected from the tragedies she had observed in the "new democratic Japan."

It is not surprising that during those years tensions would arise between a maturing Sumiko and her prominent step-mother, the young woman's primary role model and parental authority. The discord, however, was even greater than either description of this incident can suggest. Sumiko's answer to her step-mother's interference was to leave home. It seems she established an independent life working in a store, and perhaps a bank, in Osaka. In all, she stayed away from her family for almost three years, surfacing once again in June, 1950, and returning home in the fall of 1951.[3] Family life was less smooth than Shidzue tended to make it seem in retrospect.

As the GI had impolitely pointed out, Shidzue did spend a lot of time away from home during those first years as a Diet Representative. From June, 1947, until the end of June, 1948, much of this time was devoted to the cause of family planning. Although she had expected to make this the centerpiece of her elective service, she had had to delay any substantive legislative thrust on this issue until mid-1947. Early that summer Shidzue launched a new birth control organization, Japan Family Planning Dissemination Organization (Nihon kazoku keikaku fukyûkai) and became its president. One of about fifteen independent groups formed between 1946 and 1952 to consider issues of family planning and/or population increase, Shidzue's organization focused on dissemination of educational information through lectures, articles and pamphlets on contraceptives and family planning, and support of birth control clinics and instructional centers. It was a political organization and was not in competition with medically oriented groups such as the Japan Birth Control League an organization established at that time and presided over by Dr. Majima Kan.

Disappointments in the Diet

That same summer Shidzue began working toward revision of the 1941 National Eugenic Law, in cooperation with the Women's Section of the JSP and, in theory, with the backing of the entire Socialist Party. More accurately the two women Socialist Party members in the House of Councillors, Akamatsu Tsuneko and Kawasaki Natsu, the nine JSP female members in the House of Representatives,[4] and a handful of men, most prominently Oota Tenrei, could be counted on for support and votes. (In general, male JSP members could not be counted on to defend women's issues any more frequently than conservative men.) The timing of this campaign seemed appropriate, for SCAP's health officials were calling on the nation to recognize the severity of Japan's population pressures, and to take measures to stop the population increase. Also, the country's economic conditions had not improved much over the two years since the end of the war, and the basic necessities of food, clothing and shelter continued to be difficult to secure. Finally, the sitting coalition government was headed by a Socialist, as were several cabinet ministries, and Socialist Diet members, who held a plurality in both houses could introduce legislation under government sponsorship.

On August 28, 1947, a Eugenic Protection Law which would replace the 1941 law was introduced in the House of Representatives by Katô Shidzue, and two other Socialists, the physician, Oota Tenrei, and Fukuda Masako, a colleague in the JSP Women's Section. In fact, this legislation was introduced as a "private member" bill because the coalition government would not sponsor it, though it was supported by twenty-five Socialists.

This was not the bill that Shidzue wanted, for it contained significant provisions for abortion, which she opposed, and no provisions for birth control clinics or education, which she believed vital. The abortion clauses of the legislation were supported by physicians, however, who, Shidzue explained, had seen the economic pressures of housing and food which drove women to desperation. She had to agree with her physician colleagues that a medically obtained legal abortion would be preferable to the more dangerous alternatives in practice at the time. As one scholar has pointed out: "[P]ressed by stringent economic conditions and lacking the means to control conception, [the women] sought ways to end their unwanted pregnancies. Perhaps because of the atmosphere of thriving black markets, physicians were no longer threatened by the law against abortions; not only were the Ob-Gyns providing them, but other physicians and even veterinarians began performing abortions on a regular basis." In consequence, "rates for infanticide and infant abandonment rose to their highest level in postwar Japan between 1945 and 1950, nearly trebling their 1940 level."[5]

The bill was brought before the session just eight days before the closing scheduled for August 31st. SCAP, which insisted on its stated prerogative to review any bill, said it did not have adequate time to look it over. The bill was put aside. When the Diet session, which had proved legislatively ineffective, was extended for fifty days, and later extended once again until December 9th, the sponsors of the eugenics bill submitted their legislation once more. Finally, on October 1st, the bill was brought before the Welfare Committee, and the chairman asked for questions to begin the required discussion. He was met with complete silence. He held a second committee meeting and again there were no questions. According to Diet rules without discussion a bill could not be properly considered and so the bill died in committee. Shidzue believed that both Prime Minister Katayama and SCAP, the two essential power centers which could advance or inhibit legislation, lacked interest in the issue, and that resulted in the delays and the lack of committee response.[6] In fact, once the Diet session had been extended, SCAP had considered and accepted the draft as presented by the three sponsors, but by that time the session was really drawing to a close and exhausted representatives had no interest in considering this less urgent legislation.

The whole legislative session had been lackluster, at best, and Katayama had proved strikingly incapable as a leader. Many significant legislative issues which concerned both the American and Japanese leadership and which were essential to the economic well being of the impoverished nation were at a standstill. While the legislators argued over bills fundamental to industrial and agricultural recovery, the people continued to suffer daily. Workers wages were not keeping anywhere near the rampant inflation. A report of July, 1947, stated that a Tokyo family earned about 2756 yen per month and had to spend 2930 yen,[7] three quarters of it in the black market. Industrial production continued to rise at a slow rate, the trade deficit grew daily, many essential goods were simply not available, and the food crisis would not go away.[8] The Katayama government seemed unable to progress on any of these major issues. SCAP tried to get the Diet to legislate wage and price controls, rationing, and equitable distribution of the essential goods that were available. No such laws were forthcoming. In fact, the Diet deadlocked on budget legislation, basic to even the most modest level of government operations. The budget was still being debated as late as November. SCAP's reverse course on Japan's social and economic trajectory combined with Katayama's incompetence and the Socialists' lack of a majority to bring government to a virtual standstill.

Shidzue, a member of the Budget Committee, used her right of interpellation during one of the committee meetings to ask Prime Minister Katayama about his position on birth control. She posed her question within the context of the economic costs of Japan's dramatic population increase.[9] Her purpose was to obtain a public statement from Katayama for the record. The Prime Minister admitted that the nation's sudden population increase was serious and required attention. He stated frankly that the government was "so preoccupied with urgent economic and political problems that it [could] not propose concrete plans for overseas emigration or for the popularization of birth control methods."[10]

The highlight of the unproductive Diet session as far as the public was concerned was the debate in the judiciary committees of both houses over whether to change or delete Penal Code Law No. 45, Article 183, known commonly as the Adultery Law. This law provided for up to two years imprisonment for any married woman who committed adultery, but did not call for prosecution or punishment of adulterous husbands.[11] To retain adultery as a criminal offense under the new constitution the law would have to be revised so that husbands and wives were treated equally.

For the first time in Diet history a public hearing was held. On August 11th well known legal experts and women activists presented their opinion at a meeting of the lower house Judicial Affairs

Committee, a group much decreased in size because so many male members absented themselves. There was a large, interested audience, mostly young and about one-third female. On the second day of the hearing ordinary men and women, chosen on the basis of submitted statements, spoke. A young housewife, a farmer, a seaman, a teacher, an account agent, and a professor all spoke in favor of retaining criminalization of adultery. Some argued that the law should be revised to include prosecution of husbands as well as wives, and several commented that the current level of morality was so low that protection of the family demanded continuation of this law. On the other side a novelist, ex-soldier, unemployed man, legal student, ex-teacher, lawyer, primary school teacher, office worker and translator, spoke in favor of simply abolishing the law altogether. Newspapers, magazines, poll-takers, and radio programs all brought this debate before the general public.

Shidzue and Kanjû, both sitting Socialist Representatives, made headlines by opposing one another on this issue. Shidzue agreed with those who felt the time was not yet right to drop adultery from the criminal code. "If adultery is not punished," she insisted, "we cannot insure that it will not be committed openly....As an ideal the law should be abolished; but from the practical point of view, it should be preserved." Shidzue correctly surmised that Dietmen, who would vote almost unanimously for deletion of adultery from the criminal code, saw this as their only way of maintaining extra-marital relations without fear of criminal prosecution. Given Shidzue's long term illicit relationship with Kanjû, it was surprising that she took the stance she did; but she believed that providing equal application of the criminal code for adultery would better protect women and their families. The more pragmatic Kanjû wanted to do away with the law altogether. In agreement with him were many famous people like himself whose past transgression of the law was well-known to the public and would have been prosecutable under such a statute. Others never in harms way, like Yamakawa Kikue, supported abolition as well.

Shidzue was not without supporters. According to the *Women's Democratic Newspaper*, the majority of the speakers at the public Diet committee meeting advocated punishment for both male and female adulterers. But some who agreed with her low evaluation of the Japanese on the issue of morality and family unity, disagreed with her conclusion. The highly respected jurist, Wagatsuma Sakae, then head of Tokyo University's Law Department, discussed the issue in a comparative perspective for *The Housewife's Friend [Shufu no tomo]*. He praised the English system, which did not criminalize immoral conduct but rather admitted adultery as a cause for divorce. Like

Shidzue he was concerned about the current level of morality in Japan, stating that the nation "must elevate the level of her social morality and improve the economic position of women. If popular morality is elevated and social restraint made stronger, immoral conduct will gradually decrease without the necessity for legal restraint." He urged decriminalization. The final vote in both Houses was overwhelmingly in favor of deleting adultery from the Criminal Code. The debate proved there was one piece of legislation in this contentious Diet session which engaged both public and media interest and was quickly resolved.

Anticipating a more fruitful Diet session to follow, the Women's Affairs Section of the JSP carefully prepared a policy plan in January, 1948, which enumerated the issues they intended to support during the coming year. Item number five was entitled, "The expansion of the eugenics movement,"[12] and was introduced by classifying Japan amongst countries with "low cultural standards," a status evidenced by high birth and death rates. The policy paper concluded that one cause of the tragic demographic rates was the lack of national protection of mothers and children. Once again, JSP women took to task the devastating material circumstances and the oppressive workload forced upon women since the end of the war. The demographic crisis brought on by increased births and repatriation of citizens from ex-colonies, combined with the tragedy of hereditary and contagious disease, and, in a separate category, the dramatic increase in venereal disease, underscored the need to pay greater attention to the health and welfare of women. One policy suggestion included mandatory VD examinations for both boys and girls when they reached "a certain age," and for pregnant women, twice before giving birth. Although this appeared to be a policy reversal from the year before, when these same women rallied against the indiscriminate, compulsory VD examinations of women, the different circumstance they saw was the increased severity of the health problem for many Japanese. The increased number of ordinary women forced to seek economic reprieve by selling sexual favors was exposing a larger segment of the general society to VD. In addition, repatriated men from the colonies were bringing home VD and other contagious diseases. Finally, this proposal was not concerned with GI health, nor focused only on testing women. Hoping to incorporate some of these social and health issues into a legislative package, the Socialist women agreed to work for quick passage of a eugenic protection law in the new Diet session.

On March 10th the Katayama Government was replaced by another coalition government, this time headed by the Democratic Party leader, Ashida Hitoshi. The new cabinet included eight Socialists, one of whom was Katô Kanjû, as well as six members of the Democratic Party and two from the People's Cooperative Party. This time Oota, Fukuda and Katô Shidzue decided to give a Democratic Party member, Taniguchi Yosaburo, of the House of Councillors, the responsibility for introducing the eugenics bill. In this way it could be introduced as a government sponsored bill in the upper house of the Diet. Oota, Fukuda, Katô and two representatives from other parties, became the bill's primary sponsors in the House. The draft stated, "The aims of this law are to protect the life and health of mothers, to prevent the increase of inferior progeny and in consequence to contribute to physical improvement in the nation." Once again this was a eugenics bill, not a bill for family planning as Shidzue had wanted. The bill's twenty-three articles described and defined the appropriate instances for voluntary sterilization, compulsory sterilization, physicians' required reports and prohibitions, temporary contraception, interruption of pregnancy [abortion], penal regulations, and nullification of the current law.[13] The bill was officially introduced June 12th, voted on and enacted as Law 156 on June 28th, and promulgated, according to the fifteen day interim stipulated in the draft, on July 13th.

Katô Shidzue was not proud of the legislation. She had wanted a family planning law which would stress education and birth control. The Socialist Party Women's Affairs Section had placed a high priority on nation-wide clinics which would provide information for women on all aspects of family planning, similar to the sort of clinic which Shidzue had opened in Tokyo in 1937. Not only were such educational organizations missing in this law, the only mention of birth control came under Chapter Five, which spoke of "temporary contraception." Only a certified physician could prescribe "measures for temporary contraception," although "every one is free to apply such measures to himself or herself." There would be no education about birth control. In fact it would be discouraged. On the other hand there were cases in which abortion, again performed by a specially licensed physician, could be provided: in the case of a pregnancy or delivery which would endanger the life of the mother, and in the case of rape, and some instances of hereditary disease or mental illness. In 1949, after Shidzue had left the Diet, the law was amended to include a vague clause giving a designated physician supervised by a local review committee the right to recommend abortion for women who proved debilitating economic or physical circumstances, and a clause about clinics for "eugenic education" or marriage counseling. Certain offices could also propagate and provide guidance "concerning the proper method of conception adjustment."[14]

From 1949, Japanese women increased their dependency upon abortion as their primary birth control method. This was a great disappointment to Shidzue. She believed that the law which she had worked hard for had become primarily an opportunity for physicians to enrich themselves, for the clause which required that only designated physicians could legally perform abortions guaranteed a lucrative practice for a few doctors. It is no wonder that physicians had backed the original law, and that in years to come attempts to alter this physician provision or to introduce national clinics for birth control education never caught on.

A Hearing for Family Planning

Katô's attitudes about population control and family planning had not received a fair hearing in the discussion of the Eugenic Protection Law of 1948; however, on September 14, 1948, she got the opportunity to state her position before a select audience. This meeting on population problems,[15] sponsored by CIE, gathered together representatives of the Rockefeller Foundation and eleven notable Japanese interested in family planning. It began with a closed session of Americans only in which Dr. Frank Notestein of the Rockefeller Foundation asked just how deeply the Japanese were interested in birth control. Ethel Weed responded by briefly describing Katô Shidzue's work as "the Margaret Sanger of Japan." Next she spoke about the clinics established by the husband and wife team, the Doctors Amano, and about Senator Akamatsu Tsuneko's work on the Eugenics Protection Law. Herbert Passin of CIE stated that the six studies to date on Japanese attitudes toward birth control were not very useful, and Dr. Powdermaker continued that there was little real grass-roots interest in, nor much understanding of actual methods of birth control. In fact, she had found that many women believed that infanticide and abortion were forms of birth control. The American guests were then told, "While SCAP maintains a neutral policy on the question of birth control, the Japanese themselves are not restricted in any way. They may organize groups, clinics, work on legislation, etc."

At this point the Japanese[16] were invited to join the meeting and offer a brief statements describing her/his own activities in the area of overpopulation and birth control. Ironically Katô claimed an active role in securing passage of the recent eugenics bill. Apparently, since that was the only legislation on the books, she intended to take credit whether the final bill reflected her perspective or not. Amano Fumiko, an obstetrician and gynecologist, who, along with her husband, had been educated in the United States, told about the book she had published to educate doctors on the use of the diaphragm as a contraceptive. Akamatsu Tsuneko described her travels throughout Japan to explain the provisions of the new Eugenics Protection Law. Katô's sometime colleague and sometime nemesis, Dr. Majima Kan, spoke about his many years attempting to educate the public about birth control.

To begin the general discussion, Mr. Notestein posed several questions, primarily on rural women's knowledge of and receptiveness to birth control practices. The speakers suggested that the level of education about contraceptives and family planning was low, but the economic motivation to try to limit families was great. Several, including Katô, politely filled in some details.

An emotionally charged Katô Shidzue then took the floor. She began by describing the needs she felt had not been met by the current law, specifically blaming the Katayama/Ashida governments and SCAP for the deficiencies. "We have to face this problem, but unfortunately most people from the Prime Minister to the masses of people do not think seriously about this matter; they do not think about it at all. The last two Prime Ministers have been warned of the necessity of population control. At the last Diet session it was pointed out that the Japanese Government should have a plan on how to control the increase of population, but both of the Prime Ministers said that they had no ideas on it and were not planning anything on it." These officials blamed their lack of action on SCAP which had not yet issued directives. "If there are no such directives, evidently the Japanese government authorities will not bother to do anything about it." Katô continued that when she mentioned this excuse at SCAP, they said population policy was an internal matter, and as such completely up to the Japanese people. How could this be, she wondered, when SCAP had clearly declared its interest in public health issues. "SCAP has done much for typhus control and TB control, and SCAP realizes that natural resources are limited and population is increasing and that there is no balance between resources and population. This lack of balance is extremely serious and if you leave the situation as it is how can you be thinking of human welfare?" To her mind neither Americans nor Japanese were willing to take responsibility for formulating policy on population control.

While no American responded to Katô's criticism, Dr. Majima suggested that American and European researchers believed that population growth would at some point automatically decrease. This did not satisfy Katô. She found it irrelevant, if not insulting, that the Prime Minister let experts from the Population Research Institute and bureaucrats from the Welfare Ministry respond to her questions with their own statistics. Of what possible use was a debate on research supported by a ministry's manipulation of numbers. The point was that bureaucrats "should not decide on the fundamental policy of the government." This had been the government's approach before the war and to what a terrible conclusion. Now "we are building democracy [and] policies should not be decided by bureaucrats. Policies are the responsibility of the people. If the people think about human welfare seriously, they will conclude that something must be done to check the increase of population. It is too serious a problem to be left alone," or, she might well have added, to be left up to the bureaucrats.

Katô used this arena to vent all of her frustrations over the rules governing legislative action, the power of the bureaucrats over those of elected officials, the weaknesses of the prime ministers, and the disappointing inadequacy of the new eugenics law. Her ideas of democracy based on her definition of humanism had been stalemated for two years by what she considered antidemocratic abuse of power. Finally, she spoke specifically about the Eugenics Protection Law itself. "Provisions in the present law are not by any means enough to take care of the population problem, but if the bill [had been] too progressive the Diet would not [have passed] it. This [Law] should be considered as a first step. This bill must be expanded. The Government should establish clinics, financed by the government, for consultation about marriage, abortion, and birth control problems, and these clinics should not be operated on a commercial basis." No more financial largesse should be handed over to the medical profession.

After Katô gave her spirited comments, others became more aggressive and spoke out in favor of birth control education, accessible clinics funded by the government, greater leeway for legal abortions, and re-education of doctors, among other issues. These Japanese knew what direction they hoped to take the family planning questions at hand. What the Americans thought of the discussion is not recorded. The group from the Rockefeller Foundation had come to listen and the SCAP officials to moderate and introduce, but to otherwise remain silent. It would be up to Katô, Majima, Akamatsu, and the Drs. Amano to carry out their ideas from private platforms; government and SCAP support of family planning would not be forthcoming.

Political Reversals

The second half of 1948 did not go well for Shidzue, Kanjû, or for the JSP. In July, 1948, MacArthur, who felt that labor was getting out of hand and worried that its aggressive actions would turn violent, accepted the findings of the Hoover Commission that Civil Service reform must include legislation which forbade collective bargaining and strikes by government workers. Such a far reaching law would prevent labor activities by groups as diverse as railway workers, communications workers, teachers, government administrators, and custodial workers, or by employees of any one of the several government monopolies, tobacco, salt, camphor, telephone and telegraph. In effect it meant that groups here-to-fore granted collective bargaining rights by SCAP sponsored labor directives and laws would have these rescinded.[17] The directive was insisted upon by its creator, Blaine Hoover, and backed by Charles Kades and Courtney Whitney, powerful officials in the Government Section. On July 22nd the Supreme Commander sent a directive to the Ashida government demanding that they pass legislation which prohibited strikes by any civil servants or other public sector workers. This action was anathema to the Socialist Party and particularly to Katô Kanjû, the Labor Minister. He wanted to resign in protest but was talked out of it by SCAP officials. Later Kanjû, alone among the cabinet ministers, tried to argue with General Whitney against the directive, but was outmaneuvered and lost.[18] A primary result of the forced discussion of this controversial legislation was to tie up the Ashida government in debate and essentially bring about its demise by October, 1948. The weak coalition government was followed by a second Yoshida Cabinet which passed the SCAP demanded Public Service Law late in 1948.

The public workers directive was opposed by all friends of labor and that included the Women's Affairs Sections of the JSP and of the labor unions. Shidzue positioned herself solidly beside labor and used what entree she had at SCAP to create a sympathetic ear for these women's interests. During August and September she wrote her own commentaries, expressed her opinions in the media, submitted petitions by women public service workers to MacArthur and others, and discussed the issue with any SCAP official who would listen.

In one petition submitted to SCAP on August 18th, the undersigned women pled that they "keenly felt the necessity" of specifying their fears about a return to feudalistic attitudes toward women and the anticipated deterioration of the status of working women which would necessarily accompany enactment of the Public Service Law. They continued that signatures had been "speedily collected," and they were entrusting Katô Shidzue to deliver this message to GHQ. "Due to Mrs. Katô's efforts" not only did their petition reach General MacArthur, but they were given interviews with Mr. Kades, Mr. Hoover, and Mr. Salter, on August 23rd, and General Whitney on August 25th, the most influential SCAP officials on this issue. They were not aware, however, that these men were adamant in their determination that the Public Service Law be passed. Their cause was lost before they began. Still believing in the power of democratic action, Katô Shidzue accompanied the women to each meeting and introduced them. The Americans explained their position, which was essentially that "public servants have a duty to find means other than strikes to accomplish redress of their grievances." The statements were followed by questions from the women and answers from the officials.

There was no meeting of the minds. In summary the women were told that the Public Service Law would not interfere with the improvement of women's status; that there would be ways for women to insist on their rights; and that the revision could be amended in the Diet. The women listened, but came away feeling that while good will had been expressed, good will in the face of tough laws might never be acted upon. They concluded, "Now we know clearly that women's problems can be solved by the unity of women. And at the same time we notice the difference of fundamental ideas, sentiments and understanding between the Japanese who had long lived under the feudalistic system and the Americans who had never experienced such a system on their large, rich soil. The establishment of the New Japan should be done by the hands of workers and yet the actual living circumstance of the low-class public service workers has not been fully understood."[19] They were not fooled by the Americans' encouraging words. The women could see the difference between the democracy espoused in educational documents and harsh laws which countered these ideals.

The August 29th issue of the *Women's Democratic Newspaper* described the meetings and the women's concerns. Shidzue is quoted in this article explaining General Whitney's comments which emphasized SCAP's assurance that women and men would be treated equally in the public service area, that women would have equal access to the public service examinations, and would have an equal opportunity to gain promotion to the highest positions. Katô pointed out that when the women asked whether they could be appointed to the Personnel Affairs Board, as provided for in the National Public Service Law, Whitney deferred to the Japanese government, saying that this sort of detail would have to be worked out in the Diet. Working people should work through their Diet representatives. It seemed that whenever SCAP had a determined position, for example, that public unions could not strike, they ensured compliance by invoking their superior authority; but whenever they did not feel their interests were at stake, they would conveniently defer to Japanese officials. In either instance, if the women's interests did not coincide with SCAP's, they were at the mercy of the male dominated legislature and bureaucracy. As Shidzue had told Roger Baldwin the year before, a primary inhibitor of civil rights and, therefore, the future of the new democracy, was the power of the bureaucracy. The Public Service Law, which ostensibly was designed to limit the pervasive power of the bureaucratic officials, in fact had no effect on them at all, but instead destroyed the civil rights of public workers. The cracks in the "new democracy" were widening.

Successful passage of the National Public Service Law was devastating to the political life of both Katôs, but not the only difficulties which they faced at the end of 1948. Like so many in the Socialist Party and the Ashida Government the Katôs were caught up in one of several bribery scandals which added to the troubles of the coalition government and the Socialist Party. Each Katô was accused of taking illegal campaign contributions for personal use, although the accusation against Shidzue was much fuzzier than that leveled against Kanjû. The Katôs were said to have accepted some portion of 800,000 yen[20] from a textile manufacturer to be split between Kanjû and his friend and colleague, Suzuki Mosaburô. In his testimony before an investigation committee Kanjû claimed that the money was given for him but to his wife, who disposed of it legally while he was out of town during the 1947 election. He was also given a Datsun car by someone else, and since it didn't work right, he turned it in for an electric car. There seemed some confusion over just what exactly was given by whom and to whom and how the money portion was spent, but Shidzue claimed that it was used to establish a Socialist Institute for Political Studies. She did not deny receiving some money, but complained that while the bad publicity was coming toward Socialists, the conservative prime minister, Yoshida, who had accepted larger sums of money and had used his money for personal gain, was not being prosecuted or persecuted.[21]

One predictable outcome of the scandals was rejection of the JSP at the polls by a disillusioned public. Although the Ashida Government had resigned the first part of October and had been replaced by the second Yoshida Government on October 19th, new elections were not held until January 23rd. This general election was a blood bath, especially for the Socialist Party left wing. The number of JSP Representatives dropped from 143 to 48. Both Katôs lost, a terrible blow. When Shidzue ran again it was for a seat in the House of Councillors in 1950. Kanjû did not have a chance to return to the Diet until the next election for the lower house which was held in October, 1952. At that time he left his district in Aichi Province and ran for his wife's old seat in a heavily left-wing district of Tokyo and won.

After the 1949 election was over Shidzue wrote an eight page analysis of the Socialist defeat for Ethel Weed.[22] In it she stated that the most important reason the public voted the Socialists out was the inadequate attention the party had paid to educating the people about socialist principles. Secondly, the party was torn by factionalism which reflected pre-war differences that had been ignored by those determined to establish a larger, more powerful postwar party. Third, the public believed that the Party had not followed through on its promised program. Here Shidzue commented that the Socialists had been undermined by the ideological and programmatic compromises they had made in their attempts to cooperate with non-socialist parties. Furthermore, SCAP had prevented the JSP from implementing their own programs. She believed that the ideals of socialist policies clashed with the reality of SCAP's directives. In addition, what accomplishments were achieved were inadequately publicized. Under the circumstances "the Party's cooperation with Occupation policies in the name of the Japanese Government totally lost the support ... of the Japanese masses." Fourth, "[t]he Party failed to control the bureaucratic forces" which must be considered a "great menace" to the democratization of Japan. "These rotten irresponsible bureaucrats hampered the advancement of renovating policies. One of the reasons why the Party gave the impression of betraying its promises must be attributed to the resistance made from inside the administration." Finally the public expected too much of the Socialist Party. It was caught between its desires to implement socialist programs and its "responsibility to practice Occupation policies." There is no mention in this document of public scandals, nor any personal references.

Shidzue also suggested reasons for the success of the Democratic Liberals and the significant increase in seats for the Communist Party in January, 1949. The primary reason for the election of so many Democratic Liberals (269 seats won), she believed, was the popularity of its leader, Yoshida Shigeru. Furthermore, he and his party were supported because they campaigned against the Occupation. She pointed out, "Cooperating attitudes towards the Occupation Forces are becoming quite unpopular among the Japanese People. They support the action or speeches [of those] who pretend to ignore the fact of unconditional surrender." Yoshida and his party promised the people a free economy, a better life, lower taxes, reduced rationing, and so forth and this was what the people wanted to hear. The JCP also gained stature from their anti-American stance. She expressed admiration for the Communist Party's use of publicity. They had their own daily paper and several periodicals and they received positive support from intellectuals in literary fields while these same people criticized the

Socialists. Communists stayed close to the lower classes, the working people. They set up offices where these people could come and consult about tax problems or express other concerns. They helped people to fight landlords, welcomed repatriated soldiers home, entertained children, taught young people to dance and so forth, while the Socialists isolated themselves in the government. Of what worth is it, she seemed to conclude, to appear to hold power, if you do not apply that power with the good of the people in mind.

There is no doubt from this document that Katô Shidzue could rationalize her party's defeat. There is no doubt from her letters to friends, her autobiographies, and comments to mutual friends by Ethel Weed, that Shidzue was crushed by her personal elective defeat. There is also no doubt that, even though she admired her associates at SCAP, supported much of the work of the Occupation, and believed that the American style of democracy was the appropriate one for Japan, she felt that several of SCAP's autocratic directives, and their power over the Katayama and Ashida governments, were undermining all hope of socialist reform. When the authoritarian rule of Japan's bureaucrats, still alive and powerful under the new Japanese Constitution, was added to the mixture, hope of a democratic revolution seemed far off, indeed. Katô Shidzue was beginning to become disillusioned.

Notes

1. 1988a, pp. 129-131.

2. Margery Finn Brown, *Over A Bamboo Fence*, William Morrow & Co., 1951, pp. 10-14.

3. Mary Beard to Dorothy Brush, 7/17/50; *Japan Times*,, 6/6/50, Beard file, Smith. 1988a, p. 134.

4. Katô, Oishi Yoshie, Yamazaki Michiko, Matsutani Tenkoko, Fukuda Masako, Sakakibara Chiyo, Toganô Satoko, Yamaguchi Shizue, and Matsuo Toshi.

5. Samuel Coleman, *Family Planning in Japanese Society*, Princeton U. Press, 1983, pp. 18-19. Coleman's source for information in first quote is Oota Tenrei.

6. Interview, 1978.

7. $19.41 and $20.63 respectively per month. To give an idea of inflation, in March this would be $27.83 and $29.60 and the following September, $14.50 and $15.42 a month.

8. Hugh Borton, *Japan's Modern Century*, Ronald Press, 1955, pp. 414-415.

9. "6.5 million demobilized troops and repatriated civilians" had returned to Japan by 1948. Samuel Coleman, *Family Planning in Japanese Society*, p. 18

10. As quoted in *Nippon Times*, 11/12/47.

11. For public debate see RG331, Box 5248; for newspaper quotes see Publications Analysis, Box 5167; for discussion of the law and its revision see, "Revisions of the Criminal Code of Japan During the Occupation," by Howard Meyers and "Democratization of the Family Relation in Japan" by Sakae Wagatsuma, both in *Legal Reforms in Japan During the Occupation, Washington Law Review*, Seattle, 1977; and "The Family and the Law" by Yozo Watanabe, in *Law in Japan*, Arthur Taylor von Mehren, ed., Harvard University Press, 1963; see also Beard File, letter 9/10/47, Smith. Katô Shidzue does not mention this discussion in her autobiographies. There was provision for punishment of men who committed adultery with married women, but this was seldom invoked.

12. RG331, Box 5250, File: Political Parties.

13. Text of bill, Sanger Box 118, File #1194, Smith. For specific details of final law and revisions in 1949 and 1952 see Luke T. Lee and Arthur Larson, *Population and Law*, Rule of Law Press, 1971. Katô's attitude was stated clearly in our 1978 interviews, and in her autobiographies.

14. 1952 bill deleted the review committee requirement.

15. RG331, Box 5247, Birth Control & Population File.

16. Japanese attending were Akamatsu Tsuneko, Dr. Amano Fumiko, her husband, Dr. Amano Kageyasu, Hora Seki, Katô Shidzue, Professor Kitaoka Juitsu, Dr. Majima Kan, Niizuma Ito, Yamakawa Kikue, Dr. Yamamoto Sugi, Miura Sadako, Yoshizaka Shuzo. There were eight women and four men.

17. See Chapter 20 in Theodore Cohen, *Remaking Japan*, The Free Press, 1987, for a first hand account of discussions and fighting in SCAP. Cohen is scathing towards Hoover's lack of understanding of Japanese political context and of his insistence that his will be done. He blames Hoover, and Kades and Whitney, whom Hoover won over to his side, for convincing MacArthur to carry out the directive. The outcome crippled the pro-American, anti-communist labor movement and turned it against SCAP.

18. Theodore Cohen, *Remaking Japan*, p. 391 and 392.

19. RG331, Box 5248, Govt. File, National Public Service Law. Cohen says much the same. "[The Hoover Mission men] had no room in their mental baggage for the psychology and attitudes of the people for whom they had been called upon to prescribe their modern, scientific, nonfeudal administrative system." *Remaking Japan*, p. 381.

20. April, 1947 = $8,080.

21. RG331, Box 5247, File #5.

22. RG331, Box 5250, File #81.

13

Conflict over Birth Control (1949–1952)

Katô Shidzue was bitterly disappointed by her failure to gain a third term in the House of Representatives in January, 1949. The lost election, however, did not mean that she must retire from public service. She expected to work for the Socialist Party's re-establishment and to continue her own activities on selected political and social issues. She would have more time to devote to birth control education and to her birth control popularization society, not quite two years old. More and more she began to go her own way. She used her association with the Socialists when that was helpful; she sided with conservative officials, when that suited her purpose. In July, 1950, she ran successfully for a JSP seat in the House of Councillors. From then on she worked within the Diet when she saw some hope of success, but primarily she used her highly visible national profile to bolster her own causes outside the legislative process.

By the end of 1949 Katô confessed that the previous two years had been very difficult. She wrote Dorothy Brush that December bringing her up to date on the events which had transpired. "My life since the end of the war has been one of rushing for one thing and the other. Both my husband I were twice elected to the Japanese Diet. We have been very active for the democratization of Japan cooperating with the Allied people. I felt pretty satisfied in taking an active role, particularly in women's legislation. However, at the third general election which took place last January, both of us failed to be reelected. Our political party —Social Democratic Party, which we believed to be the leading force for new Japan — was bitterly attacked by both extremes. The Communist Party became a menacing force against democracy in Japan just like the reactionary forces are." She went on to tell that a life in politics had been a long time dream, so she had enjoyed her three years in the Diet; "however, life there [the Diet] is like playing a quick game of see-saw. We [JSP and the Katôs] are at present sitting at the bottom. My party has nominated me as a candidate to run a campaign for a seat in the House of Councillors next June. I feel that to have a seat in the Diet will profit our birth control movement in many ways, so if my health and funds can afford it, I shall run again."[1]

A few days later she wrote to Margaret Sanger speaking more broadly about the past year. "It seems to me that people here are spiritually very low compared to pre-war times. They can't dance to the piper's flute! People are depressed and struggling hard trying to meet these days of deflation and heavy taxation. Working people have to spend all their income for nothing but food and car fare in order to work. Deflation is just as bad as inflation for those who have no savings. I realized that when women do not have an excess of energy to think about tomorrow, being obliged to live only for today, they cannot be intelligent enough to think about their family planning." Adding a personal note she told Sanger that the last year had been an especially strenuous one politically and that she and Kanjû "felt that this was one of the worst years of our lives."[2]

Katô also told her friends a little about her family, saying that this part of her life provided her with "much joy." Both her son, Arata, now just past thirty, and her daughter, "Takko," who would be five the next March, were living at home. Arata was working at CIE and studying in his spare time. He was also responsible for his father, Ishimoto Keikichi, who had returned home from Beijing, China as a "refugee." She commented that Arata should have been anticipating a large estate from his grandfather, but Keikichi had lost it all through frivolous and imprudent financial decisions. Arata was still single because his impoverished circumstances precluded any possibility of marriage. Her little daughter, who looked more like a granddaughter, Shidzue admitted, was a great comfort to her. She felt she must look after her own health and keep alert just to care for Takko. Shidzue enclosed a picture of her daughter taken with James Killen's children at his residence. She noted that Killen had been chief of the Labor Section at SCAP when Kanjû was Minister of Labor during the summer of 1948. She did not include the fact that Killen, in agreement with Kanjû, had fought against the National Public Service Law revisions which outlawed collective bargaining and the strike by public service workers. Consequently, after that law was successfully passed, Killen had resigned in protest and been sent back to the U.S. post-haste. These were indeed difficult political times.

Shidzue added a postscript to her letter to Dorothy which revealed some of the family's material worries. "I feel shame in asking you this, but there are a number of things that our family needs. If you feel that you can spare some of the things listed below, it will be most appreciated by me." First she spoke of the items that little Takko needed, adding that she was a "rather large size for her age." She could use underwear, knitted things, all sorts of clothes and coats or material to make these. Shidzue needed suits, overcoats, sweaters, or just about anything that would fit her. She then gave her size and told her friend that she was an admirer of her taste. The household in general needed sheets, bed covers, pillow cases, towels, and they would be happy with Dorothy's discards.

Continued Economic Hardship

Times were difficult for everyone in 1949. In February of that year Joseph M. Dodge, president of a bank in Detroit, had arrived in Tokyo to advise Prime Minister Yoshida and his Finance Minister, Miyazawa Kiichi, on how to bring Japan's inflation under control through balancing the budget. Interviewed by reporters Dodge stated, "Any realistic view of the economic problem suggests a rough and rocky road which will severely test the strength, character, and loyalty of the people....There seems to be astonishingly little comprehension among the Japanese people of the real situation of their country. Nothing should have been expected as a result of the war but a long term of hardship and self-denial. The nation continuously has been living beyond its means...."[3] His program was founded on balancing the budget and included tax increases and careful tax collection as well as price and wage controls. It was a deflationary program which would cause the already squeezed population increased hardship. He expected this and pointed out at a SCAP meeting that "[a] mild increase in unemployment will...lead to increased efficiency of labor and a greater production and productivity which makes possible continued volume production at lower prices." Who would buy this increased volume of goods given the low wages and increased unemployment? Dodge expected to increase exports which would help balance the budget. And what about the necessary depression of an already low standard of living? "[The] standard of living has probably been permitted to go too high -cannot increase further- we can't give them everything they want," Dodge reasoned. "It is a tough job to halt a Santa Claus economy."[4] Few Japanese would have recognized their country in this description. Most people felt they were living on the edge of a precipice, and further cuts in their meager standard of living would force them to jump. Unfortunately not many had friends in America who might help them muddle through the difficult deflationary times.

During the same winter that Dodge was evaluating Japan's economic resources and asking the Japanese to tighten their belts once again, another advisor arrived in Tokyo to research a complementary aspect of Japan's continuing difficulty providing for the welfare of its people. Dr. Warren S. Thompson, Director of the Scripps Foundation for Research in Population Problems, began his temporary mission as technical consultant to SCAP's Natural Resources Section in January, 1949. The report of his findings, made public in March, emphasized the absolute necessity of the development of a comprehensive birth control program to curb the predicted population explosion which was well under way. Thompson was a noted expert on population growth particularly as related to questions of war and peace. In *Population and Peace in the Pacific*,[5] which he had written in 1946, he made a plea to Occupation officials to institute a "soft" peace that would look towards economic recovery and a just distribution of the world's resources. This, he believed, would put an end to economic motivations for aggression. He saw Japan's primary problems for the future as population pressures, lack of natural resources, and land area reduction to the home islands. He insisted that limitation of population was fundamental to any attempt to economically survive these three interrelated problems. Thompson's research in Japan in the winter of 1949 did not compromise his earlier findings, rather it heightened his awareness of the urgency of Japan's population problem.

In extensive newspaper interviews during the third week in March, Thompson reiterated that birth control represented the only real solution to Japan's severe population pressures.[6] He further stated that he had been encouraged during his discussions with government officials, physicians, and private citizens that there would be wide popular support for a government sponsored program on birth control education. He cautioned that Occupation authorities should not force the issue as that might leave the Americans open for criticism of an alleged "American scheme to destroy the Japanese race." An American imposed program would not be "the democratic way and I am strenuously opposed to any kind of Hitlerism." When asked whether he felt the Catholic Church would oppose such a plan he scoffed and said that in fact they also supported birth control through their rhythm method and would not deny non-Catholic Japan use of other methods to solve a serious problem. Thompson then cautioned that failure to develop a successful program to limit population would mean a more severe decrease in the Japanese standard of living and could even lead to another war. A Japan permitted to recover her industrial strength while not checking her population growth would be disastrous. Over the next few days Japanese government officials, particularly within the Welfare Ministry, spoke out in favor of Thompson's conclusion that birth control education was necessary in the fight for population control.

The following month magazines and newspapers were full of commentary on the importance of birth control education and the Chief Cabinet Secretary to Prime Minister Yoshida, Masuda Kaneshichi, spoke out in favor of birth control as a fundamental solution to Japan's population problem. He recognized that this would require reconsideration of the Eugenics Law of 1948, and he pledged the government's support for legislation amendments which would foster birth control education. On May 12, 1949, the House of Representatives expressed support for measures submitted by the Population Problem Commission and began debate on revision of the Eugenics Law. A bill was passed on May 23rd expanding acceptable reasons for aborting a pregnancy to include economic hardship of the mother, and providing for increased manufacture and sale of contraceptive medicines and devices. This revised law became effective on July 24th. While SCAP officials did not encourage any of this activity, they did not interfere.

MacArthur vs. Birth Control Advocacy

It was within this context that Katô Shidzue saw the return of Margaret Sanger to Japan as the perfect rallying point for a nation-wide campaign for birth control education. Katô, once again, was disappointed over the direction of the revision of the Eugenics Law. By default, it continued to elevate abortion above contraception, and did not emphasize education. Just the same, she believed the pronouncements in favor of a population policy and successful legislative action provided a positive environment in which her own program could grow. Publicity from a nation-wide Sanger tour and the continued magic of the Sanger name in Japan would help to popularize Katô's ideas and would mean a more encompassing and rapid success for her vision of planned parenthood education.

On May 19, 1949, Katô in a letter to Margaret Sanger:[7] "It has been my long cherished dream, to invite you and Dorothy [Brush] for a lecture tour in Japan on birth control and population problems. The Japanese Government and people are now taking a keen interest in these questions. Editorials, forums as well as the reports on investigation of public reactions on this matter occupy considerable space in newspapers now. Of course the Eugenics Law, which is such an unsatisfactory one to my mind, is stimulating the situation to a great extent." Katô then explained to Sanger that all expenses for both of the women would be paid for by the Japanese and that they would be "warmly welcomed by the people and Government."

Sanger replied immediately, accepting the invitation with great enthusiasm. In her letter she also cautioned, "I think there would have to be an official invitation, as our State Department is fearful of Catholic opposition." She sent a second letter of "acceptance" on June 14th with a copy to Lt. Weed at CIE, and a cable to Katô through Weed. She was not going to let this opportunity slip by due to problems with mail delivery. She emphasized once again the need for an official invitation but was certain that "Miss Weed would be able to advise" about State Department regulations.

Lt. Weed was actively involved almost from the beginning. She, or someone else at SCAP, did tell Katô that Occupation authorities would prefer the invitation to be issued by the Japanese, but no one attempted to put a damper on the plans. Katô wrote Sanger on June 28th, "According to my probing about GHQ reactions to your tour, I learned that they are inclined to avoid to attempt anything which raises opposition from Catholics, but if the plan is initiated by the Japanese, then the American authorities will not object." Katô proceeded with her arrangements making sure that they complied absolutely with State Department regulations. She also kept Weed advised of all new developments.

In the same letter of the 28th Katô reiterated that the timing was exactly right for Sanger's visit, an opportunity that should not be missed. Then she detailed the plans. To maximize publicity and provide adequate financial backing for large public meetings throughout both urban and rural Japan, she had approached the management at *Yomiuri Newspaper*. Baba Tsunego, the president, had accepted complete responsibility and agreed to issue the invitation. He sent a letter to Sanger setting forth the purpose of the tour - "[to] assist in improving and guiding birth control and sex education in Japan."[8] He then went on to outline current population pressures, and state that an understanding and acceptance of Sanger's ideas "would be of great help for the reconstruction of a peaceful and cultured nation." He seemed to take SCAP's cooperation for granted. "Mrs. Katô approached SCAP officials for an understanding," he assured Sanger, "and at the same time Chief Cabinet Secretary Masuda and high officials of the Welfare Ministry have promised their support for this end." The intention was to have the Population Problems Deliberative Council, a special organ instituted by the Cabinet, issue an invitation, as well. This would represent a "semi-official" welcome, since there was no precedent in occupied Japan for a formal government invitation to a foreign guest. Masuda and the Minister of Welfare, Hayashi Jôji, had already expressed agreement with the tour plans, and a three week period in October was set aside.

Meanwhile the Japanese continued to legislate, editorialize, and propagandize favorably for population limitation through birth control. Katô addressed these issues in her birth control society; the Drs. Amano discussed the issues in their Japan Birth-Control Institute; Dr. Majima Kan fostered these ideas in his Japan Birth-Control League; and others followed the progress of population control and family planning in several recently formed additional groups. Simultaneously, representatives of the Catholic Church stepped up their campaign against birth control, but focused their attacks on the Thompson report and SCAP rather than on the activities of Japanese citizens. Catholic opposition was proclaimed by the American missionary, Father William A. Kaschmitter, director of the official Catholic newspaper, *Tosei News*, the American Catholic Chaplains of Tokyo-Yokohama, The American Catholic Women's Club of Tokyo, American Catholics in the U.S., and finally, representatives of the 125,000 Japanese Catholics. On July 1st a spokesman for the Pope issued a statement alleging that Occupation authorities were encouraging the Japanese Diet to pass legislation legalizing abortion and permitting the manufacture and sale of contraceptives. "No matter who is responsible for these laws, our Christianity cannot tolerate this barbarous manner of solving a problem, no matter how crucial it can be," the Vatican statement insisted.[9]

Unable to stay out of the discussion any longer, on July 2nd MacArthur made public a letter he had written to the Tokyo Allied Catholic Women's Club in answer to their request that he address the issues raised in population control reports and that he separate the American Occupation from any conclusions which favored the use of abortion and/or contraception. MacArthur did exactly that. "In order to prevent any misunderstanding and to eradicate any misconception, the Supreme Commander wishes it understood that he is not engaged in any study or consideration of the problem of Japanese population control. Such matter does not fall within the prescribed scope of the Occupation and decisions thereon rest entirely with the Japanese themselves." He went on to say that any statements made by persons such as Dr. Thompson represented their own opinions offered within a democratic framework of free discussion. Finally, he concluded, "Birth control, with its social, economic and theological sides is, in final analysis, for individual judgement and decision.... and is certainly not within the purview of prescribed Allied policy or the defined scope of the Supreme Commander's executive responsibility or authority."[10] In effect MacArthur disavowed the Thompson report and similar reports by other Occupation advisors, and removed the entire question of population control and family planning from the Occupation's mission. One aspect of this discussion which was kept from the public's view, however, was that at this point MacArthur also scuttled the proposed Sanger visit. He certainly had no need of an American birth control advocate publicizing her views throughout the land to the delight of both the Japanese and American press.

Over the summer many letters crossed the Pacific between Katô and Sanger as they tried to resuscitate the tour. By now the salutations and closings reflected a closer relationship between these longtime associates and friends. For the first time Katô used Sanger's given name and the letters exhibited a sense of equality as well as respect, admiration and affection. Sanger's letters also revealed her increasing frustration as she was consistently refused a visa to travel to Japan. She tried to use influence in Washington to change minds at the State Department, but, of course, that was not where the roadblock existed. Katô, for her part, gained additional support for Sanger's lecture tour from prominent Japanese including the promised endorsement of Masuda, newly promoted to Minister of State. This was a significant achievement for Katô. After all she was a Socialist Party member, associated with the party's left-wing, and had recently been soundly defeated in her bid for reelection. And yet, she was being courted by a high official in a conservative government that was headed by her adversary, Yoshida Shigeru, the very same official who in the past had ignored her Diet questions regarding family planning.

As late as October Sanger wrote an optimistic letter recounting the Japanese individuals in significant public and private positions who had written her in anticipation of her lecture tour. She assured Katô, "If these various groups and individuals would cooperate with you and present a united front in requesting my visit I feel sure permission would be forth coming." She seemed happy that the delays in obtaining a visa had given her plenty of time to plan a comprehensive program which would include different lectures to specialized groups. The visit had grown in Sanger's mind. She was seventy years old, and was no longer offered an American stage to the degree the Japanese were suggesting. She had gone to Japan in the 1920s for the express purpose of a grand lecture tour, but it had been denied her. Once again, in 1936 and 1937 conditions prevented her from gaining a broad and open platform. This was an opportunity which would rectify those wrongs. She longed for a chance to profess her social cause with the fanfare and flare not offered her at home. Unfortunately a Sanger visit was not to be.

The issue of birth control for Japan, however, would not disappear. On December 30, 1949, twenty-five hundred copies of a two volume study by Dr. Edward A. Ackerman, Professor of Geography at University of Chicago, were released under SCAP's imprint. Ackerman had been invited to serve as technical advisor to SCAP's Natural Resources Section[11] and in this capacity the noted geographer had spent two years researching questions of Japan's natural resources and expectations for the future. Three years previously in a chapter entitled "Japan: Have or Have-not Nation" Dr. Ackerman had warned that if Japan expected to enter the world of free nations she must consider limits to her population. "[Japan] is a nation made relatively poor by its fecundity. So long as there are three to four children in the average Japanese family, there will be an increasingly acute resource problem in Japanese territory."[12] Ackerman's statements in his 1949 report, based on two years of cooperative research between SCAP and Japanese experts, were even more emphatic. On December 30th this scientist summarized his findings for the Japanese press. He emphasized that the crisis was so severe that population curbs must be imposed upon Japan. He further concluded that this could not be accomplished by the popularly suggested solution of emigration, and that the nation would have to concentrate on population control in concert with careful use and development of the limited resources available and with expansion of foreign trade. Although Ackerman never specifically mentioned the use of contraception in his discussion of "population control," that was the conclusion drawn by the public and by the Catholic community.

Once again birth control was in the headlines and once again GHQ had to defend itself in apparent opposition to some of its own advisors. MacArthur held firm. He would not be intimidated by his own experts, by threatening letters, by the Japanese press, or by Sanger's popularity in Japan. Claiming a neutral position on the whole issue of birth control, he refused to reconsider a Sanger tour.

In the spring of 1950, MacArthur was forced to answer questions in letters from angry or supportive Americans about the cancellation of the Sanger tour and about the Occupation's general policy toward population planning in Japan. No previous Occupation related decision had created such a flood of mail addressed to the Supreme Commander. The issue had fired up the American public far more than any involving Japan's new constitution, elective politics, dire economic distress, union strikes, or anything else SCAP had previously dealt with. Here was something the Americans could understand and something they definitely had opinions about.

MacArthur made up a flexible letter[13] to be sent in answer to the many writers, for everyone who wrote received a personal reply signed by the Supreme Commander. The longest version of the letter was four typewritten pages and began with a personal paragraph which referenced the statements in the recipient's letter. It then went on to present an explanation of SCAP's policy of non-interference and neutrality on issues of birth control for Japan, a detailed discussion of Japanese population problems past and current, Japan's recent Eugenics legislation, and some explanatory comments on the refusal of a visa for Margaret Sanger. The intent was to show that MacArthur "had yielded to pressure from neither the group in advocacy nor that in opposition to birth control." Specific references to prohibition of the Sanger visit took two tacks depending on the position of the letter writer. To those who supported the visit MacArthur showed that it was unnecessary due, for example, to the "Japanese Eugenics Law now under vigorous implementation, a product exclusively of Japanese thought, [which] in many respects goes further toward the objectives they [Sanger and other planned parenthood supporters] advocated than do the laws thus far enacted by the legislatures of our own states." Why would the Japanese need Margaret Sanger to teach them what they already knew? For those opposed to birth control the General pointed out that such a visit was not supportable under the general policies of neutrality established by the Occupation. This letter, then, could expand or contract, include or delete according to MacArthur's intended audience. The general managed to please everyone.

MacArthur's letter proved so successful in neutralizing opposition and anger that only a very few who received the letter wrote back unconvinced that he had acted appropriately. Even protesters from ACLU and Planned Parenthood groups crumbled in the face of such weighty arguments. Each recipient took from the personal letter what seemed to suit and wrote back to the effect that MacArthur was, indeed, an ally of whichever side the writer lined up with. Perhaps Eleanor Roosevelt's response to MacArthur's reply represented the most famous individual won over to the General's side. She had been a firm supporter of Planned Parenthood and had written a column in support of Sanger's proposed trip to Japan. In response to MacArthur's letter she wrote, "Thank you very much for your explanatory letter of March 10th. I entirely understand your position and I think you have made a wise decision. I shall explain it to those who wrote me. With my very best wishes, I am Very Sincerely Yours, Eleanor Roosevelt." Opposition to MacArthur's position on the Sanger tour was neutralized.

A Sanger visit would have helped Katô promote birth control education, but it was not essential to her program. On the other hand, the disappointment felt by Sanger was intense. She had dreamed of reviving her declining appeal through a successful campaign in Japan, where she had always been greatly appreciated. In fact, the relative positions of the two women had reversed, and it was Katô who could be of greater service. By February, 1950, Katô could sublimate any disappointment over the canceled trip by planning new projects or dreaming about her own travels abroad. Sanger, on the other hand, could only look forward to dissension with professional associates, and cycles of illness and convalescence in her personal life.[14]

From Depression to Elation

In the winter of 1950, while Katô lay sick in bed with influenza, she was cheered by gifts from her friends. She received dresses for Takko, a wool tweed suit, sweater, three pairs of nylons and a "smart looking" overcoat for herself from Dorothy. She was thrilled with the leather lining in the coat which zippered in and out. From Margaret she received more children's clothing, shoes that Takko could grow into, and underwear. Dr. C. J. Gamble of Planned Parenthood sent a money order for her work, suggesting that she pay poor mothers to come to a clinic for birth control education. Dorothy also sent five pairs of gloves which Shidzue found "fine in quality and luxurious looking," and Dorothy's daughter sent two bedspreads, six sheets, and pillow cases and towels. Shidzue responded with delight in her next letter. "I really don't know how to express our joy in receiving package after package full of beautiful and useful American goods! We feel as if Christmas, New Year, birthday and all other festivals have come to us at once."[15] The real import of this batch of letters, however, was Shidzue's announcement that she would be coming to the U.S. in late March or April and would get to see them all.

Like Sanger the previous fall, Katô was to be disappointed. For unstated reasons, she was prevented by SCAP from securing the necessary visa to make the trip. On February 28th, Shidzue had joyfully written to Dorothy, "[H]ere is the exciting news...I am visiting America in April." She then explained that she would be going to California to lecture to Japanese-American women's organizations and she would gather material for publication in popular Japanese magazines. She wrote to Margaret that a visit with her and other old friends would be uppermost on her schedule, but, she warned, "[T]his plan shall be kept without any publicity until I succeed in getting a passport from GHQ." On March 9th, she wrote Dorothy that her expected invitation from a California Nisei group had not yet materialized and felt they were hesitant because they had heard about "General MacArthur's attitude toward our work." She then mourned the fact that birth control workers always found themselves walking on a "road of thorns." Next she sought a substitute invitation from New York Planned Parenthood Federation, which was quickly issued, but she was still denied a visa. The April she had expected to spend in the U.S. came and went. Once again she tried for permission to leave Japan. This time Roger Baldwin and the A.C.L.U. guaranteed her expenses, and Baldwin wrote a letter of support to "his friends" at GHQ. It did not help.

Katô missed another opportunity to travel to the U.S. in the Spring of 1950. She would have been an obvious choice to join a group of Japanese women leaders that Ethel Weed escorted on a three-month study of American democratic practices. Given her political acclaim, and her close relationship with Weed, one would expect that she would have been selected to participate. She was not invited. Among those who did go were Katô's JSP associate, Senator Akamatsu Tsuneko, newly appointed chair of the Labor Committee; two members from the Women's and Minors' Bureau, Tanino Setsu and Tomita Nobuko; JSP Representative and Katô's right-wing nemesis, Toganô Satoko; and an attorney, Kume Ai. The tour provided the women with opportunities to meet with many American public figures. Tomita Nobuko and Kume Ai, for example, enjoyed an overnight at Mary Beard's home in Connecticut. Beard commented that these two women were "very intelligent and not easily fooled by the lighter-minded women who pushed them around over here." After returning to Japan, Weed calculated that the ten women combined had given a total of 164 seminars and lectures, reaching over 40,000 people.[16]

The success of this trip along with GHQ's refusal to grant Katô a visa weighed heavily on Weed's mind. In November Weed wrote sadly to Mary Beard, "Several problems have been troubling me greatly; one among them, the fact that Katô Shidzue has been unable to secure a visa to go to the States. She says that it is because of her political beliefs - a fact that she is a member of the left wing of the Social Democrat Party. I do not know whether this is so or not, but I have been unable to help her as I should like. This sort of a problem troubles my conscience and makes my presence here very uncomfortable at times. To the best of my knowledge, this is an unjust situation." Beard wrote back that while she had no way of knowing just why Katô had been consistently refused a visa, she did not think it was because of her political beliefs. Beard did feel, however, that there was a primary difference between Katô and the other Japanese who had been "visa-ed." The others had come with the "avowed purpose of studying and observing our ways," whereas Katô would be coming to lecture to the Americans. Beard suggested that American officialdom might be fearful that Katô would join the lecture circuit again for she was "acclaimed as a politico in the Diet, [and] as a birth control leader." She might even "receive an invitation to address Congress, be more of an 'exhibit' than a student."[17] She thought that this possibility for recognition and admiration must have frightened American authorities. As was often the case, Beard's devotion to Katô ran away with her imagination.

Katô had not invested all of her time during these months in her search for travel documents. In the early spring she agreed to run under the JSP banner for a seat in the House of Councillors. Once again her platform focused on family planning. She was still not satisfied with the Eugenics Law and hoped to gain support for additional revisions which would encourage government financing of birth control education and the distribution of contraceptives and birth control medicines to poor women, thereby making fewer abortions necessary. Her primary concern had always been the health and welfare of mothers and children and the right of women to make their own health and parenthood choices. Here would be a new platform from which to proclaim these principles.

In this second postwar upper house election half of the seats would be contested, and of these, fifty would be filled by candidates running at-large nationally. The rest would be filled by successful local candidates from prefectural constituencies. To run at-large a candidate needed either strong party backing or the backing of a powerful independent organization, and nation-wide name recognition. The competition was not simply among candidates of different parties, but all candidates running for the fifty seats Each voter was allowed just one vote; the fifty candidates with the highest vote total would take seats. Katô ran at-large, received the sixth highest vote total nationally, and came in first for the Socialist Party. Her political career was on the move once more; she was elated.

Reality was altogether different from anticipation. Even though Katô was well aware that the House of Councillors was considerably less powerful than the House of Representatives, she expected to find opportunities to use this prestigious office to lobby within the Diet for her concerns. In fact over this first six year term she played a minor institutional role. Although she was involved in the 1952 further revision of the Eugenics Law, in general, Katô found her career as a senator more important for the public exposure it gave her than for anything she might accomplish in the Diet.

In 1952, after Japan had regained her sovereignty, Shidzue finally realized her dream of bringing Margaret Sanger back to Japan. In January Margaret had written Shidzue to tell her that President Honda of the *Mainichi Newspaper* had invited her to come to Japan under the newspaper's sponsorship. The *Mainichi,* which had established a Population Problems Research Council in July, 1949, had begun to conduct research and sponsor study meetings on family planning, population control, and issues related to birth control. Beginning in 1950 the Council sponsored its first biennial National Opinion Survey on Family Planning. This and subsequent surveys of 3,000 couples with wives under forty-nine years of age were to become an important resource for statistical research and would serve as guidelines for making government policy as well as suggesting practical directions for private organizations.[18] It is not surprising, then, that the *Mainichi* wanted to sponsor the Sanger visit.

A package of three thousand signatures of Japanese citizens urging her to come to speak to them accompanied Sanger's invitation. She would accept, of course. She wrote how pleased she would be to meet with Shidzue, her associates, and those in other family planning organizations. She particularly mentioned Shidzue's rival, Dr. Majima Kan, who continued to head The Birth Control League, and entreated her friend, "Will you try, my dear Shidzue, to make things pleasant for Dr. Majima. He has worked hard to get these signatures in order to offset General MacArthur's insulting remarks that there were not 10 people in Japan who wanted me to come. Their signatures are splendid proof to the contrary....I am writing to you...because it was you who brought this invitation about, and I should be pleased if you could let Dr. Majima know that all will work together for my visit...." Sanger hoped her visit would smooth over old animosities in the Japanese birth control movement as well as provide a platform for her thoughts. She saw it as a profitable venture for all concerned.

In the same letter of January, 1952, Margaret had attended to private business. Shidzue had left kimonos with her after her 1951 visit and had sent some to Dorothy Brush to sell, and she had left wood-block prints for Margaret to sell as well. She wrote, "I owe you some money for the beautiful prints. I have used some and sold some, and I have $60.00 for you....I have done nothing with the kimonos. I have two here that Dorothy gave me, but so far I have not been able to sell them. I think Dorothy has put some money in the bank for you."[19] Shidzue was always eager to eke out a slightly more comfortable living by trading her exotic goods for useful dollars.

Busy with her many responsibilities Shidzue did not reply to this letter or several others, each one more urgent, which Margaret sent throughout the winter of 1952. Finally, at the end of April, Shidzue wrote, "I firmly believe that there will not be any difficulty in obtaining a visa. I will send letters of introduction to the Japanese consul-generals in San Francisco, Los Angeles and New York. I will also ask the Mainichi correspondent in New York to help you if necessary....I am sorry for my long delay in answering you. I have been extremely busy preparing for independence." In 1952 Senator Katô could exert more influence and provide more help for Sanger than the other way around. It was Sanger who approached Katô with great urgency, while Katô, whose public activities continued to grow, kept her American friend waiting until she could find a window in her busy schedule.

The visit was set. Sanger was to arrive in Yokohama on October 30th. The *Mainichi Newspaper* sent her an itinerary, which Sanger complained by return mail to Katô was totally unacceptable. She exclaimed, "I am sure that this is not what you want me to do!! I am not coming to Japan on a sightseeing tour. I want to help you all I can in consultation with those who wish to do something about birth control." She went on to say that Dr. Stone would be willing to speak with doctors and others in hospitals and "will not want to do the travel tourist joy-ride." She continued, "I would like to go down and talk with the mothers in different parts of your country, and also to broadcast if you would like me to."[20] The seventy-three year old Margaret Sanger was as feisty and stubborn as ever. Shidzue saw to changing the schedule in line with her wishes.

Sanger expected her week in Japan to be as crowded with celebrity events and speeches and discussions as her visits in 1922 and 1937, but this time with the blessing of officials. She did not see her age or deteriorating health as a handicap even after she suffered an attack of angina en route. A Honolulu physician wrote a letter urging that she "never accept two major engagements a day, that she never stand on a receiving line, that she avoid any long talks, that she have at least one hour's rest in the middle of the day, and if possible avoid any evening session where she has to take the responsibility."[21] In fact she disobeyed all instructions, maintained a strenuous pace throughout the week which was, as Sanger had requested, completely full. She met with government officials, members of the family planning movement, and other leaders; visited birth control clinics; held press conferences; participated in radio round tables; and traveled around some of the Tokyo "slums"[22] and to selected rural areas .[23] She also made a visit to two model clinics set up by Dr. Koya Yoshio, Director of the Public Health Institute of Japan. These clinics were placed in rural areas, farming, fishing, or coal mining villages, and were run with the intention of determining the effectiveness of the use of contraceptives to decrease the birth rate while reducing the number of abortions. Sanger visited one farming village on the plain and one in the mountains which had "neat little clinics all its own." She was quite impressed with Dr. Koya's project which, after just two years, had successfully educated many villagers who had experienced a definite overall reduction in birthrate.[24]

On Sanger's final day in Japan, November 8th, Katô and her JSP colleague Representative Yamaguchi Shizue took Sanger and Dorothy Brush on a tour of Tokyo. They went about the streets in a campaign style sound truck with loud speakers. The two politicians gave Sanger a taste of their educational program which borrowed from the traditional storytellers who traveled around Tokyo on bicycles with a box of story pictures, and a drawer of candy. This method of attracting a crowd to listen to stories and look at illustrations had been first adapted successfully by the Communist Party and these two Socialist women were trying to appropriate it for their own political message. They wanted to educate the populus about the democratic process and would include a word or two about family planning as well. On this occasion the loud speakers blared out "Sanger is here! Sanger is here! Sanger says no more abortions."[25] Each time the sound truck stopped a crowd gathered, the two women gave brief speeches, and then a man presented a puppet show in illustration of good family practices including the use of birth control. This final day's events seemed a fitting, if exhausting, conclusion to Sanger's week. Her return to Japan had been a triumphant one for her and a productive one for Katô Shidzue as well.

Notes

1. Katô to Dorothy Brush, 12/10/49, Smith.
2. Katô to Sanger, 12/14/49, Reel 8, Sanger, LofC.
3. Kosaka Masataka *100 Million Japanese: The Postwar Experience*, Kodansha International LTD., 1972, p.98.
4. Quotes in Jon Halliday, *A Political History of Japanese Capitalism*, Monthly Review Press, 1975, p. 189.
5 . U. of Chicago Press.
6. Restated *Nippon Times* 3/18/49.
7. All of the mentioned letters are in Smith.
8. RG331, Box 2146, July 21, 1949.
9. *Nippon Times* reports April-June, 1949. Pope's spokesman from news article, Smith.
10. Quoted in full, Nippon *Times*, 7/2/49.
11. Headed by Lt. Col. H. G. Schenck.
12. In Douglas G. Haring, ed, *Japan's Prospect*, 1946. See press reports from 12/31/49-2/50.

13. This raft of correspondence in RG331, Box 5246.

14. See last two chapters in Ellen Chesler, *Woman of Valor*, Simon & Schuster, 1992.

15. Twelve letters of February-March to and from Katô, Smith.

16. From Weed's CIE report in Beard files, Smith; names also listed in Dorothy Robins-Mowry, *The Hidden Sun*, Westview Press, p. 111. Robins-Mowry states that this trip was arranged suddenly when women complained to Weed that ten men were being sent to the U.S. but no women. See also, Beard to Dorothy [Dick] Brush, 7/17/50, Beard File, Smith

17. Weed's letter of 11/18/50, and Beard's reply, 12/3/50, Beard File, Smith.

18. Chojiro Kunii, *Humanistic Family Planning Approaches: The Integration of Family Planning and Health Goals*, UN Fund for Population Activities, 1983, p. 11 & 12.

19. Sanger to Katô, 1/30/52, Smith.

20. Sanger to Katô 10/7/52. *Mainichi*'s itinerary specified trips to Meiji Shrine, Nikko, Kamakura, Hakone, Osaka, Nara, Kyoto, the usual tourist fare, and leisurely luncheons, but only one lecture.

21. Letter from Nils P. Larsen, M.D., "To Whom Ever It May Concern," 10/20/52.

22. When Katô refers to this same event she uses the term "working class area" rather than "slums."

23. See Sanger's trip notes for details, Smith. Ellen Chesler has a brief description of this trip in *Woman of Valor*, p. 423. Because of the American focus of this book, there are only brief reference to Sanger and Japan and most of the references to Shidzue are inaccurate. This is true in all books about Sanger, for each writer draws upon Ishimoto/Katô references from the previous writer's incorrect statements.

24. Sanger's trip to Japan, 1952 notes, Box 29, File #218, Smith, and Chojiro Kunii, p. 12.

25. Sanger's trip to Japan, 1952 notes, Box 29, File #218, Smith. See essay and letter by Dorothy Brush, Box 29A, Smith.

14

"Life-Changes" (1951–1957)

Katô Shidzue's dismay over the direction which democracy had taken in post-war Japan, her disappointments about her party and legislative effectiveness, her decreased influence at SCAP in the early fifties and then loss of that base as the Americans withdrew, battles with some associates, and problems at home, all caused her to yearn for a new perspective. Like so many on the left, in the early fifties she suffered a profound loss of faith in the direction her nation was moving. For some activists this meant retreat and isolation, for others greater radicalism outside traditional political party structures, for yet others intellectual submersion and theoretical discussion divorced from action.[1] Shidzue had never been a philosophical theorist; she did not write tracts about her thinking; she believed in action based on an intuitive interpretation of what she thought was right and just. Consequently, in those days of confusion and disappointment she became receptive to a belief system which seemed to solve personal and global problems simply. The organization which appeared in answer her needs was Moral Re-Armament, which professed an ideological framework, international in focus, aggressively anti-communist, and American in concept and sympathy.

Embracing a New Ideology

By late 1949 many Japanese, including Shidzue, had become increasingly concerned about the destructive role which they saw international communism playing in a precarious world of super powers and emerging third world nations. The outbreak of the Korean War in June, 1950, confirmed their alarm, causing disruption on the political left. Although Shidzue had identified herself with left-wing socialist causes all of her adult life, she was never supportive of radical visions, and openly opposed communism. Therefore, it is not out of character that Shidzue, a strong Americanophile, and a democratic humanist with European/American philosophical underpinnings, would be attracted to a community of anti-communists in the early fifties. Circumstances dictated that the organization which found her was Moral Re-Armament. During her first intensive encounter with this organization in the summer of 1951, Shidzue concluded that the program preached by MRA's leader, Dr. Frank Buchman, including an internationalist drive for peace, a moral framework opposed to communism, and individual preparation for ethical leadership, coincided with her own ideals.

Frank Buchman was an American from Pennsylvania who had begun his adult life as a Lutheran minister. After being forced out of his church position, in the 1920s he founded an organization based on Christian evangelism but not connected with any religious denomination. The group was known during the 20s and 30s variously as the Oxford Group and Buchmanites. The "groupers," as they were called, were primarily middle-class British and Americans. Just before World War II the organization's name was changed to Moral Re-Armament or MRA. After the war the leadership under Buchman's direction modulated its close association with Christianity to make MRA more palatable to Asians and Africans and embraced an ideology which provided a counterpoint to what they termed the destructive belief of communism. The goals and ideological tenets of MRA were designed to attract political, business, and labor leaders in countries throughout the world who would attend "training" sessions at MRA owned facilities where they would receive "guidance" toward personal "life-change." These leaders would then guide others toward the ultimate goal of world-wide "moral rearmament" and the defeat of communism. The organization was most successful in Britain, Germany, Japan and America and reached its height during the anti-communist cold war years of the fifties and early sixties.[2] When Buchman died in 1961 no single individual was anointed to take his place and, by the late sixties, the organization began to lose its strength and audience.

During the Summer of 1950 a group of postwar Japanese political, labor, and business leaders were authorized to join an international meeting at MRA headquarters in Caux, Switzerland. There was a flood of applications, since this was the first opportunity Japanese had had to leave the country since the Occupation began. The group, as it was finally constituted, included the Christian Socialist, ex-Prime Minister Katayama Tetsu, and Sohmạ Yukika, daughter of the venerated twentieth century statesman, Ozaki Yukio, and a good friend of Katô Shidzue. The trip coincided with the outbreak and first months of the Korean War, and the Japanese delegates emphasized MRA's fundamental, ideological opposition to the thinking which they felt had brought this war about. In an address before the U. S. Senate a representative of Japan's prime minister stated, "The lawless aggression in Korea is again involving America in great sacrifices. We Japanese wholeheartedly support the action taken by the United Nations and pay high respect to the courageous leadership of President Truman in this matter." He then praised MRA as the truly democratic ideology which would be "the powerful answer to Communism."[3] On August 6th, the fifth anniversary of the bombing of Hiroshima, delegate Sohma Yukika spoke to the Americans. "The world does not look to America only for material aid, but also for spiritual leadership...We are so grateful to you for bringing Moral Re-Armament to Japan....We women of Japan wish to do our best to bring this spirit to our country and through her change to the world, because we believe this is the only expression of restitution for her past wrongs, and with this ideology we can build a new world."[4] It was, therefore, the combination of Shidzue's intimate friendship with Sohma Yukika, her open admiration of America, and MRA's anti-communist thrust and international framework which caused her to embrace this ideology one year later. MRA, as she interpreted it, would provide the moral underpinnings for the rest of Katô's public career and personal life.

Shidzue's initial interest in MRA was somewhat cynically related to her quest for a visa and funding to travel abroad.[5] Her application to become a delegate to the June, 1951, MRA World Assembly on Mackinac Island, Michigan, was approved immediately by the MRA leadership, but held up by Occupation authorities. Although General MacArthur, by this time, had been dismissed by President Truman, and presumably his replacement, General Matthew Ridgeway, did not have any prejudices against Shidzue, it was touch and go at GHQ. She did finally receive a visa, but later than the other delegates and had to travel alone, arriving after the conference opened on June 1st.

Mackinac Island in upper Michigan was rich in natural beauty, unique in its rustic, turn of the century atmosphere, and quiet with a few horse drawn carriages replacing banned cars. Accommodations at the Grand Hotel were magnificent compared with war devastated Tokyo, and the food plentiful, varied, and excellent. This experience should have been completely relaxing; in fact it was most intense.[6]

Shidzue listened fervently to Buchman describing early post-war MRA meetings at Caux in which the Germans and French frankly discussed their wartime animosities. She was thrilled by the wonder of these enemies coming together in friendship and understanding. Of particular import to her was the story of the French Socialist leader, Madame Irene Laure, who had been a member of the underground during

World War II and whose son had been tortured by Germans. This influential Frenchwoman's hatred of Germany had known no bounds, and yet at Caux, she had become reconciled with her enemies.[7] In fact she "apologized to the Germans for having willed the total destruction of their country." That she was a Socialist, a woman, a grieving mother, and a victim of German atrocities, and yet was able to seek unity with her enemy impressed Shidzue. MRA had changed Madame Laure's life and the lives of others, including the famous postwar German leader, Konrad Adenauer, and had moved these leaders to a higher plane of public service and personal fulfillment. Shidzue was eager to experience such a change in her own life.

The speakers from other Asian countries, especially Korea, affected Shidzue most fervently.[8] She began to understand and sympathize with colonial peoples, most especially those who had been oppressed by the Japanese. When the Korean speaker told how his people were not permitted by their Japanese rulers to study or publicly use their own language, and were considered impure and inferior by their oppressors, she was brought to tears. She experienced the same emotions when the delegates from Taiwan, Singapore, and the Malay Peninsula spoke. Then she spoke, purposefully apologizing on behalf of her whole nation to those who had been brutalized by the Japanese, and resolved to work for reconciliation with these peoples.

Accepting without compromise the four tenets of Buchman's teachings, absolute honesty, absolute integrity, absolute unselfishness, and absolute love,[9] Shidzue experienced a religious conversion. For the remainder of the conference she participated eagerly in group activities. Meetings took the form of small group discussions, or "sharing and guidance" sessions, in which about thirty participants from all over the world gave brief speeches and responses. Sharing was akin to confessing sins and guidance was assumed to come from god as interpreted by MRA leaders.

Some discussions focused on topics of family relationships—husbands and wives, parents and children—and on the family's role in society. In these intimate sessions Shidzue felt the pressure to "change"; to progress toward a moral life. She applied the message to her estrangement with her step-daughter, who had left home late in 1947. Sumiko's sudden, dramatic, and self-willed action had shocked Shidzue and Kanjû, who considered the action unfilial and selfish. At the time both of the parents were deeply involved with the downward trajectory of the Socialist Katayama Government and their own political ambitions and projects. They knew the newspapers would make scandalous reading out of this story, and so they tried to keep the event secret while conducting a quiet search for Sumiko. It was not possible to suppress the story for long and soon they were publicly disgraced by a major scandal. It hit the headlines as Kanjû took up his post as Minister of Labor, reappeared at various junctures during his tenure, and, again, throughout the JSP bribery scandals and the Katôs defeat at the polls in January, 1949. In the summer of 1950 a reporter found Sumiko working in Osaka at the Bank of America, but the family did not reconcile.

On Mackinac Island in June, 1951, the "sharing" sessions and personal confessions made Shidzue think carefully about her resentment over Sumiko's actions and wonder about her own shortcomings as a mother. She thought about Katayama's testimony and his proclamation before her discussion group, that everyone had the power to change. Buchman and his staff had looked Shidzue directly in the eye and told her that since she was a strong, career-minded woman it would be necessary for her to work especially hard to change, but that she must do so if she were to serve humankind. Like others, she should take one step at a time until she could walk easily along that moral path. She continued to think about Sumiko. The atmosphere in these meetings must have anticipated later self-help groups, or recovery groups, which cajole and pressure toward a common group goal of conversion and recovery.

Shidzue reconsidered her relationship with her step-daughter. "Although Sumiko had received love from her new parent she had also been fiercely scolded. Consequently, she had left home. If a mother is simply strict, she performs her role inadequately. I determined that I had made a mistake. I had been a bad mother."[10] She then heard a voice saying, "Sumiko forgives you." Shidzue felt that in that instant she experienced a moral change and, as tears fell, she felt at peace. Later others noticed the "life-change" commenting that even her outward appearance was different. Upon her return to Japan she commented, "I had come to America as a very proud woman, a Senator. As I sat and listened to what was being said in that room, it suddenly seemed as if I was at a funeral. I wept. It was the death of that pride of mine. But it was also the birth of a new woman, a humble woman. I had been known as a long-faced woman. My face changed, it became round and smiling."[11]

Towards the end of August Shidzue joined an MRA group which traveled to Europe and then returned to San Francisco in September, arriving at the same time as the Japanese and Allied delegations to the Peace Treaty Conference. This was especially fortuitous for the Socialist Party. The treaty signing conference included delegates from fifty-two nations pledged to sign a previously negotiated document. Prime Minister Yoshida Shigeru represented Japan, and all Japanese delegates were conservatives. The coincidental arrival of the MRA group meant that JSP members, ex-Prime Minister Katayama Tetsu, Senator Katô Shidzue, and Representative Toganô Satoko were all in the audience as observers.[12]

One reason no JSP delegates had been invited to the conference was that the party's left- and right-wings could not agree upon a response to the treaty's provisions. Yoshida, who did not want to delay the treaty, simply ignored both factions. The Peace Treaty had two major provisions: first, it ended the war and returned sovereignty over Japan to her own people; second, the added Security Agreement, urged upon Japan by the Americans in light of the Korean War and the Cold War, instituted a mutual security pact between the U.S. and Japan. The second provision gave the US government the right to maintain bases in Japan for the purposes of protecting Japan from both external attack and internal disturbances. The JSP left-wing vowed to vote against the entire document when it came before the Diet the following month. The right-wing was willing to vote for the Peace Treaty provisions, despite what they considered harsh reparations added in San Francisco, but were adamantly opposed to the Security Agreement which they felt limited Japan's sovereignty. Ordinarily the left-wing could count on Katô Shidzue's vote in the House of Councillors and the right-wing would have Toganô Satoko's vote in the House of Representatives. The two women had been adversaries throughout their Diet careers and their votes on issues which split the JSP canceled each other. In fact the two women had become close friends on this trip, and Katô, in keeping with her newly learned behaviors of reconciliation, and her strong anti-communist stance, joined Toganô and the right-wing to vote for the Peace Treaty but against the Security Agreement. On October 26th both sections of the document were passed in a special session of both houses, though by different margins representing the JSP split.[13] This vote was further evidence that Shidzue's summer of MRA training had changed her politically as well as personally.

In addition to her participation in the Diet vote Katô took two other actions immediately upon her return to Tokyo which grew out of her conversion. First, she wrote Sumiko a letter of apology "filled with feelings of love." She told her, "If you return even more joy will follow." In return she received an apology and the good news that Sumiko was coming back. Once more she became "the daughter of our house." Kanjû, always a man of few words at home, told his wife, "Thank you. I'm very happy. It is such a blessing. Sumiko has become a daughter." For Shidzue, "Katô's few words were weightier than a hundred thousand words."[14] From this time on Shidzue and her step-daughter became close.

Her second action involved formalizing MRA's connection with the Japanese. During the fall of 1951 Katô Shidzue and Sohma Yukika succeeded in urging their new American friend, Basil Entwistle, to set up a permanent MRA branch in Tokyo. Shidzue and Yukika then found a house which would serve as both the Entwistle family home and MRA headquarters. "Fireball" Katô Kanjû got the fundraising rolling when he promised that "he and his fellow Socialists would give as best they could out of their pockets." Contributions and loans from important businessmen, particularly bankers, and from politicians and professionals ensured the house purchase.[15]

In 1952 when delegates were once again selected for a May MRA World Assembly, Shidzue and Kanjû were easily at the top of the list. This meeting and the tour which followed focused almost exclusively on spreading the word about MRA. Once again Shidzue's knowledge of America and her facility with English made her sought after by the press and public, as she spoke from many platforms and eagerly responded to interview requests. Often quoted in the press, both she and her close friend, Sohma Yukika, urged their American democratic teachers to be alert to the menace of communism and to work to overcome poverty and overpopulation, society's twin devastations. Americans listened eagerly to this cold war message, that communist propaganda was manipulating the impoverished throughout the world, though only a few accepted Moral Re-Armament as the replacement ideology which could solve social problems and help make the world morally sound.[16]

MRA began to substantively influence both Shidzue and Kanjû's international activities. In 1954 Kanjû was one of four Japanese delegates in a multi-national MRA group to visit Taiwan and the Philippines, countries which retained a strong hatred for the Japanese from their periods of occupation. This mission was seen by the private Japanese delegation as an opportunity to apologize for their nation's wartime atrocities. Later, Kanjû joined a similar delegation to South America. In August, 1955, Shidzue joined what she called "a taskforce of MRA statesmen's mission" dedicated to spreading the MRA message to South Asia, the Middle East, and Africa. She proudly wrote Margaret Sanger from Cairo that she was a member of an international delegation of 194 people from 26 nations.[17]

In between trips abroad both Katôs were always ready at home to help spread the MRA message. For example, they eagerly wrote letters of good will to other nationals, especially those in countries which had experienced the brutal hand of the Japanese military and/or occupation administrators before and during the war. Perhaps the most sensitive manifestation of this gesture was their personal message sent to the

[South] Koreans in December, 1955, in which they apologized on behalf of the Japanese people for Japan's wrongdoings in the past and pledged that they personally would work devotedly for reconciliation and friendship between Japan and Korea in the future.

Shidzue's conversion to MRA was lifelong, outlasting the effectiveness and influence of that organization itself. In fact, it seemed a natural religious progression from the first teachings of Christian humanism which she had joyfully received from Nitobe at the time of her marriage to the Baron Ishimoto, through her interest in Nichiren Buddhism in the late twenties, and her religious embrace of American democratic ideals in the thirties and forties. Her spiritual needs were great and her attitude toward doctrine eclectic. She tended to add on each new revelation rather than deserting the previous faith entirely. The fact that her adherence to Buchman's principles endured speaks more to her idiosyncratic interpretation of religious values and her determination to act independently both personally and professionally than to MRA as an organization.

Family Planning for Japan and the World

Shidzue's primary interests in the fifties revolved around the general integration of her version of MRA principles into her life and public service while focusing her primary social efforts on her leadership role in the family planning movement. These two themes were closely related for her because she believed that MRA empowered people like herself to lead those of differing political persuasions toward a cooperative, common goal. Her "changed life" made it possible for Shidzue to join with leaders of other family planning organizations, even her nemesis, Majima Kan, to form a united group.

The 1955 International Planned Parenthood Conference [IPPF] was set for Tokyo and Shidzue and her associates in other birth control organizations determined to form one federated alliance in time for this event. In March, 1953, Katô, the husband and wife team, Drs. Amano, Dr. Koya of the government's National Institute of Public Health, Dr. Majima and Mr. Mihara Shinichi met with Dr. C. J. Gamble of IPPF to discuss the 1955 conference. Over the next year Katô, Majima, Koya, and Professor Kitaoka Juitsu joined forces to inaugurate a new umbrella organization for family planning which would sponsor that event. The Family Planning Federation of Japan [Nihon kazoku keikaku remmei], was born in April, 1954, and Margaret Sanger was sent to Tokyo by IPPF to welcome its arrival.

As usual Sanger's trip signaled an opportunity for Shidzue to publicize her cause. With the help of the government official, Dr. Koya, she arranged for Sanger to give a radio broadcast and organized other public events to propagate birth control education. Katô's greatest coup, however, was to arrange for Sanger to speak before an official meeting of the House of Councillors' Public Welfare Committee. No foreigner had ever before addressed a Diet body, so this was quite an honor to bestow upon her friend.[18] Although a minority party member, Katô had enough leverage in this committee to issue the precedent setting invitation, one which the aging and infirm Sanger, perhaps, did not fully appreciate nor adequately prepare for.

On April 15, 1954, Sanger spoke before the Diet committee. Her presentation was prefaced by committee chair, Kamijô Aiichi, who framed the discussion: the problem was one of population increase with conception control as a possible solution. He then introduced Sanger and commented that she would give the committee the latest information on birth control and suggest ways to educate the populace, particularly farmers, fishermen, and miners, in family planning. Sanger began. Unfortunately, she appeared to free associate as she haphazardly traced some of her accomplishments and disappointments, while at the same time both praised and criticized Japan for its various birth control practices. Unfortunately for Shidzue, Sanger applauded the Japanese for their foresight in defining family planning legislation in eugenic terms. "I congratulate you for having a sane practical eugenics law which we did not have. We did however, have the Eugenic Immigration Law but we did not follow it. Hence there has been an increase in insanity, transmittable disease, hereditary diseases, etc.." Perhaps it was fortunate that her speech, though translated, could not be easily understood by many committee members, for it was rambling, uninformative, and sometimes elitist.[19]

The question and answer period indicated that some of the Japanese were more aware of current scientific research than Sanger. Senator Yokoyama Fuku, head of the Japan Nursing Association's midwives division, posed the first question.[20] She asked about current progress in American research on contraceptive methods using a pill or injection. Sanger completely missed the point and responded with commentary on Dr. Abraham Stone's experiments with oil suppositories and, in India, applications using cooking oil. Correspondence[21] between Sanger and Katô just a few months later shows that both were well aware of Dr. Gregory Pincus' experiments with injections and oral contraceptives, but Sanger either forgot or was too tired and confused to respond to the question with this more appropriate information. Sanger was more comfortable with questions about the teaching methods applied in her own clinic and matters of financing. It soon became clear to Sanger that Japan was more advanced than the U.S. in some areas because of central support from the Ministry of Health and Welfare and its use of midwives, especially in rural areas. She admitted that her associates might do well to study the work of Senator Yokoyama's group. All in all the session was significant for its uniqueness, though not meaningful in content; it did, however, recognize Sanger's importance to Japan's birth control movement, and provided exposure for the newly formed Family Planning Federation of Japan (FPFJ).

At the same time the FPFJ was established, a new organization, the Japan Family Planning Association, was launched independently by Kunii Chôjirô. During the years to come Katô and Kunii cooperated so that these two organizations became complementary rather than competitive. In 1954 Kunii and Katô found a partial solution to their mutual problem of funding as together they carried out a project which provided their respective groups some financial stability. They sold condoms. The two colleagues approached the Okamoto Rubber Company, Japan's largest condom maker, and asked to buy their product in large quantities at reduced prices, and then resell them for a small profit. Their successful negotiations assured that from that time to the present the sale of condoms would provide both organizations with a primary source of funding. From Kunii's perspective, Senator Katô, "who was not only a famous member of the House of Councillors but a great pioneer in family planning," provided the influence through her illustrious name, while he provided the idea. Katô, on the other hand, remembers the event and the date slightly differently. "In 1956, Mr. Kunii and I put our heads together and came up with the ideal method for raising money for the JFPA while promoting its goal at the same time." Regardless of the ownership of the idea, the purchase of condoms at one-quarter of Okamoto's retail price, and their sale to couples at a 100% mark-up meant funding for family planning and a convenient supply at reasonable prices for couples who wanted to use contraceptives. Additionally the new packaging and the brand name FP, family planning, went far to erase the stigma which associated condom use with protection against venereal disease.[22]

In general 1954 was a successful year for Katô on the House of Councillors, Committee for Public Health and Welfare, where, in spite of lacking political clout, she managed to make an imprint. One success focused on nutrition for mothers and children, a long standing crusade for Katô. As late as 1954 the Japanese people continued to experience basic nutritional deficiencies in their daily living. Although the Korean War had provided an economic windfall for the nation as a whole, individuals and families continued to be hard pressed. In particular farmers and urban workers struggled to provide for their families, Shidzue learned as she traveled about the city and through the countryside talking with her constituents. On one such tour she met with dairy farmer wives in Chiba Prefecture and felt immediate sympathy for the harshness of their lives and the ceaseless nature of their work. Associating their economic problems with an inadequate vitamin intake for mothers and children nationwide, she thought of a mutually beneficial way to solve both urgent problems. She suggested to her public health committee that a small investment in equipment would make it possible for local stores and kiosks in railroad stations to provide low temperature heating for milk and that this would be adequate to make the product safe for children.[23] Easy access to relatively inexpensive milk would substantially increase a child's vitamin intake and would simultaneously provide a new outlet and increased profit for the dairy farmers, who were having difficulty convincing consumers of the benefits of drinking more milk. Some committee members opposed her program saying that Japanese culture would have to change for milk to become widely accepted, but in the end her measure was passed, providing one segment of the population with a better income and another with more nutrition.

Given the slow rate of improvement for the Katô family's own standard of living, Shidzue sought every opportunity to augment their material comforts as well. Just before Sanger was to visit in 1954 she wrote her friend and asked if she would bring a few household and clothing items with her. She accepted Margaret's kind offer of a gift for Takko saying that the nine year old wore a size ten dress, especially needed clothes for school, and liked blue or red. In her letter she enclosed clippings from an outdated Sears Catalogue of the things the family needed. Margaret found almost everything in the Tucson Sears & Roebuck, and she brought blouses, dresses, suits, sweaters, underwear, shoes, and a purse. She had sheets and pillowcases mailed for a grand total of $147.33 or about 53,000 yen, a good month's salary for someone in mid to upper management.[24]

While in Tokyo Margaret offered her hospitality for the coming year to Shidzue's stepdaughter, Sumiko, then twenty-six, who accepted immediately. According to both Margaret and Sumiko the year, beginning September, 1954, was a tremendous success. Sumiko reminisced that she and Sanger had read aloud to help with English study, had cooked western food together, and that Sanger had entertained her with parties and receptions.[25] The Tucson newspaper reported on one such event and featured Sumiko in kimono performing the tea ceremony.[26] Just after Sumiko left for home Sanger wrote Shidzue, "You will find your daughter more developed and adult. She is still a child in some emotional ways, but not like she was months ago. She has made lovely friends and people really loved her. Her romances could have been far more than usual, but she is sensible and did not take too seriously the plans that two or three young men tried to get her to share." Margaret then added, "She was a good student and if she will practice day by day she can be a good secretary. I hope you will allow her to go to work in the Conference office as soon as she arrives in Tokyo. I promised that she should have $60 a month when at work being secretary for the Conference Committee." As the American pointed out, "[Sumiko] is very anxious to be independent of her parents."[27] The stay in Tucson had been liberating for Sumiko, who yearned to be both filial and free.

Sumiko's return coincided with her stepmother's preparations for the IPPF Conference for which she had been named chair. One of three vice-presidents of the Family Planning Federation of Japan and the only woman on the Executive Board, Shidzue devoted much time to the planning of this conference.[28] She spent the rest of her busy days publicizing birth control, seeking government support for research on a contraceptive pill, pressing for greater government funding to promote family planning education, and lobbying for additional revisions to the Eugenics Law. She succeeded in each of these endeavors including adding a stipulation in the Eugenics Law which would require doctors who performed abortions to counsel patients about methods of birth control. Shidzue at fifty-eight was as energetic as ever.

The IPPF Conference, held October 24-29th, was proclaimed a tremendous success. Much of its importance can be attributed to the excitement over Dr. Pincus' first public introduction of his research on a contraceptive pill.[29] Of less international moment, but great personal satisfaction, the successful conference and Sanger's third postwar appearance in Japan gave Shidzue, her cause, and the FPFJ a bright period in the publicity limelight. Katô was both delighted and could draw an enormous sigh of relief. For at least a year preceding the conference Katô had worried that the international guests would be highly critical of Japan's Eugenics Law with its apparent emphasis on abortion.[30] Nervously she had addressed this issue in her opening remarks. In an attempt to blunt criticism she opened her comments with praise of Sanger and said that it was she "who brought us the gospel of family planning to replace abortion and the cry of unwanted children.... Women in Japan think that abortion is not the answer for mothers suffering from the burden of unwanted children. The public demand that the scientific study of population and contraception should find a place in the public programs of the political parties." At this time no other country had such free access to legal abortion, and Katô, herself, decried the implication that abortion should be seen as a birth control method. She was well aware that Japan's Eugenics Law had been cited in the foreign press as a "free pass for abortion." Consequently, she included in her statement a listing of accomplishments by the Japanese government which she believed would positively counteract this negative perception. "Today no political party... can discuss [public health] policy without stressing its readiness to support family planning. With such wide acceptance and understanding of the population problem and of family planning by our people, the Government is to make more budgetary provision for the dissemination of contraceptives and is planning to enlarge the administrative bureau further to promote this. The Japanese Diet no longer lags behind."[31]

During the conference Shidzue did, in fact, confront some difficult questions about the Eugenics Law, but these were founded more on confusion than reflecting a harsh criticism of Japanese morals as she had expected. Just the same, she spent many hours explaining Japanese policy on abortion, a difficult task given her own opposition to many aspects of this law. Her words seemed to satisfy the foreign delegates, and she managed to blunt the characterization in the foreign press, that Japan was an immoral country. One positive change in the law, which she had worked for, had been passed in the summer of 1955, and this helped to modulate foreign criticism. This extended the right to family planning field workers to sell contraceptives and thus substantially strengthened their case birth control alternatives to abortion. It also gave them financial support for further educational services. In addition, the Ministry of Health and Welfare decided to emphasize family planning among the poor by offering counseling and free contraceptives. In later years, when European countries and then America liberalized abortion laws, Katô felt Japan's family planning policies had been vindicated. Although she had never liked the idea of abortion, she believed that in an imperfect world that choice must be available to women. Her work was directed at refining the laws and diminishing the need for abortion through birth control education and economic improvement.

After the conference ended Shidzue exclaimed in a letter to Dorothy Brush that it had been a greater success than anyone had ever expected. She continued, "Margaret and I had a wonderful time together.... On her last day in Tokyo, she visited Prince and Princess Takamatsu at their residence and in the afternoon she was invited to the Imperial Garden Party, there she was presented to the Crown Prince and to His Majesty, the Emperor Hirohito. I thought this honor given to Margaret meant the recognition of our course in this country."[32] Sanger had been discouraged by friends and relatives from making the trip because of her poor health, but she had been determined. Japan was the only place left which extended to her the recognition and adulation which she believed she deserved.

More Political Victories

The year following the IPPF Conference was one of personal joy and political victory for Katô. In July, 1956, she won reelection to the House of Councillors receiving over 750,000 votes, almost twice the number of her first upper house election, and placing first among the fifty people elected at this three year interval. She was fifty-nine. Her campaign to secure her second six year term had emphasized two issues: "healthy" family planning rather than abortion; and defense of the postwar constitution against revision. She did not want to see rearmament through modifications in the anti-military provisions of the constitution for she felt women would be the losers in a Japan which jettisoned its pacifist stance. Her positions resonated with an enthusiastic public and her victory was glorious.

Although her own election campaign did not feature the anti-prostitution law which had passed the Diet in May, 1956, in fact Katô's active participation in formulating and advocating this heavily debated legislation caught the interest and support of the public and focused an even stronger national spotlight on her. Oddly, when Katô wrote about her successful reelection to Sanger in August, 1956, or reminisced about it in her autobiographies, no mention was made of the anti-prostitution legislation. On the other hand, in women's histories, which invariably ignore Katô's contributions including those in family planning, Katô's work on behalf of this legislation is likely to be cited.

Katô and other women in the JSP had worked off and on for anti-prostitution legislation from 1948. Each newly proposed bill reflected changes in their thinking, and every one was defeated in committee or in a full Diet vote.[33] In the first bill a prostitute, anyone who forced someone into prostitution, or anyone who ran a house of prostitution was classified as a criminal to be punished by imprisonment and a fine. By 1955, when a bill came very close to passing, the issue had become one of preventing prostitution without imposing criminal sanctions on prostitutes. When in May, 1956, Law No. 118, the Prostitution Prevention Law, was passed the goal was to "liberate" the women in paid sexual service while prohibiting houses of prostitution. There was also much talk about rehabilitating prostitutes, but no funds were allocated. Interestingly primary opposition to the legislation as written came from the prostitutes' union, the Tokyo Women Employees Alliance, and its two male JSP supporters, who felt that the law displaced women from their business and thus must include a compensation clause. JSP Representative Kamichika Ichiko, speaking for her associates, justified opposition to cash reimbursement for lost income. She characterized the call for compensation illogical, saying 30,000 yen a month, as proposed, was what someone in middle management could expect to earn, and prostitution was antisocial in any case. She could not see how the women could make such demands.[34] The law became effective in 1957, without compensation.

For the rest of the decade Katô devoted much of her time and energy to FPFJ becoming its chair in 1956, and helping to organize the International Japan Planned Parenthood Committee which then joined Sanger's IPPF organization. She broadened her social interests by joining the Japan Society of Prevention of Cruelty to Animals (JSPCA) [Nippon dôbutsu aigo kyôkai], which she would chair from 1964-1977. In 1957 she inaugurated and led the Society for the Study of Women's Problems, a group which had branches in Tokyo, Osaka, Kobe, Nagano, Hiroshima Yokohama and Sendai and which published a monthly magazine and a newspaper.[35] In the Diet she stiffened her resolve along with other JSP members to fight against several conservative measures which she felt would provide a set-back to the democratic postwar gains achieved by women. As she wrote Sanger in January, 1959, "we were busy trying our level best to fight for the cause of democracy against the present Japanese political power comprised of World War II culprits, which is now engaged in making laws which will eventually drag Japan into a reactionary pitfall." In this instance she was referring to the attempt of Prime Minister Kishi Nobusuke, who had been a minister in General Tôjô's cabinet, to pass a revision of the Police Duties Law. It was defeated in November, 1958. This conflict with Kishi is of particular note because later that year Katô would see Kishi as a friend of family planning, and in 1960, she would support Prime Minister Kishi against the entire JSP on an issue of much graver consequences. Even while actively participating in all of these causes Shidzue continued to provide a secure home life for her daughter, Takko, just entering her teens, and for her equally busy husband. Happily Arata and Sumiko had married and set up households elsewhere.

In 1959 Katô prepared for another visit by Margaret Sanger, who, in spite of her advanced age and infirmities, had accepted an invitation from Prime Minister Kishi and the Governor of Tokyo to make her seventh and last trip to Japan. Events provided for her included the presentation of a key to the city of Tokyo and entertainment hosted by

Katô, Mr. Mihara of FPFJ, and Mr. Honda, president of *Mainichi Newspaper*.[36] Sanger was thrilled. In these last years she began to believe that only in Japan did she enjoy the reception which she deserved. Sometime after the 1955 IPPF Conference in Tokyo she had handwritten her "last will" in which she gave instructions for disposal of her body upon her death. In this she revealed her disappointment in the treatment she had received in her home country and her appreciation for her lionization in Japan. The "will" read as follows. "In case of my death—I want to be cremated not before 2 weeks later—the heart to go to Japan to be buried in Tokyo—any place the govt. or Health and Welfare Minister together with Senator Shizue Katô wish to have it buried, as it is or in ashes. This is gratitude to the Japanese people & govt.—the only country in the world which has officially recognized me and the BC work also presented me to the Emperor."[37]

Sanger's affection for Japan was unequivocally returned through the respect and admiration which that nation showed her. On May 18, 1965, the Third Class Order of the Sacred Treasure, the highest award permitted for a foreign woman, was conferred by the Emperor and the government of Japan upon Margaret Sanger. She was much too ill to receive the award in person and so her son, Dr. Stuart Sanger, and his wife traveled to the Consul General's home in Pasadena, California, and on June 5th accepted the honor for Sanger's "distinguished services in promoting the principle of planned parenthood in Japan."[38] Margaret Sanger died in September, 1966, just short of her eight-eighth birthday. Katô Shidzue felt a great personal and professional loss at the passing of her longtime friend.

Notes

1. See J. Victor Koschmann, "Intellectuals and Politics" in Andrew Gordon, ed., *Postwar Japan As History*, University of California Press, 1993, pp. 395-423, for discussion of this change by intellectuals, in particular, its effect on the security treaty crisis of 1955-65.

2 Information on Buchman comes from Tom Dribert, *The Mystery of Moral Re-Armament: A Study of Frank Buchman and His Movement*, Alfred A. Knopf, 1965.

3. Kuriyama Chojiro, quoted in Basil Entwistle, *Japan's Decisive Decade*, Grosvenor Books, 1985, p. 51.

4. Sohma Yukika quoted in Basil Entwistle, *Japan's Decisive Decade*, p. 54.

5. See letters, spring, 1951, to Beard, Brush, and Sanger, Smith, and 1988a, p.137; 1981, pp. 163-164.

6. See Mary Beard to Ethel Weed, 6/20/51, Smith.

7. 1981 p. 165. Buchman told the story of Laure to assembled "groupers" at Mackinac Island in 1951. The event related took place in Caux in 1947 and is described also in Driberg, The *Mystery of Moral Re-Armament*, p. 122. The quote from Madame Laure in next sentence is from an article she wrote, quoted in Driberg, p. 122.

8. 1981, pp. 163-169; 1988a, pp. 132-144.

9. 1981, p. 164. In 1981 and 1988a Katô explains the tenets of MRA and the effect MRA had on her life. She uses words which translate easily to those of Driberg in his 1965 criticism of MRA, *The Mystery of Moral Re-Armament.* This book does not include anything about the World Assemblies or the role of the Japanese.

10. 1988a, p. 140.

11. As quoted in Basil Entwistle, *Japan's Decisive Decade*, p. 60.

12. See chapt. 21 in Richard B. Finn, *Winners in Peace*, U. of California Press, 1992, for Peace Treaty Conference.

13. The vote in the House of Representatives was 307 to 47 for the Peace Treaty and 284 to 71 for the Security Agreement. In the House of Councillors it was 174 to 15 for the Peace Treaty and 147 to 76 for the Security Agreement. Richard B. Finn, *Winners in Peace,* p. 307.

14. 1988a, p. 141.

15. Basil Entwistle, *Japan's Decisive Decade*, p. 62-73.

16. Letters of winter and spring, 1952, Smith.

17. 8/16/55 letter to Sanger, Smith. Shidzue wrote ten essays about her observations including several commentaries on Iran and on Moslem women, one article on Africa in general, two on Nairobi, and one on Cairo. See 1956.

18. See March-April, 1955, letters between Sanger and Katô, Smith for details on this event. Also Katô describes the event though tells nothing of the content of Sanger's speech in 1981, p. 159.

19. Sanger's speech and the questions and answers, Smith. See Chesler, *Woman of Valor*, Simon & Schuster, 1992, p. 436 for another brief description of this event. "Margaret's testimony regrettably betrayed her deteriorated health. Overwhelmed by the emotion of the occasion and by the fatigue of travel, she rambled on when given the opportunity to speak..."

20. First elected to the House of Councillors as an independent in 1953. Sally Ann Hastings, "Women Legislators in the Postwar Diet," ms., p. 16, of chapter to appear in Anne E. Imamura, ed, Re-imaging Japanese Women, U. of California Press.

21. See letters of summer, 1954, Box 58 #547, and Box 118 #1201, Smith.

22. Chojiro Kunii, *Humanistic Family Planning Approaches*, United Nations Fund for Population Activities, 1983, p. 73; Katô, 1985, pp. 101-102.

23. 1988a, pp. 156-157.

24. Sanger to Katô, 4/1/54, Smith, includes itemized list of goods.

25. As told to Ellen Chesler, *Woman of Valor*, p. 428.

26. Sanger to Katô 11/23/54, Smith. Several letters from Sanger to Katô, Smith, focus on birth control issues but refer to Sumiko's stay.

27. Sanger to Katô 7/5/55, and 7/19/55 Box 58 #547, Smith.

28. Dr. Koya and Dr. Majima were also Vice Presidents. Letters between Sanger and various Japanese about conference, Reel 128, Sanger, LofC.

29. See the *Report of the Proceedings of the Fifth International Conference on Planned Parenthood*, published by IPPF, London. See also, Ellen Chesler, *Woman of Valor*, p. 436. Two other featured speakers were the Occupation consultants who caused MacArthur such diplomatic difficulties, Warren S. Thompson and Edward A. Ackerman. See chapt. 13.

30. For Katô's concerns see 1988a, pp. 162-163.

31. See *Report of the Proceedings of Fifth International Conference on Planned Parenthood*, p. 2.

32. Katô to Dorothy Brush, 11/21/55, Box 29A, Smith.

33. For Katô's comments on prostitution in 1946, RG331, Box 5250, File #84; in 1948, RG 331, Box 5250, File: Prostitution; Kodama Katsuko, *Senko no Ichikawa Fusae*, 1985, p. 106-107, also, pp. 108-112 discuss the 1953 and 1955 legislation. After Ichikawa Fusae joins the House of Councillors in 1953, Kodama focuses exclusively on her role in the successful legislation and Katô is not mentioned. For discussion of legislation as it progressed through various forms from 1952-1956 see Itoya Toshio & Esashi Akiko, *Sengoshi to josei no kaiho* [Postwar History & Women's Liberation], pp. 194-198. For an English translation of the law see *Baishun taisaku no genkyô* [The Present Condition of Anti-Prostitution Measures], as cited in Ryuichi Hirano, "The Accused and Society: Some Aspects of Japanese Criminal Law," in Arthur Taylor von Mehren, ed., *Law in Japan*, Harvard U. Press, 1963, p. 281, ff.

34. Paraphrased from a quote in Yuki Shiga-Fujime, "The Prostitutes' Union and the Impact of the 1956 Anti-Prostitution Law in Japan" in *U.S.-Japan Women's Journal, English Supplement #5*, p. 22. This article focuses on negative affects of the 1956 law and considers it from the perspective of the prostitutes who fought against it. The two men were Iwauchi Zensaku and Takahara Asaichi, who were expelled from the JSP over this incident.

35. Allen Cole, George Totten, and Cecil Uyehara, *Socialist Parties in Postwar Japan*, Yale University Press, 1966, p. 439.

36. Letters for May, June, August from Sumiko, Shidzue, and Margaret Sanger, Smith.

37. Clipped to 1945-1946 Journal packet, box 29, File #224, Smith.

38. Copy of wire sent to American newspapers from Consulate General of Japan, Los Angeles, Reel 19, Sanger LofC.

15

A Political Maverick (1957–1995)

From Katô's perspective her most significant accomplishments during the fifties and sixties were her achievements as an ad hoc international diplomat. In this role she was particularly influenced by her firm anti-communist stance and her strong support of America. Although these attitudes were tied to her association with MRA, they had developed, as well, from her post-war ideological conflicts with marxists and members of the Japan Communist Party on the one hand, and, on the other, her revered friendship with Americans through a lifetime of collegial activities, her several trips to the United States, and the open adulation she had received from some officials during the American Occupation. In the end these ties were deeper and proved more binding than the weakening strands of Socialist Party control which demanded she follow party dictates. Shidzue had seldom found the support or inclusion she had sought in the JSP and she saw no reason to commit herself to the fixed positions as formulated and pronounced by party leadership; she had specific international goals which she would forward whether or not the JSP or the Diet found them palatable. In the thirties she had found herself isolated and she had survived, while in the forties she had teamed with different groups as suited her objectives. Her independence had been tested in the most difficult of times and she was not afraid to stand alone. She had also experienced the elation and confirmation of public praise and believed that her leadership abilities had been judged satisfactory. She was therefore not afraid to make her own way in the years to come whether that meant alone or in association with a few others of like mind.

Apologizing to the Koreans

During the fifties and sixties Shidzue was most particularly proud of her endeavors on behalf of the Republic of Korea, for whom she pressed an independent, personal campaign directed at normalizing diplomatic relations with the South Korean government and improving personal contacts between the Japanese and South Korean peoples. As she commented in 1978, "I had a chance to meet Koreans in America after the war [1951]. I extended my hand to shake in greeting but they would refuse to take it. I knew that they could speak Japanese but they preferred to converse in broken English. They told me bitter stories, many inside stories of suffering. They held bitter feelings against the Japanese. I thought it important for Japan to establish good feelings toward the Koreans. Japanese have found it easy to forget the damage which Japan did to the Korean nation but the Koreans have not forgotten." Her campaign for reconciliation, which was not officially sanctioned by either the government or her party, took on greater significance because of the prestige of her elective office and her public popularity as reflected in her strong voter appeal in 1956.

In April, 1957, an MRA sponsored conference for Asians was held in Baguio, the Philippines, and the organizers wanted a delegation from Japan to take part. This was not easy to arrange because there was no official treaty between the two countries and so travel visas required an extraordinary governmental agreement. In the end, a newly elected Prime Minister Kishi facilitated the issuance of the necessary documents and a Japanese delegation of twenty, including Katô Shidzue, was formed. At the meeting, representatives from Korea, Taiwan, and Southeast Asia poured forth their hateful memories of the treatment they had received at the hands of the Japanese. It was a forceful exhibition of bitter acrimony which the Japanese delegation listened to with tears and accepted without contest.

The most dramatic outcome of this conference, as reported in the *Yomiuri Newspaper*, was "exploratory" talks between the Koreans and Japanese toward the establishment of diplomatic relations. This was nothing short of miraculous considering that this was not an officially sanctioned gathering. Moreover, since the occurrence of inflammatory remarks in 1953 at the Third Conference between government officials of Japan and the Republic of Korea, no further talks of reconciliation had been planned. On the other hand, Prime Minister Kishi had approved travel for the MRA delegation, and he had privately agreed to the request of one delegate, Hoshijima Nirô, to use this occasion to informally seek an end to the deadlock which existed between Japan and ROK. As a senator and a member of the Foreign Affairs Committee, Katô Shidzue was the highest elected official in the Japanese delegation, and as such figured prominently in newspaper accounts. Several days of discussions among Katô, Hoshijima, an influential LDP member of the House of Representatives and chairman of the Japanese-

Korean Society, and Soon Yoong Sun, chairman of the Foreign Affairs Committee of the Korean National Assembly determined that there might be a basis for reconciliation between their nations. Undoubtedly conciliatory feelings were aided by the fact that Katô and Hoshijima apologized to the Korean for the "oppression used by the Japanese during the time of their rule in Korea," and for the stubborn and negative attitudes of previous Japanese officials during earlier official talks. (This is astonishing in light of the fact that even in 1995 Japanese government officials debate the controversial question of whether and how to apologize for its treatment and occupation of Asian nations during Word War II.) After the meeting ended the Japanese returned home. A few days later the Korean delegation arrived in Tokyo en route home. Refusing to meet the Japanese anywhere but MRA House, they were feted there by Shidzue, Kanjû and others who continued the positive discussions begun in Baguio.

After the Koreans had returned home, Hoshijima and Katô Shidzue determined to work together to move the issue of Japan/Korea normalization forward in the Diet. Hoshijima agreed to discuss the progress made at the MRA Conference with his friend, Prime Minister Kishi, and Shidzue promised to raise pertinent questions in the appropriate legislative manner of interpellation when Kishi appeared before the Foreign Affairs Committee on April 30, 1957. Katô says that she spoke privately with Kishi before the committee exchange to lay out just what she intended to say.[1] According to the proceedings of that committee meeting, Katô asked her questions within a long summary monologue of what had taken place at Baguio. She included carefully phrased criticism of Japan's wartime oppression, and the subsequent good faith actions of their associate the parliamentarian, Mr. Yoong, and his colleague in speeches before the Korean parliament. In this characteristic roundabout manner of Diet proceedings, she presented a full public account of her activities including the apology for Japan's past actions, and asked the Prime Minister to take appropriate action to begin a process of national reconciliation. The first action she requested was withdrawal of the Kubota Declaration, which claimed, among other things, that the Koreans should be appreciative of all that the colonial Japanese government had done for the Korean people. Katô then ended her statement, "I hope that in this Committee you, Mr. Prime Minister, will declare your sincerity in regard to this Kubota declaration. This statement has given the impression of superiority of the Japanese people to the Korean people. It expresses the attitude of the Japanese as a people, rather than a statement of one person, and as such I believe we should withdraw this declaration."[2]

In the 1951 Peace Treaty Japan had officially accepted the existence and independence of the Republic of Korea (ROK - South Korea). At that time, however, many government officials and other citizens believed that Japan had no obligation to apologize for its past actions in Korea because Japan's rule had been both benevolent and beneficial especially in areas of education, health, transportation, and agriculture. This attitude was evident in all three conferences between Japan and the ROK which occurred after the signing of the Peace Treaty. In 1953 Kubota Kanichiro, the chief Japanese delegate to the Third Conference on normalizing relations, had arrogantly stated that granting Korea independence before an official peace treaty was signed between the two nations was inappropriate; that the Allied Powers should be criticized for disposing of Japanese property before a peace treaty was negotiated, and that the Japanese retained the right to make compensation claims for seized property; that the Japanese had not been bad rulers and in fact in several areas the Koreans had benefited substantially from colonial rule; and, finally, that the Cairo Declaration which accused the Japanese of enslaving the Koreans was an exaggeration. The Korean reaction to this tirade was to walk out of the meeting and refuse to return. The Katô/Hoshijima diplomacy resuscitated these talks.

At the April, 1957, Foreign Affairs Committee meeting, Prime Minister Kishi, who had been primed for Katô's interpellation by Hoshijima and Katô herself, began his reply by saying that he agreed wholeheartedly with Mrs. Katô on every point as regards the normalizing of Japan-Korean relations. Then he added that in concurrence with Mrs. Katô, he believed that the most important issue was not the interpretation of the laws but the creation of trust and a spiritual understanding, and that the Japanese must take the initiative in this. He then unequivocally denounced the Kubota Declaration, and, though he insisted that it had not been an official statement but, rather, a private opinion, he officially withdrew the statement to prevent any misunderstanding.

Katô then tackled another stumbling block to reconciliation, financial claims which Japanese businesses and individuals had made for property lost when Japanese control over Korea was forfeited at the end of the war. In the exchange which followed Katô implied that the Japanese government would have to provide the compensation which these people deserved. Kishi did not so promise, but indicated such agreement might come to pass. Katô, satisfied at the progress that had been made in the face of extremely difficult problems, only asked that her government and its people "act with a humble attitude. It is so important to win the trust of the Korean people and I would like you,

Mr. Prime Minister, to promise that the Government will do its best." The interpellation achieved the anticipated policy commitments which Katô and Hoshijima had desired. In a Joint Communiqué of December 31, 1957, Kishi officially withdrew the Kubota Declaration and Japan/ROK treaty negotiations began once again. It took some time to achieve a full rapprochement, and not until February 17, 1965, under new administrations in both countries, did Japan's Foreign Minister make an official statement of regret to the ROK government and people for their unfortunate period under Japanese rule.[3]

Recognizing that Katô was a member of the minority Socialist Party and that Kishi was the penultimate conservative leader of the LDP, the completely agreeable exchange in April, 1957, on one of Japan's most sensitive issues of foreign policy, would seem an anomaly. However, considering the growing economic significance of South Korea to Japanese postwar recovery, and the conciliatory policies within the JCP and JSP toward the communist leaders of North Korea, it is not so surprising that the LDP leadership saw advantages to normalizing relations with the ROK. The crux of the issue lies in placing a 'South' in front of each mention of Korea in the exchange between Prime Minister Kishi and Senator Katô. This was not a matter of reconciliation with a people, but a matter of finding common economic and political ground which would solidify support for the South and further isolate and contain the North and her Japanese supporters on the left. Of equal importance in reviewing this most unusual LDP/JSP détente is the knowledge that Kishi was heavily influenced by, sympathized with, and soon became a part of MRA.[4] This is why Hoshijima, also LDP and MRA, was able to work so closely with Kishi and why JSP Senator Katô and Kishi appeared to be involved in a carefully choreographed dance at this particular Foreign Affairs Committee meeting. A mutual respect for MRA, combined with Kishi's foreign policy concerns and Katô's determined effort to apologize to and reconcile with the Korean people, assured that these two apparent political opponents could reach concurrence. By this time Shidzue's actions had gone beyond those of an unbridled party member; she had become a political maverick.

A Public Conflict with the Socialist Party

There is another, even more striking, example of the closeness between Katô Shidzue and Prime Minister Kishi which emerged during the bitter debate and explosive demonstrations which accompanied renegotiation of the American-Japanese Security Treaty in 1960.[5] The animosity between the sides for and against this treaty was of such intensity that it created an indelible dividing line which separated people ideologically, politically, and personally. Once again the conservative prime minister and the socialist senator found themselves unexpectedly in concert.

The treaty renewal had been approved by the U.S. Senate and President Eisenhower was to make a triumphant trip to Tokyo in June, 1960, by which time it was assumed that Kishi would have secured approval of the Japanese Diet. In fact, while the LDP majority did favor the treaty, the JSP and JCP were adamantly opposed. The left was firmly supported by many citizens who opposed the treaty's stipulation that the U.S. could station their military on Japanese soil free from any interference or control by Japan. People were further outraged that ships and planes arriving in Japan might carry nuclear weapons, and many cried foul over a possible collusion between the U.S. military and the Japanese government for a covert rearmament of the military under the guise of a Japanese self-defense force. Opposition to the treaty had the most vocal and demonstrative segments of the public on their side, and evidence further suggests that well over half of all of Japan's citizens opposed the treaty renewal.

Disapproval of this LDP sponsored legislation was formidable. Strikes were called by the most militant and largest union, Sôhyô, and demonstrations were held by the radical student organization, Zengakuren.[6] Many students, laborers and others snaked through the streets in long lines shouting their opposition to renewal. Worried about JSP/JCP tactics which might prolong the vote and cause difficulties for the Eisenhower visit, Kishi called a sudden, early morning session of the House of Representatives on May 20th, while the Socialists were boycotting the Diet on a different issue. With this trickery he succeeded in getting the treaty approved.

Public response should have been as predictable as it was extreme. The strikes and demonstrations, the clashing with police, the general public outcry were without postwar precedent. On June 4th Sôhyô organized a three hour strike of four million rail workers. On that same day the Socialists threatened to resign en masse, the students battled with police, and many anti-Eisenhower rallies were held. On June 10th students led by Zengakuren surrounded President Eisenhower's press secretary, who had just arrived at Haneda airport in advance of the President's visit. One group after another reacted forcefully in demonstration against Eisenhower's visit and treaty renewal, during these first two weeks in June. On the 15th twelve thousand Zengakuren organized students stormed the Diet; 590 were injured and one woman was killed in the process. President Eisenhower declared that the rioting and demonstrations had been fomented by international communism. Two days later, accepting Kishi's advice, Eisenhower "postponed" his visit. On June 19th, while the JSP and JCP blocked any possibility of a House of Councillors' vote on the bill, the Security Treaty automatically became law in accordance with Diet rules. On June 24th, pressed by the devastating disorder and strong public opposition to the treaty and to his methods of securing ratification, Kishi announced that he would soon resign, which he did within a month. This was an event of vastly significant proportions, and one about which the LDP and the JSP held diametrically opposed views.

One, and only one, member of the JSP stood with Kishi, and that was Senator Katô Shidzue. In a public declaration Shidzue defied her party, her husband, Kanjû, and her well known cousins Tsurumi Kazuko and Tsurumi Shunsuke, who were outspoken leaders in support of Zengakuren. Once again Shidzue took an independent road based on her moral interpretation of events without regard to the political consequences for herself or those close to her. It was a debacle from the stand-point of her future within the party and her relationships with other socialists. It was an act of courage and righteousness according to her friends in MRA. Whatever else, it was a milestone in her career and a turning point as regards any future political influence.

On June 16th Katô Shidzue issued a statement which both criticized and apologized for the actions of the JSP. Her statement was broadcast nationally, and appeared in all major and many local newspapers. The text as quoted in the *Japan Times* read as follows:

> The violent action of Zengakuren on the night of June 15 has shaken all the sound people of Japan. Watching the whole battle on television, my heart sank when I thought of the future of our country. It is cheap and off the point to discuss whether the police did too much, or whether the government was wrong. It was an extremely dangerous attempt to throw out the government by violence, planned by a small group of people run by a subversive ideology.
>
> I have been in the Japanese Diet for more than ten years now as a Socialist. I feel deeply ashamed that we have come to the point where the democracy of Japan is being exposed to the danger of destruction by such violent action.
>
> As a Socialist Party member I wish to apologize deeply to the nation for having been too cowardly these past weeks to say what I knew was right. I sat through many party meetings and when wrong decisions were taken, I didn't raise my voice. Now I wish to pledge myself to fight all out to save Japan from communism and create a real democracy.
>
> Since May 19 Japan has become the front-line of the battle between communism and democracy. The communists, with extremely active backing from Red China and Russia, have tried to destroy the Government by creating a popular front. Not only that, they have tried to lead the whole country into anti-American rioting just before the visit of President Eisenhower so that they could isolate Japan from America.

> The question of whether the revision of the security pact was right, or whether the action taken by Mr. Kishi was right, is not the central issue. The real question now is what kind of ideology we want for ourselves and our children.[7]
>
> Japan is not meant to imitate America, nor is she meant to be dominated by Red China or Russia. If we have the courage to stand up and speak out today, we can still save Japan and Asia.

There was immediate public and party reaction to Katô's statement. Journalists questioned the JSP chair of the Disciplinary Committee about the party's response to Katô Shidzue's strong criticism of the party's policy and action. The chair, Inomata Kôzô, said that he would be meeting with Mrs. Katô and would ask her just what had led up to the criticism of party policy, and some sort of party response to her action would probably be forthcoming in a week or so. By June 26th, a spokesman for the party claimed that Shidzue had apologized, but she told the reporter that she had merely acknowledged receipt of the party's warning given her over the telephone. On June 30th Shidzue told the press that she had received about six hundred letters to date and that most were favorable. She was pleased that most Japanese had retained their good sense, and that most agreed with her that the use of violence to settle issues was not to be sanctioned. She did suggest that she was sorry about the worries she had caused the JSP chair, but insisted that she would not apologize for what she had said. "I cannot yield to oppression against freedom of speech. I had fully warned the Party through International Bureau Director Sata that the anti-Treaty struggle should not become an anti-US struggle. An anti-US struggle is laid down nowhere in the Party platform. But they were exploited by the communists while they were unawares. If the Committee urges me to leave the Party, I shall have to do so. If it gives me a reprimand, I will only listen to it. If it urges me to apologize, I will not."[8]

In the next few days the party chair, Asanuma Inejirô, a good friend of both of the Katôs, asked that the case be handled with sensitivity, and the Central Executive Committee, of which Diet Representative Katô Kanjû was a member, held a meeting to decide how to handle the case. It was reported on July 5th that Shidzue was reprimanded for a violation of party regulations. For her part Shidzue stated that she had expressed her opinion within the committee meeting and would have nothing further to say and that she would remain in the JSP. She further stated that she had been told by the committee that her formal statement had provided the LDP opposition with ammunition to use against the JSP. She told the press that she had not changed her beliefs and that she felt the JSP should put the public welfare above party interests and politics in general. She was unrepentant.

According to regulations governing party discipline public deviations from a general party line or discussions in opposition to some stated party perspectives are acceptable before the party as a whole has arrived at consensus. At that point the stated position becomes policy and party discipline demands concurrence. JSP representatives and senators are then required to speak in accordance with the policy as stated, or negotiate for a modification of this policy behind closed doors. Katô Shidzue had violated this discipline in a most public and dramatic manner. There is no doubt that had she not been Kanjû's wife, she would have been asked to resign from the party. There is little doubt as well, that if she had not been Kanjû's wife, she would have resigned from the party regardless of the decision of the Disciplinary Committee. Shidzue's interest in the workings and policies of the JSP had waned, and her commitment to undermining communism, as well as her belief in the rightness of America on this issue, far outweighed any interest she might have retained in following a political party line. Her spectacular response to an international confrontation simply demonstrated the permanence of her political and ideological change over the previous decade.

There was even more to Shidzue's independent action than that illuminated by her public statement. She was not simply opposed to the methods which the JSP employed to stop the treaty renewal. Nor was the violence by the labor and student organizations, which she objected to, the primary issue. Simply put, she agreed with Kishi and disagreed with JSP policy. As she stated more candidly in private later, "I felt that Japan as a nation needed some safeguards, some protection and so the Security Treaty was reasonable." She went on to say that the demonstrations served only to please such forces as the Chinese who wanted to see the Americans humiliated. Also, the activities in the Diet proved Japan's democratic immaturity. She felt she could not sit by silently and watch those who had little understanding of the treaty destroy an important international relationship and mock the essence of freedom and democracy. Her husband had supported the demonstrations and her actions were an embarrassment to him, but she had no other moral choice. In her meeting with the Executive Committee, the party chair, Asanuma, a Christian, asked her if she had acted from her heart and whether she still believed that what she had done was right. He was concerned that her action had been a matter of conscience. She responded, "I did this from my own conviction, I obeyed the voices of my inner heart." Other committee members were less sympathetic, and, of course, the nature of the meeting meant that they asked the questions and she must answer without right of counsel. The discipline handed down at the end of the meeting was that she would not be able to run for any party position for one year. "Since I never had any party position and never had wanted one in any case," she shrugged off this penalty, for it made no impression on her whatsoever.[9]

For Shidzue, as for many who opposed the US/Japan Security Treaty, this confrontation, several years building, marked the end of a greater struggle, that for a democratic Japan.[10] Shidzue had dreamed in the late forties of a democratic revolution which would bring about a socialist democracy guaranteeing equality for men and women, economic security for families, and justice for all. Her ideas were somewhat nebulous and were far more radical than what she had observed in democratic America, but they were in line with what she believed she saw at SCAP, particularly at CIE. Like so many other Japanese on the left, she had been dismayed and to some extent defeated by the so-called "reverse course" which the Occupation officials seemed to institute as early as 1947. She was also angered by the institutional rigidity and exclusiveness of the JSP and the Diet. By 1950 she knew there would be no democratic revolution from either quarter. At the same moment she saw a more serious threat to the simple survival of democracy in the rise of communism, especially that in China. The Korean War confirmed this fear. Shidzue's support of Kishi and the treaty was the natural culmination of this train of thinking and political experience, just as opposition to this treaty was a natural progression for most others on the left, who, also, decried the death of a democratic revolution for Japan.

An Independent Road

There is no doubt that from June 1960 on, Katô Shidzue distanced herself even further from the Socialist Party and from the left. This meant apparent disagreement with her husband, Kanjû, as well, though no personal conflict was visible. Although Shidzue continued to sit as a JSP member in the House of Councillors, she had little legislative and no party influence. In the public's eye she was still well known and well liked, and gained reelection twice more. Once again in 1962 she led the Socialist Party candidates, receiving over a million votes, placing second among the fifty candidates running at-large. In 1968 she dropped in number of votes and came in twenty-first out of the fifty, and in 1974, a good election for the Socialists, she came in fifty-eighth, one of only two out of twelve Socialist at-large candidates who failed to win election. She attributed her 1974 loss to the popular reformist campaign of Ichikawa Fusae, who drew from a similar constituency. Since the top fifty vote getters gained seats in the House of Councillors, she was not in direct competition with Ichikawa, but since each voter throughout the nation only had one vote, she felt that too many, choosing between her and another women's advocate of similar age and standing, cast their vote for Ichikawa. Katô was seventy-seven in 1974 when she retired from elective politics.

Of the time spent as a senator after the 1960 debacle, Katô was most pleased with her work on the Industrial Pollution Committee and the Transportation Countermeasures Committee. Since House of Councillors committee chairs have substantially less power than their counterparts in the House of Representatives, they are often chosen from opposition parties. Katô chaired the transportation committee for two sessions in the late sixties and she chaired and then co-chaired the pollution committee once each during the early seventies,[11] a period of substantial legislative activity in this area. It was JSP pressure which caused the calling of special sessions in 1970, and, in all, during these sessions, fourteen pollution laws were enacted including five which had been modified during committee meetings. There was also a resolution passed which praised the opposition's (JSP) bills, even though they did not become law.[12] Katô felt that during this brief period she had accomplished something toward the public good even though the LDP opposed the specific legislation she had backed. She supported LDP Prime Minister Tanaka's 1971 appointment of Ooishi Buichi, M.D., to be director-general of the newly created Environment Agency, and the next year joined with him in publishing a book concerning conservation of nature, environmental pollution, and environmental health.[13] Although her legislative influence was minor, the public still valued her ideas, and she was able to add her voice to the environmental and conservation issues which were becoming a part of consumer movements for better national health and welfare in the seventies.

Katô's environmental interests grew out of her activism for the protection and humane treatment of animals, a cause which had received little attention in Japan. Beginning in 1958, Katô participated in Japan's Society for the Prevention of Cruelty to Animals, presided over the organization from 1964 to 1977, and became Chairman of the Board.[14] This small organization directs an ambitious program of education in animal protection and care, conservation, and preservation of endangered species. Much energy has been expended on programs for children and teenagers which include films, projects for "Be Kind to Animals" week, lectures and pamphlets, leaflets on care of pets, and special school programs. In addition the organization has frequently worked successfully at a local level to pressure individuals, businesses, and groups to cease activities which are harmful to animals, and it has lobbied, though not wholly successfully, for appropriate general protective legislation. Katô recalls that it took from 1965 to 1973 to pressure the Diet into passing one single animal protection law. At one point she combined her Foreign Affairs Committee assignment with her interest in animal preservation by working successfully for legislation which would support the exchange of wild birds between countries in an effort to preserve and protect wild life.

The most sensitive problems the organization has considered are those which affect the fishing industry. Passage of laws against net fishing or whaling is impossible. The organization did go on record in support of the International Whaling Commission's rulings, but at the same time they tried to show an understanding of the complex economic repercussions these would have for Japan's fishing industry. In an uphill battle Katô and her group supported the protection of dolphins caught by the indiscriminate practices of net fishermen, but such sensitive issues require cooperation. She believes, "International understanding is a very important part of animal protection. In the United States a lot of dolphins are caught by the fishing industry but this [bad publicity] is counterbalanced by organizations which study dolphin behavior and which work to protect the dolphins." This is what the JSPCA is trying to do but it is much too small, has a minuscule budget, and attracts too few sympathizers to counteract the impression left by Japan's fishing practices. According to Katô, the entire nation is blamed for animal losses caused by just one segment of society. Small victories are hard won. For example, in the early seventies the JSPCA lobbied successfully for protection of the Japanese antelope and preservation of its habitat. The primary attitude in Japan, she claims, is that "human beings come first and so there is no time or energy to commit to the protection of animals."

Regardless of whatever else Katô participated in, her primary recognition has always came from her family planning activism. She was Vice President of the Family Planning Federation of Japan from its inception and its president for the twenty-one years since 1974. In 1963 she helped establish the Western Pacific Regional Office for International Planned Parenthood in Tokyo, and in 1968 she helped inaugurate the Japanese Organization for International Cooperation in Family Planning (JOICFP) with her old LDP friend Kishi Nobusuke as chair. Katô joined the Board of Directors of this organization along with another longtime associate, Kunii Chôjirô. In 1984, after sixteen years on the Board of Directors of JOICFP, she was made Vice President. In 1974, to her great personal joy, the government recognized her work in family planning by awarding her the First Class Order of the Sacred Treasurer, an honor presented to her by Emperor Hirohito.

Katô Kanjû died on September 27th, 1980, at the age of eighty-six. In her *Reminiscences,* written four years later, Shidzue told of his last illness and her grief at his passing. At that point she resolved to move on from mourning to action, and to live her life as fully as possible, continuing her political activities while drawing strength from meditation, a program of reading, and interacting with young people.

Epilogue

From 1960, Katô has worked outside her party and outside other major organizations, as a leader of small organizations or alone on issues with minority followings. She followed her own commitments, experiencing small steps forward and occasional set-backs. This suited her post-Occupation expectation that incremental political change would result from valued individual contributions made for the general good of society. In none of these ventures has she received the accolades of the early postwar years, but she has maintained an active and personally rewarding life and believes that she has advanced the cause of public welfare. Even her greatest achievement, the creation and operation of a federation of family planning organizations, has not been as productive as she had hoped.

Although the Family Planning Federation of Japan has provided forty years of education and practical support for women and families it remains one of only three small planned parenthood organizations. All are headquartered in the same building in Tokyo, and all have small staffs, limited budgets, and no government financing. Changing the Eugenics Law continues to be difficult, and physicians still monopolize the business of abortion. The government continues to outlaw the contraceptive pill and recommend condoms over all other forms of contraception. Birth control education in Japan, though available, is still primitive, and contraception is considered the responsibility of women. Sexual activity is still mythically expected to remain within the marriage bed and extramarital, homosexual, and premarital sex are purposely ignored. Recently, a modest program of sex education has been introduced into the Ministry of Education controlled school curriculum, but it does not approach the requirements of family planning advocates

It is, however, in the arena of family planning that Katô Shidzue's name is known, through television programs, interviews, her own autobiographies (four in the eighties), and the occasional autobiographical article in newspapers and journals. She is seldom mentioned in writings by others. The story of the enormous effort which she expended to bring birth control education to Japan both before and after the war is available, then, almost exclusively through her own words. This is partly because there is little interest in family planning in Japan or recognition that this is an important part of the women's movement; partly because Katô is still alive, and therefore discussion of her is a delicate matter; and partly because the bulk of information on her is in her English letters, American Planned Parenthood publications, IPPF publications, and Occupation archival materials. Surprisingly the three family planning organizations do not maintain archives.

I would suggest that family planning has not been, in fact, Katô/Ishimoto's most significant contribution to the struggle for women's freedom and independence in Japan. Rather it is a primary part of a broader feminist role most clearly played out in the thirties and forties. Shidzue's determined and dangerous practice during the thirties of ignoring the growing oppression by the militarists and her continued courageous efforts for women's liberation must be recognized as an important, if small, counterweight to the successful government strategy of marginalizing liberal women through intimidation with "dangerous thoughts" laws and through pushing membership in government sponsored mass organizations in support of militarist policies. Admittedly Shidzue's influence was slight. Just the same her example provides a small window on what might have been had democracy survived in pre-war Japan. Additionally it underscores the faint echoes of discord which could still be heard in Japan until about 1942. Whether we suggest Japan exhibited fascism, imperial fascism, or military authoritarianism, by whatever name, official Japan in the thirties was not politically monolithic; for, as Shidzue's activities illustrate, it had cracks and chinks in the power centers .

After the war it was in Shidzue's postwar crusades for women's equality under the new constitution and for improved economic livelihood for women and children that she displayed her greatest leadership. The election of women to the Diet was a political watershed, but most of those elected were not reelected and most female Diet members were marginalized. In spite of her protestations to the contrary, Shidzue used her elected position skillfully, occasionally in the Diet itself, and more often on the outside as a lever for political influence. She was one of the most successful women in public office during the late forties, partly because of her national recognition and partly because of her acceptance by American Occupation officials. It must be expected, therefore, that her political decline followed the American "reverse course" of 1947-48, when Occupation officials switched their support to the old guard on the political right and encouraged conservatives to solidify their power. This also accounts, to a large extent, for the apparent lack of progress by newly liberated women in general. In the first year after the war it seemed that political and social gains for women would know no bounds, and women's organizations would enjoy a share of the nation's political power: women had entered the political equation and would have to be reckoned with. Shidzue's own successful, and even her failed, campaigns in those first few years certainly would have predicted this. For example, her triumphant fight for a changed civil code, and establishment of a Women's and Minors' Bureau, as well as the failed, but politically sophisticated, campaign against indiscriminate VD examinations, would all suggest the growing ability of women to use a variety of approaches to gain access to political and social power. Unfortunately the changed atmosphere at GHQ in the late forties, the cold war fears, and the strengthened position of male political conservatives shortchanged women's movements in a manner similar to that of the more carefully studied labor movement.

It would seem that a broader conception of the significance of Shidzue's role in postwar Japan is more accurate and more comprehensive than one that confines her accomplishments to her leadership in the birth control movement. The belief in democratic socialism which sustained her during the trials of the thirties and through the isolation of war, her expectation of a democratic revolution, which drove her into politics after the war and gave her the strength to circumvent the oppressive, male-dominated Diet, government bureaucracy and the exclusion of women by the JSP Central Committee, more accurately characterizes her inspiration as well as her period of most prominent activity. She was moved to act, not to theorize, and women benefited from her successes and learned from her failures. She was dynamic, active, and able until her democratic dream slipped away. At that crucial juncture she fell into the arms of MRA and lost her aggressive social/democratic political drive while gaining personal solace and peace. It was, perhaps, an unfortunate meeting. On the other hand, given the changes which had taken place under the Occupation's "reverse course," and the diminished opportunity for political liberalism and feminist advocacy, perhaps activism for social causes had had its day for the time being. Certainly Katô's life's work did not come to a standstill, though her contributions in the larger arena were curtailed.

At ninety-eight Katô Shidzue says that while her legs will not follow her commands, her mind is still alert. Her family: Ishimoto Arata, a university professor, and his wife, who live in Fukushima; Sumiko, her physician husband, Ohmori Nobuhisa and their son in

Tokyo; and Taki and her architect husband, Kurokawa Masayuki, remain close to Shidzue. She has the frequent company of Taki and her young son, for the Kurokawa family own an apartment in the same "mansion" in Tokyo as Shidzue. Katô Kanjû's son, Nobuyuki, runs a publishing company, and he and his family also reside in Tokyo. Even now Shidzue maintains contact with the public through the media, and with her professional associates through attendance at meetings. In 1994 she spoke on television, wrote an article for the *Japan Economic Newspaper [Nihon keizai shimbun]* and attended board meetings of FPFJ, adding her inspiration as president, and a word or two to the organization's plans for the future. She continues her interest in current arguments on birth control and abortion and follows the trends in the other causes she has supported. She is particularly concerned about political education of young people, and has lent her voice and energy to encouraging young women to seek careers in politics, though suggesting they do so outside the established parties, the LDP, JSP. and JCP. She believes the hope for Japan's democratic salvation lies in the currently forming new parties and realignments which she anticipates will rejuvenate Japanese political life.

Notes

1. 1978, interview.

2. For Katô's 4/20 statement,, Kishi's reply and information about 1957 Conference at Baguio, Basil Entwistle, *Japan's Decisive Decade,* Grosvenor Books, 1985, pp. 152-155.

3. Kubota Declaration and official relations between Japan and ROK, see Kwan Bong Kim, *The Korea-Japan Treaty Crisis and the Instability of the Korean Political System,* Praeger, 1971, pp. 40-77.

4. Kishi's MRA association is seldom mentioned in English or Japanese sources; an exception, John G. Roberts, *Mitsui,* Weatherhill 1973, p. 455.

5. See J. Victor Koschmann, "Intellectuals and Politics," in Andrew Gordon, ed., *Postwar Japan as History,* U. of California Press, 1993, pp. 403-414. Note references to Katô Shidzue's cousins, Tsurumi Kazuko and Tsurumi Shunsuke, children of "Uncle" Tsurumi Yûsuke, significant players in opposition to her positions.

6. National Association of Student Self-Governing Associations.

7. In Entwistle's version of this paragraph an additional sentence follows the official version quoted above. "The only such ideology I know is Moral Re-Armament." Although Entwistle does not cite the entire text or the source of those sections he quotes this is the only place where the content differs from the newspaper. Basil Entwistle, *Japan's Decisive Decade,* p. 183.

8. From *Sankei*, 6/30/60, quoted in Daily Summary of the Japanese Press for 6/60, p. 20.

9. 1978 interview. Ichikawa Fusae, in my interview, 6/17/78, stated that Katô's well known differences with JSP stemmed from "her agreement with LDP Prime Minister Kishi in favor of the US/Japan Defense Treaty and against the position of the JSP."

10. See J. Victor Koschmann, "Intellectuals and Politics" p. 406-408.

11. She was chair of Transportation Countermeasures Committee for 59th Diet's Extraordinary Session, 8/1-8/10/68 and again for 60th Diet's Extraordinary Session of 12/10-12/12. She chaired Committee on Industrial Pollution, 63rd Diet's Special Session, 1/14-5/13/70 and co-chaired with JSP associate, Kobayashi Shinichi, 64th Diet Extraordinary Session, 11/24-12/8.

12. Margaret McKean in T. J. Pempel, ed., *Policy Making in Contemporary Japan*, Cornell U. Press, pp. 228.

13. Ooishi Buichi and Katô Shidzue, *Kokudo shizen hogo ni tsuite*, [Concerning Protection of the Country's Natural Environment], 1972.

14. Founded just after the war by a foreign woman, JSPCA (Nippon dobutsu aigo-kyokai), 35-4, 3 Chome Sendagaya, Shibuya-ku, Tokyo, puts out an annual report describing activities, legislation passed, its financial status, and its officers.

Bibliography

Autobiographical Writings of Katô Shidzue
[Referenced in Text by Publication Date]

1935. [Baroness Shidzue Ishimoto]. *Facing Two Ways: The Story of My Life*. New York: Farrar & Rinehart.

1948. *Na ga wa haha; Waga hansei no ki* [Thy Name Is Mother; A Record of Half My Life). Tokyo: Kokuminsha.

1956. *Hitosuji no michi* [A Straight Road]. Tokyo: Dobuedosha.

1981. *Aru josei seijika no hansei* [Half a Life as a Stateswoman]. Tokyo. PHP Kenkyujo.

1983. Republication of *Facing Two Ways: The Story of My Life* with "Introduction" and "Afterword" by Barbara Molony. Stanford: Stanford University Press.

1984. *Omoide no furu* [Reminiscences]. Tokyo: Jiyu Shokan.

1985a. *A Fight for Women's Happiness*. Tokyo: JOICFP [Japanese Organization for International Cooperation in Family Planning].

1985b. *Futatsu no bunka no wa hazu kara* [Facing Two Ways]. Translated and edited with "Afterword" by Funabashi Kuniko. Tokyo: Seizankan.

1988a. *Ai wa jidai o koete* [Love Which Extends Beyond Time]. Tokyo: Fujinga Hosha.

1988b. *Saiai no hito Kanjû e* [To My Dearly Beloved Kanjû] 1937-1938 Diary entries transcribed and edited with afterword by Funabashi Kuniko. Tokyo: Shindosha.

Archives
[Referenced in Text by Abbreviations]

Princeton University Libraries, Roger Baldwin Papers, Princeton, New Jersey. [Baldwin Papers]

Sophia Smith Collection, College Archives, Smith College, Northampton Massachusetts. [Smith]

United States Library of Congress, Margaret Sanger Archives. [Sanger, LofC]

United States National Archives, National Records Center, Suitland Maryland. The archival material from the American occupation of Japan which relates to

Katô Shidzue is found primarily in Record Group 331 [RG331], in the files of the Government Section and of Civil Information and Education Section [CIE].

Secondary Sources

Akamatsu Yoshiko. 1977. *Nihon fujin mondai shiryô shûsei* [Collection of Documents on Japanese Women's Questions], Vol. 3. Domesu Shuppan.

Amano Masako and Sakurai Atsushi. 1992. *"Mono to onna" no sengoshi* [A Postwar History of "Objects and Women"]. Tokyo: Yûshindô Takabunsha.

Andô Yoshio, ed. 1966. *Shôwa keizaishi e no shôgen*. [Testimonies for an Economic History of the Shôwa Era]. Tokyo: Mainichi Shimbunsha.

Arahata Kanson: Hito to jidai [Arahata Kanson: The Man and His Era]. Tokyo: Marukushu Sha.

Arima, Tatsuo. 1969. *The Failure of Freedom: A Portrait of Modern Japanese Intellectuals*. Cambridge: Harvard University Press.

Awaya Kentarô. 1983. *Shôwa no rekishi: Shôwa no seitô* [History of Shôwa: Shôwa's Political Parties] Vol. 6. Tokyo: Shôgakukan.

Barnhart, Michael A. 1987. *Japan Prepares for Total War: The Search for Economic Security 1919-1941*. Ithaca: Cornell University Press.

Barrett, Brendan F. D. and Riki Therivel. 1991. *Environmental Policy and Impact Assessment in Japan*. London: Routledge Press.

Beard, Charles A. 1923. *The Administration and Politics of Tokyo*. New York: The Macmillan Company.

Beard, Mary Ritter. 1924. "The New Japanese Woman." *The Woman Citizen*. January 12.

____. 1953. *The Force of Women in Japanese History*. Washington DC: Public Affairs Press.

____. 1955. *The Making of Charles A. Beard: An Interpretation*. New York: Exposition Press.

Beckman, George M. and Genji Okubo. 1969. *The Japanese Communist Party 1922-1945*. Stanford: Stanford University Press.

Berger, Gordon Mark. 1977. *Parties Out of Power in Japan 1931-1941*. Princeton: Princeton University Press.

Bernstein, Gail Lee. 1976. "The Russian Revolution, The Early Japanese Socialists and the Problems of Dogmatism." *Studies in Comparative Communism* 9:4; 327-348.

Blewett, John E., S.J., ed. and trans. 1965. *Higher Education in Postwar Japan*. Ministry of Education, 1964 White Paper, *Monumenta Nipponica Monograph* #22. Tokyo: Sophia University Press.

Borton, Hugh. 1955. *Japan's Modern Century*. New York: The Ronald Press.

Brown, Margery Finn. 1951. *Over A Bamboo Fence*. New York: William Morrow & Company.

Chamberlain, William Henry. 1937. *Japan Over Asia*. Boston: Little Brown & Co.

____. 1939. "Japan at War." *Foreign Affairs*, April; 465-488.

Chesler, Ellen. 1992. *Woman of Valor: Margaret Sanger and the Birth Control Movement in America*. New York: Simon & Schuster.

Cohen, Theodore. 1987. *Remaking Japan: The American Occupation As New Deal.* New York: The Free Press.

Colbert, Evelyn S. 1952. *The Left Wing in Japanese Politics.* New York: Institute of Pacific Relations.

Cole, Allen Burnett, George O. Totten, and Cecil H. Uyehara. 1966. *Socialist Parties in Postwar Japan.* New Haven: Yale University Press.

Coleman, Samuel. 1991. *Family Planning in Japanese Society: Traditional Birth Control in a Modern Urban Culture.* Princeton: Princeton University Press.

Cook, Haruko Taya, and Theodore F. Cook. 1992. *Japan at War, An Oral History.* New York: The New Press.

Cott, Nancy F. 1980. "Mary Ritter Beard," in Barbara Sicherman and Carol Hurd Green, eds, *Notable American Women: The Modern Period, pp. 71-73.* Cambridge: Harvard University Press.

____., ed. 1991. *A Woman Making History: Mary Ritter Beard Through Her Letters.* New Haven: Yale University Press.

Drea, Edward J. 1979. *The 1942 Japanese General Election: Political Mobilization in Wartime Japan.* International Studies, East Asian Series, Research Publication, #11, Center for East Asian Studies, University of Kansas. New York: Paragon Book Gallery.

Driberg, Tom. 1965. *The Mystery of Moral Re-Armament, A Study of Frank Buchman and His Movement.* New York: Alfred A. Knopf.

Education in Japan. 1937. Tokyo: Tokyo Municipal Office.

Endô Shûsaku. 1983. "Meijijo no kyôkiyun; Katô Shidzue" [The Heart of a Meiji Woman, Katô Shidzue]. *Bungei Shunjû* July; 345-357.

Entwistle, Basil. 1985. *Japan's Decisive Decade.* London: Grosvenor Books.

Finn, Richard B. 1992. *Winners in Peace: MacArthur, Yoshida, and Postwar Japan.* Berkeley: University of California Press.

Fujiwara Akira. 1982. *Shôwa no rekishi: nitchû zenmen sensô* [History of Shôwa: The All-Out War between Japan and China] Vol. 5. Tokyo: Shôgakukan.

Furuta Hikari, Sakuta Keiichi, Ikimatsu Keizô, eds. 1971. *Kindai nihon shakai shisôshi* [A History of Social Thought in Modern Japan]. Tokyo: Yûhikaku.

Garon, Sheldon. 1987. *The State and Labor in Modern Japan.* Berkeley: University of California Press.

____. 1993a. "Women's Groups and the Japanese State: Contending Approaches to Political Integration, 1890-1945." *Journal of Japanese Studies* 19:1; 5-41.

____. 1993b. "The World's Oldest Debate? Prostitution and the State in Imperial Japan, 1900-1945." *American Historical Review* 98:3; 710-732.

Gordon, Andrew. 1991. *Labor and Imperial Democracy in Prewar Japan.* Berkeley: University of California Press.

Haas, Margaret P. [undated]. "The First Birth Control Movement in Japan, 1902-1937," unpublished manuscript.

Halliday, Jon. 1975. *A Political History of Japanese Capitalism.* New York: Monthly Review Press.

Hastings, Sally Anne. 1995. "Women Legislators in the Postwar Diet," ms. to appear in Anne E. Imamura, ed., *Re-imaging Japanese Women.* Berkeley: University of California Press.

Havens, Thomas, R. H. 1986. *Valley of Darkness, The Japanese People and World War Two.* Lanham: University Press of America.

Hino Ashihei. [pseud. for Tamai Katsunori]. 1939. *Wheat and Soldiers*, trans. Baroness Shidzue Ishimoto. New York: Farrar & Rinehart.

____. 1939. *Barley and Soldiers*, trans. Lewis Bush. Tokyo: Kenkyûsha.

____. 1972. "Mugi to Heitai" in *Hino Ashihei shû; Nihon bungaku zenshû*, Volume 67, pp. 56-150.

Hirano, Ryuichi. 1963. "The Accused and Society: Some Aspects of Japanese Criminal Law," in Arthur Taylor von Mehren, ed., *Law in Japan*, pp. 274-295. Cambridge: Harvard University Press.

Hopper, Helen M. 1982. "Katô Shidzue, Socialist MP, and Occupation Reforms Affecting Women" in Thomas W. Burkman, ed., *The Occupation of Japan: Educational and Social Reform*, pp. 375-399. Norfolk, Virginia: Gatling Publishing Company.

____. 1989. "Shidzue Ishimoto and Margaret Sanger in Japan, August, 1937." *Phoebe: An Interdisciplinary Journal of Feminist Scholarship, Theory & Aesthetics* 1:1; 34-50.

____. 1993. "A Case Study in Democratic Activism: Women Protest Indiscriminate, Forced Examinations for Venereal Disease (November-December, 1946)." Paper presented at the Midwest Japan Seminar, Pittsburgh.

____. 1995. "Katô Shidzue: Activist, Socialist, and Political Maverick." Paper presented at the American Historical Association, Chicago.

Hoyt, Edwin P. 1986. *Japan's War*. New York: McGraw-Hill.

Huston, Perdita. 1992. *Motherhood by Choice: Pioneers in Women's Health and Family Planning*. New York: Feminist Press.

Ichikawa Fusae, ed. 1977. *Nihon fujin mondai shiryô shûsei* [Collection of Documents on Japanese Women's Questions]; Vol. 2. Tokyo: Domesu Shuppan.

Inoue, Kyoko. 1991. *MacArthur's Japanese Constitution: A Linguistic and Cultural Study of Its Making*. Chicago: University of Chicago Press.

Itoya Toshio and Esashi Akiko. 1977. *Sengoshi to josei no kaihô* [Postwar History and Women's Liberation]. Tokyo: Gôdô Shuppan.

Itoya Toshio, ed. 1982. *Nihon shakaishûgi undô shisôshi* [An Intellectual History of Japan's Socialist Movement]. Volume 3. Tokyo: Hosei Daigaku Shuppan.

Kanda Fuhito. 1979. *Nihon no tôitsu senzen undô* [Japan's Popular Front Movement]. Tokyo: Aoki Shoten.

____. 1983. *Shôwa no rekishi: Senryô to minshushugi* [A History of Shôwa: Occupation and Democracy], Vol. 8. Tokyo: Shôgakukan.

Katô Kanjû. 1936. "Koe naki taishû no daibensha to shite" ["Spokesman for the Voiceless Masses."] *Chûô Kôran* 51:4; 209-215.

____. 1936b. *Tôitsu sensen o tenbô* [The Outlook for a United Front]. Tokyo: Kikyoku Shimbunsha.

Keene, Donald. 1976. "Japanese Literature and Politics in the 1930s." *Journal of Japanese Studies* 2:2; 225-248.

____. 1978. "The Barren Years." *Monumenta Nipponica* 33:1, 67-112.

____. 1984. *Dawn to the West: Japanese Literature of the Modern Era*. New York: Holt, Rinehart, and Winston.

Keenleyside, Hugh L. and A. F. Thomas. 1937. *History of Japanese Education and Present Educational System*. Tokyo: Hokuseido Press.

Kim, Kwong Bong. 1971. *The Korea-Japan Treaty Crisis and the Instability of the Korean Political System*. New York: Praeger.

Kodama Katsuko. 1985. *Senko no Ichikawa Fusae* [The Postwar Ichikawa Fusae]. Tokyo: Shinshuku Shobô.

Koschmann, J. Victor. 1993. "Intellectuals and Politics" in Andrew Gordon, ed., *Postwar Japan As History*, pp. 395-423. Berkeley: University of California Press.

Koyama Shizuko. 1994. "The 'Good Wife and Wise Mother' Ideology in Post-World War I Japan." *U.S.-Japan Women's Journal, English Supplement No. 7* ; 31-52.

Kunii, Chôjirô. 1983. *Humanistic Family Planning Approaches: The Integration of Family Planning and Health Goals*. United Nations Fund for Population Activities.

____. 1987. "Katô Shidzue to taishô demokurashi" [Katô Shidzue and Taishô Democracy]. *Sakaito Gikai*. Part 1, February: 5-14; Part 2, March: 5-14.

Large, Stephen S. 1981. *Organized Workers and Socialist Politics in Interwar Japan*. Cambridge: Cambridge University Press.

Lee, Luke T. and Arthur Larson. 1971. *Population and Law*. Durham, North Carolina: Rule of Law Press.

Lippit, Noriko Mizuta and Kyoko Iriye Selden, eds. and trans. 1991. *Japanese Women Writers*. Armonk, New York: M. E. Sharpe, Inc.

Maruoka Hideko and Yamaguchi Miyoko, eds. 1980. *Nihon fujin mondai shiryô shûsei: Kindai nihon fujin mondai nenpyô* [Collection of Documents on Japanese Women's Questions: A Chronology of Modern Japanese Women's Questions], Vol. 10. Tokyo: Domesu Shuppan.

Maruoka Hideko. 1982. *Fujin shisô keiseishi nôtô* [Notes on the History of the Formation of Women's Ideas], Vol. 2. Tokyo: Domesu Shuppan.

Masataka, Kosaka. 1972. *100 Million Japanese: The Postwar Experience*. Tokyo: Kodansha International Ltd.

Masumi, Junnosuke. 1985. *Postwar Politics in Japan, 1945-1955*. Berkeley: University of California Press.

Mayo, Marlene. 1988. "The War of Words Continues: American Radio Guidance in Occupied Japan" in Thomas W. Burkman, ed., *The Occupation of Japan: Arts and Culture*, pp. 45-83. Norfolk, Virginia: General Douglas MacArthur Foundation.

McKean, Margaret A. 1977. "Pollution and Policymaking," in T. J. Pempel, ed., *Policy Making in Contemporary Japan*, pp. 201-238. Ithaca: Cornell University Press.

____. 1987. "Japan's Rationing Economy in War: Cheating vs. Cooperation in Adversity." Paper presented at the Association for Asian Studies, Boston.

Meyers, Howard. 1977. "Revisions of the Criminal Code of Japan During the Occupation," in *Washington Law Review: Legal Reforms in Japan During the Allied Occupation*, pp. 66-96. Seattle: Washington Law Review.

Mitchell, Richard H. 1976. *Thought Control in Prewar Japan*. Ithaca: Cornell University Press.

____. 1983. *Censorship in Imperial Japan*. Princeton: Princeton University Press, 1983.

____. 1992. *Janus-Faced Justice, Political Criminals in Imperial Japan*. Honolulu: University of Hawaii Press.

Mitsui Reiko. 1963. *Gendai fujin undôshi nenpyô 1868-1960* [A Chronology of the Modern Women's Movement]. Tokyo: Sanichi Shobô.

Miyake, Yoshiko. 1991. "Doubling Expectations: Motherhood and Women's Factory Work Under State Management in Japan in the 1930s and 1940s," in Gail Lee Bernstein, ed., *Recreating Japanese Women, 1600-1945*, pp. 267-295. Berkeley: University of California Press.

Miyamoto, Ken. 1975. "Itô Noe and the Bluestockings." *The Japan Interpreter* 10:2; 190-204.

Miyazawa Toshiyoshi, et. al., eds. 1971. *Nihon shakaishûgi undô shisôshi* [An Intellectual History of Japan's Socialist Movement] Vol. 2. Tokyo: Kabushiki Kaisha.

Miyoshi, Masao. 1991. *Off Center: Power and Culture Relations between Japan and the United States*. Cambridge: Harvard University Press.

Molony, Barbara. 1995. "Gender and the Politics of Morality in the Parliamentary Career of Ichikawa Fusae (1893-1981)." Paper presented at the American Historical Association, Chicago.

Mori Shôzô. 1946. *Fusetsu no hi: Shôwa junnansha retsudan* [The Memorial of a Storm: Biographies of Martyrs of the Shôwa Era]. Tokyo: Masu Shobô.

Murray, Patricia. 1975. "Ichikawa Fusae and the Lonely Red Carpet." *The Japan Interpreter* 10:2; 171-189.

Nagy, Margit. 1991. "Middle-Class Working Women During the Interwar Years," in Gail Lee Bernstein, ed., *Recreating Japanese Women, 1600-1945*, pp. 199-216. Berkeley: University of California Press.

Nolte, Sharon H. 1986. "Women's Rights and society's Needs: Japan's 1931 Suffrage Bill." *Comparative Studies in Society and History* 28:4; 690-714.

Nomura, Gail M. 1978. *The Allied Occupation of Japan: Reform of Japanese Government Labor Policy on Women*. Ph.D. Dissertation, University of Hawaii.

Nore, Ellen. 1983. *Charles A. Beard: An Intellectual Biography*. Carbondale: Southern Illinois University Press.

Ooe Shinobu, 1976. *Nihon no rekishi: Sengo henkaku* [History of Japan: Postwar Reform] Vol. 31. Tokyo: Kabushiki Kaisha Shôgakukan.

Ooishi Buichi and Katô Shidzue. 1972. *Kokudo shizen hogo ni tsuite* [Concerning Protection of the Country's Natural Environment]. Tokyo: Ozaki Yukio Kinen Zaidan Toron Shûkai Shirizu No. 5.

Pharr, Susan J. 1980. "Ethel Berenice Weed," in Barbara Sicherman and Carol Hurd Green, eds., *Notable American Women: The Modern Period*, pp. 721-723. Cambridge: Harvard University Press.

____. 1987. "The Politics of Women's Rights," in Robert E. Ward and Sakamoto Yoshikazu, eds., *Democratizing Japan: The Allied Occupation*, pp. 221-252. Honolulu: University of Hawaii Press.

Phillips, Susan. 1987. "Beyond Borders: Class Struggle and Feminist Humanism in Banshû heiya [The Banshû Plain]." *Bulletin of Concerned Asian Scholars* 19:1; 56-65.

Roberts, John G. 1973. *Mitsui: Three Centuries of Japanese Business*. New York: Weatherhill.

Robins-Mowry, Dorothy. 1983. *The Hidden Sun: Women of Modern Japan*. Boulder: Westview Press.

Rodd, Laurel Rasplica. 1991. "Yosano Akiko and the Taishô Debate Over the 'New Woman'," in Gail Lee Bernstein, ed., *Recreating Japanese Women, 1600-1945*, pp. 174-198. Berkeley: University of California Press.

Roden, Donald T. 1980. *Schooldays in Imperial Japan: A Study in the Culture of a Student Elite*. Berkeley: University of California Press.

Roth, Andrew. 1946. *Dilemma In Japan*. London: Victor Gollancz Ltd.

Sato, Barbara Hamill. 1983. "Modan gaaru no jidaiteki imi [The Modern Girl in a Historical Context]," in Minami Hiroshi, ed., *Gendai no esupuri - Nihon modanizumu* [Present-Day Spirit - Japan's Modernism] 188: 84-85.

____. 1993. "The *Moga* Sensation: Perceptions of the *Modan Gaaru* in Japanese Intellectual Circles during the 1920s." *Gender and History* 5:3; 363-381.

____. 1994. "Cultivating a Different Modern: Women and *Shûyô* [cultivated professionals] in the 1920s." Paper presented at the Association for Asian Studies, Boston.

Scalapino, Robert A. 1967. *The Japanese Communist Movement, 1920-1966*. Berkeley: University of California Press.

Seidensticker, Edward. 1983. *Low City, High City: Tokyo, 1867-1923*. New York: Alfred A. Knopf.

Shapcott, Jennifer. 1987. "The Red Chrysanthemum: Yamakawa Kikue and the Socialist Women's Movement in Pre-war Japan" in *Papers on Far Eastern History* (Australia) 35: 1-30.

Shibagaki Kazuo. 1983. *Shôwa no rekishi: kôwa kara kôdo seichô* [History of Shôwa: From Peace to the Heights of Growth], Vol. 9. Tokyo: Shôgakukan

Shiga-Fujime, Yuki. 1993. "The Prostitutes Union and the Impact of the 1956 Anti-Prostitution Law in Japan." *U.S. - Japan Women's Journal, English Supplement No. 5*, 3-27.

Shillony, Ben-Ami. 1981. *Politics and Culture in Wartime Japan*. Oxford: Clarendon Press.

Shôwa nimannichi no zenkiroku [A Complete Record of Shôwa Day by Day], Vol. 7, 1945-1946. Tokyo: Kodansha.

Sievers, Sharon L. 1983. *Flowers in Salt: The Beginnings of Feminist Consciousness in Modern Japan*. Stanford: Stanford University Press.

Silverberg, Miriam. 1991. "The Modern Girl as Militant," in Gail Lee Bernstein, ed., *Recreating Japanese Women, 1600-1945*, pp. 239-266. Berkeley: University of California Press.

Smethurst, Richard J. 1978. "The Army, Youth, and Women" in Edward R. Beauchamp, ed., *Learning To Be Japanese*, pp. 137-166. Hamden, Connecticut: Linnet Books.

Starr, Mark. 1947. "Leaders of Labor in New Japan." *Labor and Nation*, 3:1, pp. 51-53.

Starr, Mark. 1947. "The Japanese Labor Movement and Its Leaders." *Labor and Nation*, 3:2, pp. 14-16.

Stein, Gunther. 1938. "'Totalitarian' Japan." *Foreign Affairs*, January; 294-308.

Steinhoff, Patricia. 1988. "Tenkô and Thought Control," in Gail Lee Bernstein and Haruhiro Fukui, eds., *Japan and the World*, pp. 78-94. New York: St. Martin's Press.

____. 1991. *Tenkô: Ideology and Societal Integration in Prewar Japan*. New York: Garland Press.

Suzuki, Tomin. 1936. "Japan and the Front Populaire." *Contemporary Japan*, December; 443-448.

Takahashi Hikohiro. 1977. *Nihon no shakai minshûshûgi seitô* [Japan's Social-Democratic Parties]. Tokyo: Hosei Daigaku Shuppan.

Takeda, Kiyoko. 1967. "Ichikawa Fusae: Pioneer for Women's Rights in Japan." *Japan Quarterly* 22:3-4; 410-415.

Takemae, Eiji. 1987. "Early Postwar Reformist Parties," in Robert E. Ward and Yoshikazu, Sakamoto Yoshikazu, eds., *Democratizing Japan: The Allied Occupation*, pp. 339-365. Honolulu: University of Hawaii Press.

Tama, Yasuko. 1994. "The Logic of Abortion: Japanese Debates on the Legitimacy of Abortion As Seen in Post-World War II Newspapers." *U.S.-Japan Women's Journal, English Supplement No. 7* , 3-30.

Tipton, Elise. 1990. *Japanese Police State, Tokkô in Interwar Japan*. Honolulu: University of Hawaii Press.

Tolischus, Otto D. 1943. *Tokyo Record*. New York: Reynal & Hitchcock.

Toshitani, Nobuyoshi. 1994. "The Reform of Japanese Family Law and Changes in the Family System." *U.S.-Japan Women's Journal, English Supplement No. 6* , 66-82.

Totten, George O. 1966. *The Social Democratic Movement in Prewar Japan*. Yale University Press.

Tsurumi, Kazuko. 1970. *Social Change and the Individual: Japan Before and After Defeat in World War II*. Princeton: Princeton University Press.

Tsurumi, Shunsuke. 1986. *An Intellectual History of Wartime Japan*, 1931-1945. London: Kegan Paul International.

____. 1987. *A Cultural History of Postwar Japan*, 1945-1980. London: Kegan Paul International.

Tsurumi, Yûsuke. 1924. *Present Day Japan*. New York: Columbia University Press.

____. 1927. *Contemporary Japan*. Tokyo: The Japan Times.

____. 1932. *The Mother*. New York: Rae D. Henkle.

Uno, Kathleen S. 1993. "The Death of 'Good Wife, Wise Mother'?" in Andrew Gordon, ed., *Postwar Japan As History*, pp. 293-322. Berkeley: University of California Press.

Wagatsuma, Sakae. 1977. "Guarantee of Fundamental Human Rights Under the Japanese Constitution" in *Washington Law Review: Legal Reforms in Japan During the Allied Occupation*, pp. 124-145. Seattle: Washington Law Review.

Watanabe, Yozo. 1963. "The Family and the Law: The individualistic Premise and Modern Family Law" in Arthur Taylor von Mehren, ed., *Law in Japan*, pp. 364-398. Cambridge: Harvard University Press.

Wohr, Ulrike. 1993. "Between Revolution and Reaction: The Japanese Women's Movement in the Taishô Era" in Ian Neary, ed., *War Revolution & Japan*, pp. 50-73. Sandgate, Great Britain: Japan Library.

Women's Movements in Postwar Japan. 1968. Trans. Wake A. Fujioka. [Selected articles from Shiroyo: Sengo nijû-nen shi - Source Book on Twenty Postwar Years in Japan]. Occasional Papers of Research Publications and Translations No. 29. Honolulu: East-West Center.

Wray, William D. 1972. "The Japanese Popular Front Movement, July 1936-February 1938" in *Papers on Japan 6*, 102-142. Cambridge: Harvard University.

Yamakawa Kikue. 1979. *Nihon fujin undô shôshi* [A short History of Japan's Women's Movement]. Tokyo: Yamato Shobô.

Yoneda Sayoko. 1972. *Kindai nihon joseishi* [A History of Women in Modern Japan], Vol. 2. Tokyo: Shin Nihon Shuppansha.

Yoshimi Kaneko. 1977. *Nihon fuashizuma to josei* [Japanese Fascism and Women]. Tokyo: Gôdô Shuppan.

About the Book and Author

This perceptive, detailed biography traces the life of Katô Shidzue, one of Japan's most powerful female activists and politicians. Katô's activism initially was sparked by her friendship with Margaret Sanger, who inspired Katô to found a Japanese birth control movement in the 1920s. Katô then opened one of Japan's first birth control clinics in the 1930s and worked for women's rights up to World War II despite the growing oppression of the country's militarists. After the war, she returned to public life, running for elective office. She served as a representative and as a senator, and with her entrée to the offices of the American Occupation she became one of the most effective women in postwar politics.

Although primarily a political biography, this book also traces Katô's joys and sorrows as wife and mother. Helen Hopper movingly describes Katô's solitary struggle when her formerly radical husband abandoned her for imperialist adventurism; her secret liaison with the political labor leader Katô Kanjû during the 1930s; her despair at sending her first son to war and watching the second succumb to tuberculosis; and her delight with her wartime marriage to Katô Kanjû and the birth of a daughter during the U.S. firebombing of Tokyo. Still active at ninety-eight, Katô Shidzue continues to speak out forcefully for the causes she espouses. Scholars of Japan and of women's history will find this book a richly documented and engaging view of women's issues and political life in Japan.

Helen M. Hopper is adjunct professor of history at the University of Pittsburgh.

Index